Evidence-Based Adjunctive Treatments

Evidence-Based Adjunctive Treatments

Edited by

William T. O'Donohue
Department of Psychology, University of Nevada, Reno

and

Nicholas A. Cummings
The Cummings Foundation for Behavioral Health, Reno

AMSTERDAM • BOSTON • HEIDELBERG • LONDON • NEW YORK • OXFORD
PARIS • SAN DIEGO • SAN FRANCISCO • SINGAPORE • SYDNEY • TOKYO

Academic Press is an imprint of Elsevier

Academic Press is an imprint of Elsevier
30 Corporate Drive, Suite 400, Burlington, MA 01803, USA
84 Theobald's Road, London WC1X 8RR, UK
525 B Street, Suite 1900, San Diego, CA 92101-4495, USA

First edition 2008

British Library Cataloguing in Publication Data
A catalogue record for this book is available from the British Library

Library of Congress Cataloging-in-Publication Data
A catalog record for this book is available from the Library of Congress

ISBN: 978-0-1208-8520-6

For information on all Academic Press publications
visit our website at books.elsevier.com

Printed and bound in United States of America
08 09 10 11 12 10 9 8 7 6 5 4 3 2 1

CONTENTS

3

PSYCHOEDUCATION IN CONJUNCTION WITH PSYCHOTHERAPY PRACTICE

NICHOLAS A. CUMMINGS AND JANET L. CUMMINGS

4

MUTUAL-HELP GROUPS

JOHN F. KELLY AND JULIE D. YETERIAN

5

ADJUNCTIVE E-HEALTH

CRISSA DRAPER, MANDRA RASMUSSEN HALL, AND WILLIAM T. O'DONOHUE

6

SUPPORT GROUPS

MICHAEL A. CUCCIARE

7

THE ADDICTION SEVERITY INDEX MULTIMEDIA VERSION

SIMON H. BUDMAN, STEPHEN F. BUTLER, AND ALBERT J. VILLAPIANO

8

EXERCISE AS AN ADJUNCTIVE EVIDENCE-BASED TREATMENT

BRIE A. MOORE AND AMANDA ADAMS

9

MEDITATION AND RELAXATION

KENNETH KUSHNER AND MARK MARNOCHA

10

THE USE OF SELF-MONITORING AS A TREATMENT INTERVENTION

CLAUDIA AVINA

11

EXPRESSIVE WRITING

DEBORAH NAZARIAN AND JOSHUA SMYTH

12

HOLISTIC AND ALTERNATIVE MEDICINE AS ADJUNCTIVE TO PSYCHOTHERAPY

JANET L. CUMMINGS AND NICHOLAS A. CUMMINGS

13

ADJUNCTIVE TREATMENTS FOR CHILDHOOD DISORDERS

BRIE A. MOORE AND LAUREN W. TOLLE

14

ADJUNCTIVE THERAPIES WITH ETHNICALLY DIVERSE POPULATIONS

ADITI VIJAY, MELANIE P. DUCKWORTH, AND IREON LEBEAUF

15

ADJUNCTIVE TREATMENTS FOR RURAL POPULATIONS

DENNIS F. MOHATT, CANDICE M. TATE, AND MIMI MCFAUL

16

ADJUNCTIVE TREATMENTS FOR SEVERE MENTAL ILLNESS (SCHIZOPHRENIA)

JENNIFER D. GOTTLIEB AND KIM T. MUESER

Contributors

Amanda Adams (161) Department of Psychology, California State University, Fresno, 2576 East San Ramon Ave., ST11, Fresno, California 93740–8039.

Claudia Avina (207) Social Science Division, Pepperdine University, 24255 Pacific Coast Highway, Malibu, California 90263.

Simon H. Budman (141) Inflexxion, Inc., 320 Needham Street, Suite 100, Newton, Massachusetts 02464.

Stephen F. Butler (141) Inflexxion, Inc., 320 Needham Street, Suite 100, Newton, Massachusetts, 02464.

Michael A. Cucciare (123), VA Palo Alto Health Care System and Stanford University, School of Medicine 3801 Miranda Avenue (116B), Palo Alto, California 94304.

Nicholas A. Cummings (1) (41) (243) The Cummings Foundation for Behavioral Health, 4781 Caughlin Parkway, Reno, Nevada 89519.

Janet L. Cummings (41) (243) The Nicholas and Dorothy Cummings Foundation, 4400 North Scottsdale Road #305, Scottsdale, Arizona 85251.

Crissa Draper (107) Department of Psychology/298, University of Nevada, Reno, Nevada 89557.

Melanie Duckworth (285) Department of Psychology/298, University of Nevada, Reno, Nevada 89557.

Jennifer D. Gottlieb (339) ELMHC Freedom Trail Clinic Schizophrenia Research Program, 25 Staniford Street, Boston, Massachusetts 02114.

Mandra Rasmussen Hall (107) University of Nevada, Reno, Nevada 89557.

Negar Nicole Jacobs (7) Department of Psychiatry and Behavioral Sciences, University of Nevada School of Medicine/354, 401 W. 2nd Street, Suite 216, Reno, Nevada 89503.

John F. Kelly (61) MGH-Harvard, Center for Addiction Medicine, 60 Staniford Street, Boston, Massachusetts 02114.

Kenneth Kushner (177) University of Wisconsin, School of Medicine, Wingra Family Medical Center, 777 Mills Street, Madison, Wisconsin 53715.

Ireon Lebeauf (285) Department of Psychology, University of Nevada, Reno, Nevada 89557.

Mark Marnocha (177) Clinical Psychologist, Fox Valley Family Medicine Residency Program, UW Health Fox Valley Family Medicine, 229 S. Morrison Street, Appleton, Wisconsin, 54911-5725.

Mimi McFaul (317) WICHE, Mental Health Program, 3035 Center Green Drive, Boulder, Colorado 80301.

Dennis F. Mohatt (317) WICHE, Mental Health Program, 3035 Center Green Drive, Boulder, Colorado 80301.

Brie A. Moore (161) (261) Department of Psychology, University of Nevada, Reno, 4781 Caughlin Parkway, Reno, Nevada, 89519.

Elizabeth Mosco (7) Veteran's Administration Sierra Nevada Health Care System, Reno, NV.

Kim T. Mueser (339) NH-Darthmouth Psychiatric Research Center, Main Building, 105 Pleasant Street, Concord, New Hampshire 03301.

Deborah Nazarian (221) Department of Psychology, Huntington Hall, Syracuse University, Syracuse, New York 13244-2340.

William O'Donohue (1) (107) Department of Psychology, University of Nevada, Reno, Nevada 89557.

Joshua Smyth (221) Department of Psychology, Huntington Hall, Syracuse University, Syracuse, New York 13244-2340.

Candice M. Tate (317) WICHE, Mental Health Program, 3035 Center Green Drive, Boulder, Colorado 80301.

Lauren W. Tolle (261) Department of Psychology, University of Nevada, Reno, Nevada 89557.

Aditi Vijay (285) Department of Psychology/296, University of Nevada, Reno, Nevada 89557.

Albert J. Villapiano (141) Inflexxion, Inc., 320 Needham Street, Suite 100, Newton, Massachusetts 02464.

Julie D. Yeterian (61) MGH-Harvard, Center for Addiction Medicine, 60 Staniford Street, Boston, Massachusetts 02114.

1

Evidence-Based Adjunctive Therapy

Introduction

William T. O'Donohue* and
Nicholas A. Cummings†

*University of Nevada, Reno
†The Cummings Foundation for Behavioral Health

Psychotherapy is often thought of as solely a dyadic phenomenon. To be sure, there are group psychotherapy models and family systems models that involve additional people, but the prototypical depiction of psychotherapy is that it almost exclusively involves just two individuals: the patient and the therapist. One of the implications of this model is that most of the benefit that the patient will receive from this interaction would directly flow from what the therapist can provide. The therapist's skills "in the room" are essentially the best and only hope the client has to make progress on their problems. Thus, any limitations in this skill set will limit the benefit the client can receive from therapy. Additionally, the one-on-one format is labor-intensive and thus expensive to the patient.

One obvious critique of this approach is that it is risking too much on the particular therapist, as we know that therapists vary considerably. These variations include such dimensions as

(1) professional degree (psychiatrist, doctoral psychologist, masters level psychologist, social worker, counselor, marriage/family therapist);
(2) general level of experience (intern, newly licensed, mid or advanced career);
(3) level of experience with the particular presenting problem;
(4) theoretical orientation or "school" of psychotherapy;
(5) general competence at the proper diagnosis and treatment for the client's particular array of problems;
(6) skills at the nonspecifics;
(7) gender, race, and other cultural variables;

(8) expense (fee charged) and availability on patient's insurance panel;
(9) personal qualities such as intelligence, general problem-solving ability, life experience, sensitivity, relatedness, charisma.

We have named just a few relevant variables. One can imagine particular combinations of these (and other variables) having a felicitous influence on a particular client's prospects for change. On the other hand, one can also imagine arrays of these variables which would not be the cause for optimism, and may even have a negative effect.

In an attempt to compensate for this, variation has been the movement toward treatment by *teams* of professionals. These teams often comprise individuals from diverse professional backgrounds (e.g., physicians, substance abuse specialists, behavioral medicine specialists) and, indirectly, will often be diverse on one or the other helper dimensions listed above. A basic premise of this approach is that a client may need not just the expertise of a single discipline but the nature of the client's problem is best suited for a multidisciplinary approach. For example, an individual who is depressed, has gained weight and has been drinking too much may need a team consisting of a primary care physician (to monitor general health issues), a psychiatrist (to prescribe antidepressants), a substance abuse specialist (to address the problematic drinking), a nutritionist (to address obesity), and a psychologist (to provide psychotherapy for the depression and to help with a self-control obesity program). A key to such teams is that the treatment is in fact coordinated as opposed to each independently working with little or no knowledge of the others. An advantage of this model is that there can be many eyes on the case; so if some professional is dropping the ball, others can notice. Such coordination does not come automatically or even easily but must be planfully structured. These teams again may be more or less successful due to other classes of variables (e.g., cohesiveness of the team, experience in working together, and actual competence of individual members).

There are two serious problems with the team approach: (i) It can be very labor-intensive and thus prohibitively expensive. Third-party payers are unlikely to approve the expenditure unless highly justified, forcing the patient to pay out of pocket. Few patients are in a position to assume such expense, especially if there are cheaper alternatives. (ii) It can be unavailable. There are many rural and frontier areas or other areas underserved by healthcare professionals, making such teams simply not available.

THE ADJUNCTIVE MODEL: THERAPIST AS STRATEGIST

This volume is predicated on the view that the therapist needs to develop a case formulation, address these issues, and respond to questions such as the following:

(1) What constitutes a comprehensive assessment plan, case formulation, and treatment design for this client?

(2) What does the client (and others legitimately affected) prefer with respect to the above?
(3) What comprises a good financial value for the client and other payers?
(4) What is the minimally intrusive intervention for this client?
(5) As a therapist, what are my strengths and limitations with respect to the above and how can the latter be offset by other resources?

We believe these questions will provide a strategic vision for the therapist regarding each case. The second premise of this book is that evidence-based adjunctive therapies should be considered in this strategic vision as they can be (1) helpful, (2) client preferred, (3) less expensive, (4) less intrusive, (5) offsetting of the therapist's weaknesses, and (6) more comprehensive.

"Adjunctive" is defined by the Webster's dictionary as "something attached to another in a dependent or subordinate position." Thus, we are not thinking of adjunctive interventions as replacing needed face-to-face therapy, but something most often in addition to usual therapy.

A CASE ILLUSTRATION

Steve is a 42-year-old recently divorced father of two boys aged 6 and 9 years. He has graduated from college and runs a small computer repair business. He presents with complaints of crying, fatigue, and anger. He was divorced about 6 months ago after discovering that his wife was having a longstanding affair with her boss for 15 years. He has gained about 25 lbs in the last 9 months. His Beck Depression Inventory (BDI) is 16 with no indications of suicide ideation and a history of suicidal behavior. He reports that his depression is a reaction to his divorce, and he states he has no history of depression. His primary care physician recently diagnosed him with type 2 diabetes and reports that he is having trouble being treatment compliant. He lives in a small rural community about 1 hour's drive from the therapist's office, and there are no other mental health professionals practicing closer to his home. He was previously on his wife's insurance plan, and since the divorce he has no health insurance coverage.

One option would be for the therapist to attempt to treat all of Steve's problems. He could come in for evidence-based cognitive behavior therapy (CBT) for his mild depression and the therapist could also treat his diabetes noncompliance, his obesity, and his anger. In addition, he could help him cope with his divorce and his feelings of loss. Some of these targets, of course, may dissolve with success at initial treatment targets. However, this therapy could be rather long term and expensive in both time and money.

An option to be considered by the therapist in this case would be to assess "what is the best use of my professional expensive time in this case and what adjunctive resources can be used to leverage the client's money, time, and commitment?" This option might result in the therapist recommending the client to read David Burn's *Feeling Good* (an evidence-based bibliotherapy book) for his mild depression, recommending involvement in a diabetes disease management group at the local hospital based on the work of Dr Kate Lorig at Stanford, and seeing the client for six individual therapy sessions to treat his anger and difficulty in coping with the divorce. The client was presented with both options and he chose the second. However, he was told the diabetes self-management group is full and instead was recommended that he participate in the Internet version: Self-Management @ Stanford: Healthier Living With Diabetes (Internet) http://patienteducation.stanford.edu/internet/diabetesol.html

It is this kind of strategic vision we would like this book to help encourage in therapists. The therapist discerns the options and gives the client a choice. In so doing, the therapist is responding to the person's financial and time constraints and offers adjuncts that are sensitive to these. However, all the while the therapist is insisting that the treatment options be evidence-based (Fisher & O'Donohue, 2006).

We believe this treatment can be

(1) helpful (the evidence would suggest improvement in the all the treatment targets);
(2) client preferred (the client appreciated the wide scope of different expertise as well as the convenience and much lower costs of some of the methods of service delivery);
(3) less expensive (the book *Feeling Good* was less than $10 and the Internet group was less than $300);
(4) less intrusive. Both the book and the Internet therapy allowed less intrusion into his busy schedule, with less stigma and more privacy.
(5) Offsetting of the therapist's weaknesses. The therapist was not trained in diabetes disease management and thus was grateful that this client's need could be handled through other expertise.
(6) More comprehensive. The client's depression, diabetes management, and coping problem with the divorce were handled by the therapist. These three treatment targets were thought to be sufficient initially, as the therapist did not want the client overwhelmed. If the depression could be reduced, the client's health problems (and obesity) would improve along with his adjustment to the divorce be improved. With these changes it was likely that the client would no longer need therapy, as his life would be much more satisfactory to him.

ADJUNCTIVE THERAPY IN A STEPPED CARE MODEL

However, there may be times when what is considered here as an adjunctive therapy may serve as the main intervention. For example, if someone presents with concerns about a very low level depression, a stepped care model could involve something like

(1) watchful waiting;
(2) self-monitoring;
(3) bibliotherapy;
(4) Internet therapy (such as Seligman's AuthenticHappiness.com);
(5) prescription of exercise;
(6) support group;
(7) psychotherapy group;
(8) individual psychotherapy;
(9) medication;
(10) inpatient treatment.

As one goes up these steps, intrusiveness, cost, and in general treatment intensity increase. The following chapters will describe these in more detail and provide the evidence base. Stepped care is partly based on the following notions:

(1) Many of the problems we as mental health professionals deal with have very large incidence rates (e.g., depression, anxiety, obesity, oppositional defiant disorder) and thus would overwhelm the mental health system if all who suffered from these would present for tertiary care. Thus, public health approaches that are scalable to large numbers are needed. It is not an overall good strategy to perpetuate the present system based on the expectation that most individuals suffering from a problem simply will not present for treatment.
(2) Triage to the appropriate step may be necessary. However, in many cases it is permissible to "fail up," i.e., what appears to be a reasonable step for a particular individual (say bibliotherapy) is initiated, and if this fails, a higher step is then attempted (e.g., Internet therapy).
(3) Client preferences can also play a role in what step is tried. In stepped care, clients are given a lot of options. There is not a "one size fits all" mentality that is too common in our profession—the one size being one-to-one therapy for most mental health professionals or medications for medical professionals.
(4) Stepped care is a more affordable way to treat populations of individual suffering with many problems.

It is also possible that a client is from the start given a lower step therapy that we here consider adjunctive. This would normally be the case for clients whose problems are less intense, who may prefer these modalities, who cannot access higher level steps (geographical or financial reasons), or who may not want the stigma of psychotherapy (e.g., military personnel). This is common in many aspects of healthcare. Consider, for example, how often a urologist, after thoroughly examining an octogenarian male with a benignly enlarged prostate gland, recommends watchful waiting instead of a prostectomy. The same urologist might recommend watchful waiting in a very elderly man who already has early prostate cancer inasmuch as the cancer is so slow-growing that it will outlive the life span of the patient. The surgeon may further ascertain that allowing the slow-growing prostate cancer has a better prognosis than subjecting a man of very advanced age to the side effects of major surgery. Such determinations are common throughout medicine and surgery, but are uncommon in mental healthcare. This book addresses the importance of both adjunctive therapies and stepped care.

THE ORGANIZATION OF THIS BOOK

The book is broadly organized into two sections. The first gives a general overview of the major adjunctive modalities, whereas the second concentrates on a systematic description of their role in the treatment of a number of special populations.

The authors were asked to write their chapters in the following format:

(1) Basic description of the intervention with some examples.
(2) Outcome data:
   (a) Cost-efficiency;
   (b) Demonstrated range of applicability;
(3) The key process variables.
(4) The role in comprehensive treatment planning or stepped care and the coordination issues.
(5) The research agenda.
(6) The dissemination agenda.

REFERENCE

Fisher, J.E. & O'Donohue, T. (2006). *Practitionar's Guide to Evidence-Based Psychotheraphy*. New York: Spaiwuer.

2

Bibliotherapy as an Adjunctive Treatment

Read All About It

Negar Nicole Jacobs* and Elizabeth Mosco†

*Department of Psychiatry and Behavioral Sciences,
University of Nevada School of Medicine, Reno, NV
†Veteran's Administration Sierra Nevada Health
Care System, Reno, NV

There are many obvious advantages to bibliotherapy over traditional psychotherapy such as the ability to self pace, allowing individuals who are unable to receive mental health services due to geographical or transportational barriers receive treatment, cost-effectiveness for those who cannot afford psychotherapy or pharmacotherapy, providing individuals with privacy that can lessen stigmatization or labeling, and providing individuals with coping skills available after treatment has ended (Scogin et al., 2003). Despite these benefits, there are still many unknowns in the area of bibliotherapy such as for whom it is effective, for which psychological problems it is effective, what degree of adjunctive professional or nonprofessional help is needed, and what role can bibliotherapy play in integrated health care systems. We are defining bibliotherapy in this chapter as psychotherapeutic programs presented in a written self-help format as opposed to fictional stories or religious texts.

This chapter is intended to address these issues: First, the research literature regarding the clinical effectiveness and cost-effectiveness of bibliotherapy for a wide variety of problems will be outlined. Second, the literature on process variables leading to therapeutic change in patients utilizing bibliotherapy will be discussed. Third, the role of bibliotherapy within the context of a stepped care and integrated care environment will be addressed. Finally, research and dissemination agendas for the use of bibliotherapy as an adjunctive treatment will be proposed.

OUTCOME DATA

COST-EFFICIENCY

The economic impact of mental health problems nationwide is staggering. The financial burden exceeds $148 billion annually [National Institute of Mental Health (NIMH), 2000]. The costs associated with depression alone have increased from $44 billion in 1990 (Greenberg et al., 1993) to $83 billion in 2000 (Greenberg et al., 2003). Depression and anxiety disorders are associated with an increased use of general medical services, which in turn results in decreased resources for other patients, as well as increased costs to the patient, other taxpayers, and the insured public (Chiles et al., 1999). The intricate nature of integrated healthcare makes it difficult, if not impossible, to accurately predict the cost-effectiveness of a psychological intervention for the provider or the patient. Factors such as costs of implementing the intervention (salaries of providers, written or video materials, medication costs including testing for efficacy and safety, etc.), costs of subsequent medical utilization, and costs to the patient such as lost wages and productivity at work all must be considered when determining the cost-effectiveness of a psychological intervention (Gabbard et al., 1997).

Besides the obvious cost decrease when reading a $10 book as opposed to 12 sessions of psychotherapy with a psychologist billing at $150 per session, bibliotherapy may have more subtle financial benefits for patients and health care systems. One must remember that it is not only the monetary cost of therapy (e.g., $90/h) but also the transportation, child care, and opportunity costs that must be included in the comparison. As many as 25% of primary care outpatient visits can be accounted for by psychological factors that cause physiological disturbance with no permanent organ damage (migraines, functional bowel disease, types of chronic pain), and this rate rises to 50% if this is broadened to include conditions where actual physiological changes occur (hypertension, asthma, chronic skin disorders; Paulter, 1991). Researchers have found that brief psychotherapy can reduce patient stress levels, related physical symptoms, and overall medical costs (Cummings, 1993).

Jones (2002) evaluated the role of bibliotherapy in reducing health anxiety, which can lead to panic attacks, inability to cope, or depression. Health anxiety arises from the misinterpretation of bodily symptoms, leading patients to seek assurance from medical professionals and draining medical resources (Barsky et al., 1991). Smit et al. (2006) found that adding minimal contact bibliotherapy to the usual care of patients seen in primary care with subthreshold depression resulted in improved outcomes and generated lower costs over a 1-year period. The intervention resulted in a 30% decreased risk of developing a full-blown depressive disorder among participants.

In an interesting study of a manual-based behavioral therapy for obesity, different levels of therapist contact had minimal impact on the overall effectiveness of the treatment (Pezzot-Pearce et al., 1982). Obesity can lead to numerous costly physiological and psychological complications including hypertension, diabetes, cancer, osteoarthritis, stroke, sleep apnea, depression, and eating disorders, among many more. Researchers found that a 15-minute investment of therapist time during treatment resulted in a maintained 11-pound loss 6 months later. A 60-minute investment resulted in no additional loss, and a 300-minute investment resulted in 1 additional lost pound. The authors note that the findings "should make all therapists involved in obesity treatment seriously question not only the program effectiveness but perhaps more important, program efficiency as well (p. 449)." This study is a clear example of additional intervention not necessarily resulting in better outcomes. Fifteen minutes of a therapist's time versus 300 minutes of a therapist's time would have huge cost implications for the patient and the health care system resources. Clearly, bibliotherapy can play a significant role in reducing costs in integrated health care systems.

DEMONSTRATED RANGE OF APPLICABILITY

Treatment outcome studies involving bibliotherapy have proliferated over the past couple of decades. These studies encompass a wide range of psychological disorders and severities, as well as different levels of therapist assistance. The following is a representative review of the current research utilizing bibliotherapy with some of the most prevalent mental health problems.

Mood Disorders

Depression

Depression is now the leading cause of disability in the United States (NIMH, 2000). The World Health Organization (WHO) expects depression to be the most serious medical disease by the year 2020 (Murray & Lopez, 1997). Given these sobering statistics, it is no surprise that researchers have been evaluating treatments for depression, including bibliotherapy, for decades. Several meta-analyses of bibliotherapy for depression have also been conducted in order to examine the numerous research findings, with mostly promising results. Scogin et al. (2005) meta-analyzed four cognitive bibliotherapy treatment studies for geriatric depression (Floyd et al., 2004; Landreville & Bissonnette, 1997; Scogin et al., 1987, 1989). Each of the studies utilized David Burns' *Feeling Good* (1980), and typically involved reading and written exercises to be completed away from a clinic at the participant's own pace over a 4-week period. Researcher or therapist contact consisted of weekly telephone checkups of less than 5 minutes. All these studies led to significant improvement in depressive symptoms among participants.

Cuijpers (1997) also found in a meta-analysis of six studies addressing bibliotherapy for depression that overall bibliotherapy was as effective as individual or group therapy. McKendree-Smith et al. (2003) also reviewed several bibliotherapy studies for depression and concluded that those who have been used in clinical trials have effect sizes that are equivalent to the average effect sizes in traditional psychotherapy studies. In yet another meta-analysis,

Gregory et al. (2004) evaluated 29 cognitive bibliotherapy studies for depression. Bibliotherapy was found to be effective in improving depressive symptomatology in adolescent, adult, and older adult age groups. With the adolescent depression rate rising, as well as suicide and suicide attempts among adolescents (National Center for Health Statistics, 1992), finding means to provide treatments such as bibliotherapy to possibly reluctant teens is crucial. Ackerson et al. (1998) found a 4-week bibliotherapy with weekly telephone calls to be beneficial for adolescents experiencing mild and moderate depressive symptomatology.

Initial improvements gained from bibliotherapy for depression also appear to hold up at follow-up assessments. Floyd et al. (2006) conducted a 2-year follow-up of a study examining bibliotherapy versus individual psychotherapy with depressed older adults (Floyd et al., 2004). Although the individuals who participated in bibliotherapy had more recurrences of depression during the 2-year period, overall treatment gains on depression scale scores were maintained with no significant differences between treatment groups. Jamison and Scogin (1995) also found that bibliotherapy resulted in statistically and clinically significant improvement initially, and treatment gains were maintained at a 3-year follow-up (Smith et al., 1997). This research is encouraging to support bibliotherapy as a treatment for depression.

Although the research is promising, it is also important to be critical of the conclusions drawn from bibliotherapy research. For example, Anderson et al. (2005) evaluated 11 randomized control trials of bibliotherapy for depression. The authors found some evidence supporting the use of bibliotherapy; however, the studies they used in their analyses had relatively small sample sizes and "were overall of a poor quality" (p. 390). The authors also caution about the generalizability of bibliotherapy research to the primary care setting, where many, if not the majority of patients, are seeking and receiving treatment for depression as well as a myriad of other mental health problems (Cummings, 2003).

Anxiety Disorders

Estimates by the US Department of Health and Human Services (2006) indicate that approximately 44 million adults in the United States currently meet criteria for an anxiety disorder. DuPont et al. (1996) reported that anxiety disorders are the most costly mental illness ($46.4 billion), accounting for 31.5% of total expenditures for mental illness. As in the case of depression, these data have led to numerous evaluations of bibliotherapy for anxiety in an effort to meet the mental health demand. Several of these studies have utilized brief, non-psychotherapeutic contact, which proved to have a positive effect on treatment outcomes. Reeves and Stace (2005) examined the use of an assisted self-help treatment package for mild to moderate stress/anxiety with an adult population referred by their general practitioner. Assisted bibliotherapy consisted of 8 weeks of intervention, during which time participants read a cognitive-behavioral bibliotherapy package and engaged in 7 weekly 20-minute one-to-one "coaching sessions." There was significant improvement at posttreatment and at a 3-month follow-up. The researchers also found that 75% of participants found the bibliotherapy materials "very helpful," lending to bibliotherapy's face validity for potential consumers. Bowman et al. (1997) evaluated self-examination therapy (SET) in a bibliotherapeutic format over 4 weeks with therapist contact only to answer questions about carrying out the written material with no therapy provided. SET participants had a significant reduction in anxiety symptoms versus a delayed treatment condition, and these gains were maintained at a 3-month follow-up. The use of bibliotherapy in the treatment of anxiety disorders appears to be valuable, at least in some cases.

Febbraro (2005) investigated the effectiveness of bibliotherapy and minimal contact interventions in the treatment of panic attacks. Minimal contact in this study consisted of phone calls lasting no more than 15 minutes at weeks 2, 4, 6, and 8 of the 8-week intervention period. Results indicated that individuals receiving bibliotherapy and bibliotherapy with phone contact exhibited significant reductions on panic cognitions and fear of having a panic attack at posttreatment as well as clinically significant improvement on most dependent measures as compared with that in phone contact alone. Individuals in the bibliotherapy with phone contact condition demonstrated reduced panic symptoms and avoidance posttreatment. However, a significantly higher proportion of participants in the bibliotherapy with phone contact condition were more panic free than participants in the bibliotherapy-alone condition at posttreatment.

Sharp et al. (2000) investigated different levels of therapist contact using a cognitive-behavioral therapy (CBT) manual for panic disorder and agoraphobia in primary care over 12 weeks. A total of 104 patients were assigned to either standard therapist contact (eight 45-minute sessions), minimum contact (six 30-minute sessions), or bibliotherapy alone. Results indicated that bibliotherapy alone showed the weakest overall treatment response. Although this group showed significant improvements in global symptom severity and disruption in social life, there were no significant improvements in disruption of work and home life. The minimum contact group showed significant improvement on all measures, albeit modest. The standard contact group demonstrated the most significant and comprehensive treatment response, with a huge improvement in global symptom severity. This research emphasizes the use of bibliotherapy as an adjunct to, as opposed to stand alone, treatment in some cases.

Wright et al. (2000) investigated a bibliotherapy approach to relapse prevention in panic attacks. The study involved three phases: Phase 1 examined the effectiveness of assessment and feedback; Phase 2 examined the effectiveness of bibliotherapy and monitoring; and Phase 3 involved incorporating a self-help relapse prevention program for individuals completing the first two phases of the study with phone contact. The results of Phase 3 indicated that ongoing minimal phone contact with participants may be necessary for bibliotherapy-based interventions to be effective for individuals with panic problems.

In some cases, bibliotherapy has not proven to be as effective as standard psychological treatments but is significantly more effective than no treatment. Rapee et al. (2006) compared standard group therapy, waitlist, or a bibliotherapy version of treatments for childhood anxiety. Bibliotherapy was found to be beneficial to children compared with the waitlist group, but standard group treatment was found more effective in reducing anxiety. Nonetheless, relative to the waitlist condition, bibliotherapy with no therapist contact still resulted in approximately 15% more children being free of an anxiety disorder diagnosis after 12 and 24 weeks. Thus, bibliotherapy may be an effective option when traditional treatment is not immediately accessible, such as when clients are on a waitlist.

Hirai and Clum (2006) found in a meta-analytic study of self-help approaches for anxiety problems that self-help interventions were helpful and produced slightly less effect sizes than therapist-directed interventions. This study also found that dropout rates were comparable in both groups and were not related to diagnostic criterion. This implies that individuals with more severe anxiety problems can view self-help interventions as a viable treatment option as well as those with less severe symptoms. Den Boer et al. (2004) also conducted a meta-analysis of self-help treatments for mood disorders. Their analysis also showed a robust effect for bibliotherapy as a treatment for anxiety and depression, which might be chronic and recurrent.

In a review of bibliotherapy studies of anxiety disorders, Newman et al. (2003) found that bibliotherapy was the most effective for specific phobias. Pure self-help for panic disorder was not significantly different from a self-monitoring or waitlist condition, and self-help for obsessive-compulsive disorder (OCD) led to minimal change. However, when minimal therapist contact (check-ins, teaching to use self-help, rationale) was included, self-help was found to be more effective than waitlist for OCD and generalized anxiety disorder (GAD). This type of self-help also showed improvement in mixed anxiety disorder samples. The authors concluded that participants were most likely to respond to minimal contact self-help if they were motivated, their symptoms were not extremely severe, they were not too disabled from their symptoms, they were younger, had no personality disorders, and had not had recurrent bouts of anxiety. Treatment studies of bibliotherapy in the treatment of anxiety disorders has yielded encouraging results.

Alcohol Abuse

Between the years of 2001 and 2002, 9.7 million adult Americans met the DSM-IV criteria for alcohol abuse and 7.9 million Americans for alcohol dependence (Grant et al., 2004). Alcohol problems are notoriously difficult to treat, which has led researchers to focus on brief interventions that can be widely disseminated to prevent severe and difficult-to-treat cases of alcohol problems (Bien et al. 1993).

Apodaca & Miller (2003) conducted a meta-analysis of the effectiveness of bibliotherapy for alcohol problems using 22 research studies. They defined bibliotherapy as any written format of therapeutic intervention with a maximum of one session with a therapist, physician, or other health case worker. A relatively large effect size of 80 was found for bibliotherapeutic interventions. With the populations studied in bibliotherapy research, average effect size does not seem to increase significantly by adding more therapist intervention to bibliotherapy. Studies with longer follow-up periods (up to 8 years) have consistently shown little reversal in any of the initial reductions in drinking. Maintenance gains in one study were better for bibliotherapy over extensive outpatient treatment (Miller et al., 1980). These astonishing results led Miller to conclude: "There appears to be a segment of North American and European populations with heavy drinking and alcohol-related problems who will access self-help materials if readily available, but who are unlikely to seek counseling from agencies or telephone services" (p. 301).

Cunningham et al. (2002) assessed the effectiveness of a self-help book and a personalized assessment-feedback session, both separately and together, in the general population. Personalized assessment feedback (PAF) interventions are designed to increase motivation for change by providing normative feedback to individuals regarding their alcohol consumption compared with the alcohol consumption of others (heavy drinkers typically overestimate the consumption of others). The study found that at a 6-month follow-up, the combination of self-help book, and PAF had significantly improved drinking outcomes. However, research utilizing bibliotherapy for alcohol problems is mixed, and longer follow-up periods may be necessary to determine the effectiveness of these interventions.

Smoking

An estimated 20.9% (45.1 million) of adults in the United States are smokers (CDC, 2005). The research to date utilizing bibliotherapy for smoking cessation has indicated that bibliotherapy alone may not be effective but may become more effective when used as an adjunct to other modes of therapy. In a review of 60 randomized trials of different forms of self-help materials for smoking cessations, Lancaster and Stead (2006) concluded that self-help materials tailored to the individual may increase quit rates compared with no intervention, but the effect is likely to be small. The authors did not find any additional benefit gained when self-help was used in conjunction with other interventions such as advice from a professional or nicotine replacement therapy.

Curry et al. (2003) also studied self-administered treatments for smoking cessation. They found that there was no evidence that self-help manuals alone were effective. However, self-help manuals increase quit rates when combined with personalized adjuncts such as written feedback and outreach telephone counseling. Population-based estimates are that fewer than 5% of smokers use self-help materials, and those that those who do tend to be heavier, more addicted smokers with limited social support and poor health status. These factors may contribute to the limited effectiveness of bibliotherapy in the treatment of nicotine addiction.

Eating Disorders

It is estimated 1.5% of women and 0.5% of men reported having bulimia, and 3.5% of women and 2% of men reported having binge-eating disorder at some point in their lives (Hudson et al., 2007). In a study of a 12-week CBT bibliotherapy for bulimia and binge-eating disorder (Ghaderi, 2006), self-help had a moderate effect on the patients' eating problems. No significant difference was found between pure self-help and guided self-help. Carter and Fairburn (1998) evaluated a 12-week bibliotherapy study of pure self-help, guided self-help, or a waitlist control condition for binge-eating disorder. In the pure self-help condition, participants were mailed the bibliotherapy materials. Guided self-help involved six to eight 25-minute sessions in which a nonspecialist therapist facilitated the participants in using the bibliotherapy materials. Both pure and guided self-help were effective at reducing binge-eating behavior, and these gains were maintained at a 6-month follow-up. Guided self-help was more potent than pure self-help on many secondary outcomes, and compliance was higher in the guided group (92% read the whole book) versus the pure group (71% read the whole book).

Carter and colleagues (2003) evaluated two unguided self-help books, one cognitive-behavioral and one nonspecific, in the treatment of bulimia nervosa. The results indicated that both self-help conditions produced modest reductions in the primary behavioral symptoms of binge eating and purging for a subgroup of participants. In this study, neither condition was associated with a decrease in general psychopathology such as depression and anxiety. However, Bailer et al. (2004) found that an 18-week guided self-help bibliotherapy for bulimia and an 18-week 1.5 hours per week cognitive-behavioral group therapy conditions were both effective at decreasing binge eating and vomiting frequencies, as well as depressive symptomatology. Self-help had significantly higher remission rates, however, at follow-up than did the CBT condition. Cooper et al. (1996) also found guided self-help to be effective at reducing bulimic episodes. The researchers also found that those who had poorer outcomes or dropped out of treatment were more than twice as likely to have a history of anorexia nervosa and were somewhat more likely to have a personality disorder. Given the notorious difficulty of treating eating disorders and the difficulty in getting eating-disordered individuals to attend treatment, the above studies indicate that bibliotherapy may be a viable treatment option.

Sexual Dysfunction

Sexual dysfunction rates from a national probability sample indicate that 43% of women and 31% of men experience sexual dysfunction (Laumann et al., 1999). Given the feelings of shame or embarrassment that individuals experiencing sexual dysfunction may experience, bibliotherapy would appear to be a prime treatment venue for this problem. van Lankveld et al. (2001) investigated a 10-week bibliotherapeutic intervention for sexual dysfunctions. Males endorsed an improvement in their sexual functioning at both posttreatment and follow-up.

Females reported improvement in their sexual functioning at posttreatment, but not at follow-up. Several gains demonstrated at posttreatment eroded at follow-up including complaints about infrequency of sexual interaction and male ratings of distress associated with sexual dysfunction.

In a meta-analysis of bibliotherapy for sexual dysfunctions, van Lankveld (1998) found bibliotherapy to be initially effective for orgasmic disorders, but the gains were generally not maintained at follow-up. van Lankveld also cautioned, as did Rosen (1987), that improper diagnosis could damage the participant's health and well-being. The studies all examined in this meta-analysis included some sort of pretreatment assessment to exclude individuals with sexual problems for whom the treatment manuals would be inappropriate. Bibliotherapy appears to have demonstrated efficacy in the treatment of sexual dysfunctions. The effectiveness could be improved by having therapist contact to ensure proper diagnosis as well as provide encouragement to engage in follow-up reading to maintain gains.

Meta-analyses

Meta-analyses have also been conducted looking at a range of different psychological problems. In a meta-analysis of bibliotherapy studies by Marrs (1995), the author found that bibliotherapy appeared more effective for certain problem types (assertion training, anxiety, sexual dysfunction) than for others (weight loss, impulse control, and studying problems). Overall, it was found that the amount of therapist contact did not seem to relate to effectiveness, but there was evidence that certain problem types (weight loss and anxiety reduction) responded better with increased therapist contact. Gould and Clum (1993) conducted a meta-analysis of self-help treatment approaches, the majority of which were bibliotherapeutic in nature (audiotape, videotape were also included). The effect size of self-help treatments was nearly as large as therapist-assisted interventions within the same studies. Self-help problems seemed to be most effective with problems associated with skill deficits and diagnostic problems such as fears, depression, headache, and sleep disturbance rather than habit disorders such as smoking, drinking, and overeating. Overall, the research regarding the use of bibliotherapy as an adjunct, as well as a stand-alone treatment, is promising and lends support for its use for a myriad of problems.

KEY PROCESS VARIABLES

Research on bibliotherapy has focused on questions of effectiveness while largely ignoring identification of process variables. Cohen (1994) stated that bibliotherapy is "a combination of two poorly researched and understood phenomena: reading and psychotherapy" (p. 40). Marrs (1995) noted in his meta-analysis that most of the studies he examined did not include information on potential moderating variables, such as reading ability or education level of the participants, how much the subjects used the bibliotherapy materials, or personality variables of the readers. This problem parallels the state of research in traditional psychotherapy, where mediating and moderating variables have not been clearly demonstrated. For example, Whisman (1993) has observed that even with cognitive therapy for depression, which has been extensively researched and repeatedly found to be efficacious, conclusions regarding mediators of change "should be viewed as tentative" due to mixed results for the cognitive mediation hypothesis and small-effect sizes across studies for the effects of cognitive therapy on cognitive phenomena (p. 258).

The literature of the 1950s and 1960s defined bibliotherapy as a treatment modality consisting of three main components: Identification, insight, and catharsis (Lenkowsky, 2001). Schrank and Engels (1981) explained that identification involves developing an affiliation with the literature and may lead to perspective taking, which can help readers develop a sense of normalization and validation. Identification may also help readers learn vicariously through the experience of others. Catharsis occurs through vicarious experience and may lead to insight. Insight is the result of readers seeing their own experiences described in the literature. This insight is hoped to allow for positive change in attitude and behavior. Despite the popularity of defining bibliotherapy by these three components, there is no clear data to substantiate them as process variables.

Cohen (1994) interviewed readers of self-materials about how the literature was helpful to them and found some common themes including: Recognition of self, ways of feeling, and ways of knowing. Ways of feeling involved shared experience (normalization), validation, hope, comfort, inspiration, and catharsis. Ways of knowing included understanding (insight) and gathering of information such as specific techniques for dealing with problematic situations. Readers also identified escape functions and seeing bibliotherapy as an alternative form of therapy, likening reading to being in a support group or meeting with a psychotherapist.

While there are no clear conclusions on what variables account for change in bibliotherapy, some studies have shed light on putative process variables. Overall, these studies point to nonspecific processes thought to exist in almost all therapies, variables that may be the ingredients of change in more traditional psychotherapies, and factors specific to bibliotherapy such as amount of therapist contact, content of bibliotherapy, and understanding of reading materials.

Most treatment modalities involve a variety of nonspecific factors which have been linked to treatment outcomes. Frank (1982) noted that these nonspecific process variables include the therapeutic relationship, having a designated healing setting, provision of a rationale for symptoms and an explanation of treatment procedure, and the treatment procedure itself. These factors were thought to remoralize clients and restore hope for clinical improvement. Ilardi and Craighead (1994) proposed that all of Frank's nonspecific processes could be boiled down to hope. The authors referred to the body of literature supporting placebo effects, stating that such effects were likely due to expectancy effects, or hope.

Along these lines, Marrs' (1995) meta-analysis of bibliotherapies found that studies which used placebo control groups had smaller effect sizes than those using no treatment controls, suggesting that part of the effectiveness of bibliotherapy may be due to expectation effects.

Other factors that are common to most forms of treatment and likely to be active ingredients of change include compliance issues. Compliance with treatment has been related to positive treatment outcome, with results showing clear dose-response patterns. For example, in a study assessing the effectiveness of a self-help approach in the treatment of bulimia nervosa and binge-eating disorder, Ghaderi (2006) found that 40% of the variance in the outcome variable could be explained by the number of stages of the treatment program the subject had worked through. Compliance with treatment was assessed by asking participants on a weekly basis to identify the stage of the program they were currently in, rate how well they felt they were able to follow the program, and identify what elements in the program they thought to be most helpful in reducing problematic eating behaviors. In another study, Burns and Nolen-Hoeksema (1992) found that compliance with the cognitive therapy protocol for depression, as evidenced by completion of homework, was positively related to outcome. However, the authors noted that further research was needed to determine the factors underlying this correlation and suggested the possibility of learning of coping skills. They also suggested that homework completion could be reflective of a third variable, such as motivation, which could in turn cause clinical improvements. Alternatively, they hypothesized that clinical improvements could cause motivation to do homework assignments, which could then account for clinical improvements. Since compliance is likely a rich process variable, research on bibliotherapy should routinely ask readers to identify how much they have read and include some measure of the extent to which the materials were applied in the reader's daily life (such as amount of time spent or number of skills used per week).

Issues around demographic factors, client characteristics, and diagnostic variables are also likely to be related to treatment outcomes for both traditional psychotherapies and bibliotherapies. Treatments may be differentially effective based on demographic variables such as age, gender, educational level, socio-economic status, and ethnicity. Personality characteristics such as levels of insight, psychological-mindedness, and motivation are also likely to be predictive of treatment outcome. Furthermore, variables around type of diagnosis, severity of symptoms, and possible comorbidity of other mental health problems would be expected to relate to treatment outcome in bibliotherapy just as in traditional psychotherapy. Although there is little systematic research on these variables as mediators or moderators of change in bibliotherapy, some authors have commented on these factors as indications and contraindications for recommendation of bibliotherapy (see below).

Just as the therapeutic relationship is thought to be a nonspecific factor accounting for change in traditional psychotherapy, amount of therapist contact may be an important process variable in bibliotherapy. And, just as the jury is still out on the importance of the therapeutic relationship in traditional psychotherapy as an essential ingredient of change, there is mixed data in the field of bibliotherapy on level of therapist contact and effectiveness of the treatment. Several meta-analyses have discovered that there are no significant differences between self-administered and therapist-administered treatments (i.e., Cuijpers, 1997; Marrs, 1995; Scogin et al., 1990). For example, in a meta-analysis analyzing the effectiveness of bibliotherapy, Marrs (1995) found no overall relationship between amount of therapist contact and effectiveness during bibliotherapy. However, it was noted that all of the studies, by virtue of having the subjects respond to recruitment efforts, had at least some contact with a therapist. The effectiveness of bibliotherapies bought from bookstore shelves could not therefore be determined. Marrs (1995) also cautioned that most of the studies in the meta-analysis did not use samples from a clinical population and that the conclusions of the study could not be generalized to more severe clinical concerns. On the other hand, several studies found that higher levels of therapist contact were increasingly effective in treating anxiety problems (i.e., Sharp et al., 2000). Other meta-analyses have come to different conclusions. For example, Gould and Clum's (1993) meta-analysis showed that the combination of bibliotherapy plus therapy was more effective than minimal therapist contact treatment modalities. Similarly, Pantalon et al. (1995) concluded that bibliotherapy is best used when combined with other therapeutic modalities.

Obviously, the actual content of the bibliotherapeutic materials is a likely ingredient of change. Content factors that could be process variables include provision of validation, normalization, and support; education about new coping skills; knowledge and understanding of the materials discussed; changes in attitudes, thoughts, and behaviors; and changes in self-efficacy. First, although there is no research to indicate that providing validation, normalization, or support is an active ingredient of change, early researchers in the field have identified "identification," which may be a form of validation or normalization, as a possible process variable (see Schrank & Engels, 1981, see above). Validation, normalization, and support may come through the process of providing psychoeducation about the symptoms, the course of the disorder, and the likely effects the problems may have on the reader's life. Reading about others with similar problems and how they are coping may also help in that readers can develop perspective about their own problems.

Second, learning new skills to manage symptoms may be another process variable. For example, Whisman (1993) proposed that mediators of change in cognitive therapy for depression would be cognitive mediation through changes in automatic thoughts, attributional style, and challenging negative expectancies. However, Ilardi and Craighead (1994) outlined studies showing that much of the change in outcome scores in cognitive therapy for depression was found early in treatment, before the introduction of cognitive restructuring techniques, and thus attributed this change to the nonspecific factors and not to cognitive mediation.

Third, the reader's knowledge and understanding of the materials read is a putative process variable. Lichstein (1994) termed this "receipt," or accuracy of the reader's comprehension of the treatment, and noted that deficits in receipt would jeopardize the internal validity of a treatment. Scogin et al. (1998) developed a test of cognitive bibliotherapy knowledge in order to test whether the extent to which a reader exhibits mastery of the knowledge thought to be important for a treatment is actually an active ingredient of treatment. Despite the hypothesis that increases in knowledge in a psychoeducationally oriented cognitive therapy program should be related to positive outcomes, the study found no such relationship. However, the authors suggested that knowledge without application of that knowledge could be a "necessary but not sufficient" ingredient for change.

Fourth, changes in attitudes, thoughts, and behaviors targeted by the bibliotherapy materials may be active ingredients of change. Several reviews of bibliotherapy research have linked bibliotherapy with attitude change (i.e., Schrank & Engels, 1981; Stevens & Pfost, 1982) whereas other reviews have found mixed results (i.e., Riordan & Wilson, 1989).

Finally, a change in self-efficacy (Bandura, 1977), an individual's belief that he or she can successfully respond to a particular situation, may be an active ingredient of change in bibliotherapy. Buenaver et al. (2006) reviewed literature assessing the effectiveness of a mixture of self-help treatments for a variety of chronic pain conditions and found that self-efficacy appeared to be a mediating variable in the effectiveness of self-help therapies in reducing pain.

Understanding what variables account for change in bibliotherapy is likely a very complex question that depends on many factors, like those mentioned above and others yet to be identified. As outlined in the outcomes section above and as shown in Papworth's (2006) second-order review of meta-analyses of the effectiveness of self-help approaches, bibliotherapy has been shown to have varying levels of effectiveness depending on these types of variables and the interactions between these variables. Despite Glasgow and Rosen's (1978) call to researchers to identify subject predictors of treatment outcomes, almost 30 years of subsequent research on bibliotherapy has produced no clear results on the matter.

There is a significant unmet need for further research to identify the critical ingredients of change, including mediating and moderating variables that may shed light on processes of change in bibliotherapy. As discussed in the *Research Agenda* section below, researchers could use time-series methodology designs with frequent data points measuring putative process variables and then test to see whether these covary with change in the outcome variable, precede that change in time, and change only within the treatment condition that contains the intervention (Hollon et al., 1990). Researchers could also use component analysis studies to systematically identify the active ingredients of change. Whisman (1993) suggested task analysis studies, such as those analyzing the effects of important interactional sequences between therapist and client on client change.

Researchers could also use sophisticated methodologies such as structural equation modeling to identify causal pathways of change in bibliotherapy. Eliciting qualitative feedback from readers of the elements thought to be useful could also help identify process variables that could later be tested through quantitative methods.

ROLE IN COMPREHENSIVE TREATMENT PLAN AND STEPPED CARE ISSUES

Some researchers have proposed a "stepped care" approach as a feasible alternative to traditional models of service delivery (i.e., Lovell & Richards, 2000; Newman, 2000). In this model, patients would first be offered the most effective yet least intensive and restrictive therapeutic interventions and gradually "stepped" up to more complex treatments should monitoring of treatment outcomes indicate that they become necessary (NICE, 2002). Stepped care models of treatment are advantageous in that they identify and initially utilize the least expensive and time-consuming treatment options, promising cost-effective treatment.

There are several other advantages to using bibliotherapy in the context of a stepped care approach. For many patients with mild to moderate symptoms, "full-blown therapy" may not be necessary or even appropriate. Such symptoms may be "subclinical" but significantly distressing. Bibliotherapy offered as an initial step in a stepped care model is a good treatment option for many patients. Scogin (2003, p. 249) notes that one of the potential benefits of bibliotherapy is its ability to reach populations who may be experiencing "non-reimbursable subsyndromal difficulties." Another advantage of bibliotherapy is its potential to prevent such subclinical difficulties from developing into full-blown clinically significant disorders (Scogin, 2003). In addition, the demand for mental health services currently outweighs the supply of mental health practitioners properly trained to deliver those services. Bibliotherapy delivered in the context of a stepped care mental health model is a potential solution to the need for effective and efficient treatment (Den Boer et al., 2004; Lovell & Richards, 2003). Furthermore, Glasgow and Rosen (1979) noted that bibliotherapy would be useful in a stepped care strategy to provide some self-help materials to clients that may otherwise be placed on a waitlist in a busy practice.

The use of bibliotherapy in the context of a stepped care model addresses many of the criticisms that have been aimed at this form of self-help. Since the treatments in a stepped care model are administered and monitored by professional providers, issues around appropriate assignment of treatment, quality of bibliotherapeutic approaches, potential iatrogenic effects, and negative treatment outcomes are addressed by the provider. Providers would be able to screen patients in order to ensure that they meet inclusion and exclusion criteria for assignment to treatments. Through familiarity with the literature on evidence-based self-administered treatments, providers could ensure recommendation of the most efficacious treatments available. In addition, the approach would be self-correcting via monitoring of patient outcomes. Should bibliotherapy be harmful or fail to ameliorate the patient's presenting complaints, higher levels of care would be offered sequentially until treatment progress were made and maintained.

Literature in the field of bibliotherapy offers many examples of the use of this treatment modality in the context of a stepped care approach. Two representative examples are presented here. First, Newman (2000) outlined the use of a self-administered treatment in a stepped care model for the treatment of GAD, proposing that individuals with moderate levels of GAD and meeting certain exclusion criteria (no evidence of personality disorders, interpersonal problems, or emotional avoidance) be provided with a computer-assisted therapy and that those with more severe GAD symptoms be offered the traditional but more intensive 12–14 sessions of individual CBT for anxiety. Second, Tolfin et al. (2005) found preliminary evidence supporting a stepped care model for treatment of OCD. Twenty percent of subjects responded well to the initial step of treatment, involving assignment to a cognitive-behavioral bibliotherapy approach focusing on exposure and ritual prevention. Of the remaining subjects who were then assigned to therapist-assisted bibliotherapy (in which the therapist provided CBT education and advice but did not participate in exposure exercises), 29% were responders. The remaining patients were then assigned to traditional therapist-administered CBT and 67% of these patients responded well. The authors also noted that the stepped care model of treatment they proposed demonstrated cost-effectiveness.

BIBLIOTHERAPY IN PRIMARY CARE SETTINGS

Given the variety of mental health related presenting complaints made to primary care providers and given that the majority of mental health problems are treated in the primary care setting, it is crucial that a wide range of appropriate and effective treatment options be available to patients in this setting. Use of a stepped care model to address mental health problems in the primary care setting is one way to meet this demand. Gilbody et al. (2003) have suggested that using a self-help approach, such as bibliotherapy, as the first element in a stepped care model in a primary care setting would make sense, especially if primary care providers had appropriate training in the use of this approach (Whitfield & Williams, 2003). Lovell et al. (2003) have documented the effectiveness of using a stepped care model in the primary care setting for treating mental health problems. They showed that use of the stepped care model decreased the number of patients seen in primary care while proving to have similar effectiveness as traditional mental health services.

Bibliotherapy has been used extensively in primary care settings, often in the context of a stepped care model. For example, Scogin et al. (2003) proposed a stepped care model for the treatment of depression in primary care settings, citing evidence for the effectiveness of such treatment in individuals with mild to moderate levels of depression (i.e., Scogin et al., 1987). In this model, they suggested that depression first be assessed using screening instruments such as the Beck Depression Inventory (BDI; Beck et al., 1961). They recommended that bibliotherapy be used as a first-line treatment approach for individuals shown by screening to have mild to moderate levels of depression. Patients who did not show full remission in depression with bibliotherapy alone would then move to the next level in the stepped care model, involving the combination of antidepressant medication plus bibliotherapy. If this level of care did not prove to be effective, antidepressant medication plus evidence-based psychotherapy would then be recommended. The highest level of care in the stepped care model would be evaluation of medication and therapy options. The authors noted that adherence to treatment in this model could be improved by having providers thoroughly explain the stepped care approach to treating depression, and that the approach should only be used for patients who expressed a willingness to participate in a bibliotherapy approach. They also noted that providers using this approach should develop a system of tracking progress in patients and suggested the use of weekly phone calls. Researchers have demonstrated the effectiveness of bibliotherapy in primary care settings for a wide range of clinical disorders including anxiety (i.e., Reeves & Stace, 2005), panic disorder and agoraphobia (i.e., Power et al., 2000), and depression (i.e., Willemse et al., 2004).

FACTORS TO CONSIDER WHEN RECOMMENDING BIBLIOTHERAPY

On the basis of their research on the use of bibliotherapy in a stepped care model of treatment delivery for depression, Scogin et al. (2003) argue that self-administered treatments should be considered for some types of mental health problems and for certain types of consumers. Although no systematic research has been done on appropriate inclusion and exclusion criteria for users of bibliotherapy, some authors have commented on indications and contraindications for therapists to consider when recommending bibliotherapy. In research analyzing matching effects for various client characteristics with treatment techniques, Beutler et al. (1991) found that clients high in reactance and resistance had better treatment outcomes with self-administered treatments such as bibliotherapy. Some authors have suggested that bibliotherapy would be most appropriate for clients with mild to moderate levels of depression as well as for clients interested in the self-management of more chronic depression (i.e., Anderson et al., 2005). Campbell and Smith (2003) have noted that individuals with internalized coping styles tend to use bibliotherapy more successfully than those with externalized coping styles. They note that there has been no systematic research to match reader variables with bibliotherapeutic treatments, but they suggest that providers could extrapolate from research matching clients to traditional psychotherapy treatments (i.e., Beutler et al., 1991).

With respect to contraindications for use of bibliotherapy, some studies (i.e., Newman, 2000; Reeves & Stace, 2005) have noted that factors such as symptom severity, personality disorders, emotional avoidance, interpersonal distress, and comorbid psychological symptoms be taken into account when deciding whether to assign a client to bibliotherapy. Specifically, they recommended that bibliotherapy be offered to clients with moderate symptom severity, screening negative for personality disorders, low levels of emotional avoidance, and low levels of interpersonal problems. Mains and Scogin (2003) note that in treatments for depression, factors that likely reduce the effectiveness of self-administered treatments include severe depression, suicidality, comorbidity, and defensiveness. With respect to comorbid psychological problems, it has been suggested that clients with a high risk of harm to self or others, alcohol or drug misuse, and psychosis be excluded. Of course, clients who are not able to read or comprehend the language used in the assigned reading materials at a sufficient level should not be offered bibliotherapy.

With respect to principles to follow when assigning self-help books, Katz and Watt (1992) use a drug analogy, likening recommendation of bibliotherapy to the prescription of psychotropic medications. They suggest that both books and medications should be prescribed with consideration of the patient's problems, characteristics, and the likely effects of the treatment recommended. Furthering the drug analogy, they note that compliance with medications is best in the context of a good therapeutic relationship and when the doctor has a good attitude toward the intervention, and they suggest that the same would apply to recommendation of a book. Additionally, they note that as with prescription of a drug, providers recommending bibliotherapy should address patients' expectations of the treatment and address any potential problems a patient may encounter when making use of the recommended treatment.

Mains and Scogin (2003) also offer a number of recommendations practitioners should follow when making use of bibliotherapy as an adjunctive treatment. First, they suggest that response to treatment and progress should be monitored. They note that changes in symptomatology may necessitate changes in treatment, as in a stepped care model. Second, they state that maintenance programs should be implemented if individuals are progressing with the self-administered treatment. Third, they note that the characteristics of individuals should be considered when assigning self-help as a treatment modality and only individuals that would be good candidates (i.e., highly motivated) for bibliotherapy should be recommended that treatment modality. Fourth, they observed that generally speaking, self-administered treatments involving some degree of therapist contact were more effective than such treatments alone. Fifth, they documented variable effectiveness in self-administered treatments for different disorders, noting that bibliotherapy may not be effective for certain disorders (see above). Finally, they warned providers about the lack of research on self-administered treatments and encouraged them to recommend self-help books that have been tested for efficacy, such as *Feeling Good* (Burns, 1980). However, they cautioned practitioners that self-administered treatments proving to be effective in a research context may not be as effective in a real-world context. Given the lack of research on the effectiveness of most bibliotherapies on the market, the authors encouraged providers to use "caution and clinical judgment" in the recommendation of self-administered treatments (Mains & Scogin, 2003, p. 245).

In summary, given the mixed data on the effectiveness of bibliotherapy, it is advisable to use bibliotherapy as an adjunct as opposed to as a stand-alone treatment. Pardeck and Pardeck (1984) argue that such adjunctive bibliotherapy should be utilized with the guidance of a therapist at *every* stage, including selection of the self-help material, reading and understanding of that material, and integration of the material into the rest of the therapeutic process. In fact, Hynes and Hynes-Berry (1986) contend that the essential ingredient of change involved in bibliotherapy is not the materials themselves but the process of discussing the materials with the therapist.

RESEARCH AGENDA

Although consumers have a variety of options when selecting a self-help program, the proliferation of self-help literature may be ahead of its empirical evaluation. Several researchers have addressed the paucity of empirical research in regard to the efficacy of self-help material (Craighead et al., 1984; Glasgow & Rosen, 1978; Riordan & Wilson, 1989; Schrank & Engels, 1981; Stevens & Pfost, 1982).

In a search of www.amazon.com by Rosen et al. (2003), 137 self-help books were listed for just the letter "A." In a subsequent search of PsychInfo, in response to the key words "self-help books," only 83 references were listed since 1970. More promisingly, a search of "bibliotherapy" found 472 references. However, in the decade from 1990 to 1999, 205 records were listed, and after excluding dissertations, book chapters, commentaries, and review articles on the use of bibliotherapy, only 15 references remain. This is an astoundingly low number of studies considering the thousands of self-help books available at www.amazon.com. Thus, despite the handful studies that have evaluated self-help programs, a massive gap exists in the self-help literature between the number of programs available and the number of programs evaluated for effectiveness. The problem with unevaluated self-help literature is that there is not only no guarantee that these treatments will be effective, but that these treatments could be iatrogenic.

Gordon Paul asked the critical psychotherapy research question nearly 40 years ago, "What treatment, by whom, is the most effective for this individual with that specific problem, and under which set of circumstances, and how does that come about?" (Paul, 1969). Unfortunately, there are no official standards for self-help materials. However, several authors have offered suggestions for the evaluation of self-help materials. "The only way to know the effectiveness of well-intentioned instructional materials, when they are entirely self-administered, is to test those specific materials in the context of their intended usage. Psychologists who write self-help manuals based on methods they find in office settings have no assurance that the public can successfully apply these procedures on their own," (Rosen et al., 2003, p. 410). Stevens and Pfost (1982) offer some guidelines to address when evaluating and publishing studies examining bibliotherapy. These are (1) clearly define the type of literature (imaginative vs didactic, oral vs written); (2) clearly state the amount of therapist contact (therapist-directed bibliotherapy vs minimal, contact vs no contact); (3) describe the client characteristics for whom the bibliotherapy is evaluated (age, intelligence, presenting problem, gender, socioeconomic status); (4) clearly define the therapeutic goals (attitude change, behavior change, values clarification); (5) clearly define the duration of bibliotherapy; and, (6) state whether bibliotherapy is used alone, or as an adjunct to another treatment. These guidelines address Rosen et al. (2003) recommendations that "the value of a self-help program can only be known by testing the specific content and instructions of that program under the conditions for which it is intended" (p. 408).

On the other hand, some researchers argue that we may be holding bibliotherapy up to standards to which traditional psychotherapy is not held accountable (Floyd et al., 2004). Regardless of the position one takes on the current status of bibliotherapy research, few would argue that further research on bibliotherapeutic interventions is not warranted. There are many potent questions regarding the usefulness of bibliotherapy as a stand-alone or an adjunct treatment:

- What psychological problems are effectively addressed with bibliotherapy?
- Are there certain characteristics of responders versus non-responders to bibliotherapy?
- How much therapist contact is needed?
- Can bibliotherapy be used as a preventative measure?
- What are the mechanisms of action (process variables) operating in bibliotherapy?
- Is bibliotherapy cost-effective for the provider and consumer?

There are countless potential variations of bibliotherapy research that could address these questions: The following are four ways to address these potential areas:

TIME-SERIES METHODOLOGY

As described in an earlier section, there is an abundance of promising research demonstrating the benefit of bibliotherapy interventions for many psychological problems. Mood disorders such as depression and anxiety appear to particularly receptive to self-help intervention, especially cases which are of mild to moderate severity. The trouble is other psychological problems, such as addictive disorders, which repeatedly show resistance to self-help. According to Hayes et al. (1999), if a problem is complex and resistant to treatment, the task is not of just evaluation but also of more sophisticated forms of case analysis and technique development. Time series methodology, also called single-case designs, is a way to systematically evaluate these hard-to-treat cases. Because of course, for every hard-to-treat case, there are many more to follow, clogging up the health care systems and stymieing clinicians.

Group comparison approaches to psychological research rely on calculating a central tendency of scores within a sample. The major argument for this approach is that the sample results generalize to a population, thereby maximizing external validity. One trouble of this method is that with complicated psychological problems or new venues for delivering psychological treatment (such as primary care), group comparison designs do not provide data regarding exactly what is contributing, or where there is an obstacle, to behavioral changes as a result of treatment. Single case designs monitor a handful of participants very carefully, frequently assessing behavioral change and what is contributing to it. These types of designs also allow the researcher to add or drop different facets of the treatment in order to determine what is contributing to change (such as therapist contact). The majority of bibliotherapy research today includes treatment packages evaluated at a group level. It is difficult, if not impossible to pinpoint exactly what the key process variables are and what variables may be mediating or moderating treatment outcomes.

For example, what we know from group level comparisons is that problem drinking is extremely difficult to treat with a self-help book alone. Perhaps by examining this behavior in a single case design, different interventions and combinations of interventions can be implemented and then frequently assessed for treatment gains and pitfalls. Group comparison designs generally allow too many variables to interfere with answering these questions, but single case designs can provide a systematic starting point.

PRIMARY CARE

As many as 90% of people with a mental health problem are managed solely in primary care (Goldberg & Huxley, 1992). Other researchers have found that approximately half of the cases of depression are treated by general practitioners (Munoz et al., 1994). With integrated healthcare now the norm, treating mental health problems in primary care is essential. The benefit of integrated care is that mental health screenings are discovering problems such as anxiety and depression which may have been overlooked until the symptomatology became severe and required intensive intervention. The problem is that there is a limited number of mental health professionals and space for mental health professionals in primary care settings. Thus, bibliotherapy, in particular treatments that can be administered and monitored by nonmental health care providers, ideal in this type of environment.

For example, in a pilot study of nurse-facilitated self-help for agoraphobia (Lovell et al., 2003), results indicated that 89% of clients were clinically significantly improved at posttreatment. In another study by Kupshik and Fisher (1999), assisted bibliotherapy for anxiety with a nurse led to clinically significant improvements, with increased improvement in symptoms with increased level of contact (72% showing clinically significant improvement when meeting with a nurse every week).

If we refer back to Paul's question posed earlier, we cannot assume that treatments effective in other settings with other patients will generalize to the primary care setting, primary care patients, and primary care providers. Psychotherapy research within this setting is needed to determine what will work with the symptomatology and resources in primary care, and bibliotherapy is a logical intervention to research given the time and resource constraints within this milieu.

PREVENTION

Prevention research is particularly tricky in any modality due multiple outcome variables. For example, in alcohol prevention research, alcohol-involved problems become intermediate variables such as traffic crashes or alcohol-related health problems which can alter distal variables such as utilization of emergency health services for injuries or future inpatient and outpatient medical costs due to chronic alcohol-related health problems (Holder, 2002).

In a study mentioned previously in this chapter, Smit et al. (2006) found that adding minimal contact bibliotherapy to the usual care of patients seen in primary care with subthreshold depression resulted in a 30% decreased risk of developing a full-blown depressive disorder. Of course, preventing depressive symptomatology has positive repercussions for the patient and the health care system as a whole. Yeater et al. (2004) found that bibliotherapy participants reported less participation in risky dating behaviors and improvement in sexual communication strategies across a variety of dating situations; however, the self-help book was no more effective than the waitlist control in reducing rates of sexual victimization. Clearly, there are many possible benefits as well as room for improvement in prevention research. Prevention efforts are typically most effective when reaching a large audience, making bibliotherapy an optimal choice for disseminating prevention interventions. Stepped care models used in primary care settings would be perfect to study the effectiveness of bibliotherapy in prevention. Of course, empirical evaluation of these interventions is the first step.

GENERALIZABILITY

Several bibliotherapeutic interventions have proven effective for mood disorders among other psychological problems in well-controlled research settings. However, the question of generalizability remains: How do these interventions work in the bookstore sample? How effective are these interventions when individuals not assessed for their participation in a study pick up a self-help book and start reading? How effective is the lay person at self-diagnosis and choosing an effective self-help book? How compliant are readers with no one calling to assess their progress in completing the book and monitoring their symptomatology? There are no obvious answers nor are there obvious ways of evaluating these questions. A book like *Feeling Good*, which has been found highly effective over and over again in research settings, could be overlooked for a flashier title in the self-help aisle. Individuals suffering with depressive symptomatology could pick up a book about bipolar disorder and become frustrated when the intervention is not relevant to their problem. Individuals with severe OCD could become discouraged and hopeless when they are unable to follow-through with the self-help intervention techniques on their own. Even worse, these problems could lead to iatrogenic effects, as cautioned by Rosen (1987). A handful of newer self-help books are including postcards to return to the publisher regarding readers' satisfaction with the self-help book. These postcards could also invite readers to participate in further research to analyze the effectiveness of the book. The obvious problem with this method is a self-selection bias in terms of those individuals completing and returning the postcards.

There are no current methods of evaluating the bookstore sample of self-help book utilizers. Despite the obvious difficulty in developing methods to conduct this research, as psychological researchers it would be useful to begin thinking of different ways to approach this issue in the near future.

Of course this is by no means an exhaustive list, but rather a sample of valuable routes bibliotherapy research could take given the literature currently available and the changing trends in the mental health field in general.

Jacobs and O'Donohue (2007) offer a case example that could be used as a model for the research agenda of bibliotherapy. The authors noticed a significant gap in the self-help literature for quality treatment of the emotional aspects of infertility, such as depression, anxiety, and relationship problems. Heeding Miller's (1969, p. 1074) call to "give psychology away," the authors drew upon existing evidence-based techniques for the treatment of depression (i.e., Beck et al., 1979; Burns, 1980; Lewinsohn et al., 1984, 1992), anxiety (i.e., Bernstein & Borkovec, 1973; Carlson & Bernstein, 1995; Linehan, 1993a, 1993b), and marital conflict (i.e., Jacobson & Margolin, 1979) and adapted them to issues specific to the infertility experience. The self-help book, *Coping with Infertility: Clinically Proven Ways of Managing the Emotional Roller Coaster* (CWI), was then evaluated for content validity by presenting the written materials to both focus groups of infertility patients and to consultants with known expertise in the area(s) of infertility, CBT, and/or bibliotherapy. Feedback was incorporated into revisions of the book. The book was then evaluated in a randomized clinical trial to analyze the efficacy of the materials in addressing the emotional aspects of infertility. One hundred and fifteen female participants self-identifying with infertility-related emotional distress were recruited from a fertility clinic and randomly assigned to either the bibliotherapy condition or to a waitlist control condition. Dependent variables included measures of depression, anxiety, relationship satisfaction, hope, self-efficacy, treatment compliance, motivation to stay in fertility treatment, number of conceptions, and satisfaction with the bibliotherapy approach. These measures were collected at pretreatment, posttreatment, and at 3-month follow-up. Results demonstrated that *CWI* was effective in significantly reducing depression, increasing self-efficacy to cope with infertility-related distress, increasing motivation to stay in treatment, and increasing satisfaction with overall infertility experience relative to controls. In addition, there was some evidence to support the effectiveness of *CWI* in decreasing state anxiety, improving hope, and keeping marital satisfaction from deteriorating, in comparison to subjects in the control condition. No significant differences between groups were found with respect to number of conceptions or treatment compliance. Finally, bibliotherapy subjects were highly satisfied with *CWI*. The authors concluded that *CWI* appeared to be a viable, generally effective, inexpensive (with respect to money, time, and effort expended), and satisfying treatment approach to helping individuals with fertility problems to better understand and manage the emotional aspects of their infertility experience. Following this example, it is recommended that authors of bibliotherapeutic materials also draw upon existing evidence-based treatments and adapt them to new mental health concerns, get feedback from both consumers (through focus groups) and expert consultants to evaluate content validity, and go on to conduct sound clinical trials of the self-help materials that have been developed. In addition to measuring effectiveness of the materials, researchers should also include measures of satisfaction and potential process variables.

DISSEMINATION AGENDA

Rosen (1987, 1993; Rosen et al., in press) have written extensively about the use of bibliotherapy in the field of psychology. Commenting on the origins of dissemination efforts for bibliotherapy, Rosen (1987, 1993) noted that George Miller, past president of the American Psychological Association, urged psychologists in his 1969 Presidential Address to "give psychology away" (Miller, 1969, p. 1074) by developing self-help programs in which people could be empowered to change themselves. Rosen further noted that in 1978, the American Psychological Association's Task Force on Self-Help Therapies (APA, 1978) echoed Miller's sentiments and encouraged psychologists to use their unique training to advance self-help technologies. The task force argued that psychologists training in diagnosis and treatment of emotional disorders, coupled with their scientific knowledge in program evaluation, put them in a perfect position to both develop and evaluate self-help programs. However, Rosen commented "The 1970's started as a decade of excitement and promise in the field of self-help, but ended with the realization that giving psychology away was more complicated than early investigators had thought. Unbridled enthusiasm was tempered by reality, when research demonstrated that not all self-help programs promote the public's welfare" (Rosen, et al., in press). Rosen (1987, 1993) argued that psychology has failed to properly advance self-care by violating professional standards with respect to failing to appropriately evaluate self-help methodologies and exaggerated claims of effectiveness. Despite clear recommendations made by the 1978 Task Force on Self-Help Therapies (Rosen, 1993) to address these problems, Rosen pointed out that most psychologists, including many members of the APA's Board of Professional Affairs, have failed to endorse any of these standards.

QUALITY ISSUES

Issues around the quality of self-help materials must be considered in the dissemination agenda for bibliotherapy. Over 2000 self-help books are published each year (Marrs, 1995, p. 843) but less than 10% of self-help materials have undergone any type of outcome research (Quackenbush, 1991). Floyd et al. (2004) note that lack of quality control is a major problem in the field of self-administered treatments. Books with no empirical support are allowed to be marketed to the lay public. However, they liken this problem to the lack of empirical support for most current therapist-administered psychotherapies and note that requiring empirical support to market self-help treatments would be holding self-administered treatments to a higher standard than is required for other forms of psychotherapy. They argue that despite lack of sound empirical support for self-help treatments, they are "at least benign and potentially helpful for most consumers" (p. 115). However, the authors concede that the potential for harming the public with self-administered materials should be addressed. The authors argue that the burden of demonstrating the efficacy of self-administered treatments should fall on the authors of such products (Scogin, 2003).

On the other hand, Rosen argued that review boards for self-help materials should carry the burden of developing standards of quality for such materials. As editor of a journal that frequently reviewed self-help materials, Rosen (1981) proposed a number of standards that should be used by other reviewers of self-help methods. First, the title and contents of the materials should be analyzed to determine whether they are identified as a do-it-yourself treatment. Second, reviewers should determine whether the author has clearly and accurately communicated information regarding any empirical support for the materials, as well as if the author determined whether the readers' expectations were accurate. Third, reviewers should comment on whether the materials provide a method for readers to diagnose themselves and whether these methods of self-diagnosis have been evaluated. Fourth, there should be discussion of whether the techniques presented in the self-help materials have been empirically supported.

Fifth, the reviewers should discuss whether the book itself has been subjected to empirical evaluation of clinical efficacy as well as the conditions under which these evaluations have been conducted. Sixth, the accuracy of any claims made in the self-help materials should be evaluated in the context of the above criteria. Finally, reviewers should make comparisons between the materials under review and any other self-help materials on similar topics. It is highly recommended that these standards be followed by authors as well as reviewers of bibliotherapeutic materials in order to ensure quality of those materials.

EXPANDING THE USE OF BIBLIOTHERAPY BY HEALTH CARE PROVIDERS

As discussed above, bibliotherapy is an excellent form of a self-help treatment with demonstrated efficacy, which behooves health care providers to make use of it on a more frequent basis. Several authors have made specific book recommendations, based on surveys of psychologists of bibliotherapeutic materials most commonly recommended to their clients for a variety of disorders (i.e., Campbell & Smith, 2003; Quackenbush, 1991). Although it is beyond the scope of this chapter to delineate specific bibliotherapeutic resources, the interested reader is referred to these bibliographies of selected bibliotherapy resources. Providers wishing to use bibliotherapeutic materials as an adjunct to psychotherapy should stock their personal libraries with such resources, which would facilitate making such recommendations to clients.

Before considering how the use of bibliotherapy could be promoted amongst health care providers, it is important to first analyze possible barriers to its use. Concerns about validity of bibliotherapy amidst the mass of nonscientifically based and faddish materials may be a barrier to the use of bibliotherapy by some providers. However, as is pointed out by Scogin (2003), the many evidence-based self-administered treatments that exist should not be overshadowed by the over-hyped and poorly constructed treatments that have become popularized in the bookstores. Another possible impediment to the use of bibliotherapy by mental health providers may be the fear that self-administered treatments could threaten their livelihood. However, therapists who fear being replaced by self-help materials should understand the role of bibliotherapy in a stepped care model. These therapists should also be aware that much of the research backing bibliotherapy supports its use as an adjunctive and not as a stand-alone treatment.

EXPANDING USE OF BIBLIOTHERAPY BY MENTAL HEALTH PROVIDERS

Understanding current prescriptive practices of mental health providers can assist in developing an agenda for more widespread dissemination of bibliotherapy. Starker (1988) surveyed 123 psychologists in practice across 36 states and found that 59.8% of them prescribed self-help books "occasionally," 23.9% "often" recommended them, and 12% suggested them "regularly." The author concluded that the practice of prescribing self-help books was "widespread" because 97.7% of psychologists surveyed prescribed self-help books at least regularly. Another survey questioned therapists about the frequency and reasons for prescribing self-help books (Adams & Pitre, 2000). The authors found that 68% of respondents indicated that they used bibliotherapy in their practices and cited the following top three reasons for doing so: To encourage clients to take further responsibility for therapeutic outcomes, to improve the process of therapy, and because their clients requested the self-help materials. Campbell and Smith (2003) found that the top three purposes rated by psychologists for recommending self-help books were to encourage insight/awareness, to provide reinforcement of materials discussed in session, and to encourage readers to make lifestyle changes. Other highly rated reasons for recommending bibliotherapy included empowering clients, providing support and knowledge for family members, improving client motivation, and educating clients about diagnosis and treatment.

Several studies (Adams & Pitre, 2000; Smith & Burkhalter, 1987) have found that more experienced therapists have a higher tendency to prescribe bibliotherapy than therapists with fewer years of clinical experience, hypothesizing that this finding could be due in part to a failure of training programs to formally teach and promote use of bibliotherapy such that therapists have to come upon it on their own in practice. It is thus recommended that mental health professionals be trained in the use of self-administered treatments as an adjunct to traditional psychotherapy (Lampropoulos & Spengler, 2005). Curricula for graduate school training programs for all mental health professions should be changed such that formal training in use of bibliotherapy occurs systematically, along with training in other treatment modalities such as traditional psychotherapy. The aim of this training should be on getting providers to be familiar with various empirically supported bibliotherapies, with a focus on being able to discriminate between good and poor quality reading materials. Another aim of this training should be on knowing when to recommend bibliotherapy, as discussed above.

EXPANDING USE OF BIBLIOTHERAPY BY PRIMARY CARE PROVIDERS

Because the primary care medical setting is where many, if not most, patients seek and receive treatment for common mental health problems such as depression and anxiety (Cummings, 2003), it would be advisable to include primary care physicians in the dissemination agenda for promotion of bibliotherapy. Although most primary care physicians deliver treatment for mental health problems through pharmacotherapy (Moore, 2004), Antonuccio et al. (1999) have noted that medical interventions for depression often come with significant risks and side effects. Encouraging primary care physicians to consider prescription of bibliotherapy as an alternative to pharmaceutical interventions for treatment of mental health problems would offer both the doctor and his or her patients a viable treatment option (Frude, 2005). A recent study (Naylor et al., in press) investigating "behavioral prescriptions" for evidence-based cognitive-behavioral bibliotherapy for depression in primary care settings found promising outcomes for patients and suggested that it was feasible to encourage primary care physicians to prescribe such bibliotherapy. It is thus recommended that medical and nursing school curricula be modified to systematically include training in identifying mental health problems and prescribing bibliotherapy in the context of a stepped care model, as described above. As with training for mental health professionals, training for primary care providers should focus on using high quality empirically supported materials.

EXPANDING USE OF BIBLIOTHERAPY BY RELIGIOUS LEADERS

Many individuals who do not seek help from mental health professionals or primary care providers may look to members of the religious community, such as clergy or rabbis, for help with mental health problems. Bibliotherapy could be an excellent referral option for this population. Thus, religious leaders should be systematically trained in the use of bibliotherapy, as has been suggested for mental health and primary care providers above.

EXPANDING USE OF BIBLIOTHERAPY TO THE LAY PUBLIC

Bibliotherapy has the potential to deliver effective mental health treatments to the general public, especially to those who may otherwise not utilize mental health services such as the elderly, members of certain ethnic groups, those who cannot afford traditional psychotherapy, and those living in areas where mental health services are not readily available. Given this tremendous potential of bibliotherapy to help the masses, it should be more widely marketed to the lay public. However, Rosen (1987) has passionately criticized self-help authors for marketing untested programs and for making exaggerated claims about the effectiveness of their self-help materials. Rosen challenged psychologists as follows, "not to sell psychology, but to apply the skills of our profession to the development of self-help treatments to ensure that professional standards, rather than commercial factors, have a bearing on the marketplace" (Rosen, 1987, p. 50). He proposed a set of criteria that should be taken into account by reviewers of self-help materials (Rosen, 1981, see below), Rosen argued that techniques presented in self-help books as well as the books themselves should be subjected to empirical evaluation. He cautioned psychologists not to make any false claims about effectiveness in the title or contents of the self-help materials. Thus, while bibliotherapy resources should be widely marketed, authors and publishers should heed Rosen's call to promote self-help materials in an ethical manner.

REFERENCES

Ackerson, J., Scogin, F., McKendree-Smith, N., & Lyman, R.D. (1998). Cognitive bibliotherapy for mild and moderate depressive symptomatology. *Journal of Consulting and Clinical Psychology, 66*, 685–690.

Adams, S.J. & Pitre, N.L. (2000). Who uses bibliotherapy and why? A survey from an underserviced area. *Canadian Journal of Psychiatry, 45*(7), 645–649.

American Psychological Association Task Force on Self-Help Therapies (1978). Task force report on self-help therapies. Unpublished manuscript. Washington D.C.: American Psychological Association.

Anderson, L., Lewis, G., Araya, R., et al. (2005). Self-help books for depression: How can practitioners and patients make the right choice? *British Journal of General Practice, 55*, 387–392.

Antonuccio, D.O., Danton, W.G., DeNelsky, G.Y., et al. (1999). Raising questions about antidepressants. *Psychotherapy and Psychosomatics, 68*, 3–14.

Apodaca, T.R. & Miller, W.R. (2003). A meta-analysis of the effectiveness of bibliotherapy for alcohol problems. *Journal of Clinical Psychology, 59*, 289–304.

Bailer, U., de Zwaan, M., Leish, F., et al. (2004). Guided self-help versus cognitive-behavioral group therapy in the treatment of bulimia nervosa. *American Journal of Psychiatry, 160*, 973–978.

Bandura, A. (1977). Self-efficacy: Toward a unifying theory of behavioral change. *Psychological Review, 84*, 191–215.

Barsky, A.J., Wyshank, G., Latham, K.S., & Klerman, G.I. (1991). Hypochondriacal patients, their physicians and their medical care. *Journal of General Internal Medicine, 6*, 413–419.

Beck, A.T., Rush, A.J., Shaw, B.F., & Emery, G. (1979). *Cognitive Therapy of Depression.* New York: Guilford Press.

Beck, A.T., Ward, C.H., Mendelson, M., et al. (1961). An inventory for measuring depression. *Archives of General Psychiatry, 4*, 53–63.

Bernstein, D.A. & Borkovec, T.D. (1973). *Progressive Relaxation Training: A Manual for the Helping Professions.* Champaign, Illinois: Research Press.

Beutler, L.E., Engle, D., Mohr, D., et al. (1991). Predictors of differential response to cognitive, experiential, and self-directed psychotherapeutic procedures. *Journal of Clinical and Consulting Psychology, 59*, 333–340.

Bien, T.H., Miller, W.R., & Tonigan, J.S. (1993). Brief interventions for alcohol problems: A review. *Addiction, 88*, 315–336.

Bowman, D., Scogin, F., Floyd, M., et al. (1997). Efficacy of self examination therapy in the treatment of generalized anxiety disorder. *Journal of Counseling Psychology, 44*, 267–273.

Buenaver, L.F., McGuire, L., & Haythornthwaite, J.A. (2006). Cognitive-behavioral self-help for chronic pain. *Journal of Clinical Psychology: In Session, 62*(11), 1389–1396.

Burns, D.D. (1980). *Feeling Good.* New York: Signet.

Burns, D.D. & Nolen-Hoeksema, S. (1992). Therapeutic empathy and recovery from depression in cognitive-behavioral therapy: A structural equation model. *Journal of Consulting and Clinical Psychology, 60*, 441–449.

Carlson, C.R. & Bernstein, D.A. (1995). Relaxation skills training: Abbreviated progressive relaxation. In W.T. O'Donohue & L. Krasner (Eds.), *Handbook of Psychological Skills Training: Clinical Techniques and Applications.* Boston: Allyn and Bacon.

Campbell, L.F. & Smith, T.P. (2003). Integrating self-help books into psychotherapy. *Journal of Clinical Psychology, 59*, 177–186.

Carter, J.C. & Fairburn, C.G. (1998). Cognitive-behavioral self-help for binge-eating disorder: A controlled effectiveness study. *Journal of Consulting and Clinical Psychology, 66*, 616–623.

Carter, J.C., Olmstead, M.P., Kaplan, A.S., et al. (2003). Self-help for bulimia nervosa: A randomized controlled trial. *American Journal of Psychiatry, 160* , 973–978.

Centers for Disease Control and Prevention. (2005) Tobacco use among adults—United States, 2005. *Morbidity and Mortality Weekly Report, 55*, 1145–1148.

Chiles, J.A., Lambert, M.J., & Hatch, A.L. (1999). The impact psychological interventions on medical cost offset: A meta-analytic review. *Clinical Psychology: Science and Practice*, *6*, 204–220.

Cohen, L.J. (1994). Bibliotherapy: A valid treatment modality. *Journal of Psychosocial Nursing*, *32*(9), 40–44.

Cooper, P.J., Coker, S., & Fleming, C. (1996). An evaluation of the efficacy of supervised cognitive behavioral self-help for bulimia nervosa. *Journal of Psychosomatic Research*, *40*, 281–287.

Craighead, L., McNamara, K., & Horan, J. (1984). Perspectives on self-help and bibliotherapy: You are what you read. In S. Brown and R. Lent (Eds.), *Handbook of Counseling Psychotherapy*. New York: John Wiley and Sons, 878–929.

Cuijpers, P. (1997). Bibliotherapy in unipolar depression: A meta-analysis. *Journal of Behavior Therapy & Experimental Psychiatry*, *28*, 139–147.

Cummings, N. (1993). Somatization: When physical symptoms have no medical cause. In D. Goleman & J. Gurin (Eds.), *Mind Body Medicine*. New York: Consumers Union.

Cummings, N.A. Advantages and limitations of disease management (2003). In N.A. Cummings, W.T. O'Donohue, K.E. Fegason (Eds.), *Behavioral Health as Primary Care; Beyond Efficacy to Effectiveness* (pp. 31–44). Reno, NV: Context Press.

Cunningham, J.A., Koski-Jannes, A., Wild, C., & Cordingley, J. (2002). Treating alcohol problems with self-help materials: A population study. *Journal of Studies on Alcohol*, *63*, 649–654.

Curry, S.J., Ludman, E.J., & McClure, J. (2003). Self-administered treatment for smoking cessation. *Journal of Clinical Psychology*, *59*, 305–319.

Den Boer, P.C.A.M., Wiersma, D., & Van Den Bosch, R.J. (2004). Why is self-help neglected in the treatment of emotional disorders? A meta-analysis. *Psychological Medicine*, *34*, 959–971.

DuPont, R.L., Rice, D.P., Miller, L.S., et al. (1996). Economic costs of anxiety disorders. *Anxiety*, *2*, 167–172.

Febbraro, G. (2005). An investigation into the effectiveness of bibliotherapy and minimal contact interventions in the treatment of panic attacks. *Journal of Clinical Psychology*, *61*, 763–779.

Floyd, M., Rohen, N., Shackelford, J.A.M., et al. (2006). Two-year follow-up of bibliotherapy and individual cognitive therapy for depressed older adults. *Behavior Modification*, *30*, 281–294.

Floyd, M., McKendree-Smith, N., & Scogin, F. (2004). Remembering the 1978 and 1990 task forces on self-help therapies: A response to Gerald Rosen. *Journal of Clinical Psychology*, *60*, 115–117.

Floyd, M., Scogin, F., McKendree-Smith, N., et al. (2004).Cognitive therapy for depression: A comparison of individual psychotherapy and bibliotherapy for depressed older adults. *Behavior Modification*, *28*, 297–318.

Frank, J.D. (1982). Therapeutic components shared by all psychotherapies. In J.H. Harvey & M.M. Parks (Eds.), *Psychotherapy Research and Behavior Change* (pp. 5–37). Washington DC: American Psychological Association.

Frude, N. (2005). Book prescriptions: A strategy for delivering psychological treatment in the primary care setting. *The Mental Health Review*, *10*(4), 30–33.

Gabbard, G.O., Lazar, S.G., Hornberger, J., & Spiegal, D. (1997). The economic impact of psychotherapy: A review. *American Journal of Psychiatry*, *154*, 147–155.

Ghaderi, A. (2006). Attrition and outcome in self-help treatment for bulimia nervosa and binge eating disorder: A constructive replication. *Eating Behaviors*, *7*, 300–308.

Gilbody, S., Whitty, P., Grimshaw, J., & Thomas, R. (2003). Educational and organizational interventions to improve the management of depression in primary care. *Journal of the American Medical Association*, *289*, 3145–3151.

Glasgow, R.E. & Rosen, G.M. (1978). Behavioral bibliotherapy: A review of self-help behavior therapy manuals. *Psychological Bulletin*, *85*, 1–23.

Glasgow, R.E. & Rosen, G.M. (1979). Self-help behavior therapy manuals: Recent developments and clinical usage. *Clinical Behavior Therapy Review*, *1*, 1–20.

Goldberg, D.P. & Huxley, P. (1992). *Common Mental Disorders: A Bio-Social Model*. Tavistok, London.

Gould, R.A. & Clum, G.A. (1993). A meta-analysis of self-help treatment approaches. *Clinical Psychology Review*, *13*, 169–186.

Grant, B.F., Dawson, D.A., Stinson, F.S., et al. (2004). The 12-month prevalence and trends in DSM-IV alcohol abuse and dependence: United States, 1991-1992 and 2001-2002. *Drug and Alcohol Dependence, 74*, 223–234.

Greenberg, M.A., Kessler, R.C., Birnbaum, H.G., et al. (2003). The economic burden of depression in the United States: How did it change between 1990 and 2000? *Journal of Clinical Psychiatry, 64*(12), 1465–1475.

Greenberg, P.E., Stiglin, L.E., Finkelstein, S.N., & Berndt, E.R. (1993). The economic burden of depression in 1990. *Journal of Clinical Psychiatry, 54*, 405–418.

Gregory, R.J., Canning, S.S., Lee, T.W., & Wise, J.C. (2004). Cognitive bibliotherapy for depression: A meta-analysis. *Professional Psychology, 35*, 275–280.

Hayes, S.C., Barlow, D.H., & Nelson-Gray, R.O. (1999). *The Scientist Practitioner: Research and Accountability in the Age of Managed Care*. Boston: Allyn and Bacon.

Hirai, M. & Clum, G.A. (2006). A meta-analytic study of self-help interventions for anxiety problems. *Behavior Therapy, 37*, 99–111.

Holder, H. (2002). Prevention research and its actual application to health services. *Journal of Behavioral Health Services and Research, 28*, 118–129.

Hollon, S.D., Evans, M.D., & DeRubeis, R.J. (1990). Cognitive mediation of relapse prevention following treatment for depression: Implications of differential risk. In R.E. Ingram (Ed.), *Contemporary Psychological Approaches to Depression* (pp. 117–136). New York: Plenum Press.

Hudson J.I., Hiripi E., Pope H.G., & Kessler R.C. (2007). The prevalence and correlates of eating disorders in the National Comorbidity Survey Replication. *Biological Psychiatry, 61*, 348–358.

Hynes, A.M. & Hynes-Berry, M. (1986). *Bibliotherapy – The Interactive Process: A Handbook*. Boulder, CO: Westview Press.

Ilardi, S.S. & Craighead, W.E. (1994). The role of nonspecific factors in cognitive-behavioral therapy for depression. *Clinical Psychology: Science and Practice, 1*(2), 138–156.

Jacobs, N.N. & O'Donohue, W.T. (2007). *Coping with Infertility: Clinically Proven Ways of Managing the Emotional Roller Coaster*. New York: Routledge.

Jacobson, N.S. & Margolin, G. (1979). *Marital therapy: Strategies based on social learning and behavior exchange principles*. New York: Brunner/Mazel.

Jamison, C. & Scogin, F. (1995). Outcome of cognitive bibliotherapy with depressed adults. *Journal of Consulting and Clinical Psychology, 63*, 644–650.

Jones, F.A. (2002). The role of bibliotherapy in health anxiety: An experimental study. *British Journal of Community Nursing, 7*, 499–503.

Katz, G. & Watt, J.A. (1992). Bibliotherapy: The use of books in psychiatric treatment. *Canadian Journal of Psychiatry, 37*(3), 173–178.

Kupshik, G.A. & Fisher, C.R. (1999). Assisted bibliotherapy: Effective, efficient treatment for moderate anxiety problems. *British Journal of General Practice, 49*, 47–48.

Lampropoulos, G.K. & Spengler, P.M. (2005). Helping and change without traditional therapy: Commonalities and opportunities. *Counselling Psychology Quarterly, 18*(1), 47–59.

Lancaster, T. & Stead, L.F. (2006). Self-help interventions for smoking cessation, *Evidence Based Medicine, 11*, 48.

Landreville, P. & Bissonnette, L. (1997). Effects of cognitive bibliotherapy for depressed older adults with a disability. *Clinical Gerontologist, 17*, 35–55.

Laumann, E.O., Paik, A., & Rosen, R.C. (1999). Sexual dysfunction in the United States: Prevalence and predictors. *Journal of the American Medical Association, 281*, 537–544.

Lenkowsky, R.S. (2001). Bibliotherapy: A review and analysis of the literature. *The Journal of Special Education, 21*(2), 123–132.

Lewinsohn, P.M., Antonuccio, D.O., Breckenridge, J.S., & Teri, L. (1984). *The Coping with Depression Course*. Eugene, OR: Castalia Publishing Co.

Lewinsohn, P.M., Munoz, R.F., Youngren, M.A., & Zeiss, A.M. (1992). *Control Your Depression*. New York: Simon and Schuster.

Lichstein, K.L. (1994). Fair tests of clinical trials: A treatment implementation model. *Advances in Behaviour Research and Therapy, 16*, 1–29.

Linehan, M.M. (1993a). *Cognitive-Behavioral Treatment of Borderline Personality Disorder.* New York: Guilford Press.

Linehan, M.M. (1993b). *Skills Training Manual for treating borderline personality disorder.* New York: Guilford Press.

Lovell, K., Cox, D., Garvey, R., et al. (2003). Agoraphobia: nurse therapist-facilitated self-help manual. *Issues and Innovations in Nursing Practice, 43,* 623–630.

Lovell, K. & Richards, D.A. (2000). Multiple access points and levels of entry: Ensuring choice, accessibility, and equity for CBT services. *Behavioural and Cognitive Psychotherapy, 28,* 379–391.

Lovell, K. & Richards, D. (2003). Multiple Access Points and Levels of Entry (MAPLE): ensuring choice, accessibility and equity for CBT services. *Behavioural and Cognitive Psychotherapy,* 728, 379–391.

Lovell, K., Richards, D.A., & Bower, P. (2003). Improving access to primary care mental health: Uncontrolled evaluation of a pilot self-help clinic. *British Journal of Clinical Psychology, 59,* 275–288.

Mains, J.A. & Scogin, F.R. (2003). The effectiveness of self-administered treatments: A practice-friendly review of the research. *Journal of Clinical Psychology/In Session, 59*(2), 237–246.

Marrs, R.W. (1995). A meta-analysis of bibliotherapy studies. *American Journal of Community Psychology, 23,* 843–870.

McKendree-Smith, N.L., Floyd, M., & Scogin, F.R. (2003). Self-administered treatments for depression: A review. *Journal of Clinical Psychology,* 59, 275–288.

Miller, G.A. (1969). Psychology as a means of protecting human welfare. *American Psychologist, 24,* 1063–1075.

Miller, W.R., Taylor, C.A., & West, J.C. (1980). Focused versus broad spectrum behavior therapy for problem drinkers. *Journal of Consulting and Clinical Psychology, 48,* 590–601.

Moore, T.J. (2004). *Drug safety research: Special report. Medical use of antidepressant drugs in children and adults: 1998-2001.* Paper presented at the Feb. 2, 2004 FDA hearing on the use of antidepressants in children. Retrieved on March 2, 2004 from http://drugsafetyresearch.com/downloads/med_use_antidep.pdf

Munoz, R.F., Hollon, S.D., McGrath, E., et al. (1994). On the AHCPR depression in primary care guidelines: Further considerations for practitioners. *American Psychologist, 49,* 42–61.

Murray, C.J.L. & Lopez, A.D. (1997). Global mortality, disability, and the contribution of risk factors: Global Burden of Disease Study. *Lancet, 349,* 1436–1442.

National Institute for Clinical Excellence (2002). *Guidance on the Use of Computerised CBT for Anxiety and Depression.* Department of Health, London.

National Center for Health Statistics (1992). Advance report of final mortality statistics, 1989 (Publication No. PHS 92-1120). Hyattsville, MD: Public Health Service.

National Institute of Mental Health (NIMH) (2000, July 6). Translating behavioral science into action: Report of the National Advisory Mental Health Council Behavioral Science Workgroup. Available: http://www.nimh.nih.ov/council/bswsummary.cfm

Naylor, E.V., Antonuccio, D.O., Johnson, G., et al. (2007). A pilot study investigating behavioral prescriptions as a treatment for depression. *Journal of Clinical Psychology in Medical Settings, 14*(2), 152–159.

Newman, M.G. (2000). Recommendations for a cost-offset model of psychotherapy allocation using generalized anxiety disorder as an example. *Journal of Consulting and Clinical Psychology, 68,* 549–555.

Newman, M.G., Erickson, T., Przeworski, A., & Dzus, E. (2003). Self-help and minimal contact therapies for anxiety disorders: Is human contact necessary for therapeutic efficacy? *Journal of Clinical Psychology, 59,* 251–274.

Pantalon, M.V., Lubetkin, B.S., & Fishman, S.T. (1995). Use and effectiveness of self-help books in the practice of cognitive and behavioral therapy. *Cognitive and Behavioral Practice, 2,* 213–222.

Papworth, M. (2006). Issues and outcomes associated with adult mental health self-help materials: A "second order" review or "qualitative meta-review." *Journal of Mental Health, 15*(4), 387–409.

Pardeck, J.A. & Pardeck, J.T. (1984). An overview of bibliotherapeutic treatment approach: Implications for clinical social work practice. *Family Therapy*, *11*, 241–252.

Paul, G.L. (1969). Behavior modification research: Design and tactics. In C.M. Franks (Ed.), *Behavior Therapy: Appraisal and Status*. New York: McGraw Hill.

Paulter, T. (1991). A cost-effective mind-body approach to psychosomatic disorders. In K.N. Anchor (Ed.), *Handbook of Medical Psychotherapy: Cost-Effective Strategies in Mental Health*. New York: Hogrefe & Huber.

Pezzot-Pearce, T.D., LeBow, M.D., & Pearce, J.W. (1982). Increasing cost-effectiveness in obesity treatment through the use of self-help behavioral manuals and decreased therapist contact. *Journal of Consulting and Clinical Psychology*, *50*, 448–449.

Power, K.G., Sharp, D.M., Swanson, V., & Simpson, R.J. (2000). Therapist contact in cognitive behaviour therapy for panic disorder and agoraphobia in primary care. *Clinical Psychology and Psychotherapy*, *7*, 37–46.

Quackenbush, R.L. (1991). The prescription of self-help books by psychologists: A bibliography of selected bibliotherapy resources. *Psychotherapy*, *28*, 671–677.

Rapee, R.M., Abbott, M.J., & Lyneham, H.J. (2006). Bibliotherapy for children with anxiety disorders using written materials for parents: A randomized control trial. *Journal of Consulting and Clinical Psychology*, *74*, 436–444.

Reeves, T. & Stace, J.M. (2005). Improving patient access and choice: Assisted bibliotherapy for mild to moderate stress/anxiety in primary care. *Journal of Psychiatric and Mental Health Nursing*, *12*, 341–346.

Riordan, R.J. & Wilson, L.S. (1989). Bibliotherapy: Does it work? *Journal of Counseling and Development*, *67*, 506–508.

Rosen, G.M. (1981). Guidelines for the review of do-it-yourself treatment books. *Contemporary Psychology*, *26*, 189–191.

Rosen, G.M. (1987). Self-help treatment books and the commercialization of psychotherapy. *American Psychologist*, *42*, 46–51.

Rosen, G.M. (1993). Self-help or hype? Comments on psychology's failure to advance self-care. *Professional Psychology: Research and Practice*, *24*(3), 340–345.

Rosen, G.M., Glasgow, R.E., & Barrera, M. (2007). Good intentions are not enough: Reflections on past and future efforts to advance self-help. In P.L. Watkins & G.A. Clum (Eds.), *Handbook of Self-Help Therapies*. (p. 25–39). Mahwah, NJ: Lawrence Erlbaum.

Rosen, G.M., Glasgow, R.E., & Moore, T.E. (2003). Self-help therapy: The science and business of giving psychology away. In S.O. Lilienfeld, S.J. Lynn, & J.M. Lohr (Eds.), *Science and Pseudoscience in Clinical Psychology*. (399–424). New York: The Guilford Press.

Schrank, F.A. & Engels, D.W. (1981). Bibliotherapy as a counseling adjunct: Research Findings. *Personnel and Guidance Journal*, *60*, 143–147.

Scogin, F. (2003). Introduction: The status of self-administered treatments. *Journal of Clinical Psychology*, *59*(3), 247–249.

Scogin, F., Bynum, J., & Stephens, G. (1990). Efficacy of self-administered treatment programs: Meta-analytic review. *Professional Psychology: Research and Practice*, *21*, 42–47.

Scogin, F., Hamblin, D., & Beutler, L. (1987). Bibliotherapy for depressed older adults: A self-help alternative. *The Gerontologist*, *27*, 383–387.

Scogin, F.R., Hanson, A., & Welsh, D. (2003). Self-administered treatment in stepped-care models of depression treatment. *Journal of Clinical Psychology*, *59*, 341–349.

Scogin, F., Jamison, C., Floyd, M., & Chaplin, W.F. (1998). Measuring learning in depression treatment: A cognitive bibliotherapy test. *Cognitive Therapy Research*, *22*(5), 475–482.

Scogin, F., Jamison, C., & Gochneaur, K. (1989). Comparative efficacy of cognitive and behavioral bibliotherapy for mildly and moderately depressed older adults. *Journal of Consulting and Clinical Psychology*, *57*, 403–407.

Scogin, F., Welsh, D., Hanson, A., et al. (2005). Evidence-based psychotherapies for depression in older adults. *Clinical Psychology: Science and Practice*, 12, 222–237.

Sharp, D.M., Power, K.G., & Swanson, V. (2000). Reducing therapist contact in cognitive behaviour therapy for panic disorder and agoraphobia in primary care: Global measures of outcome in a randomized controlled trial. *British Journal of General Practice*, *50*, 963–968.

Smit, F., Willemse, G., Koopmanschap, M., et al. (2006). Cost-effectiveness of preventing depression in primary care patients. *British Journal of Psychiatry*, *188*, 330–335.

Smith, D. & Burkhalter, J.K. (1987). The use of bibliotherapy in clinical practice. *Journal of Mental Health Counseling*, *9*, 184–190.

Smith, N.M., Floyd, M.R., Scogin, F., et al. (1997). Three-year follow-up of bibliotherapy for depression. *Journal of Consulting and Clinical Psychology*, *65*, 324–327.

Starker, S. (1988). Psychologists and self-help books: Attitudes and prescriptive practices of clinicians. *American Journal of Psychotherapy*, *42*(3), 448–455.

Stevens, A.J. & Pfost, K.S. (1982). Bibliotherapy: Medicine for the soul? *Psychology: A Quarterly Journal of Human Behavior*, *19*, 21–25.

Tolfin, D.F., Diefenbach, G.J., Maltby, N., & Hannan, S. (2005). Stepped care for obsessive-compulsive disorder: A pilot study. *Cognitive and Behavioral Practice*, *12*, 403–414.

U.S. Department of Health and Human Services. (2006, rev.). Anxiety disorders (NIH Publication No. 06-3879). Washington, D.C.: Author.

van Lankveld, J.J.D.M. (1998). Bibliotherapy in the treatment of sexual dysfunctions: A meta-analysis. *Journal of Consulting and Clinical Psychology*, *66*, 702–708.

van Lankveld, J.J.D.M., Everaerd, W., & Grotjohann, Y. (2001). Cognitive-behavioral bibliotherapy for sexual dysfunctions in heterosexual couples: A randomized waiting-list controlled clinical trial in the Netherlands. *The Journal of Sex Research*, *38*, 51–67.

Whisman, M.A. (1993). Mediators and moderators of change in cognitive therapy of depression. *Psychological Bulletin*, *114*(2), 248–265.

Whitfield, G. & Williams, C.J. (2003). The evidence base for CBT in depression: Delivering CBT in busy clinical settings. *Advances in Psychiatric Treatment*, *9*, 21–30.

Willemse, G.R.W., Smit, F., Cujipers, P., et al. (2004). Minimal-contact psychotherapy for sub-threshold depression in primary care: Randomized trial. *British Journal of Psychiatry*, *185*, 416–421.

Wright, J., Clum, G.A., Roodman, A., & Febbraro, G.A.M. (2000). A bibliotherapy approach to relapse prevention in individuals with panic attacks. *Journal of Anxiety Disorders*, *14*, 483–499.

Yeater, E.A., Naugle, A.E., O'Donohue, W., & Bradley, A.R. (2004). Sexual assault prevention with college-aged women: A bibliotherapy approach. *Violence and Victims*, *19*, 593–612.

3

Psychoeducation in Conjunction with Psychotherapy Practice

NICHOLAS A. CUMMINGS AND JANET L. CUMMINGS

University of Nevada, Reno, and The Nicholas and Dorothy Cummings Foundation

Once regarded as apart from psychotherapy, in the past 25 years there has been a rapid emergence of psychoeducational programs that combine treatment, information dissemination, and behavioral techniques directed at inducing lifestyle changes, all within a time-limited group model. Following a period of initial resistance, there emerged a wide use of such programs as research (to be discussed below) began to demonstrate their effectiveness with a number of psychological and medical conditions, and have been replacing much of the work that previously was done in one-on-one psychotherapy. In a surprisingly wide range of chronic medical and psychological conditions, they have been shown to be more effective than individual psychotherapy, and cost significantly less than does individual psychotherapy, and even brief individual psychotherapy, for the same conditions. In this era of cost containment, approaches that yield positive research for both therapeutic effectiveness and cost efficiency are bound to increase in use and application.

Many practitioners today view any interest in cost containment with suspicion as they slavishly cling to the 50-minute hour as the only true psychotherapy. Yet, several therapist researchers who predate the advent of managed care have held that the responsibility of the practitioner is to render our interventions more effective and efficient *for the sake of the patient*, and that effective psychotherapy results in cost containment without making economics the primary focus of care. Long before the Institute of Medicine (2001) published its landmark recommendations for closing the quality chasm, these visionaries began addressing the need for psychotherapy to surmount its self-imposed strictures and anticipated by decades the recommendations of the President's New Freedom Commission on Mental Health (Hogan, 2003). In Great Britain, Michael Balint(1957) stated that physicians should become more like psychologists, and psychologists more like physicians. Cummings and Follette (1968) demonstrated that effective psychotherapy as an integral part of the health system could save billions in medical surgical care. Pioneers in effective short-term psychotherapy (Budman & Gurman, 1988; Cummings, 1977; Davenloo, 1978; Erickson, 1980; Hoyt, 1995; Malan, 1976; Sifneos, 1987) were either scorned or accorded only passing interest as mainstream psychology had no real interest in addressing the inefficiency and cost of long-term psychotherapy. In looking back, one APA president (Fox, 2004) stated that psychology brought managed care on itself by doing nothing in the areas of quality, effectiveness, efficiency, and accountability.

Several movements converged to produce the current enthusiasm for psychoeducational programs: Brief psychotherapy, time-limited group therapy, and skills training. How these forces all converged is more than just a matter of historical interest, as psyochoeducational models, which by precedent should have been the province of psychology, are driven by nurse practitioners and other health professionals as they continue to evolve.

DEFINITION OF PSYCHOEDUCATION

As described in this chapter, *psychoeducation is health psychology combined with behavioral counseling and even psychotherapy, and is applied in a group setting that is specific to a diagnosis, and is both structural and open-ended as may be therapeutically appropriate.* The behavioral counseling component of psychoeducation deals with emotions, perceptions, coping, relaxation, and self-care, whereas the educational component imparts knowledge about the physical or psychological condition that is shared by the participants in the group. There are four components in psychoeducation, which may vary in their concentration depending upon the condition being addressed, but it is not psychoeducation unless all four components are present:

- *Treatment* of the condition.
- *Management* of the condition, especially those that are chronic and intractable.
- *Compliance* with the medical and psychological regimen.
- *Prevention* of progression, exacerbation, or relapse.

The group format provides an esprit among patients afflicted with the same condition, who are experiencing similar limitations and pain, and are usually in despair about the future. They can learn from and be inspired by group members who are doing exceptionally well, and can empathize with those who are lagging behind. So potent is this group spirit that the Kaiser Permanente Health Plan on the West Coast uses the group format for routine medical visits (Kent & Gordon, 1997), and for first session psychological emergencies (Cummings & Sayama, 1995).

HISTORICAL PERSPECTIVE

HEALTH EDUCATION

The late 1950s saw the emergence of health educators whose avowed purpose was to enhance individual health by turning consumers into enlightened participants in their own good health. Hospitals and health insurance plans conducted "health fairs" that drew little interest and were poorly attended. In time there emerged health newsletters available at nominal subscription cost, and were published and continue to be published by such renowned medical centers as Harvard, Johns Hopkins, and Mayo. These have had greater influence than earlier face-to-face health education, but fall short of eliminating the drawbacks that plague all of healthcare: Non-compliance with medical regimen and persistently unhealthy lifestyles.

These health letters continue to be mailed to subscribers, but with the advent of the Internet, there are a number of websites from which health information can be obtained online. The biggest among them by far is WebMD.com, which averages 40 million users a month. Even the National Institutes of Health have a site, NIH.gov, and behind WebMD are MayoClinic.com and AboutHealth.com, the latter owned by the *New York Times*. On Google one can type in a search word, such as "sore throat," and the user is led to potential diagnoses and information about potential causes and risks, treatments and tests, and alternative medicines. A new site was established in 2007 in this crowded market by none other than the founder of AOL, RevolutionHealth.com, indicating the wide use of Internet health information by consumers (Freudenheim, 2007).

Perhaps the most successful health education campaign was conducted by the recent charismatic Surgeon General C. Everett Koop who succeeded in getting 40 million Americans to quit smoking. Yet, despite the decades since 1978 of intense health education by both the government and the private sector healthcare, one-third of the population continues to smoke, and people are becoming increasingly sedentary and obese. It seems that health education in its several iterations is speaking to the same segment of the population. In all these efforts, little has been done to address the challenges known as "health literacy," with its enormous problem of functional illiteracy, and also the widespread disregard for self-care and personal health responsibility (Gottfredson, 2002, 2004). As will be seen in this chapter, these are problems best addressed by psychoeducational approaches rather than education alone.

Psychoeducational group programs began in psychology as skills training and yielded considerable success. This also laid the practical groundwork for disease management programs that were to come later. However, third-party payers took psychologists at their word, that this was skills training rather than psychotherapy, and thus was not reimbursable through health insurance. Without an economic base, the future of skills training was limited. One of the earliest psychological group management programs to qualify for reimbursement was that of Hardy (1970) with agoraphobia. Hardy was a psychiatrist who amalgamated psychoeducation and cognitive-behavioral therapy into a group program protocol called Terrap (short for "territorial apprehension," an alternative name to the frightening term agoraphobia). Terrap became a national therapeutic chain, with psychologists trained by Hardy and working in their own offices in a loose kind of franchise that spanned the continent. During the 1960s and 1970s, agoraphobia was seemingly epidemic and Terrap flourished. As has happened with others of psychology's ostensible epidemics (e.g., multiple personality disorder, repressed memories of incest) by the 1980s the incidence of agoraphobia diminished, and with the passing of Arthur Hardy, so did Terrap. But this laid the format for a series of later group protocols that addressed the treatment and management of a wide range of psychological conditions.

What we now call disease management may well have been born with the work of Kate Lorig, an innovative nurse who was concurrent in the 1970s with Hardy and who established the first disease management program in the nation (see Lorig et al., 1989, 2001). Her first such program in arthritis became the basis for disease management programs established by others with programs for such chronic diseases as asthma, chronic obstructive pulmonary disease (COPD), diabetes, hypertension, ischemic heart disease, and rheumatoid arthritis, as only a few examples of the many chronic disease programs that now exist. In fact, disease management has burgeoned into a multibillion dollar industry and one that should have been the province of psychology rather than its being dominated by nursing. Because of the minor role played by psychologists, disease management protocols are too often absent—the degree of behavioral input that would render them more effective.

Psychologists, however, have developed two very successful group programs for psychological conditions that address (1) assertiveness training (Gambrill, 2002), and (2) anger management (Novaco, 2002). The latter has become a favorite resource for overwhelmed courts to refer troublesome rage patients who have committed only minor offenses. Also, entering an anger management program has become a place where tarnished celebrities can say they are sorry and thereby hopefully recoup their popularity. Both assertiveness training and anger management programs have been adopted by psychotherapists and accepted by society far beyond their proven usefulness or efficacy.

USES AND LIMITATIONS OF DISEASE MANAGEMENT

Research has demonstrated that just understanding the facts about one's chronic physical or psychological condition of itself can be therapeutic (Budman & Gurman, 1988), but education alone has a limited impact. This includes even exhortation. Were it otherwise, the appearance of the warning label on a pack of cigarettes would have eliminated smoking in the 1960s. Signs warning of the dangers to the fetus of drinking alcoholic beverages while pregnant are mandatory in every bar and restaurant in California and several other states, but they have not reduced the incidence of fetal alcohol syndrome. Every physician is aware of the extent of noncompliance to medical regimen, and each has been exasperated when their advising or even sternly lecturing the patient has been of no avail. Often such well-meaning exhortation backfires, causing the patient to totally disregard the regimen (Nitzen & Smith, 2004). Resistance and denial are psychological problems, and they require psychological interventions.

Psychoeducational programs are of value to several categories of patients, spanning chronic physical disease, intractable psychological conditions, and certain life situations. There are widely used disease and population management programs and protocols for each of the following:

- *Major chronic physical diseases*, such as asthma, cancer, COPD, diabetes, hypertension, ischemic heart disease, and rheumatoid arthritis (including fibromyalgia).
- *Prolonged, chronic, or intractable psychological conditions*, such as borderline personality disorder (BPD), schizophrenia, chronic or lifelong depression, obsessive-compulsive and perfectionist personality, agoraphobia, multiple phobias, and panic attacks. One of the most intractable conditions is obesity. Many programs succeed in getting the weight off, only to have it return.
- *Sudden tragic situations* with sustained emotional reaction, such as bereavement (especially in marriages of long standing), and parents' loss of a child. Bereavement is a natural response to such situations, and it is best helped through its natural course. Thus, it should be addressed separately and differently than depression.
- *Somatizers*, defined as psychologically driven high utilizers of medical and surgical services.
- *Pre- and postsurgery*, especially in procedures followed by extensive limitations and prolonged recovery (heart and other transplants, amputations).
- *Preaddiction program*, for those substance abusers who are not yet ready to admit or accept their addictive state.
- *Immediate group.* As previously mentioned, patients who must be seen immediately can very effectively be treated in a group. The patient can attend up to four consecutive days, so patients are rotating in and out, assuring there will always be previous days' attendees to instill confidence in newcomers.

It is important in disease and population management that each group comprises patients sharing the same condition. Mixing various conditions, no matter how much overlap, deprives the solidarity that comes from shared pain and experience. A caveat often ignored is that borderline personality-disordered patients must be seen in their own special groups. Not only is there a program for management of borderline personalities, but there must be separate programs for borderline asthmatics, borderline diabetics, borderline arthritics, and so on. This is because borderline patients are so competitive and narcissistic that they will disrupt the entire program and prevent others from benefiting if they cannot be the center of attention.

The groups are time-limited, with the patients beginning and terminating at the same time. The number of sessions and its spacing depends on the disease or condition addressed. Groups vary from four to twelve members, with eight being the mode. Each disease management protocol has a set number of sessions ranging from 5 to 24, with the optimum number for each condition having been determined by research and practice. The protocols are modular, allowing mixing and matching among protocols.

The Substance Abuse and Mental Health ServicesAdministration (SAMHSA, 2004) has identified an interesting aspect of patient noncompliance. Patients have come to expect far more than imperfect medical science can deliver, and as their aches, pains, and other distressing symptoms persist and even increase, they are prone to disregard the prescribed regimen, shrugging "what's the use?". In every psychoeducation program, it is important to have an ongoing behavioral component that addresses this futility aspect, as well as a broader tendency to noncompliance.

Perhaps the greatest problem is the existence of undiagnosed and untreated psychiatric disorders that are often comorbid to the medical condition being treated, which can be as high as 44% (Fulop et al., 1998). Almost always overlooked is the inevitable accompaniment to any chronic illness of a subclinical depression that fosters a feeling of futility (Cummings et al., 1997). An important part of psychoeducation is to elicit and treat this comorbidity with its accompanying feelings of futility. Behavioral interventions, medication, or outright psychotherapy are often necessary along with psychoeducation.

In the psychoeducational groups addressing persistent behavioral conditions, there is frequently an important element of psychological resistance to the patient's confronting underlying emotional problems, while those suffering chronic physical illnesses do not wish to see emotional factors that are exacerbating their disease. Especially, this is extant in somatizers who do not want their belief in the physical cause of all their problems to be challenged (Cummings & Cummings, 1997).

Because most disease management is administered by other than psychologists, it continues to be plagued by insufficient emphasis on behavioral interventions. The teaching of coping strategies and problem-solving skills, though vitally important, cannot be the only or even major thrust. The emphasis on educative counseling, coupled with the lack of psychological knowledge, renders disease management susceptible to the one-size-fits-all fallacy (Kent & Gordon, 1997). It is as if invariably all participants will behave or respond the same way whether they are neurotic, alcoholic, borderline personality disordered, or sociopaths. Patients are lumped together whether they fall into Axis I or Axis II diagnoses, resulting in a high degree of failure or dropout rate. Even worse, borderline patients who remain in the program often wreck it, preventing anyone from benefiting.

ECONOMIC CONSIDERATIONS IN DISEASE MANAGEMENT

Had disease management not been shown to be effective, economic considerations would now be a secondary consideration. In this cost-conscious era, however, the combination of a method that not only is efficacious but also cost-effective is a win–win situation, accounting for the burgeoning of disease management programs since 1995. Unfortunately, psychologists do not think in such terms, resulting in their not having grasped the economy of scale that disease management accords. Taking an average of eight patients in each group over 2 hours equals four patients seen in individual psychotherapy over 4 hours. Not only is disease management more efficient time wise, research (to be discussed below) demonstrates it is also more effective than one-on-one therapy with some conditions (chronic physical illnesses, bereavement, BPD) and is superior in reducing medical/surgical costs (especially the High Utilizer Program).

As health costs continue to rise, the healthcare corporations have become cautious and are oriented toward return on investment (ROI). They want to know in advance if they invest $1 now, how many dollars will they get back and when? This caution has led to a common practice of parachuting one disease management program into an otherwise traditional setting, which by its very limited nature mitigates against any impressive ROI. Favorite programs are depression and obesity, and although there is a favorable saving in the program itself, it is so small that it resembles a drop of red paint into a 5-gallon bucket of white paint. The red dot is completely lost, with disappointment that the bucket of white did not turn pink. On the other hand, and as will be seen, infusing a wide range of disease/population management programs into a large-scale delivery system yields unprecedented savings.

In individual practices, and even in small group practices, there is the problem of achieving the critical mass necessary to form these groups. This critical mass can be achieved by psychotherapists pooling their patients, and practitioners conducting each program in rotation. In rural settings, it is impossible to achieve critical mass, and there are individual treatment versions for most programs. However, it must be emphasized that applied individually the results are seldom as positive as they are in group format.

RESEARCH FINDINGS

Considerable research has been conducted on single programs, and there have been three meta-analyses of these, but there is a paucity of studies involving large-scale health systems. Despite this deficiency, research has established the efficacy of a wide variety of programs that address the gamut of chronic physical diseases and psychological conditions. Space limitations permit only a sampling of the single program studies, which will be followed by large scale health delivery systems that have employed psychoeducational models extensively.

An early randomized study (Spiegel et al., 1989) of metastatic breast cancer patients used what the authors called "psychosocial treatment" because the term "psychoeducation" had not yet been coined. The women in the experimental group lived an average of 36.6 months beyond the randomization, whereas the women in the control group lived half as long, or 18.9 months. The authors attributed this highly significant difference to better patient and family coping skills in the treatment group, along with social support, more effective control of anxiety and depression, improved compliance, and a better working relationship with the oncology staff.

Randomized married patients with bipolar disorder and their spouses demonstrated improved medication compliance accompanied by improved functioning attributed to that compliance (Clarkin et al., 1998). This is important, as bipolar patients experience a lowered intensity of their cycle, and when entering the lessened hypomanic phase they often refrain from their medication in order to experience the high. As the mood invariably goes out of control, the patient doubles and triples the dosage in a futile effort to restore equilibrium. It is often too late, as the patient is hospitalized not only with mania but lithium toxicity as well. In another study Miklowitz et al. (2000) confirmed the value of family-focused group psychoeducation with bipolar patients.

Illustrating the broad range of issues addressed by psychoeducational research are the following examples: postprostate surgery (Mishel et al., 2002), chronic pain (Gatchel & Turk, 1996), lifestyle approaches to hypertension (Blumenthal et al., 2005), childhood diabetes (Delameter et al., 2001), self-management of chronic illnesses (Creer & Holroyd, 1997), depression (Antonnuccio & Naylor, 2005), and pediatric obesity (Moore & O'Donohue, 2005).

Three meta-analyses of studies addressing psychoeducational programs have been conducted to date. A meta-analysis of 102 psychoeducational studies with hypertension (Devine & Reifschneider, 1995) concluded that substantial and beneficial effects on blood pressure were the result of increased compliance with both medication and healthcare appointments. Similarly, a meta-analysis of 37 studies of the effect of psychoeducation for coronary heart disease suggested a 34% reduction in cardiac mortality (Dusseldorp et al., 1999). In another reported meta-analysis of 153 studies assessing the effectiveness of psychoeducation on compliance in chronic diseases (e.g., diabetes, cancer, hypertension, mental health problems), the authors concluded that the educative focus was most effective when combined with cognitive, behavioral, and affective components (Roter et al., 1998).

PSYCHOEDUCATION IN COMPREHENSIVE HEALTHCARE DELIVERY SYSTEMS

Studies of single psychoeducational programs have been important in establishing the efficacy of a broad range of such programs. However, the ultimate value of group psychoeducation is its cost/therapeutic effectiveness, defined as demonstrable benefit to the patient coupled with cost-efficiency over that of traditional methods. There are inherent difficulties in measuring cost savings (termed "medical cost offset;" see Cummings et al., 2002) in single entity research as just described, primarily because of the drop of paint in the bucket effect. Even so, many single program studies suggest there is such savings. For example, a recent review of the medical literature (Ketterer et al., 2004) strongly indicates that when angina patients are treated for distress, medical care utilization is reduced as measured by shorter hospital lengths of stay and fewer readmissions. However, the full impact of medical cost offset is best demonstrated in extensive, comprehensive health delivery systems. Unfortunately, only a handful of such studies have been conducted because there are few comprehensive, integrated healthcare systems in existence.

The pioneer has been the Kaiser Permanente Health System on the West Coast, the original HMO before the term "health maintenance organization" was coined. Covering several million lives, a 20-year experience was described by Cummings and VandenBos (1981) and more recently by Kent and Gordon (1997). It was here that the medical cost offset phenomenon was discovered (Cummings & Follette, 1968); but because this innovative health plan was reluctant to deny care to the control patients as required of randomized research, its findings were based on retrospective studies using comparison groups.

The first such randomized, controlled study on a comprehensive healthcare delivery system was the Hawaii Medicaid Project, over a 7-year period and involving the entire Medicaid (N = 36 000) and federal employees (N = 90 000) populations of Oahu, i.e., Honolulu (Cummings et al., 1993; Pallak et al., 1994). Termed the "Hawaii Medicaid Project" by the government, it was a three-way contract among the Health Care Financing Administration (HCFA), the State of Hawaii, and the Foundation for Behavioral Health through which a new delivery system was created within a 6-month initial period. A series of clinics termed "Biodyne Centers" (from two Greek words meaning "life change") delivered an array of innovative behavioral interventions through 68 protocols, which included over two dozen psychoeducational programs. The 126 000 Medicaid/federal employee population was randomized into two-thirds experimental (eligible for Biodyne services), and one-third control (the standard liberal benefit of 52 individual sessions per year, renewable every year). The treatment situation, rather than being compared with that in no treatment, was contrasted with a liberal traditional psychotherapy benefit.

The defining difference in the Biodyne Model, along with extensive training of the providers and an intensive collaboration between psychotherapists and physicians, was the inclusion of individual-focused psychotherapy and psychoeducational group programs. Using the latter, 50% of the therapists' time involved delivery of these programs, so that the overwhelming majority of patients were seen in groups. Rather than waiting for patients to enter the system, a sensitive, but aggressive outreach program directed at the 15% highest users of healthcare increased the penetration rate at several times the national average. Some feared that this unprecedented use of psychotherapy services would bankrupt the system. To the contrary, the resulting savings in medical, surgical, emergency room visits, and hospital stays enabled Biodyne to recoup within 18 months the $8 million in government funds needed to launch the delivery system. The medical cost offset continued to accrue through the remainder of the experiment.

Contrast this experience with that of the Fort Bragg Study (Bickman, 1996). Insisting that the removal of all restrictions to access would result in similar medical cost offset, proponents of traditional psychotherapy persuaded the government to finance such an experiment with Champus (now called TriCare) in the Fort Bragg, North Carolina area. The experiment was a disaster: Within 3 years, an $8 million existing program increased ten-fold into an $80 million fiasco. The experimenters admitted that this out-of-control cost did not improve services one bit. The spectacular contrast between the Hawaii Project results and those of the Fort Bragg Study attest to the value of innovation, including as a cornerstone psychoeducational group programs.

The Hawaii Project with its system of care and its range of psychoeducational programs was so successful that the model later transposed into a national organized behavioral health system that in 7 years grew to 14.5 million covered lives in 39 states, and eventually to over 20 million in all 50 states. Named American Biodyne, it was clinically driven, with psychologists not only delivering the services, but also serving in every decision-making executive capacity. No matter how high in management practitioners rose, they were required to spend at least one, and more often two full days per week in hands-on therapeutic services to maintain their acumen as professionals. Medical cost offset continued to be high, with a 20% reduction in medical/surgical costs, and there were no malpractice suits or patient complaints that had to be adjudicated. The national system secured the first Medicare contract ever awarded in behavioral care and in response a number of psychoeducational programs that would be applicable to the large elderly population were added, including an outreach bereavement program (Hartman-Stein, 1997).

Following the success of these early behavioral delivery systems, Kaiser-Permanente in the 1990s established a behavioral medicine service and added a number of new psychoeducational programs, including the innovative “skills not pills” to wean patients off medication and into behavioral solutions to their aches, pains, and limitations (Kent & Gordon, 1997). By the turn of the twenty-first century, Kaiser-Permanente was so impressed with the results of the collaboration between medicine and behavioral care, along with its extensive repertoire of psychoeducational programs, that it embarked on a full-scale integration of behavioral health and primary care for its 4.2 million enrollees in Northern California. In these settings primary care physicians (PCPs) and behavioral care providers (BCPs) work side-by-side, colocated in the primary care setting (Stephen Tulkin, personal communication, July 2005). The Group Health Cooperative of Puget Sound, now a part of Kaiser-Permanente in the Seattle area, was another healthcare system that early adopted a model of integrated healthcare, along with psychoeducational models and colocation of behavioral health in primary care (Strosahl et al., 1997).

The thrust continues to gain momentum. The U.S. Air Force has integrated all 167 of its hospital and medical facilities throughout the world (Runyan et al. 2003), and TriCare and the Veterans Administration are in the early stages of also doing so (Chaffee, 2005). In the private sector, lagging behind Kaiser-Permanente, several large healthcare companies are in the planning stages.

PROVEN PSYCHOEDUCATIONAL PROGRAMS

More than a dozen psychoeducational programs were integral to the success of the Biodyne Model. All were in protocol form, but far from being cookbooks, the protocols had the necessary latitude for clinical judgment to be operative as appropriate. No other array of group programs has had the successful field experience with a national delivery system with over 20 million covered lives. These programs are divided into three groups corresponding to whether they address chronic physical disease, psychological conditions, or problems of addiction. A high utilizer outreach of the 15% highest users of healthcare often precedes the patient's assignment to one of these programs, along with physician and self-referral. All patients receive one to three individual sessions to prepare them for the group format.

CHRONIC PHYSICAL DISEASES

- Asthma, with separate programs for asthmatics and parents of asthmatic children.
- COPD.
- Diabetes, with separate programs for parents of childhood diabetics.
- Essential hypertension.
- Ischemic heart disease, with a separate program for patients who have had a heart attack and another for patients after heart surgery.
- Rheumatoid arthritis, including fibromyalgia.
- Depressions that typically accompany chronic disease are treated within each separate group program.
- Patients with BPD are treated in special groups for each chronic disease entity.

PSYCHOLOGICAL CONDITIONS

- Bipolar depression treated as endogenous depression, with separate groups for family and spouses of bipolar patients.
- Reactive depression resulting from loss or setback, with special programs for parents who have lost a child.

- Chronic depression, especially that which resulted from early childhood loss, such as of a parent.
- Anniversary depression, occurring regularly on the anniversary of the loss of a parent, spouse, child, or important situation.
- Bereavement treated as a natural but painful healing process that is apart and different than depression.
- Agoraphobia, with special tailoring for housebound patients. Includes field desensitization.
- Multiple phobias and panic attacks. Includes desensitization.
- BPD, with separate groups for men and women for reasons attendant to the disorder.
- Perfectionist personality, including obsessive-compulsive disorder (OCD).
- Independent living for schizophrenics, including field outings.
- Parenting and stepparenting groups.
- Adolescent defiant disorder.
- Antisocial personality disorder (adults), with special groups for ex-felons.
- Intractable somatization disorder, or patients who have failed every other intervention and persist in manifesting somatized symptoms.

ADDICTIVE AND SUBSTANCE ABUSE

In this model, contrary to the manner in which different types of depression are segregated, it is preferred that addictions be mixed. In this way, it can be demonstrated that addiction is a way of life despite the variation in addiction. Furthermore, the extreme denial typical of addicts is not enhanced by like-addicts rationalizing for each other. A rivalry often develops (i.e., my addiction is worse than your addiction), and in other ways, patients begin to "police" each other in ways that the therapist would not be able to do.

- Preaddictive program for those who are not yet convinced they are addicted. This can enhance motivation and cut through the denial, resulting in fewer dropouts in the addictive program.
- Addictive program that includes alcoholics, drug addicts, foodaholics, and compulsive gambling. There are separate programs for adolescents, but no effort is made to separate upscale users from those who have hit bottom.
- Morbid obesity, usually £300 or more.

ESSENTIAL CHARACTERISTICS OF PSYCHOEDUCATION PROGRAMS

As stated before, all psychoeducation programs must address four components, in varying degrees depending on the condition: (1) treatment, (2) management, (3) prevention, and (4) compliance. In addition to these overall considerations, and in order to accomplish them, there are a number of essential characteristics that make psychoeducational programs effective (taken from Cummings & Cummings, 1997, 2005).

(1) *Educational component.* For each program, information clearly describing the condition to the patient, along with its psychological concomitants, is of discernible relief to the patient and becomes the foundation upon which management of the chronic physical disease or psychological condition is built. It introduces the patient to the all-important link between emotions and illness.

Much information will be found in usable form in such books as *Mind–Body Medicine* (Goleman & Gurin, 1993), but care must be exercised to update the medical information by booklets readily available from various charitable organizations (e.g., American Heart Association, American Diabetes Association). Self-help books have proliferated since 1995, and a number of good, readable ones exist for each condition being addressed. A caveat, however, is that many self-help books are of questionable validity, and even faddish, and caution should be exercised in assigned readings. There is evidence that gaining a better understanding of one's condition in itself is therapeutic (Budman & Gurman, 1988), but the patient has a right to expect accurate information.

Practitioners are admonished to frankly impart information about each patient's disorder, including borderline personality-disordered patients. Withholding or avoiding unpleasant facts will boomerang in the end, but if sensitively and candidly presented, this will enhance the patient's ability to anticipate and comprehend the condition, and to cope with it.

(2) *Counseling Component.* The extensive use of evidence-based cognitive and behavioral interventions is paramount in the treatment and management of chronic disease and pervasive psychological conditions. Anticipating relapse or exacerbation is important to prevention, and these interventions directly address compliance. Flexibility is important, and the broadest range of proven cognitive and behavioral interventions as they may specifically apply to each condition being addressed is recommended. An excellent resource is Fisher and O'Donohue (2006).

(3) *Psychotherapy Component.* This is the component that is most often absent, perhaps because most leaders of psychoeducational and disease management groups are nurses, health educators, or other healthcare professionals not trained in psychotherapy. There are psychological variables that mitigate against success, not the least of which may be the patient has a vested interest in remaining ill (e.g., psychological secondary gain, monetary compensation, reluctance to address and grapple with unpleasant realty). Furthermore, the depressed patient feels futile and pessimistic, and unless the depression is treated, will not benefit from the program. The fear of facing the environmental factors that are causing or exacerbating the illness (e.g., marital unhappiness, job dissatisfaction) most likely

is addressed in psychotherapy. The ability to recognize a borderline personality-disordered participant who may be sabotaging the program may also require the deftness of a skilled psychotherapist. Perhaps more than any other factor, the absence or inadequacy of a psychotherapy component accounts for failure of disease management.

(4) *Treatment of depression.* The depression that typically accompanies chronic illness reflects the context in which the depression is occurring and is best addressed within that context. These depressions should not be seen as primarily a medical condition for which an antidepressant is prescribed; rather, the psychological etiology and behavioral components of the depression must be treated if the patient is to understand how emotions determine illness or undermine physical health. This most often requires an experienced psychotherapist, often lacking in these programs, resulting in limited or no success.

(5) *Support System.* Group programs provide a necessary support system that is important to all patients, but especially to social isolates who lack family and friends. Learning from others with the same condition that "I am not the only one feeling like this" results in a therapeutic group spirit. It also underscores the importance of having cohesive groups limited to one primary disease or condition. The protocols also pair patients into a buddy system, encouraging each patient to call one's buddy when the going gets rough between group meetings.

(6) *Borderline personality disorder (BPD).* Most borderline personalities seen in the mental health system are women inasmuch as most BPD males are remanded to the criminal justice system because of their propensity to break the law with readily punishable offenses. The primary behavioral characteristics of these patients are projective identification (ascribing the worst of oneself to those around her and provoking them until they respond in negative fashion) and splitting (ingratiating oneself to half the group, while antagonizing the other half, and then pitting one half against the other). So pervasive are these mechanisms, and so adept and unrelenting are these patients, that they will wreck any group, preventing everyone along with themselves from getting help. It is strongly recommended that borderline patients be seen in separate groups, not only when they are being treated for their psychological condition, but also when being seen for a chronic physical illness. Therefore, BPD with diabetes is treated in diabetic borderline groups, BPD with arthritis is treated in arthritic borderline groups, and so forth. The same holds true when borderline patients are being treated with depression, panic attacks, agoraphobia, or any other psychological symptoms. BPD patients can be very charming, making the diagnosis difficult and enabling them to slip inappropriately into a group and past a group leader who lacks psychotherapy training. The Borderline-Disordered Personality group therapy protocol tested by the authors and widely used nationally for circa 1975 to 1995 may be of helpful (see Cummings & Sayama, 1995, pp. 241–8).

(7) *Pain Management* is a part of any program that addresses a painful chronic illness.

(8) *Stress Management* is an important part of all programs, but especially for those who anticipate sudden panic and anxiety attacks, and for recovering addicts who are taking it one day at a time.

(9) *Relaxation Techniques*, including breathing exercises, guided imagery, and a variety of other techniques can be helpful in all the conditions addressed.

(10) *Self-evaluation Component.* This includes not only physical monitoring (e.g., blood pressure and blood sugar), but psychological monitoring as well (e.g., stress levels, panic levels, exercise regimen). Training patients to monitor blood pressure or blood sugar is relatively easy with the current home apparatuses available, but they can also be trained to evaluate psychological progress, such as the ten-point scale of panic attacks, or a five-point scale of compliance to their own exercise regimen. Such monitoring of behavioral progress markedly improves compliance, because patients share results of all self-monitoring in the group.

(11) *Homework* is given to each patient after every session. There is no cookbook of homework assignments, and homework is tailored to help the patient (and the group) attain the next level of understanding and mastery.

(12) *Self-efficacy* (after Bandura, 1977) refers to the belief that one can perform a specific action or complete a task. Although this involves self-confidence in general, it is the confidence to perform a specific task. Positive changes can be traced to an increase in self-efficacy brought about by a carefully designed protocol that will advance the sense of self-efficacy.

(13) *Learned Helplessness* (after Seligman, 1975) is a concept that holds helplessness is learned and can be unlearned. Some patients with chronic illnesses fall into a state of feeling helpless in the face of their disease. A well-designed protocol will enable a patient to confront and unlearn helplessness.

(14) *A Sense of Coherence* (after Antonovsky, 1987) is required for a person to make sense out of adversity. Patients with chronic mental or physical illness feel not only that their circumstances do not make sense, but neither does their life. The ability to cope often depends on the presence or absence of this sense of coherence, and the protocol should be designed to enhance it.

(15) *Exercise* is an essential component of every protocol, and is the feature that is most often neglected by patients. Unfortunately, because many practitioners also lead sedentary lives, they are less diligent in enforcing this component than they should be. Exercise helps ameliorate depression, raises the sense of self-efficacy, and promotes coping behavior. The patient should be encouraged to plan and implement his or her own exercise regimen, and then to stick to it.

(16) *Diagnosis of Comorbidity* is necessary inasmuch as often its presence was not detected until a group program is underway, and a patient may have to be reassigned to a more appropriate program (e.g., alcoholism, BPD).

(17) *Modular Formatting* enables a protocol to serve different but similar populations and conditions by inserting or substituting condition-specific modules. There is utility in deriving protocols that facilitate mixing and matching.

SUMMARY AND CONCLUSIONS

The legendary John Maynard Keynes, who dominated economic thought for decades, frequently stated, "The difficulty lays not so much in developing new ideas as in escaping old ones" (Case, 2007). New ideas abound in psychology, and among these are proven psychoeducation models and their outgrowth disease management. These have been shown to be not only efficacious, but even superior to traditional therapy in certain instances. The problem remains, however, that practitioners are mired in the 50-minute hour, preferring to treat the worried well with familiar interventions. Practice is declining; yet, psychotherapists doggedly cling to one-on-one therapy, and many express hostility toward anything other than traditional long-term treatment, stating anything less is not real psychotherapy and may even be unethical.

Third-party payers, beset by double-digit healthcare inflation, are reluctant to embark on new methods that might escalate costs further. Other than Kaiser-Permanente, private sector plans have lagged behind, with the military, government programs, and the Veterans Administration taking a decisive lead. Nonetheless, disease management, an outgrowth of psychoeducation models and one that should have been the province of psychology, has burgeoned into a multibillion dollar industry. Because of the lack of participation by psychology, disease management tends to suffer from a lack of behavioral therapeutic acumen, causing it to fall short of its full potential.

In summary, psychoeducation has been shown to improve health outcomes and reduce healthcare costs with patients with chronic physical diseases, a wide variety of psychological conditions, high utilizers (somatizers) of medical services, substance abusers, and patients pre- or postsurgery. Beginning with one-on-one programs administered by nurses and health educators, psychoeducation has moved to sophisticated group programs extensively used in disease management and other settings. Effectiveness is somewhat limited in most group programs because of an over-reliance on educative features and a lack of intensive behavioral interventions, especially when the skills of a psychotherapist are required.

REFERENCES

Antonnuccio, D.O. & Naylor, E.V. (2005). Behavioral prescriptions for depression in primary care. In N.A. Cummings, W.T. O'Donohue, & E.V. Naylor (Eds.), *Psychological Approaches to Disease Management* (pp. 209–224). Vol. 8, Cummings Foundation for Behavioral Health: Healthcare Utilization and Cost Series. Reno, NV: Context Press.

Antonovsky, A. (1987). *Unraveling the Mystery of Health: How People Manage Stress and Stay Well.* San Francisco: Jossey-Bass.

Balint, M. (1957). *The Doctor, his Patient, and the Illness.* New York: International Universities Press.

Bandura, A. (1977). Self-efficacy: Toward a unified theory of behavioral change. *Psychological Review*, *84*, 191–215.

Bickman, L. (1996). A continuum of care: More is not always better. *American Psychologist, 51*, 689–701.

Blumenthal, J.A., Sherwood, A., LaCaille, L.J., et al. (2005). Lifestyle approaches to the treatment of hypertension. In N.A. Cummings, W.T. O'Donohue, & E.V. Naylor (Eds.), *Psychological Approaches to Chronic Disease Management* (pp. 87–116). Vol. 8, Cummings Foundation for Behavioral Health: Healthcare Utilization and Cost Series. Reno, NV: Context Press.

Budman, S.H. & Gurman, A.S. (1988). *Theory and Practice of Brief Therapy*. New York: Guilford.

Case, D. (2007). Unlearning curve. *Worth,* p. 8.

Chaffee, B. (2005). Implementing integrated behavioral health in TRICARE. In N.A. Cummings, W.T. O'Donohue & M.A. Cucciare (Eds.), *Universal Healthcare: Readings for Mental Health Professionals* (pp. 111–126). Vol. 9, Cummings Foundation for Behavioral Health: Healthcare Utilization and Cost Series. Reno, NV: Context Press.

Clarkin, J., Carpenter, D., Hull, J., et al. (1998). Effects of psychoeducational intervention for married patients with bipolar disorder and their spouses. *Psychiatric Services, 49*(3), 305–313.

Creer, T.L. & Holroyd, R.A. (1997). Self-management. In A. Baum, S. Newman, J. Weinman, R. West & C. McManus (Eds.), *Cambridge Handbook of Psychology, Health, and Medicine* (pp. 225–258). Cambridge: Cambridge University Press.

Cummings, N.A. (1977). Prolonged (ideal) versus short-term (realistic) psychotherapy. *Professional Psychology, 8*, 491–501.

Cummings, N.A. & Cummings, J.L. (1997). The behavioral health practitioner of the future: The efficacy of psychoeducational programs in integrated primary care. In N.A. Cummings, J.L. Cummings, & J.N. Johnson (Eds.), *Behavioral Health in Primary Care: A Guide for Clinical Integration* (pp. 325–346). Madison, CT: Psychosocial Press (International Universities Press).

Cummings, N.A. & Cummings, J.L. (2005). Behavioral interventions for somatizers within the primary care setting. In N.A. Cummings, W.T. O'Donohue, & E.V. Naylor (Eds.), *Psychological Approaches to Chronic Disease Management.* Vol. 6, Cummings Foundation for Behavioral Health: Healthcare Utilization and Cost Series (pp. 49–70). Reno, NV: Context Press.

Cummings, N.A., Cummings, J.L., & Johnson, J.N. (1997). *Behavioral Health in Primary Care: A Guide for Clinical Integration.* Madison, CT: Psychosocial Press.

Cummings, N.A., Dorken, H., Pallak, M.S., & Henke, C.J. (1993). The impact of psychological interventions on healthcare costs and utilization: The Hawaii Medicaid Project. In N.A. Cummings & M.S. Pallak (Eds.), *Medicaid, Managed Behavioral Health and Implications for Public Policy.* Vol. 2, Healthcare Utilization and Cost Series (pp. 3–23). South San Francisco: Foundation for Behavioral Health.

Cummings, N.A. & Follette, W.T. (1968). Psychiatric services and medical utilization in a prepaid health plan setting: Part 2. *Medical Care, 6*, 31–41.

Cummings, N.A., O'Donohue, W.T., & Ferguson, K.E. (2002). *The Impact of Medical Cost Offset on Practice and Research: Making it Work for You.* Vol. 5, Cummings Foundation for Behavioral Health: Healthcare Utilization and Cost Series. Reno, NV: Context Press.

Cummings, N. & Sayama, M. (1995). *Focused Psychotherapy: A Casebook of Brief, Intermittent Psychotherapy Throughout the Life Cycle.* New York: Brunner/Mazel.

Cummings, N.A. & VandenBos, G.R. (1981). The twenty year Kaiser-Permanente experience with psychotherapy and medical utilization: Implications for national health policy and national health insurance. *Health Policy Quarterly, 1*, 159–175.

Davenloo, H. (1978). *Basic Principles and Techniques in Short-Term Dynamic Psychotherapy.* New York: Spectrum.

Delameter, A.M., Jacobson, A.M., Anderson, B., et al. (2001). Psychosocial therapies in diabetes: Report of the Psychosocial Therapies Working Group. *Diabetes Care, 24*, 1286–1292.

Devine, E. & Reifschneider, E. (1995). A meta-analysis of the effects of psychoeducational care in adults with hypertension. *Nursing Research, 44*(4), 237–245.

Dusseldorp, E., van Elderin, T., Maes, S., et al. (1999). A meta analysis of psychoeducational programs for coronary heart disease patients. *Health Psychology, 18*(5), 506–519.

Erickson, M.H. (1980). *Collected papers* (Vols. 1–4), E. Rossi (Ed.), New York: Irvington.

Fisher, J.E. & O'Donohue, W.T. (2006). *Practitioner's Guide to Evidence-Based Psychotherapy.* New York: Springer.

Fox, R.E. (2004). It's about money: Protecting and enhancing our incomes. *Independent Practitioner, 24*(4), 158–159.

Freudenheim, M. (2007, April 16). AOL founder hopes to build new giant among a bevy of health care websites. *New York Times*, B1 and 5. *Practitioner, 24* (4), 158–159.

Fulop, G., Strain, J., Fahs, M., et al. (1998). A prospective study of the impact of psychiatric comorbidity on length of hospital stays of elderly medical-surgical persons. *Psychosomatics 39*(3), 273–280.

Gambrill, E. (2002). Assertion training. In M. Hersen & W. Sledge (Eds.), *Encyclopedia of Psychotherapy,* Vol. 1, 309–315.

Gatchel, R.J. & Turk, D.C. (1996). *Psychological Approaches to Pain Management: A Practitioner's Handbook.* New York: Guilford.

Goleman, D. & Gurin, J. (Eds.) (1993). *Mind–Body Medicine.* Yonkers, NY: Consumer Reports Books.

Gottfredson, L.E. (2002). g: Highly general and highly practical. In R.J. Sternberg & E.L Grigorenko (Eds.). *The general factor of intelligence: How general is it?* (pp. 331–380). Mahwah, NJ: Erlbaum.

Gottfredson, L.E. (2004). Intelligence: Is it the epidemiologists' elusive "fundamental cause" of social class inequalities in health? *Journal of Personality and Social Psychology, 44*, 615–629.

Hardy, A. (1970). *The Terrap Manual.* Menlo Park, CA: TERRAP.

Hartman-Stein, P.E. (Ed.) (1997). *Innovative Behavioral Healthcare for Older Adults.* San Francisco: Jossey-Bass (Wiley).

Hogan, M.F. (2003). New Freedom Commission Report: The President's New Freedom Commission – Recommendations to transform mental health care in America. *Psychiatric Services, 54,* 1467–1474.

Hoyt, M.F. (1995). *Brief Psychotherapy and Managed Care.* San Francisco: Jossey-Bass.

Institute of Medicine (2001). *Crossing the Quality Chasm: A New Health System for the 21st Century.* Washington, DC: National Academy of Sciences.

Kent, J. & Gordon, M. (1997). Integration: A case for putting Humpty Dumpty together again. In. N.A. Cummings, J.L. Cummings, & J.N. Johnson (Eds.), *Behavioral Health in Primary Care: A Guide for Clinical Integration* (pp. 103–120). Madison, CT: Psychosocial Press (imprint of International Universities Press).

Ketterer, M.W., Mahr, G., Cao, J.J., et al. (2004). What's "unstable" in unstable angina? *Psyhchosomatics, 45*(3), 1–12.

Lorig, K., Ritter, P., Stewart, A., et al. (2001). Chronic disease management program: 2-year status and health care utilization outcomes. *Medical Care, 39*(11), 1217–1223.

Lorig, K., Selesnick, M., Lubeck, D., et al. (1989). The beneficial outcomes of the arthritis self-management course are not adequately explained by behavior change. *Arthritis and Rheumatism, 32*, 91–95.

Malan, D.H. (1976). *The Frontiers of Brief Psychotherapy: An Example of the Convergence of Research and Clinical Practice.* New York: Plenum.

Miklowitz, D., Simoneau, T., George, E., et al. (2000). Family-focused treatment of bipolar disorder: 1-year effects of a psychoeducational program in conjunction with pharmacology. *Biological Psychiatry, 48*(6), 582–592.

Mishel, M., Belyea, M., Germino, B., et al. (2002). Helping patients with localized prostatic carcinoma manage uncertainty and treatment side-effects: Nurse delivered psychoeducational intervention over the telephone. *Cancer, 94*(6), 1854–1866.

Moore, B.A. & O'Donohue, W.T. (2005). Examining family-based treatments for pediatric obesity: A detailed review of the last 10 years. In N.A. Cummings, W.T. O'Donohue, & E.V. Naylor (Eds.), *Psychological Approaches to Chronic Disease Management* (pp. 225–270) Vol. 8. Cummings Foundation for Behavioral Health: Healthcare Utilization and Cost Series. Reno, NV: Context Press.

Nitzen, J.L. & Smith, S.A. (2004). *Clinical Preventive Services in Substance Abuse and Mental Health Update: From Science to Services.* Washington, DC: Substance Abuse and Mental Health Services Administration.

Novaco, R.W. (2002). Anger control therapy. In M. Hersen & W. Sledge (Eds.), *Encyclopedia of Psychotherapy,* Vol. 1 (pp. 41–48). San Diego, CA: Academic Press (Elsevier).

Pallak, M.S., Cummings, N.A., Dorken, H., & Henke, C.J. (1994). Medical costs Medicaid, and managed mental health treatment: The Hawaii Study. *Managed Care Quarterly*, *2*, 64–70.

Roter, D., Hall, J., Merisca, R., et al. (1998). Effectiveness of interventions to improve patient compliance: A meta-analysis. *Medical Care*, *36*(8), 1138–1161.

Runyon, C.N., Fonseca, V.P., & Hunter, C. (2003). Integrating consultative behavioral healthcare into the Air Force medical system. In N.A. Cummings, W.T. O'Donohue, & K.E. Ferguson (Eds.), *Behavioral Health in Primary Care: Beyond Efficacy to Effectiveness* (pp. 145–164). Vol. 6, Cummings Foundation for Behavioral Health: Healthcare Utilization and Cost Series. Reno, NV: Context Press.

Seligman, M.E.P. (1975). *Helplessness: On Depression, Development and Death.* San Francisco: W.H. Freeman.

SAMHSA (2004). *Substance Abuse and Mental Health Update.* Washington, DC: Author.

Sifneos, P.E. (1987). *Short-Term Dynamic Psychotherapy: Evaluation and Technique* (2nd Ed.). New York: Plenum.

Spiegel, D., Kraemer, H., Bloom, J., & Gottheil, E. (1989). Effects of psychosocial treatment on survival of patients with metastatic breast cancer. *The Lancet*, *2*, 888–891.

Strosahl, K., Baker, N.J., Braddick, M., et al. (1997). Integration of behavioral health and primary care services: The Group Health Cooperative Model. In N.A. Cummings, J.L. Cummings, & J.N. Johnson (Eds.), *Behavioral Health in Primary Care: A Guide for Clinical Integration* (pp. 61–86). Madison, CT: Psychosocial Press (International Universities Press).

4

MUTUAL-HELP GROUPS

JOHN F. KELLY* AND JULIE D. YETERIAN†

**Massachusetts General Hospital, Department of Psychiatry, Center for Addiction Medicine; and Harvard Medical School*

†Massachusetts General Hospital, Department of Psychiatry, Center for Addiction Medicine

INTRODUCTION

WHAT ARE MUTUAL-HELP GROUPS?

Consumer-provided therapeutic help comes in many forms, such as self-help groups (SHGs) and mutual-help groups (MHGs); consumer-operated services, such as drop-in centers and residential programs; and mental health counseling provided by trained consumers in traditional clinical settings (Davidson et al., 1999). The different types of help, and the various terms used to describe such help, reflect differences in the relationships between those involved (e.g., mutual helping, nonmutual mentoring). The terms "self-help groups" and "mutual-help groups" are often used interchangeably. However, the term "self-help" is frequently used to denote a variety of interventions targeting self-change using *individual-focused* workbooks or reading materials. Understood from that viewpoint, the term "self-help group" is arguably somewhat of an oxymoron, because the "help" that one acquires is derived not from the "self" at all, but rather through the presence, support, and shared experience of others present in a *group*. Thus, in order to more accurately reflect both the purported therapeutic processes at work in such organizations, and to minimize confusion in both professional and public discourse, SHGs are increasingly referred to as "mutual help" (or sometimes "mutual aid") groups (Kelly et al., 2004). In keeping with this trend, we use the term "MHG" to describe this particular adjunctive therapy.

There are numerous MHG organizations that address many different problems. Some groups, such as Alcoholics Anonymous (AA) and Narcotics Anonymous (NA), have an exclusive focus on substance use disorders (SUDs), whereas others, such as Double Trouble in Recovery (DTR) and Dual Recovery Anonymous (DRA), are aimed at people who have comorbid substance use and psychiatric disorders (i.e., "dual diagnoses"). Other groups address mental illness or emotional problems in a general way [e.g., Recovery, Inc. (RI), GROW], whereas some are focused on specific psychiatric disorders [e.g., Depression and Bipolar Support Alliance (DBSA), Schizophrenics Anonymous (SA)]. Others focus on helping family members who are affected by the illness of a loved one (e.g., Alanon).

Although the foci of these organizations are quite diverse, all share common features. Specifically, MHGs contain individuals with a common experience or problem (e.g., alcohol dependence, depression) who come together to share their experiences and/or to provide help and support to one another. The groups are typically led and organized by consumers rather than professionals, although professionals sometimes may be involved in advisory roles (e.g., in DBSA chapters). Groups are available free of charge, although many ask for voluntary contributions from those who attend (Humphreys, 2004). Some unique advantages of MHGs include the fact that group meetings, such as AA, are often locally accessible several times a day in many communities, notably also in the evenings and on weekends when professional care is often not available. Many also foster the development of additional group-member support by telephone that can be accessed "on demand" between meetings. The World Wide Web (WWW) has also given rise to "online" meetings. Restriction of professional services covered by managed care means that these free, flexible, available, and accessible community resources serve an increasingly important role in public health.

HOW COMMON ARE MUTUAL-HELP GROUPS?

How numerous are MHGs in the United States and how many people participate in such organizations? Due to the informal and often anonymous nature of many MHG organizations, group and membership estimates can be difficult to obtain and those estimates that are obtained may underestimate true membership. However, in a broad national survey focusing on mental health mutual support groups, self-help organizations, and consumer-operated services, Goldstrom et al. (2006) estimated that as of 2002, there were nearly 7500 such consumer- and family-run mental health organizations in the United States, nearly twice the national estimate for traditional mental health organizations such as hospitals and clinics. In addition, it was estimated that as many as 41 000 people have participated in mental health mutual-support groups and over 1 million people belong to mental health self-help organizations. Although these consumer-run services may be more numerous than professional mental health services, virtually none of the groups surveyed reported that they viewed their services as a substitute for professional services, and 94% reported receiving referrals from professionals, highlighting the complementary and collaborative nature of the two types of services. Nevertheless, as detailed below, for some individuals these groups are not merely "adjunctive," but instead "replacement" therapies (e.g., Timko et al., 1999). The striking number of consumer organizations is made even more impressive if one takes into account addiction- and dual diagnosis-focused MHGs, such as AA, NA, and DTR. AA alone has approximately 60 000 groups meeting each week in the United States, and more than 1 million active members (AA, 2005).

We begin this chapter by describing the goals and key therapeutic processes of MHGs presumed to facilitate improvement and/or maintenance of functioning. We then review and evaluate available outcome data pertaining to MHGs' effectiveness in helping individuals manage or recover from their respective disorders, including any evidence in support of the key therapeutic processes. We then describe the role MHGs may play in a formal treatment plan and describe how professionals might facilitate and coordinate participation in these groups. In the final sections, we describe opportunities for further research and what might be done to help disseminate knowledge about MHGs and their potential utility. Within the first two sections we provide information about various MHGs divided into three distinct, but related, problem areas: (1) substance dependence (e.g., alcohol, cocaine); (2) mental illness (e.g., schizophrenia, depression); and, (3) dual diagnosis (i.e., substance dependence in combination with mental illness). For ease of reference and due to space limitations inherent in a single chapter on this topic, we have constructed several summary tables containing brief descriptions of the MHGs of the types covered in the chapter, website and contact information, degree of evidence for the MHGs, and several other indices that we hope will facilitate easy comparisons of organizations along multiple lines (see Tables 4.1–4.3). We had considered also including more detailed MHG information in the text regarding other compulsive behaviors (e.g., gambling, sex, eating behaviors) and family-related MHGs (e.g., Alanon, Naranon). However, given space confines we were unable to pursue these in detail. As a compromise, however, we have included a summary table of MHGs for each of these additional domains (Tables 4.4 & 4.5).

KEY PROCESS VARIABLES

MHG organizations operate on certain assumptions about the causes, maintaining conditions, and therapeutic factors needed to manage, reduce, or eliminate the suffering caused by the particular condition of focus. To varying degrees, each MHG organization adheres broadly to an overarching theoretical framework and describes specific therapeutic targets (e.g., abstinence from alcohol/drugs, recovery) and strategies believed necessary to reach those goals. This forms the idiosyncratic or "specific" components of each MHG organization (e.g., the "12-steps" in AA). In addition, nearly all MHGs by definition involve helping others. This has been more formally conceptualized as the "helper principle" (Riessman, 1965). From this viewpoint, those who help others help themselves by reinforcing their own dedication to change, increasing the perception of their importance to others and their self-esteem, and enhancing their social status and sense of independence. Positive associations between helping and emotional well-being have been found in the general population (e.g., lower depression and higher self-esteem; Piliavin, 2003). However, the degree of emphasis on helping others as an essential curative process varies substantially across MHG organizations.

MHGs also possess further nonspecified, "common" therapeutic factors that are likely to operate across all MHGs and are rarely mentioned explicitly. These nonspecified common factors might be conceptualized as transtheoretical therapeutic effects inherent in group process (e.g., Yalom, 1995).

Group therapy theory as outlined by Yalom (1995) posits several therapeutic elements of groups. Some of these are "altruism"—a principle aligned with the helper principle mentioned above, "universality"—a sense of belonging and identification, "imitative behavior"—observing and "trying on" various behaviors and ways of coping, "instillation of hope"—feeling more hopeful, "imparting information"—giving and getting tips and learning skills, and "catharsis"—expressing thoughts and emotions. Because MHGs *are* groups, it is likely that they will all possess similar group process elements such as those specified by Yalom (1995). However, as alluded to above, each MHG also possesses unique elements. Such processes are those therapeutic elements deemed to apply only to that particular MHG, such as the four-point program of Self-Management And Recovery Training (SMART) Recovery or the "spiritual awakening" of AA and other 12-step organizations. Below, we outline the key "specific" process variables for MHGs categorized, as mentioned earlier, by their particular focus, starting with those focusing primarily on alcohol/drug dependence.

KEY PROCESS VARIABLES OF MUTUAL-HELP GROUPS FOCUSING PRIMARILY ON SUBSTANCE DEPENDENCE

Alcoholics Anonymous and Other 12-Step-Based Mutual-Help Groups

We begin by describing the specific key process variables espoused within the 12-step model that originated in AA in the 1930s, and that have been widely adopted and adapted to several other drugs besides alcohol (e.g., Marijuana Anonymous, NA, Cocaine Anonymous), to alleviate other kinds of compulsive behaviors (e.g., Sex Addicts Anonymous, Overeaters Anonymous, Gamblers Anonymous), mental health conditions (e.g., SA) and dual diagnosis issues (e.g., DTR, DRA), and to help affected family members (e.g., Alanon, Families Anonymous, Naranon).

The purported mechanism of recovery from alcohol addiction according to AA is through a "psychic change" (AA, 2001, p. xxvi) or "spiritual experience" or "spiritual awakening" (AA, 2001; Appendix II) achieved by following a sequential 12-step program. A clear definition of what exactly is meant by "a spiritual experience" or "awakening" has been confusing to many. However, AA states broadly that this is most often characterized by a gradual change of an "educational variety" that leads to "… a profound alteration in [his] reaction to life" (AA, 2001, Appendix II). At times it is associated with a "higher power" (e.g., a "God consciousness") and at other times it has a much more practical approach regarding a change in one's specific attitudes and behaviors.

TABLE 4.1 Substance Focused Mutual-help Groups

Name and year founded	Target population	Number and location of groups in the US	Overarching theoretical orientation	Therapeutic goal(s)	Evidence base* (0–3)	Degree of professional involvement in groups	■ Website ■ E-mail ■ Phone number ■ Basic text
Alcoholics Anonymous (AA) 1935	People with a drinking problem	52 651 groups in all 50 States	12-Step	Abstinence	1, 2, 3	Consumer-run	■ www.alcoholics-anonymous.org ■ In the US/Canada: Look for "Alcoholics Anonymous" in any telephone directory. ■ (212) 870-3400 ■ *Alcoholics Anonymous (The Big Book)*
Narcotics Anonymous (NA) 1940s	People with an addiction to any drug, including alcohol	Approx. 15 000 groups in all 50 States	12-Step	Abstinence	1, 2	Consumer-run	■ www.na.org ■ (818) 773-9999 ■ *Narcotics Anonymous, Basic Text*
Cocaine Anonymous (CA) 1982	People with an addiction to cocaine/crack and/or any other "mind-altering substance"	Approx. 2000 groups in most States; 6 online meetings at www.ca-online.org	12-Step	Abstinence	0	Consumer-run	■ www.ca.org ■ (310) 559-5833 ■ *Hope, Faith, & Courage*

(*Continues*)

TABLE 4.1 (*Continued*)

Name and year founded	Target population	Number and location of groups in the US	Overarching theoretical orientation	Therapeutic goal(s)	Evidence base* (0–3)	Degree of professional involvement in groups	■ Website ■ E-mail ■ Phone number ■ Basic text
Nicotine Anonymous (NicA) 1980s	People with an addiction to nicotine	Approx. 450 groups in most States; Numerous online (www.nicotine-anonymous.org/meetings_internet_meetings.asp) and telephone meetings	12-Step	Abstinence	3 (but Ps in the NicA condition also received psycho-educational tx)	Consumer-run	■ www.nicotine-anonymous.org ■ info@nicotine-anonymous.org ■ (415) 750-0328 ■ *Nicotine Anonymous*
Methadone Anonymous (MA) 1990s	People who use or have used methadone	Approx. 100 groups in 25 States; Online meetings at http://methadone-anonymous.org/chat.html	12-Step	Abstinence from mind-altering, nonprescribed drugs; Methadone use is accepted as it is seen as a medication	1, 2	Consumer-run	■ www.methadone-anonymous.org ■ www.methadone anonymous.info
Marijuana Anonymous (MA) 1989	People with an addiction to marijuana	Approx. 200 groups in 24 States; Online meetings at www.ma-online.org	12-Step	Abstinence	0	Consumer-run	■ www.marijuana-anonymous.org ■ office@marijuana-anonymous.org ■ 1-800-766-6779 ■ *Life With Hope*

Rational Recovery (RR) 1988	People with an addiction to alcohol and/or drugs	No group meetings or mutual helping; Emphasis is on *individual* control and responsibility	Cognitive-behavioral	Abstinence	1, 2	No groups, but program is antiprofessional and emphasizes using only RR techniques for recovery	■ www.rational.org ■ (530) 621-2667 ■ *The Small Book*
Self-Management and Recovery Training (SMART Recovery) 1994	People with all types of addictive behaviors	Approx. 250 groups in 40 States; 19 online meetings at www.smart recovery.org/ meetings/ olschedule.htm	Cognitive-behavioral; 4-point program	Abstinence is recommended, but moderation is acknowledged as a possibility	1, 3	Advised by addiction professionals	■ www.smart-recovery.org ■ 1-866-951-5357 ■ info@smartrecovery.org
Secular Organization for Sobriety, a.k.a. Save Our Selves (SOS) 1986	People with an addiction to alcohol and/or drugs	Approx. 480 groups in all 50 States; Online chat at www.sossobriety. org/sos/chat.htm	Humanistic/ Existential	Abstinence	1	Consumer-run	■ www.sossobriety.org ■ www.secularsobriety. org ■ sos@cfiwest.org ■ (323) 666-4295 ■ *Recovery without Religion*

(Continues)

TABLE 4.1 (*Continued*)

Name and year founded	Target population	Number and location of groups in the US	Overarching theoretical orientation	Therapeutic goal(s)	Evidence base* (0–3)	Degree of professional involvement in groups	■ Website ■ E-mail ■ Phone number ■ Basic text
Women for Sobriety (WFS) 1976	Women with an addiction to alcohol	150–300 groups in the US; Online meetings at http://groups.msn.com/WomenforSobriety	Cognitive (focus on self-esteem; Affirmations, positive thinking	Abstinence	1	Consumer-run	■ www.womenforsobriety.org ■ newlife@nni.com ■ (215) 536-8026 ■ *Turnabout: New Help for the Woman Alcoholic*
Moderation Management (MM) 1994	Problem drinkers who are not dependent on alcohol	Most meetings are online at www.angelfire.com/trek/mmchat/; Approx.16 face-to-face meetings in 12 States	Cognitive-behavioral	Moderate use (not more than 3 drinks/day or 9 drinks/week for women and not more than 4 drinks/day or 14 drinks/week for men)	1	Consumer-run; Professionals may help to start groups	■ www.moderation.org ■ mm@moderation.org ■ (212) 871-0974 ■ *Responsible Drinking: A Moderation Management Approach for Problem Drinkers*

* 0 = None; 1 = Descriptive studies only; 2 = Observational (correlational, longitudinal); 3 = Experimental (random assignment, controlled).

Of course, the other major feature of all 12-step organizations is the *fellowship*. This social context in which recovery is learnt and supported is less explicitly documented as an essential curative component in the main texts of AA (probably because there was only a very small number of members initially when the texts were written), but is captured in the preamble read at the start of nearly all AA meetings (AA Grapevine, 1947):

> Alcoholics Anonymous is a fellowship of men and women who share their experience, strength and hope with each other that they may solve their common problem and help others to recover from alcoholism. The only requirement for membership is a desire to stop drinking. There are no dues or fees for A.A. membership; we are self-supporting through our own contributions. A.A. is not allied with any sect, denomination, politics, organization or institution; does not wish to engage in any controversy; neither endorses nor opposes any causes. Our primary purpose is to stay sober and help other alcoholics to achieve sobriety.

This preamble emphasizes the aspects of mutual "sharing" or communication of experiences in an attempt to help oneself and others. As alluded to in the preamble's last sentence, perhaps more than any other MHG, a central curative process of 12-step organizations is the "helper principle" (Riessman, 1965), essentially the notion that "helping you helps me". As AA states: "Practical experience shows that nothing will so much insure immunity against drinking as intensive work with other alcoholics" (AA, 1939, 2001, p. 89). Indeed, early AA members believed that reaching out to other alcoholics was vital to facilitate ongoing recovery. AA cofounder Bill W's formal recognition and documentation of this fact was a driving force behind AA's active outreach to hospitals and institutions that helped other alcoholics find sobriety and led to the growth of AA (AA, 1939). This also formed the basis of AA's "12th step" of passing on the AA recovery program to other alcoholics to help maintain one's own sobriety.

In summary, the two major processes in all 12-step organizations that are purported to facilitate recovery are the 12-step *program* and the *fellowship* accessible through attendance at meetings. Another important element that facilitates working through the 12-step program is the fellowship mentor or "sponsor" who serves as a coach and guide for new members.

Although not directly related to individuals' sobriety or healthy functioning, per se, AA's "12 Traditions" (AA, 1953) are the group-level equivalent of how to facilitate healthy functioning of 12-step meetings and the larger 12-step organization. Essentially, they consist of 12 statements derived from the experiences of early groups that form a template for how groups may wish to structure themselves and operate. These conclusions were based on the early AA groups' growing pains that resulted in a consensus regarding the best way to function as groups and as an organization. The formulation and documentation of the 12 Traditions provided a successful, adaptable, template for myriad other 12-step organizations to grow and flourish.

Self Management and Recovery Training (SMART) Recovery

The stated goals of SMART Recovery are to "support individuals who have chosen to abstain, or are considering abstinence from any type of addictive behavior (substances or activities), by teaching how to change self-defeating thinking, emotions, and actions; and to work towards long-term satisfactions and quality of life." It teaches self-empowerment and self-reliance and views addictions/compulsions as complex maladaptive behaviors with possible physiological factors. It teaches tools and techniques for self-directed change and encourages individuals to recover and live satisfying lives. The SMART Recovery meetings have a contemporary cognitive-behavior orientation, are educational, and include open discussions. It also explicitly advocates the appropriate use of prescribed medications and psychological treatments. It draws on evidence-based practices and "evolves as scientific knowledge evolves." The main processes of recovery stated by SMART are enhancing and maintaining motivation to abstain, coping with urges, problem solving (e.g., managing thoughts, feelings, and behaviors), and lifestyle balance achieved and reinforced through meeting participation.

Secular Organization for Sobriety

Secular Organization for Sobriety (SOS) refers to itself as "a self-empowerment approach to recovery" without any spiritual or religious involvement. Its therapeutic processes and general organizational principles are quite similar to AA however, and much of the organizational language is very similar to AA's 12 Traditions. It does not possess a clear, sequential program of action, like AA, but does advocate honest sharing, association with others including other alcoholics, and a focused "Sobriety Priority" of not drinking "no matter what." The course of action needed to achieve sobriety is largely left up to the individual to decide for himself or herself but is encouraged to be sought using the experience of those SOS members who have found it.

Moderation Management

Moderation Management (MM) is the only substance-focused MHG that explicitly advocates moderation and not complete abstinence from alcohol. It embodies four principles: Self-management, balance, moderation, and personal responsibility. MM's main aim is to share strategies for successful moderation and the "restoration of balance," which include both changes in behavior and the management of emotions. Its main therapeutic process is through self-monitoring of drinking to keep within healthful limits. This is supported by MM group participation. A primary tool used in MM is "awareness." Daily drink charting is intended to bring an unconscious habit back to consciousness and within control. The very act of counting the number of drinks consumed each week is one of the key processes of therapeutic change. MM advocates nine steps (http://www.moderation.org/readings.shtml#9steps) that include an initial 30-day period of abstinence during which the member can assess how alcohol has affected them, set drinking limits, and begin to make lifestyle changes. Even after moderate drinking is begun within the context of MM, MM still recommends not drinking every day, but rather to abstain from alcohol completely on at least 3–4 days per week.

Rational Recovery

Rational Recovery (RR) claims to have made MHGs "obsolete" through a technique called the "addictive voice recognition technique" (AVRT). Thus, it is not officially a "mutual-help group," but is mentioned here because RR once sponsored an extensive recovery group network offering a cognitive-behavioral mutual-help approach along with an undeveloped version of AVRT, and is quite well-known nationally. Following some internal conflict, the organization split into RR and SMART Recovery (see above). RR now operates solely through the Internet, by mail, and through literature. The goal is abstinence, and the key assumption is recognizing and dealing with the internal "addictive voice." Thus, it is an explicitly cognitive approach somewhat similar to the rational emotive therapy espoused by Albert Ellis.

KEY PROCESS VARIABLES OF MUTUAL-HELP GROUPS FOCUSING PRIMARILY ON MENTAL ILLNESS

Recovery, Inc.

Recovery, Inc. (RI) uses cognitive-behavioral techniques and unique language to help individuals "regain and maintain their mental health" and cope with difficult situations in everyday life. The Recovery model, established by Abraham A. Low, MD, in 1937, emphasizes accepting personal responsibility for one's successes and failures, exerting willpower and control over one's impulses and cognitions, and countering negative, self-defeating thoughts with self-endorsing, wellness-promoting ones. These factors may be viewed as ways of strengthening one's internal locus of control (Murray, 1996). The RI basic text, *Mental Health through Will Training* (Low, 1950) is problem-focused, with an emphasis on affective problems such as depression and anxiety and on cognitive strategies for coping (McFadden et al., 1992). As such, the philosophy behind the Recovery program suggests that change occurs through personal responsibility and effort rather than through relinquishing control to a "Higher Power" outside of oneself, as in 12-step programs.

GROW

GROW strives to provide "a sharing and caring community" to help persons with mental illnesses and emotional problems work toward personal growth and recovery. Within this community, the program focuses on changing maladaptive cognitions and behaviors, as well as on helping members to work toward the "five foundations of maturity": Understanding, acceptance, confidence, control, and love. GROW literature (*The Program of Growth to Maturity and Readings for Mental Health*) emphasizes spirituality and striving to reach one's highest potential, and offers advice in a nonauthoritarian way (McFadden et al., 1992). The program also offers a structured group format to help meetings run smoothly,

TABLE 4.2 Mental Illness Focused Mutual-Help Groups

Name and year founded	Target population	Number and location of groups in the US	Overarching theoretical orientation	Therapeutic goal(s)	Evidence base (0–3)*	Degree of professional involvement in groups	■ Website ■ E-mail ■ Phone number ■ Basic text
Depression and Bipolar Support Alliance (DBSA; formerly MDDA) 1986	People with mood disorders (depression and bipolar) and their families*	Over 1000 groups in most States; Online chat at www.dbsalliance.org/site/PageServer?Pagename=support_chatindex	Focus on sharing experiences and providing support	Management of mental illness Improving quality of life	0	Groups are consumer-run but advised by professionals	■ www.dbsalliance.org ■ chapters@dbsalliance.org (info on support groups and chapters) ■ info@dbsalliance.org (other questions) ■ 1-800-826-3632 or (312) 642-0049
Depression and Related Affective Disorders Association (DRADA) 1986	People with mood disorders (depression and bipolar) and their families*	75 groups in MD, VA, DC, DE, & PA	Focus on sharing experiences and providing support	Management of mental illness	0	Groups are led by professionally trained consumers	■ www.drada.org ■ info@drada.org ■ (703) 610-9026 ■ *The Manual for Mood Disorder Support Groups* (for group leaders)
Depressed Anonymous (DA) 1985	People with depression	19 groups in 10 States	12-Step	Overcoming depression and preventing relapse	0	Consumer-run	■ www.depressedanon.com ■ info@depressedanon.com ■ (502) 569-1989 ■ *Depressed Anonymous*

Recovery, Inc. (RI) 1937	People with psychiatric illnesses and those who need help coping with difficulties in everyday life	Over 700 groups in 44 States	Cognitive-behavioral	Management of mental illness Learning coping strategies for problems in everyday life	1, 2	Consumer-run	■ www.recovery-inc.com ■ inquiries@recovery-inc.org ■ (312) 337-5661 ■ *Mental Health through Will Training*, By Abraham A. Low, MD
GROW, Inc. 1957 in Australia, 1978 in USA	People with psychiatric illnesses or life problems (e.g., stress, grief)	Approx. 140 groups in IL, NJ, and RI; Approx. 650 groups worldwide	Based on 12 Steps (not same as AA's Steps) and 5 Foundations of Maturity	Recovery from mental illness Personal growth to maturity	1, 2	Groups are usually consumer-led but occasionally led by professionals	■ www.grow.net.au (Australian site); www.growinamerica.org (American site) ■ 1-888-741-GROW ■ *Program of Growth to Maturity (Blue Book)*
Emotions Anonymous (EA) 1971	People with emotional difficulties	1430 groups in all 50 States	12-Step	Emotional well-being	0	Consumer-run	■ www.emotions anonymous.org ■ info@emotions anonymous.org ■ (651) 647-9712 ■ *Emotions Anonymous (Big Book)*

(*Continues*)

TABLE 4.2 (*Continued*)

Name and year founded	Target population	Number and location of groups in the US	Overarching theoretical orientation	Therapeutic goal(s)	Evidence base (0–3)*	Degree of professional involvement in groups	■ Website ■ E-mail ■ Phone number ■ Basic text
Schizophrenics Anonymous (SA) 1985	People with schizophrenia or schizophrenia-related illness	Approx. 170 groups in 26 States	Based on 6 Steps; Spiritual	Management of mental illness Adherence to treatment and medication	1	Consumer-run but "adminis-tered in partnership with the National Schizophrenia Foundation"	■ www.nsfoundation.org/sa/index.html ■ Consumer Line: 1-800-482-9534 ■ *Schizophrenics Anonymous: A Self-Help Support Group (Blue Book)*
Obsessive-Compulsive Anonymous (OCA)	People with obsessive-compulsive disorder	40 groups in 17 States	12-Step	Reduction or elimination of obsessions and compulsions	0	Consumer-run	■ http://members.aol.com/west24th/ ■ (516) 739-0662 ■ *Obsessive Compulsive Anonymous*

*DBSA and DRADA also have MHGs for family members.

Note: See Anxiety Disorders Association of America's website (www.adaa.org/gettinghelp/supportgroups.asp) for listings of approximately 200 support groups for various anxiety disorders.

See also American Self-Help Group Clearinghouse website (http://mentalhelp.net/selfhelp/) to further explore MHGs in existence for a vast variety of diseases and disorders.

* 0 = None; 1 = Descriptive studies only; 2 = Observational (correlational, longitudinal); 3 = Experimental (random assignment, controlled).

which includes the sharing of one member's personal story of recovery or growth, practical problem-solving tasks, follow-up reports on members' progress, and education and discussion about the program itself. To develop and maintain the desired "sharing and caring community," GROW members are encouraged to interact with each other outside of weekly meetings and to take an interest in each other's lives and well-being. Thus, the social, spiritual, and cognitive-behavioral aspects of the group are thought to be important to members' personal growth and recovery from their illnesses.

Depression and Bipolar Support Alliance

In the United States, there are over 1000 consumer- and family-operated support groups affiliated with the DBSA that aim to help people with mood disorders and their families cope with these illnesses. DBSA groups provide lifetime support to members, and are not viewed as an alternative to professional care, but rather are suggested for use only "following proper diagnosis and treatment." Although the groups are peer-led, mental health professionals from the community serve as advisors and board members. Unlike other MHGs, DBSA groups are not based on steps, a basic text, or specific techniques for change, and vary in content according to the needs of members of each individual group. Despite intragroup differences, members view interpersonal support and help with coping with problems as common benefits of group participation, and note that support groups improve their understanding of medications and treatment and motivate them to follow their treatment plan (DBSA, 2004).

Schizophrenics Anonymous

SA is a consumer-run MHG for people with schizophrenia and schizophrenia-related illnesses that is affiliated with the National Schizophrenia Foundation. The organization aims to provide members with support, information, and a sense of dignity and purpose, as well as to help improve attitudes toward the illness and make progress toward recovery. SA views recovery as functioning at one's own highest potential as opposed to an objectively defined cessation of symptoms. To help members achieve these goals, SA has a 6-step program for recovery, which includes admitting that help is needed, taking responsibility for one's choices, believing in oneself, forgiving oneself and others, understanding the need for changes in cognition, and finally, turning one's life over to a self-defined Higher Power. The themes of spirituality and relinquishing control are similar to those found in the 12 steps of AA, although SA steps seem to place more emphasis on internal processes and abilities. Thus, although it is based on a 12-step, "Anonymous" template, it has substantially adapted it to fit this particular disorder.

KEY PROCESS VARIABLES OF MUTUAL-HELP GROUPS FOCUSING PRIMARILY ON DUAL DIAGNOSIS

As noted in Table 4.3, all the dual diagnosis MHGs are based on the 12-Step and 12-Tradition template of AA. However, there are some important emphases

TABLE 4.3 Dual Diagnosis Focused Mutual-help Groups

Name and year founded	Target population	Number and location of groups in the US	Overarching theoretical orientation	Therapeutic goal(s)	Evidence base (0–3)*	Degree of professional involvement in groups	■ Website ■ E-mail ■ Phone number ■ Basic text
Double Trouble in Recovery (DTR) 1989	Dually diagnosed individuals	200 (Highest number of groups in NY, GA, CA, CO, NM, FL)	12-Step	Abstinence Management of mental illness	1, 2	Consumer-run	■ www.doubletroublein recovery.org ■ HV613@aol.com ■ (718) 373-2684 ■ *Double Trouble in Recovery Basic Guide*
Dual Recovery Anonymous (DRA) 1989	Dually diagnosed individuals	345 (Highest number of groups in CA, OH, PA, MA)	12-Step	Abstinence Management of mental illness	0	Consumer-run	■ www.draonline.org ■ Toll Free: 1-877-833-2332 ■ *The Twelve Steps and Dual Disorders*
Dual Disorders Anonymous 1982	Dually diagnosed individuals	48 (28 in IL)	12-Step	Abstinence Management of mental illness	0	Consumer-run	■ www. msnusers. com/dualdisorders anonymous ■ dualdisordersanonymous @www.msnusers.com ■ (847) 781-1553
Dual Diagnosis Anonymous (DDA)	Dually diagnosed individuals	56 (38 in CA)	12-Step; 5 additional steps	Abstinence Management of mental illness	0	Consumer-run	■ www.ddaworldwide.com ■ info@ddaworldwide.com ■ Toll Free: 1-800-359-1216 ■ *DDA for Adults*

* 0 = None; 1 = Descriptive studies only; 2 = Observational (correlational, longitudinal); 3 = Experimental (random assignment, controlled).

that come into play in these dual diagnosis groups. The burden of two complex psychiatric conditions (i.e., substance dependence and a mental illness) raises additional issues, because the signs and symptoms of comorbid conditions require specific dialogue outside of the realm of alcohol or other drug dependence, and often benefit from psychotropic medication. AA's official position on medication use is that it should be handled by qualified medical professionals and that decisions about such medication use should be decided between the patient and his or her doctor (AA, 1984). The lack of emphasis on medications and other psychiatric symptoms has led many dually diagnosed individuals to seek out MHGs that focus more explicitly on medication compliance and management of symptoms, although many also attend AA or NA (Ouimette et al., 1998). The three dual diagnosis-focused MHG organizations – DTR, DRA, and Dual Diagnosis Anonymous (DDA) all emphasize the fact that many dually diagnosed individuals may need and want to address their dual recovery in an integrated and holistic way. Thus, in addition to the regular 12-step MHG format, other key processes involve medication compliance and acknowledgment of the need for appropriate professional help to manage symptoms.

OUTCOME DATA

At first glance, the very notion of "mutual help" for individuals whose mental capabilities and reality testing may be less than optimal appears to be a little incongruous. With satirical cries of "the blind leading the blind," it is not hard to see how one might scratch one's head and wonder how on earth this could be? Yet, during the past 25 years, accumulating evidence indicates that many individuals attending MHGs derive benefit.

In this section, we describe evidence pertaining to any benefits individuals derived from MHG participation including any research on subgroups of individuals for whom MHGs may or may not work particularly well. We also review research relating to cost-effectiveness where available. There is a growing body of literature that addresses substance use and/or mental health outcomes in MHGs, as well as the factors that mediate these outcomes. However, it should be noted that there are a number of methodological issues related to the study of MHGs. For instance, randomized controlled trials (RCTs) in this context are relatively rare and may not be the most appropriate way to examine outcomes because of the nature of the groups themselves (McCrady & Miller, 1993). Random assignment of people to MHG participation would interfere with the voluntary, self-initiated manner in which participation naturally occurs, thereby limiting generalizability to naturally occurring MHGs (Davidson et al., 1999). Conversely, it can be seen as unethical to prevent people in a control group from participating in freely available community MHGs if they so desire (Kelly, 2003). Therefore, straightforward causal conclusions about the effects of participation in MHGs on mental health and/or substance use outcomes cannot be easily drawn. However, prospective, longitudinal study designs that control for major confounding variables (e.g., baseline functioning, addiction/psychiatric severity, participant motivation, professional interventions) are also important sources of evidence, even though the data are correlational. More of these types of studies are beginning to emerge. With this said, we now focus on what is currently known about the utility and benefits of MHGs beginning first with those MHGs focusing on substance dependence.

OUTCOME DATA FOR MUTUAL-HELP GROUPS FOCUSING ON SUBSTANCE DEPENDENCE

Alcoholics Anonymous is the most commonly sought source of help for an alcohol problem in the United States (Room & Greenfield, 1993). Being the oldest, largest, and most influential of all mutual-help organizations, the preponderance of empirical work has been focused on AA, including three meta-analyses. As mentioned previously, because of the problems inherent in using RCTs to test the efficacy of MHGs, efficacy trials have been conducted using a professional therapy constructed to facilitate their use and to which clinical research participants can be randomly assigned (e.g., *Twelve-Step Facilitation Therapy*, Nowinski et al., 1992). We include such studies herein. We begin with a review and evaluation of meta-analyses (Emrick et al., 1993; Kownacki & Shadish, 1999; Tonigan et al., 1996), followed by RCTs (e.g., Project MATCH Research Group, 1997) and effectiveness studies. The evidence is then reviewed regarding what is known about who may or may not benefit from AA or other MHG involvement, with a focus on four specific areas: Psychiatric comorbidity, religious orientation, gender, and age (youth). Attention is then turned to studies attempting to elucidate how or why MHG involvement may or may not be beneficial. Finally, we review studies that have examined cost-effectiveness.

Meta-Analyses

Emrick and colleagues' (1993) review was the first to estimate the effectiveness of AA using meta-analytic techniques. A total of 107 studies were included. Studies were excluded that blended alcohol and other drug use disorder clients into a single sample or included participants who had gone to both AA and NA. Thus, their review was exclusively of primary alcoholics and AA. The authors concluded that AA had a positive, but moderate, salutary effect on drinking behavior and psychosocial functioning. In an attempt to examine some of the conditions under which AA may be more or less beneficial, a further meta-analytic review was conducted by Tonigan et al. (1996) examining moderators of AA's effectiveness. Two major variables were examined as potential moderators of AA findings: (1) treatment source of the sample (i.e., inpatient vs outpatient) and (2) study quality.

Tonigan et al. (1996) found that studies of outpatient samples identified stronger relationships between AA involvement and drinking outcomes, and between AA attendance and improved psychosocial outcomes than studies of inpatient samples. However, absolute attendance levels may be much higher among inpatients. Stronger relationships may be observed among outpatient samples because there is a greater range of substance use severity and attendance rates among outpatients. These findings have implications today, given the large scale move from inpatient programs to outpatient/intensive outpatient programs in many countries.

Tonigan et al. (1996) also found that better quality studies evinced relationships between severity and AA involvement (e.g., more severe patients were more likely to attend), but poorer quality studies found no such relationship. Better designed studies found moderate and positive relationships between AA attendance and improved psychosocial functioning, whereas such relationships were much weaker in studies with less rigor. However, more rigorous studies provided less support than poorly designed studies for AA's effects in relation to abstinence after treatment. The authors argue that global AA profiles or blanket statements about the effectiveness are not supported. Instead, the extent to which AA is helpful may depend on many variables. As noted earlier, the exclusion of studies that included participants with drug use disorders or who attend MHGs other than AA, such as NA, limits the generalizability of findings from these meta-analyses beyond fairly homogenous, alcohol-dependent samples attending AA.

The problems with RCTs and MHGs notwithstanding, Kownacki and Shadish (1999) completed a meta-analytic review of only controlled trials of AA in order to minimize selection bias in an attempt to establish AA's efficacy in a cause–effect way. The review focused on 12-month alcohol-related outcomes and examined several potential moderator variables to aid in interpreting the results: Method of assignment to conditions, attrition, type of control group used, type of outcome measure, and voluntary versus coerced admission to conditions. Studies were subgrouped into studies of conventional outpatient AA meetings, AA-based residential treatment, and components of AA. Participants in the 21 studies tended to be male (92%) and Caucasian (79%).

The review concluded that randomized trials were almost completely confounded with coerced status, i.e., randomized controlled studies used subjects *required* to attend AA. Such individuals fared worse than individuals receiving other treatment or no treatment. Individuals forced to attend AA, often by the judicial system, may find AA difficult to accept and, because coerced attendance is a violation of the membership requirement of "a desire to stop drinking" (AA, 1953), such individuals may not be openly accepted by other voluntary members. However, as pointed out by Kownacki and Shadish (1999), these individuals may do better if they were coerced into other kinds of treatment (e.g., see Kelly et al., 2005). Because most existing controlled trials have studied attendees coerced through the criminal justice system, the generalizability of their findings to individuals who are free to choose is limited.

TABLE 4.4 Non Substance Focused Addictive Behavior Mutual-Help Groups

Name and year founded	Target population	Number and location of groups in the US	Overarching theoretical orientation	Therapeutic goal(s)	Evidence base (0–3)*	Degree of professional involvement in groups	■ Website ■ E-mail ■ Phone number ■ Basic text
Gamblers Anonymous (GA) 1957	People with compulsive gambling problems	Approx. 1000 chapters in all 50 States	12-Step	Abstinence from gambling	1, 2	Consumer-run	■ www.gamblersanonymous.org ■ (213) 386-8789 ■ isomain@gamblersanonymous.org
Sex Addicts Anonymous (SAA) 1977	People with compulsive sexual behaviors	Approx. 700 meetings in most States; Online meetings at www.sexaa.org/online.htm; Telephone meetings	12-Step	Abstinence from addictive sexual behavior; Becoming "sexually healthy"	0	Consumer-run	■ www.sexaa.org ■ info@saa-recovery.org ■ 1-800-477-8191 ■ *Sex Addicts Anonymous*

Sex and Love Addicts Anonymous (SLAA) 1976	People with an addiction to sex, love, relationships, and/or fantasy, or those with "sexual anorexia"	Approx. 1320 groups worldwide (including in all 50 States), Online meetings at www.slaafws.org/online/onlinemeet.html; regional teleconference calls	12-Step	Abstinence from one's "own personal bottom-line addictive behavior"; Changing the pattern of compulsive sex and love behavior	0	Consumer-run	■ www.slaafws.org ■ info@slaafws.org ■ (210) 828-7900 ■ *Sex and Love Addicts Anonymous*
Overeaters Anonymous (OA) 1960	People with compulsive eating problems	Thousands of meetings in all 50 States; Numerous online (www.oa.org/pdf/OnlineMeetingsList.pdf) and telephone meetings (www.oa.org/pdf/phone_mtgs.pdf)	12-Step	Abstinence from compulsive eating; Following an eating plan	1	Consumer-run	■ www.oa.org ■ info@oa.org ■ (505) 891-2664 ■ *Overeaters Anonymous, 2nd Ed. (Brown Book)*

* 0 = None; 1 = Descriptive studies only; 2 = Observational (correlational, longitudinal); 3 = Experimental (random assignment, controlled).

Randomized Controlled Trials

Further evidence of the effectiveness of MHG participation was generated in a large multisite RCT of treatment for alcohol dependence (Project MATCH Research Group, 1993). This was the largest RCT of individual psychotherapies for any disorder ever undertaken, comprising more than 1700 male and female patients. In this study, a professionally delivered 12-Step Facilitation (TSF) treatment was compared with motivational enhancement therapy (MET) and cognitive-behavioral therapy (CBT). Ethical concerns about *requiring nonattendance* at AA were ameliorated through the use of comparison treatments (MET, CBT) that neither actively encouraged nor discouraged MHG attendance. Although the TSF condition was not a test of MHG involvement itself, the study examined the feasibility and effects of a professional facilitation of its use. Results revealed the feasibility of the TSF approach, as well as its superior efficacy with respect to abstinence, relative to the more empirically supported CBT and MET (Project MATCH Research Group, 1997). A larger effect was observed regarding patients' social networks; outpatients with social networks supportive of drinking, measured at treatment intake, had better long-term outcomes in TSF than in the other treatment conditions (Longabaugh et al., 1998).

The superior outcomes attained by these patient subgroups when treated in TSF appeared to be explained by MHG attendance during the follow-up period. Such attendance may have buffered the negative effect from the existing social network and provided a new abstinence-focused social network (Project MATCH Research Group, 1997, 1998). In addition, the study found that regardless of which original treatment patients received, individuals who attended 12-step MHGs, such as AA, had significantly better drinking outcomes (Tonigan et al., 2003). Interestingly, at the 3-year follow-up, 58% of TSF patients had attended an AA meeting in the prior 90 days, but 45% of the clients assigned to MET and 39% of the clients assigned to CBT had also attended meetings. Thus, despite a lack of professional encouragement to participate in AA, many patients nevertheless elected to attend AA. Importantly, the independent effect of MHG participation indicates AA may be a valuable adjunct to addiction treatment participants—*even in professional treatment programs where it is not formally emphasized.* However, as mentioned below, clinician's behavior can substantially increase the likelihood that patients will participate and benefit from MHGs.

A similar multisite, controlled trial sponsored by the National Institute of Drug Abuse (NIDA) was completed with cocaine-dependent patients (Crits-Christoph et al., 1999). This Collaborative Cocaine Treatment Study randomized 487 patients to one of four manual-guided treatments: Individual drug counseling (12-step-focused), individual cognitive therapy, individual supportive-expressive therapy, or a group drug-counseling condition (all of the individual conditions also received the group drug counseling in addition to the individual therapy sessions). Although patients assigned to the individual drug-counseling (12-step) condition attended significantly fewer therapy sessions than did patients in either of the other two psychotherapy conditions, they experienced the best drug use outcomes of any group at 1 year post discharge. Again, although not a test of 12-step MHG involvement per se, a principal goal of the individualized drug-counseling condition was to facilitate active involvement in 12-step MHGs. Better drug use outcomes, despite lower levels of professional treatment engagement, may be accounted for by increased 12-step mutual-help involvement. A further study of the same sample showed that those in the individualized 12-step treatment condition were attending 12-step MHG meetings at significantly higher levels at the end of the active (6 month) treatment phase (Weiss et al., 2000).

Observational Studies

A complementary effectiveness study to the highly controlled efficacy designs used in Project MATCH and the cocaine collaborative studies, was carried out in the Department of Veterans Affairs (Ouimette et al., 1997). This naturalistic study was of treated individuals but examined MHG participation as an important adjunct to treatment. In this study of 15 VA-Veterans Affairs SUD inpatient treatment programs, 5 of which were 12-step, 5 cognitive-behavioral, and 5 eclectic in program philosophy and practices, patients treated in professional 12-step-oriented treatment programs were more likely to be abstinent at a 1-year follow-up than those treated in cognitive-behavioral or eclectic programs. Furthermore, patient involvement in MHGs during the follow-up period was again associated with better alcohol/drug and psychosocial outcomes *irrespective of the type of professional treatment they had received.* Similar findings emerged in a subsample of 927 cocaine-dependent patients from the national Drug Abuse Treatment Outcome Studies (DATOS) enrolled in outpatient, residential, and short-term inpatient programs. At least twice-weekly attendance, on average, at 12-step MHG meetings during the follow-up year was associated with significantly reduced likelihood of relapse during the follow-up year (Etheridge et al., 1999).

A recent rigorously conducted longitudinal study with 227 alcohol-dependent patients following outpatient SUD treatment examined the influence of addiction MHG participation on alcohol use outcomes across a 3-year period. The study found that even when controlling for pretreatment levels of drinking, early posttreatment levels of drinking, addiction severity, motivation, professional treatment utilization during the follow-up period, and a variety of other factors, MHG participation was still independently associated with better alcohol use outcomes (Kelly et al., 2006). The study also sought to examine whether there were important subgroups of patients for whom addiction MHGs might be particularly helpful or unhelpful. The study examined gender, religiosity, psychiatric comorbidity, and prior MHG participation, but did not find any evidence that these variables affected the degree of benefit derived from MHGs: Women derived as much benefit as men, those with psychiatric comorbidity derived as much benefit as those without, and MHG novices derived as much benefit as MHG "veterans."

TABLE 4.5 Family-Focused Mutual-help Groups

Name and year founded	Target population	Number and location of groups in the US	Overarching theoretical orientation	Therapeutic goal(s)	Evidence base (0–3)*	Degree of professional involvement in groups	■ Website ■ E-mail ■ Phone number ■ Basic text
Al-Anon/Alateen 1951	Families and friends of alcoholics	Approx. 15 000 groups in all 50 States; Online meetings at www.ola-is.org	12-Step	Improving well-being Stopping enabling behaviors	1, 2, 3	Consumer-run	■ www.al-anon.alateen.org ■ wso@al-anon.org ■ (757) 563-1600 ■ *The Al-Anon Family Groups*
Nar-Anon 1967	Families and friends of persons with addictions	Approx. 440 groups in 47 States	12-Step	Recovery "from the effects of living with an addicted relative or friend"	3 (Study of Nar-Anon facilitation therapy)	Consumer-run	■ www.nar-anon.org ■ naranonwso@hotmail.com ■ 1-800-477-6291 ■ *Nar-Anon Blue Booklet*
Families Anonymous (FA) 1971	Families and friends of persons with addictions to drugs and/or alcohol	Approx. 220 groups in 36 States	12-Step	"Recovery from the effects of a loved one's addictions"	0	Consumer-run	■ www.familiesanonymous.org ■ famanon@familiesanonymous.org ■ 1-800-736-9805 ■ *Today a Better Way*

National Alliance for the Mentally Ill (NAMI)* 1979	People with serious mental illnesses and their families	Over 1200 groups in all 50 States; Several online communities at www.nami.org/template.cfm?section=communities	Focus on sharing experiences and providing support	Improving quality of life through support, education, and advocacy	1, 2	Consumer-run; Professionals may be involved in groups	■ www.nami.org ■ info@nami.org ■ Main Tel.: (703) 524-7600 ■ Helpline: 1-800-950-NAMI
Gam-Anon/ Gam-a-Teen	Family and friends of compulsive gamblers	Approx. 300 groups in 40 States	12-Step	Resolving problems "Creation and preservation of serenity"	2 (cross-sectional corr.)	Consumer-run	■ www.gam-anon.org ■ info3@gam-anon.org ■ (781) 352-1671 ■ *The Gam-Anon Way of Life: A Gam-Anon Manual; Living with the Compulsive Gambler*

(*Continues*)

TABLE 4.5 (*Continued*)

Name and year founded	Target population	Number and location of groups in the US	Overarching theoretical orientation	Therapeutic goal(s)	Evidence base (0–3)*	Degree of professional involvement in groups	■ Website ■ E-mail ■ Phone number ■ Basic text
COSA (Codependents of Sex Addicts or Co-Sex Addicts) 1980	People whose lives have been affected by another's compulsive sexual behavior; People who are codependent upon a sex addict	Approx. 110 groups in 29 States; Online discussions on Yahoo; Telemeetings (www.cosacall. com)	12-Step	Installation of hope Caring for one's own well-being	0	Consumer-run	■ www.cosa-recovery.org ■ info@cosa-recovery.org ■ (763) 537-6904

* Also known as "National Alliance on Mental Illness"

* 0 = None; 1 = Descriptive studies only; 2 = Observational (correlational, longitudinal); 3 = Experimental (random assignment, controlled).

A further study by McKellar and colleagues (2003) with 2319 male patients followed for 2 years following intensive SUD treatment, assessed causal links between AA involvement and substance use outcomes with the aid of structural equation modeling. Findings supported the assertion for a causal link after controlling for confounds of patient motivation for abstinence, level of comorbid psychopathology, and demographic variables, i.e., AA involvement leads to better outcomes.

Smaller quasi-experimental studies also have been carried out recently. Fiorentine and Hillhouse (2000) examined 360 outpatient clients of SUD treatment facilities followed up for 8 months and found that those who participated concurrently in both drug outpatient treatment and 12-step MHGs had higher rates of abstinence than those who participated only in treatment or MHGs alone. Thus, in this population, there was an additive effect for combining aftercare/outpatient treatment with MHG activity. Similarly, Miller et al. (1997) found that posttreatment AA attendance during the first year uniquely accounted for 14% of the variance in substance use among outpatients, after controlling for patients' pretreatment, outpatient, and posttreatment factors. In a study by Morgenstern et al. (1997), AA attendance following inpatient treatment predicted better 1- and 6-month outcomes controlling for other possible demographic, treatment, and symptom confounds.

An intriguing long-term study examining the unique effects of AA participation on drinking outcomes in 466 problem drinkers compared four groups of individuals who had self-selected either (a) no treatment at all, (b) AA only, (c) professional treatment only, or (d) professional treatment plus AA (Timko et al., 2000). Compared to the untreated cohort, those receiving formal treatment or attending AA only were more likely to be abstinent at 1-, 3-, and 8-year follow-ups. The AA-only cohort also was more likely to be abstinent than the professional treatment cohort at 1- and 3-year follow-up, and was equivalent at 8-year follow-up. Additionally, the AA-only cohort was equally likely to be abstinent at 1-, 3-, and 8-year follow-up when compared with the professional treatment plus AA cohort. Thus, individuals choosing to "go it alone" appear less likely to show improvement: those choosing to attend AA only appear to fare at least as well as those who choose professional treatment.

Although observational studies are only one piece of the evidence base, they are nevertheless an important piece, especially when they are carefully conducted. When evidence from meta-analytic, observational, and efficacy studies is viewed conjointly, a consistently beneficial effect emerges for involvement in these organizations on various substance use and psychosocial outcomes measured at various time points.

Cost-Effectiveness Studies

MHGs are typically completely free of charge, except for voluntary contributions, making them extremely cost-effective interventions. Although we were unable to find any studies explicitly addressing the cost-effectiveness of MHGs, there have been studies that have shown involvement in MHGs may reduce healthcare costs. A 3-year prospective study by Humphreys and Moos (1996) found that problem drinkers who chose to attend only AA had overall treatment costs that were 45% lower than for problem drinkers who chose to attend outpatient treatment; yet, outcomes were similar for both groups. There was no initial index treatment episode; so, this difference reflects only the treatment costs during the 3-year follow-up period. Two further studies by Humphreys and Moos (2001; 2007), using a large multisite sample of veterans receiving treatment for SUDs, found that compared with patients treated in CBT programs, those treated in professional 12-step treatment programs had significantly greater 12-step MHG involvement at follow-up. Patients treated in CBT programs averaged almost twice as many outpatient continuing care visits after discharge than did 12-step patients, and also received significantly more days of inpatient mental health care relating to their SUD/psychiatric status, resulting in 64% higher annual costs for CBT programs. In contrast, psychiatric and substance use outcomes were comparable across the two treatments, except that 12-step-oriented treatment program patients had higher rates of abstinence at follow-up.

Findings on potential cost-savings for health care systems are intriguing but preliminary. Further study is needed to more accurately specify under which circumstances MHG groups may serve as a sufficient substitute for professional care without negatively affecting patient outcomes. Certain patient subgroups, for example, may adjust more readily to and derive greater benefit from MHGs than others, whereas some patients may need greater professional attention. To emphasize this point, evidence regarding subgroups of individuals who may or may not benefit from MHGs is examined next.

For Whom are Substance-Focused Mutual-Help Groups Particularly Helpful or Not Helpful?

Clinical concerns have been raised in relation to the member-group fit with certain MHG organizations. For example, do individuals with both an SUD and another comorbid psychiatric diagnosis benefit from the regular 12-step MHGs, such as AA or NA? This section examines the evidence regarding four persistent areas of concern: Psychiatric comorbidity, religiosity, gender, and age (youth).

Psychiatric Comorbidity

Studies of general population as well as clinic samples have revealed that SUDs frequently co-occur with psychiatric illnesses (e.g., affective, anxiety, psychotic, and personality disorders; Kessler et al., 1996, 1997; Mowbray et al., 1995; RachBeisel et al., 1999). Although the quantity and quality of integrated professional treatment services designed to concurrently address both types of disorders has increased, concerns have been raised about member-group fit of dual-diagnosis patients with typical 12-step MHGs such as AA (e.g., Laudet et al., 2000a, 2000b). Cited barriers have included some 12-step members' putative opposition toward individuals taking psychotropic medication; however, empirical evidence is scarce. One survey found that the majority (86%) of 277 sampled AA members thought that the use of medications intended to reduce relapse risk (e.g., naltrexone, disulfiram) was either a good idea or might be a good idea. However, 29% of those sampled stated they themselves had been pressured to stop taking medications of one kind or another (Rychtarik et al., 2000). A further related barrier is 12-step participants' uncertainty and confusion about which clinical syndromes require professional treatment versus subclinical states that are likely to respond to application of the 12 steps.

Preliminary studies suggest that participation in and effects from traditional substance-focused MHGs for dually diagnosed patients may be moderated by the type of comorbid diagnosis. A large prospective Icelandic study (N = 351) found similar rates of attendance at AA for all comorbid diagnoses, except for persons diagnosed with schizophrenia who went less often (Tomasson & Vaglum, 1998). Similarly, a study by Noordsy and colleagues (1996) of outpatients suffering from psychotic spectrum disorders and substance dependence did not find evidence for beneficial effects of 12-step group involvement at a 4-year follow-up, although the sample size was very small (N = 18). Kelly et al. (2003) found that compared with SUD patients without a psychiatric diagnosis, patients with major depressive disorder in addition to their SUD did not become as socially involved in self-help fellowships as their noncomorbid counterparts and derived progressively less benefit from traditional 12-step groups during the 2-year follow-up, despite similar levels of self-help involvement. In contrast, Ouimette et al. (2001), using the same dataset, found that patients with comorbid SUDs and posttraumatic stress disorder (PTSD) participated in, and benefited from, 12-step groups as much as SUD-only patients. A further study by Bogenschutz and Akin (2000) found that severely mentally ill patients with comorbid SUDs attended MHGs at rates comparable with the general addiction treatment population, but reported more difficulties at meetings regarding their comorbid status. Thus, particular diagnostic comorbid subgroups may differ in rates of attendance, involvement, and derived benefits, but the knowledge base is currently limited, especially given the large comorbid overlap between SUDs and other Axis I diagnoses.

As noted in this chapter, MHGs specifically designed for dual-diagnosis patients have begun to emerge (e.g., DTR—http://doubletroubleinrecovery.com and DRA—http://draonline.org) and may be a better fit (Vogel et al., 1998). Because medication compliance is such a critical issue in the treatment of mental illness, explicit attention to and support for such compliance within a dual-diagnosis MHG context may be important. A study by Magura et al. (2002), of 240 dually diagnosed individuals attending DTR meetings, found that, in contrast to attendance at other 12-step meetings, consistent attendance at DTR meetings was associated with better medication compliance, even after controlling for possible confounds of psychiatric severity, stressful life events, and supported housing. Improved medication compliance, in turn, was associated with less hospitalization.

One randomized study compared the efficacy of intensive outpatient rational emotive behavior therapy (REBT) treatment with a 12-step/disease-oriented treatment for severely impaired dual-diagnosis patients (Penn & Brooks, 2000). Both conditions strongly emphasized ongoing MHG attendance at their respective philosophy-concordant meetings. Results revealed that those in REBT had lower ratings on need for psychiatric treatment and fewer patients in this condition needed inpatient hospitalization at follow-up. However, those in 12-step treatment showed greater improvement on the addiction severity index (ASI) alcohol composite, a greater decrease in the perceived need for alcohol treatment by the 12-month follow-up, and less overall substance use at the 3-month follow-up. Although the sample size was small (N = 50), results suggest elements of REBT may have greater salutary influence on psychiatric symptoms, whereas 12-step treatment may have greater positive influence on substance use outcomes for severely impaired dually diagnosed patients.

Religiosity

Given the spiritual/"quasi-religious" terminology and concepts used in 12-step MHGs, some clinicians and researchers have suggested that referral to 12-step organizations should take into account religious background. Practice guidelines from the American Psychiatric Association (APA), for example, have recommended clinicians refrain from referring nonreligious people to 12-step groups. However, the only large-scale study to examine this issue (Winzelberg & Humphreys, 1999) did not support this view. In a sample of 3018 male veterans, degree of religiosity did not affect attendance rates or related substance use outcomes.

Additionally, one of the matching hypotheses predicted in Project MATCH was that participants high in religiosity would fare better in TSF. However, degree of religiosity did not interact with treatment orientation in relation to drinking outcomes; patients low in religiosity fared as well as those high on this dimension (Connors et al., 2001). A study by Brown et al. (2001) of a sample of 153 individuals with drug use disorders found no relationship between religious involvement and frequency of 12-step attendance. Also, a study by Kelly et al. (2006) with a sample of 227 alcohol-dependent outpatients did not find any evidence for religiosity influencing the degree of derived benefit from addiction MHGs. However, further study is needed to determine whether religiosity may interact with the type of MHG philosophy—for example, whether nonreligious people experience better outcomes in groups without explicit spiritual themes (e.g., SMART Recovery).

Women

There is a dearth of information regarding attendance at, and effects from, all forms of MHG involvement among women. In the meta-analytic review by Emrick et al. (1993), women were vastly underrepresented. The average sample size for men was 116, whereas for women it was 9. This disparity is remarkable given that women have consistently made up about one-third of AA members (AA, 2005) and about one-third of SUD treatment admissions (SAMHSA, 2005). Some have expressed concerns over the fit of women, particularly in 12-step organizations because of the 12-step emphasis on "powerlessness" and the minority status of women in 12-step groups, which may make issues specific to women more difficult to discuss. Related to these notions, a matching hypothesis in Project MATCH was that women would fare better in CBT than in TSF, in part, because of its emphasis on tackling negative affect, which is found to be more prevalent in women, and on increasing self-esteem and self-efficacy, rather than emphasizing powerlessness (Del Boca & Mattson, 2001). However, no gender by treatment interaction was found. In fact, women attended AA meetings at least as frequently as men and often became more involved in AA than men.

Youth

Demographic data from AA's latest triennial survey (AA Alcoholics Anonymous Membership Survey, 2005) revealed the average age of members to be 46 years old, with only 2% under age 21 years. Consequently, the sharing of specific experiences at meetings by older members may not be perceived by youth as helpful or relevant in dealing with their own life-stage recovery issues. Nonattendance at and dropout from 12-step groups among youth are high (Kelly et al., 2000).

Emrick et al. (1993) did not find any studies examining use of AA by persons under 21 years of age. However, some evidence suggests that this approach may be helpful. Adolescent samples studied by Brown and colleagues (e.g., Brown et al., 1990; Vik et al., 1992) found that 12-step MHG attendance was associated with more favorable outcomes at 1-year follow-up. Also, in a study by Kelly et al. (2002), youth with more severe substance use problems became involved more frequently and benefited more from involvement in AA and NA. Finally, a multisite study by Hsieh et al. (1998) found that among 2317 adolescents who received inpatient treatment for substance use problems, 12-step MHG participation was the most powerful predictor of abstinence from substances at 6 and 12 months posttreatment.

How or Why Do Substance-Focused Mutual-Help Groups Work?

Increasing scientific attention has been drawn to understanding not just *whether* MHGs work, but *why*. Reflecting methodological advances, studies have begun to elucidate mechanisms of action responsible for salutary effects within MHG organizations. To date, such mediational studies have only been carried out on 12-step organizations. Variables that have been investigated have been related to AA-prescribed activities (e.g., getting a sponsor, working the steps), psychological "common process" variables (e.g., self-efficacy, motivation, coping; Connors & Tonigan, 2001; Kelly et al., 2000, 2002; Morgenstern et al., 1997; Morgenstern & Bates, 1999; Owen et al., 2003), interpersonal or social variables (e.g., Bond et al., 2003; Humphreys & Noke, 1997; Kaskutas et al., 2002), and spirituality (Owen et al., 2003).

AA-Prescribed Behaviors and Common Process Mediators

Morgenstern and colleagues (1997) found that the positive effects from an aggregated measure of AA affiliation (e.g., AA attendance, talking with a sponsor, engaging in service, reading AA literature, seeking advice from AA sources) on 6-month substance use outcomes were mediated by a set of psychological, common process factors measured at 1-month posttreatment (i.e., self-efficacy, motivation, and active coping). A similar study by Kelly et al. (2002) studied the degree to which 12-step program behaviors (i.e., working the 12 steps, having a sponsor, engaging in social activities with fellow members) in the first 3 months posttreatment explained increases in common process variables, measured at 3 months, and whether these common process variables explained the effects of AA on subsequent substance use outcomes in an adolescent inpatient sample. Similar to the Morgenstern et al. (1997) study, youth who attended more 12-step meetings during the first 3 months following treatment showed increases in motivation for abstinence, coping, and self-efficacy, a relationship that was explained by the degree of active 12-step involvement. However, in this younger cohort, it was motivation for abstinence, and not self-efficacy or coping, that mediated the effect of 12-step involvement on substance use outcomes in the ensuing 3 months. Humphreys et al. (1999) also found that active coping efforts partially mediated the effect of 12-step participation on outcome in a large VA sample 1 year after inpatient treatment, although the variables were all assessed and analyzed during the same 90-day window, limiting causal inferences (Kazdin & Nock, 2003). Two further studies by Connors and Tonigan (2001) and Tonigan (in Owen et al., 2003) examined self-efficacy as a mediator of AA participation using the Project MATCH sample. The first study found that greater addiction severity was associated with greater AA involvement in the 6 months after treatment, which, in turn, was associated with more subsequent abstinence and less substance use. The latter relationship was found to be explained by increases in self-efficacy. The second study examined the effect of AA participation on self-efficacy at the 3-year follow-up and found that self-efficacy was also a mediator of the effect of AA on outcome at this later time point.

Thus, one of the processes by which AA may work is by increasing or maintaining motivation for abstinence and by enhancing self-efficacy and coping skills. Interestingly, although self-efficacy looks to be a promising mediator among adults, it was not found to mediate AA's effects when tested in an adolescent sample. This could be due to methodological or measurement differences in the studies. Another possible explanation is that AA may benefit different individuals in different ways, and/or at different times in recovery. Hence, these common process mediators (e.g., self-efficacy) may, themselves, be moderated by other factors such as age, addiction severity, or length of time in recovery ("moderated mediation"; Muller et al., 2005).

Social Mediators

The study by Humphreys et al. (1999), mentioned above, which found that active coping was a partial mediator of AA's effects also found that patients' friendship networks (e.g., friends' support for abstinence) partially mediated the effect of 12-step participation on 1-year outcome. Kaskutas et al. (2002) studied 1-year outcomes in relation to AA participation and found that although general support from well-meaning others was associated with improvement in other functioning, only specific support from AA members mediated abstinence. Again, this study examined variables during the same period, thereby limiting casual conclusions. Other studies have examined the influence of social network characteristics, particularly with regard to abstinent role models (e.g., Bond et al., 2003; Witbrodt & Kaskutas, 2005) and found that among alcohol-dependent persons, having a higher number of sober individuals in the social network was predictive of abstinence, but did not formally test mediation. Although not an analysis of the mechanisms of AA, per se, a related finding from analysis of Project MATCH data indicated that outpatients with higher network support for drinking at treatment intake had significantly better 3-year outcomes in TSF than in MET, an effect that was mediated by 12-step involvement (Longabaugh et al., 1998). Similarly, an inpatient study examined disease and common process model variables and found that commitment to AA and belief in a higher power was associated with reduced relapse intensity (Morgenstern et al., 1996). Thus, the social aspects of 12-step fellowships may affect changes in substance use behavior through providing a social network of friends who are supportive of abstinence and who model and reinforce alternative sober activities.

Spirituality

AA's philosophy and content is explicitly spiritual in nature. Its 12 steps contain overtly spiritual or religious language, its stated mechanism of action for recovery is the attainment of a "spiritual awakening" achievable by working through the 12-step program, and there is continued emphasis on spiritual growth. Most AA meetings also include prayers adopted from formal religious organizations (AA, 1984). The spiritual essence of AA has been difficult to operationalize and measure. Thus, although a central focus of AA, few studies have formally tested spirituality as a mediator of AA's effects. Two large clinical studies examined the degree of patient religiousness as a moderator of AA benefits but did not find evidence that atheists or agnostics who attended AA benefited less than patients who were more religious (Tonigan et al., 2002; Winzelberg & Humphreys, 1999). However, both studies found that less spiritual/religious individuals were less likely to attend. One study examining a 12-step-based, dual diagnosis MHG found that spirituality was not a mediator of 12-step affiliation on substance use outcomes (Magura et al., 2003).

Summary

For many years, although AA and other similar organizations spread, some clinicians and researchers were unconvinced that such fellowships were actually helpful and some believed they might even be harmful. However, during the past 20 years, the empirical evidence for addiction MHGs, particularly 12-step MHGs, has grown dramatically in quantity and quality. In fact, the APA and the Department of Veteran's Affairs Health Care System now include standard referral to MHGs, such as AA or NA, in their clinical practice guidelines. Current evidence indicates that many patients are likely to participate and benefit (e.g., Emrick et al., 1993; Kelly, 2003; Kelly et al., 2006), that women benefit at least as much as men and may assimilate more easily and participate more often (e.g., Del Boca & Mattson, 2001); that some addiction patients with certain comorbid psychiatric conditions (e.g., PTSD) may attend and benefit as much as those without comorbidity (Ouimette et al., 2001) whereas other addicted clients, such as those with psychosis or recurrent major depressive disorder, may not benefit as readily as those without a comorbid condition (Kelly et al., 2003); and that some adolescents may also benefit following treatment, particularly those with more severe substance involvement (e.g., Kelly et al., 2000, 2004). Contrary to popular belief, many atheists and nonreligious persons also attend and benefit from the spiritually based, 12-step organizations (Winzelberg & Humphreys, 1999). Non-12-step organizations, such as SMART Recovery and Women for Sobriety, have been slow to spread and gain acceptance. These other organizations are likely to hold similar potential benefits to groups such as AA, but await empirical study.

OUTCOME DATA FOR MUTUAL-HELP GROUPS FOCUSING ON MENTAL ILLNESS

At present, there is only a limited amount of research on MHGs that focus on mental illness. In a review of the existing research on mental illness MHGs, Davidson et al. (1999) concluded that attending such groups is generally associated with positive outcomes such as less hospitalization and less psychiatric symptomatology, but that the available data are correlational and come largely from unpublished, uncontrolled studies that are reliant on retrospective self-reports. Davidson et al. also note that mental illness MHGs are underutilized and plagued by high rates of attrition and discuss a number of factors that may contribute to the limited use of peer support (e.g., skepticism about the effectiveness of peer-provided help, the belief that only intensive professional treatment can help the seriously mentally ill).

Two mental illness MHGs in which outcomes have been studied to a limited degree are GROW and RI. In a study of 98 GROW members with serious mental illnesses, Roberts et al. (1999) examined the association between giving and receiving help (observationally coded) and self-reported and interviewer-rated psychosocial adjustment. Overall, participants showed significant improvements over time in psychiatric symptomatology and social adjustment. The amount of help given, but not received, was predictive of better social functioning (both self-reported and interviewer-rated) at follow-up, although help given was not related to psychiatric symptomatology. There was an interaction between help received (low vs high) and feelings of group integration on adjustment outcomes, such that those who felt integrated into the group and received high levels of help had better adjustment outcomes than those who felt integrated but received low levels of help, whereas the opposite was true for those who did not feel integrated into the group, where higher levels of help were associated with poorer adjustment. These results suggest that the way help is perceived within a mutual-help setting may be more important than the actual amount of help received, as receiving help may not be interpreted positively if the recipient does not feel connected to the people who are providing the help. In addition, this study found that the amount of emotional support given was unrelated to later adjustment outcomes, whereas guidance given (in the form of direct and specific suggestions for actions) was related to better self-reported social functioning at follow-up. These results imply that informational guidance and support may be more beneficial to members than emotional support, perhaps as a result of direct reinforcement and reminders of one's own goals and strategies for coping.

Galanter (1988) examined psychosocial and treatment-related outcomes in Recovery members and leaders as compared with a control sample. In this study, the leaders (N = 201) had been participating in Recovery for an average of 14 years, whereas the members (N = 155) had been participating for an average of 1.5 years. Both members and leaders reported lower neurotic distress scores since joining Recovery, although pre-Recovery neurotic distress ratings were made retrospectively and may not reflect the actual level of distress at a time several years (or over a decade) in the past. Leaders were lower in neurotic distress, higher in well-being, used fewer outside helping resources than newer members, and did not differ from controls in terms of well-being. In addition, the majority of Recovery participants reported a high degree of belief in and commitment to the principles of the program itself. This affiliation with Recovery was positively correlated with well-being and improvement in neurotic distress scores.

OUTCOME DATA FOR MUTUAL-HELP GROUPS FOCUSING ON DUAL DIAGNOSIS

The only dual diagnosis MHG in which outcomes have been empirically studied is DTR. DTR is a 12-Step, completely consumer-run mutual-help program for persons with both chemical dependency and mental illness (dual diagnoses). Dual diagnoses are common among individuals with SUDs, where some 59% of people with a lifetime history of substance abuse or dependence also have a lifetime history of a mental disorder (Kessler, 1995). Perhaps unlike substance-only 12-Step groups such as AA, DTR provides a forum for the open discussion of medication use and compliance, psychiatric symptoms, and psychiatric hospitalization in addition to issues related to substance abuse. DTR is organized according to versions of the 12 Steps and 12 Traditions of AA that have been modified to include the issue of mental illness (e.g., Step 1 states, "We admitted we were powerless over mental disorders and substance abuse—that our lives had become unmanageable").

A single research group has used a prospective, longitudinal design to study outcomes of DTR participation, as well as the factors that mediate those outcomes, in a sample of over 300 DTR members in New York City. Overall, DTR participation appears to be associated with positive outcomes. For instance, longer DTR attendance was related to decreased mental health distress and substance use, as well as to increased perceived social support and understanding. In addition, more frequent participation in DTR was related to greater personal well-being, whereas attendance at single-focus 12-step meetings (e.g., AA, NA) was associated with lower levels of well-being in this sample (Laudet et al., 2000b). DTR attendance was also positively correlated with adherence to psychiatric medication even after controlling for baseline variables that were related to adherence, such as living in supported housing, having fewer stressful life events, and having lesser psychiatric symptomatology. Greater medication adherence, in turn, was related to the absence of hospitalization during a 1-year follow-up period (Magura et al., 2002).

These researchers have also conducted several studies of factors that mediate or are associated with the relationships between DTR attendance and substance use and mental health outcomes. For instance, Magura et al. (2003) examined the association between abstinence and three theoretically important benefits to MHG participation: Helper therapy (the idea that providing help to others can reaffirm one's own commitment to change and recovery), reciprocal learning (the process of obtaining information and skills relevant to one's own problem from others' experiences with the same problem), and emotional support (supportive approval and reinforcement from the group). They found that helper therapy and reciprocal learning processes, but not emotional support, were positively correlated with drug and alcohol abstinence at follow-up, independent of other factors that were also predictive of abstinence (e.g., abstinence at baseline, DTR involvement, self-efficacy), similar to the findings obtained by Roberts et al. (1999) within the context of GROW.

Additionally, Magura et al. (2003) studied four process factors that were hypothesized to mediate the relationship between DTR affiliation and outcomes related to abstinence and health-promoting behaviors: Internal locus of control (LOC; including internal motivation for change, coping skills, and self-efficacy), social support, installation of hope, and spirituality. Results showed that internal LOC was the only variable to fully mediate the relationship between DTR affiliation and abstinence, whereas social support was a partial mediator. In terms of the relationship between DTR affiliation and health-promoting behaviors (i.e., medication adherence, medical care, and self-care), internal LOC, installation of hope, and spirituality all fully mediated this relationship, whereas social support was a partial mediator. However, these mediational results should be viewed cautiously, because analyses were conducted with variables measured during the same period. Hence, it is hard to determine the direction of the relationship between the mediator and the outcome (see Kazdin & Nock, 2003).

Finally, Laudet et al. (2004) more specifically examined the role of social support in the relationship between DTR participation and drug and alcohol abstinence during a 2-year follow-up period. They found that although there was no significant relationship between social support at baseline and the amount and frequency of DTR attendance in the first year, DTR attendance was related to a change in social support from baseline to 1-year follow-up, such that participants who reported more DTR attendance also reported high levels of social support and participants who reported less DTR attendance reported decreased levels of social support. In addition, DTR attendance during the first year of the study and social support at 1-year follow-up were unique predictors of decreased substance use during the second year of the study. Therefore, it appears that DTR can contribute to abstinence among this dually diagnosed population by providing social support, a forum for learning from others' shared experiences, and the opportunity to help oneself by helping others. Participants' own motivation, coping skills, and self-efficacy also appear to contribute to positive outcomes related to abstinence and self-care.

ROLE IN COMPREHENSIVE TREATMENT PLAN OR STEPPED CARE AND COORDINATION ISSUES

MHGs can be viewed as valuable, free adjuncts to formal interventions conducted in professional settings. In most cases, these resources will be complements to, rather than replacements for, formal care. Their flexibility, accessibility, and cost-effectiveness make them enduring and valuable allies in the fight against relapse, dysfunction, and rehospitalization. However, compared to a more formal approach used by most professionals, clinicians sometimes feel at odds with the more informal, mutual-help approaches. Some of this discomfort may have arisen from hearing a negative anecdote or perhaps having negative personal experiences with such organizations. However, perhaps more frequently, discomfort arises from not knowing much about MHG organizations and how they may be useful as an adjunct to professional services. Some clinicians also lack awareness that they, as health care professionals, can exert a big influence on the extent to which patients engage in and benefit from these organizations. At least two experimental studies have systematically varied the type and extent of professional MHG facilitation carried out by clinicians (Sisson & Mallams, 1981; Timko et al., 2006). Findings from this work indicate that clinicians who take a few extra steps to help patients, such as introducing them to existing MHG members, can make a substantial difference to the likelihood that a patient will utilize and benefit from such organizations.

Below, we recommend seven ways in which clinicians might help maximize the benefits available from community MHG organizations, which are adapted from Kelly et al. (2004).

1. *Keep an open mind*: Preconceived notions or negative anecdotes may distort perceptions of the utility of these groups. It is important to be informed about a variety of MHGs. Strict adherence to one theoretical orientation or model of care may deprive the client of potential help. Keeping an open mind about the potential of nonmainstream groups (e.g., SMART Recovery, GROW, SOS) may be a lifeline for some who do not wish to attend more mainstream groups.

2. *Recognize the validity and importance of MHGs*: Hundreds of published studies reveal that MHGs help patients maintain treatment gains and have better outcomes (e.g., Emrick et al., 1993; Kelly, 2003). It is thus appropriate and potentially very beneficial for clinicians to introduce to clients the idea of participation in these groups. Clinicians can add legitimacy to and reinforce the value of these groups. Furthermore, the chronic nature of most mental disorders suggests a good fit with similarly "chronic" ongoing forms of support, which are specifically focused on their condition and that can be flexibly accessed, free of charge, in their local community. The clinician may help further by addressing any misperceptions about MHGs that patients may have and help them give groups a fair try.

3. *Become familiar with local MHGs*: Clinicians may feel more confident and comfortable discussing these groups if they themselves have attended (e.g., 8–10 meetings). Doing some local MHG research can also inform the clinician about the format, content, size, and composition of local meetings so that they are better equipped to make referrals that their clients may perceive as a good fit.

4. *Make contacts and actively facilitate attendance*: It is a good idea to keep a list of former clients who attend MHGs, who would be willing to act as contacts. Having these personal connections can make a powerful difference. One study found that compared with clients who were simply encouraged to attend MHGs (i.e., "standard referral"), clients who were encouraged and proactively linked with current mutual-help attendees by their therapist during treatment were much more likely to attend and continue attending (Sisson & Mallams, 1981).

5. *Ask patients to get involved early in treatment*: Having the patient sample meetings early in treatment allows for early reactions and experiences to be processed and discussed during therapy sessions. Some clinicians ask patients to keep a formal log of their meeting experiences and reactions and bring it to sessions to discuss. If the client has not begun to attend these groups during treatment, it is very unlikely that the patient will begin to access these groups posttreatment.

6. *Bring in other materials to complement your skills*: Many resources are available for clinicians, often free of charge, from the National Institutes of Health. For example, there are now empirically supported manuals available for TSF available from the National Institute of Alcohol Abuse and Alcoholism (NIAAA). Even if these are not followed exactly, they provide useful information

and handouts that can help with facilitation. The Internet is a further infinite source of information on practically every mutual-help organization that exists with most organizations having a website that includes meetings list, contact, and other information (see Tables 4.1–4.5).

7. *Prepare clients about what to expect*: This is where knowing more about the groups to which you are referring your clients is important. The better informed you are about the issues your client may encounter, the better facilitator you will be. For example, if your client is an adolescent or young adult, you may do well to find and refer your client to a young person's meeting (Kelly et al., 2005). If they are dually diagnosed, you may need to warn them about the potential for misunderstandings or resistance from some MHG members. You may wish to refer these clients to dual recovery–focused meetings or meetings you know are medication-friendly. Knowing your clients' religious/spiritual background may help you prepare your client for MHGs that are very spiritually based or not spiritual enough.

Thus, remaining open-minded, obtaining educating about these organizations, attending groups, preparing clients about what to expect, and actively putting clients in touch with current members and continuing to monitor and discuss client progress, are some of the ways clinicians can help clients obtain maximum benefits from these organizations.

RESEARCH AGENDA

As mentioned above, research on most MHG organizations is lacking. Even in the addiction field, where most of the work to date has been conducted, the amount of good quality research pales in comparison with the magnitude and influence of MHGs, such as AA. Despite the prodigious numbers of individuals with mental illness in the United States and globally (Lopez et al., 2006), empirical information about the effectiveness of MHGs that address mental illness is too scarce, and the availability of some of these MHGs in some regions is very low. This creates a potential "Catch-22" scenario whereby these other organizations do not grow because of lack of referrals, and referrals are rarely made because of a lack of availability and low clinical confidence in these groups' effectiveness. Future research detailing participant composition, meeting types, and the effectiveness of MHGs, especially those focusing on mental illness, could highlight their presence and legitimacy among treatment providers and potentially increase referrals and organizational growth. Given the high prevalence of mental disorders, efficacy and comparative effectiveness studies of clinical MHG facilitation efforts for MHGs focusing on mental illness (e.g., DBSA, GROW) might be conducted to help determine how well such efforts lead to participation and improved outcomes. Further studies examining which types of patients, in particular, are more or less likely to benefit from which MHGs and why are also needed to help increase the effectiveness of referrals and our understanding of the therapeutic mechanisms of action inherent in specific organizations. More published research on MHGs would raise professional awareness of their benefits and limitations, and increase clinical confidence that precious clinical resources devoted to facilitating MHG participation will pay dividends for the patient in the short- and long-term.

DISSEMINATION AGENDA

Clearly, more empirical evidence regarding the effectiveness of these resources would highlight their presence and increase clinical confidence in their utility. Clinicians, managers, and policy makers, curious about these resources can now readily obtain information through the World Wide Web. The Internet age has provided immediate access to information in a central location from practically anywhere on the globe. Perhaps the best way to find out more about them is to go online and access their websites. These websites, which are listed in the tables provided in this chapter, provide a wealth of information about MHG organizations' origins and early history, broad theoretical orientation, therapeutic goals, and practices and principles. They also contain detailed group meeting lists, and information about how to start your own groups in your own community. There is often specific information directed at professionals. In many cases, one can also obtain literature for free or to purchase, and some sites have links to their own literature downloadable for free, such as the main text of AA (the *Big Book*; http://www.aa.org/bigbookonline/).

The past 25 years has seen increasing attention focused on the influence of MHG organizations in public health. In fact, an expert consensus panel was recently convened to address policy issues pertaining to MHGs (Humphreys et al., 2004). Although the focus of the workgroup was on addictions, many of the recommendations apply equally well to MHGs focusing on other conditions. A statement was produced regarding the evidence on the effectiveness of MHGs and presented potential implications for clinicians, treatment program managers, and policy makers. It was concluded that, because longitudinal studies associate MHG involvement with reduced substance use, improved psychosocial functioning, and lessened health care costs, there are humane and practical reasons to develop MHG supportive policies. The policies described in the consensus statement that could be implemented by clinicians and program managers include making greater use of empirically validated MHG referral methods, such as those mentioned above, and developing a menu of locally available MHG options that are responsive to patients' needs, preferences, and cultural backgrounds. The workgroup also offered possible MHG supportive policy options (e.g., supporting mutual-help clearinghouses) for state and federal decision makers. It is likely that implementing such policies would strengthen MHG organizations and thereby enhance the national response to the serious public health problems of substance misuse and mental illness.

SUMMARY AND CONCLUSIONS

When one reflects on the magnitude of mental health and addiction problems in the United States and in other countries around the world, it is quite clear that despite sometimes quite generous provision of formal healthcare resources, professional efforts alone cannot cope with the burden of disease attributable to these conditions (Lopez et al., 2006). Perhaps the emergence and growth of the mutual-help movement is many societies' tacit recognition of, and response to, this unsettling truth. In the United States, a lack of health insurance parity and restrictions in existing coverage for substance use and other mental disorders has impacted the extent of professionally delivered care available for these pervasive and endemic conditions. Consequently, freely available MHG organizations may play an increasingly important role as their availability grows and evidence of their effectiveness continues to emerge. We encourage health care providers to inform their patients about these organizations, to help them give them a fair try, and to monitor patients' responses.

REFERENCES

Alcoholics Anonymous (1939). *Alcoholics Anonymous: The Story of How Thousands of Men and Women Have Recovered from Alcoholism* (1st Ed.). New York: Alcoholics Anonymous World Services.

Alcoholics Anonymous World Services (1947, June). Alcoholics Anonymous preamble. *AA Grapevine*.

Alcoholics Anonymous (1953). *Twelve Steps and Twelve Traditions*. New York: Alcoholics Anonymous World Services.

Alcoholics Anonymous (1984). *Pass It On: The Story of Bill Wilson and How the A.A. Message Reached the World*. New York: Alcoholics Anonymous World Services.

Alcoholics Anonymous (2001). *Alcoholics Anonymous: The Story of How Thousands of Men and Women Have Recovered from Alcoholism* (4th Ed.). New York: Alcoholics Anonymous World Services.

Alcoholics Anonymous (2005). *2004 Membership Survey: A Snapshot of A.A. Membership*. New York, NY: Alcoholics Anonymous World Services.

Bogenschutz, M.P. & Akin, S.J. (2000). 12-Step participation and attitudes toward 12-step meetings in dual diagnosis patients. *Alcoholism Treatment Quarterly*, *18*(4), 31–45.

Bond J., Kaskutas, L.A., & Weisner, C. (2003). The persistent influence of social networks and alcoholics anonymous on abstinence. *Journal of Studies on Alcohol*, *64*(4), 579–588.

Brown, B.S., O'Grady, K.E., Farrell, E.V., et al. (2001). Factors associated with frequency of 12-Step attendance by drug abuse clients. *American Journal of Drug and Alcohol Abuse*, *27*(1), 147–60.

Brown, S.A., Mott, M.A., & Myers, M.G. (1990). Adolescent alcohol and drug treatment outcome. In R.R. Watson (Ed.), *Drug and Alcohol Abuse Prevention. Drug and Alcohol Abuse Reviews* (pp. 373–403). Clifton, NJ: Humana Press, Inc.

Connors, G.J. & Tonigan, J.S. (2001). A longitudinal model of intake symptomatology, AA participation and outcome: Retrospective study of the project MATCH outpatient and aftercare samples. *Journal of Studies on Alcohol*, *62*(6), 817–25.

Connors, G.J., Tonigan, J.S., & Miller, W. (2001). *Religiosity and Responsiveness to Alcoholism Treatments*. Bethesda, MD: Department of Health & Human Services.

Crits-Christoph, P., Siqueland, L., Blaine, J., et al. (1999). Psychosocial treatments for cocaine dependence: National Institute on Drug Abuse Collaborative Cocaine Treatment Study. *Archives of General Psychiatry*, *56*(6), 493–502.

Davidson, L., Chinman, M., Kloos, B., et al. (1999). Peer support among individuals with severe mental illness: A review of the evidence. *Clinical Psychology: Science and Practice*, *6*(2), 165–87.

Del Boca, F.K. & Mattson, M.E. (2001). The gender matching hypothesis. In Longabaugh, R. & Wirtz, P.W. (Eds.), Project MATCH Hypotheses: Results and Causal Chain Analysis. Project MATCH Monograph Series, Vol. 8. Bethesda, MD: National Institute on Alcohol Abuse and Alcoholism.

Depression and Bipolar Support Alliance (2004). *DBSA Support Groups: An Important Step on the Road to Wellness*. [Brochure]. Chicago: Author.

Emrick, C.D., Tonigan, J.S., Montgomery, H., & Little, L. (1993). Alcoholics Anonymous: What is currently known? In B.S. McCrady & W.R. Miller (Eds.), *Research on Alcoholics Anonymous: Opportunities and Alternatives* (pp. 41–76). Piscataway, NJ: Rutgers Center of Alcohol Studies.

Etheridge, R.M., Craddock, S.G., Hubbard, R.L., & Rounds-Bryant, J.L. (1999). The relationship of counseling and self-help participation to patient outcomes in DATOS. *Drug and Alcohol Dependence 57*, 99–112.

Fiorentine, R. & Hillhouse, M.P. (2000). Drug treatment and 12-step program participation: The additive effects of integrated recovery activities. *Journal of Substance Abuse Treatment*, *18*(1), 65–74.

Galanter, M. (1988). Zealous self-help groups as adjuncts to psychiatric treatment: A study of Recovery, Inc. *American Journal of Psychiatry*, *145*(10), 1248–1253.

Goldstrom, I.D., Campbell, J., Rogers, J.A., et al. (2006). National estimates for mental health mutual support groups, self-help organizations, and consumer-operated services. *Administration and Policy in Mental Health and Mental Health Services Research*, *33*(1), 92–103.

Hsieh, S., Hoffmann, N.G., & Hollister, C.D. (1998). The relationship between pre-, during-, post-treatment factors, and adolescent substance abuse behaviors. *Addictive Behaviors*, *23*(4), 477–488.

Humphreys, K. (2004). *Circles of Recovery: Self-help Organizations for Addictions*. Cambridge, UK: Cambridge University Press.

Humphreys, K., Mankowski, E., Moos, R.H., & Finney, J.W. (1999). Do enhanced friendship networks and active coping mediate the effect of self-help groups on substance abuse? *Annals of Behavioral Medicine*, *21*(1), 54–60.

Humphreys, K. & Moos, R.H. (1996). Reduced substance-abuse-related health care costs among voluntary participants in Alcoholics Anonymous. *Psychiatric Services*, *47*(7), 709–713.

Humphreys, K. & Moos, R.H. (2001). Can encouraging substance abuse patients to participate in self-help groups reduce demand for health care? A quasi-experimental study. *Alcoholism: Clinical and Experimental Research*, *25*(5), 711–716.

Humphreys, K. & Moos, R.H. (2007). Encouraging posttreatment self-help group involvement to reduce demand for continuing care services: Two-year clinical and utilization outcomes. *Alcoholism: Clinical and Experimental Research*, *31*(1), 64–68.

Humphreys K. & Noke J.M. (1997). The influence of posttreatment mutual help group participation on the friendship networks of substance abuse patients. *American Journal of Community Psychology*, *25*, 1–16.

Humphreys, K., Wing, S., McCarty, D., et al. (2004). Self-help organizations for alcohol and drug problems: Toward evidence-based practice and policy. *Journal of Substance Abuse Treatment*, *3*(26), 151–158.

Kaskutas L.A., Bond J., & Humphreys K. (2002). Social networks as mediators of the effect of Alcoholics Anonymous. *Addiction*, *97*(7), 891–900.

Kazdin, A.E. & Nock, M.K. (2003). Delineating mechanisms of change in child and adolescent therapy: Methodological issues and research recommendations. *Journal of Child Psychology and Psychiatry*, *44*(8), 1116–1129.

Kelly, J.F. (2003). Self-help for substance use disorders: History, effectiveness, knowledge gaps and research opportunities. *Clinical Psychology Review*, *23*(5), 639–663.

Kelly, J.F., Abrantes, A.M., & Brown, S.A. (2004). *An 8-year follow-up of 12-step group involvement among treated adolescents*. Presentation at the Research Society on Alcoholism, Vancouver, Canada, June 26–30.

Kelly, J.F., Finney, J.W., & Moos, R.H. (2005). Substance use disorder patients who are mandated to treatment: Characteristics, treatment process, and 1- and 5-year outcomes. *Journal of Substance Abuse Treatment*, *28*(3), 213–233.

Kelly, J.F. Humphreys, K.N., & Youngson, H. (2004). Mutual Aid Groups. In *Alcohol and Drug Problems: A Practical Guide for Counsellors* (3rd Ed.). Toronto: Centre for Addiction and Mental Health.

Kelly, J.F., McKellar, J.D. & Moos, R. (2003). Major Depressive Disorder in patients with substance use disorders: Effects on 12-step self-help involvement and substance use outcomes. *Addiction*, *98*, 499–508.

Kelly, J.F., Myers, M.G. & Brown, S.A. (2000). A multivariate process model of adolescent 12-step attendance and substance use outcome following inpatient treatment. *Psychology of Addictive Behaviors*, *14*(4), 376–389.

Kelly, J.F., Myers, M.G., Brown, S.A. (2002). Do adolescents affiliate with 12-step groups? A multivariate process model of effects. *Journal of Studies on Alcohol*, *63*(3), 293–304.

Kelly, J.F., Myers, M.G., & Brown, S.A. (2005). The effects of age composition of 12-step groups on adolescent 12-step participation and substance use outcome. *Journal of Child & Adolescent Substance Abuse*, *15*(1), 67–76.

Kelly, J.F., Stout, R., Zywiak, W. & Schneider, R. (2006). A 3-year study of addiction mutual-help group participation following intensive outpatient treatment. *Alcoholism: Clinical and Experimental Research*, *30*(8), 1381–1392.

Kessler, R.C. (1995). The national comorbidity survey: Preliminary results and future directions. *International Journal of Methods in Psychiatric Research*, *5*(2), 139–151.

Kessler, R.C., Crum, R.M., Warner, L.A., et al. (1997). Lifetime co-occurrence of DSM-III-R alcohol abuse and dependence with other psychiatric disorders in the National Comorbidity Survey. *Archives of General Psychiatry*, *54*(4), 313–321.

Kessler, R.C., Nelson, C.B., McGonagle, K.A., et al. (1996). The epidemiology of co-occurring addictive and mental disorders: Implications for prevention and service utilization. *American Journal of Orthopsychiatry*, *66*(1), 17–31.

Kownacki, R.J. & Shadish, W.R. (1999). Does Alcoholics Anonymous work? The results from a meta-analysis of controlled experiments. *Substance Use & Misuse*, *34*(13), 1897–1916.

Laudet, A.B., Cleland, C.M., Magura, S., et al. (2004). Social support mediates the effects of dual-focus mutual aid groups on abstinence from substance use. *American Journal of Community Psychology*, *234*(3–4), 175–185.

Laudet, A.B., Magura, S., Vogel, H.S., & Knight, E. (2000a). Recovery challenges among dually diagnosed individuals. *Journal of Substance Abuse Treatment*, *18*(4), 321–329.

Laudet, A.B., Magura, S.,Vogel, H.S., & Knight, E. (2000b). Support, mutual aid and recovery from dual diagnosis. *Community Mental Health Journal*, *36*(5), 457–476.

Longabaugh, R., Wirtz, P.W., Zweben, A., & Stout, R.L. (1998). Network support for drinking, Alcoholics Anonymous and long-term matching effects. *Addiction*, *93*(9), 1313–1333.

Lopez, A.D., Mathers, C.D., Ezzati, M., et al. (Eds.) (2006). *Global Burden of Disease and Risk Factors*. New York: Oxford University Press.

Low, A.A. (1950). *Mental Health through Will Training: A System of Self-Help in Psychotherapy as Practiced by Recovery, Incorporated*. Boston, MA: Christopher Publishing.

Magura S., Knight, E., Vogel, H.S., et al. (2003). Mediators of effectiveness in dual-focus self-help groups. *American Journal of Drug and Alcohol Abuse*, *29*(2), 301–322.

Magura, S., Laudet, A.B., Mahmood, D., et al. (2002). Adherence to medication regimens and participation in dual-focus self-help groups. *Psychiatric Services*, *53*(3), 310–316.

Magura, S., Laudet, A.B., Mahmood, D., et al. (2003). Role of self-help processes in achieving abstinence among dually diagnoses persons. *Addictive Behaviors*, *28*, 399–413.

McCrady, B.S. & Miller, W.R. (Eds.) (1993). *Research on Alcoholics Anonymous: Opportunities and Alternatives*. New Brunswick, NJ: Rutgers Center of Alcohol Studies.

McFadden, L., Seidman, E., & Rappaport, J. (1992). A comparison of espoused theories of self- and mutual-help: Implications for mental health professionals. *Professional Psychology*, *23*(6), 515–520.

McKellar, J.D., Stewart, E. & Humphrey, K.N. (2003). Alcoholics Anonymous involvement and positive alcohol-related outcomes: Cause, consequence, or just a correlation? A prospective 2-year study of 2,319 alcohol-dependent men. *Journal of Consulting and Clinical Psychology*, *71*(2), 302–308.

Miller, N.S., Ninonuevo, F.G., Klamen, D.L., & Hoffmann, N.G. (1997). Integration of treatment and post-treatment variables in predicting results of abstinence-based outpatient treatment after one year. *Journal of Psychoactive Drugs*, *29*(3), 239–248.

Morgenstern, J. & Bates M.E. (1999). Effects of executive treatment. *Journal of Studies on Alcohol*, *60*, 846–855.

Morgenstern, J., Frey, R.M., McCrady, B.S., et al. (1996). Examining mediators of change in traditional chemical dependency treatment. *Journal of Studies on Alcohol*, *57*(1), 53–64.

Morgenstern, J., Labouvie, E., McCrady, B.S., et al. (1997). Affiliation with Alcoholics Anonymous after treatment: A study of its therapeutic effects and mechanisms of action. *Journal of Consulting and Clinical Psychology*, *65*(5), 768–777.

Mowbray, C.T., Solomon, M., Ribisl, K.M., et al. (1995). Treatment for mental illness and substance abuse in a public psychiatric hospital. Successful strategies and challenging problems. *Journal of Substance Abuse Treatment*, *12*(2), 129–139.

Muller, D., Judd, C.M., & Yzerbyt, V.Y. (2005). When moderation is mediated and mediation is moderated. *Journal of Personality and Social Psychology*, *89*, 852–863.

Murray, P. (1996). Recovery, Inc., as an adjunct to treatment in an era of managed care. *Psychiatric Services*, *47*(12), 1378–1381.

Noordsy, D.L., Schwab, B., Fox, L., & Drake, R.E. (1996). The role of self-help programs in the rehabilitation of persons with severe mental illness and substance use disorders. *Community Mental Health Journal*, *32*(1), 71–81.

Nowinski, J., Baker, S., & Carroll, K.M. (1992). *Twelve-Step Facilitation Therapy Manual: A Clinical Research Guide for Therapists Treating Individuals with Alcohol Abuse and Dependence*. NIAAA Project MATCH Monograph Series Vol. 1. DHHS Pub. No. (ADM)92-1893. Rockville, MD: National Institute on Alcohol Abuse and Alcoholism.

Ouimette, P., Humphreys, K., Moos, R.H., et al. (2001). Self-help group participation among substance use disorder patients with posttraumatic stress disorder. *Journal of Substance Abuse Treatment*, *20*(1), 25–2.

Ouimette, P.C., Finney, J.W., & Moos, R.H. (1997). Twelve-step and cognitive-behavioral treatment for substance abuse: A comparison of treatment effectiveness. *Journal of Consulting and Clinical Psychology*, *65*(2), 230–240.

Ouimette, P.C., Moos, R.H., & Finney, J.W. (1998). Influence of outpatient treatment and 12-step group involvement on one-year substance abuse treatment outcomes. *Journal of Studies on Alcohol*, *59*(5), 513–22.

Owen, P.L., Slaymaker, V., Tonigan, J.S., et al. (2003). Participation in AA: Intended and unintended change mechanisms. *Alcoholism: Clinical and Experimental Research*, *27*, 524–32.

Penn, P.E. & Brooks, A.J. (2000). Five years, twelve-steps, and REBT in the treatment of dual diagnosis. *Journal of Rational-Emotive & Cognitive-Behavior Therapy*, *18*(4), 197–208.

Piliavin, J.A. (2003). Doing well by doing good: Benefits for the benefactor. In: Keyes, C.L. M. & Haidt, J. (Eds.) *Flourishing, Positive Psychology and the Life Well-lived* (pp. 227–247). Washington, DC: American Psychological Association.

Project MATCH Research Group. (1993). Project MATCH (Matching Alcoholism Treatment to Client Heterogeneity): Rationale and methods for a multisite clinical trial matching patients to alcoholism treatment. *Alcoholism: Clinical Experimental Research*, *17*(6), 1130–1145.

Project MATCH Research Group. (1997). Matching alcoholism treatments to client heterogeneity: Project MATCH posttreatment drinking outcomes. *Journal of Studies on Alcohol*, *58*(1), 7–29.

Project MATCH Research Group (1998). Matching alcoholism treatments to client heterogeneity: Project MATCH three-year drinking outcomes. *Alcoholism: Clinical and Experimental Research*, *22*(6), 1300–1311.

RachBeisel, J., Scott, J., & Dixon, L. (1999). Co-occurring severe mental illness and substance use disorders: A review of recent research. *Psychiatric Services*, *50*(11), 1427–1434.

Riessman, F. (1965) The 'helper therapy' principle. *Social Work*, *10*, 27–32.

Roberts, L.J., Salem, D., Rappaport, J., et al. (1999). Giving and receiving help: Interpersonal transactions in mutual-help meetings and psychosocial adjustment of members. *American Journal of Community Psychology*, *27*(6), 841–867.

Room, R. & Greenfield, T. (1993). Alcoholics Anonymous, other 12-step movements and psychotherapy in the US population, 1990. *Addiction*, *88*(4), 555–562.

Rychtarik, R.G., Connors, G.J., Dermen, K.H., & Stasiewicz, P.R. (2000). Alcoholics Anonymous and the use of medications to prevent relapse: An anonymous survey of member attitudes. *Journal of Studies on Alcohol*, *61*(1), 134–138.

SAMHSA (2005). Treatment Admissions for Alcohol Abuse, Alone and with a Drug Problem. US Department of Health and Human Services. Arlington: Office of Applied Studies.

Sisson, R.W. & Mallams, J.H. (1981). The use of systematic encouragement and community access procedures to increase attendance at Alcoholic Anonymous and Al-Anon meetings. *American Journal of Drug and Alcohol Abuse*, *8*(3), 371–376.

Timko, C., DeBenedetti, A., & Billow, R. (2006). Intensive referral to 12-step self-help groups and 6-month substance use disorder outcomes. *Addiction*, *101*(5), 678–688.

Timko, C., Moos, R.H., Finney, J.W., & Lesar, M.D. (2000). Long-term outcomes of alcohol use disorders: Comparing untreated individuals with those in Alcoholics Anonymous and formal treatment. *Journal of Studies on Alcohol*, *6*(4), 529–540.

Timko, C., Moos, R.H., Finney, J.W., et al. (1999). Long-term treatment careers and outcomes of previously untreated alcoholics. *Journal of Studies on Alcohol*, *60*(4), 437–447.

Tomasson, K. & Vaglum, P. (1998). Psychiatric co-morbidity and aftercare among alcoholics: A prospective study of a nationwide representative sample. *Addiction*, *93*(3), 423–431.

Tonigan, J.S., Connors, G.J., & Miller, W.R. (2003). Participation and involvement in Alcoholics Anonymous. In Babor, T.F., & Del Boca, F.K. (Eds.). Treatment Matching in Alcoholism (pp. 184–204). New York: Cambridge University Press.

Tonigan, J.S., Miller, W.R., & Schermer, C. (2002). Atheists, agnostics, and Alcoholics Anonymous. *Journal of Studies on Alcohol*, *63*, 534–541.

Tonigan, J.S., Toscova, R., & Miller, W.R. (1996). Meta-analysis of the literature on Alcoholics Anonymous: Sample and study characteristics moderate findings. *Journal of Studies on Alcohol*, *57*(1), 65–72.

Vik, P.W., Grizzle, K.L. & Brown, S.A. (1992). Social resource characteristics and adolescent substance abuse relapse. *Journal of Adolescent Chemical Dependency* *2*(2), 59–74.

Vogel, H.S, Laudet, A.B., & Magura, S. (1998). Double trouble in recovery: Self-help for people with dual diagnoses. *Psychiatric Rehabilitation Journal*, *21*(4), 356–364.

Weiss, R.D., Griffin, M.L., Gallop, R., et al. (2000). Mutual aid group attendance and participation among cocaine dependent patients. *Drug and Alcohol Dependence*, *60*, 169–77.

Winzelberg, A. & Humphreys, K. (1999). Should patients' religiosity influence clinicians' referral to 12-step self-help groups? Evidence from a study of 3,018 male substance abuse patients. *Journal of Consulting and Clinical Psychology*, *67*(5), 790–4.

Witbrodt, J. & Kaskutas, L.A. (2005). Does diagnosis matter? Differential effects of 12-step participation and social networks on abstinence. *American Journal of Drug and Alcohol Abuse*, *31*, 685–707.

Yalom, I.D. (1995). *The Theory and Practice of Group Psychotherapy* (4th Ed.). New York: Basic Books.

5

ADJUNCTIVE E-HEALTH

CRISSA DRAPER, MANDRA RASMUSSEN HALL, AND WILLIAM T. O'DONOHUE

University of Nevada, Reno

Definitions of psychotherapy vary greatly. Some are a bit cynical, such as Victor Raimy's: "Psychotherapy is an undefined technique applied to unspecified cases with unpredictable results. For this technique, rigorous training is required." Given the wide range of quality and evidence for the safety and effectiveness of psychotherapy might be quite justified. Other definitions are less cynical although these are very general: "Psychotherapy is a set of techniques used to treat mental health and emotional problems and some psychiatric disorders (http://www.nhsdirect.nhs.uk/articles/article.aspx?articleId=659). Note that this definition does not preclude typical e-health interventions. Certainly, the paradigmatic image of therapy is of a psychotherapist and a client sitting face-to-face for 50 minutes discussing, and trying to improve the client's psychological problems. However, the paradigmatic version of travel in the eighteenth century was either by walking or by horse. Things change, sometimes for good reasons.

Relatively recently developed technologies allow new possibilities. Often as with any alternative, there are trade-offs (walking allows superior opportunities for exercise, air travel allows speedier transit). In this chapter, we will discuss some of the advantages and disadvantages of e-health as part of a therapist's toolbox for trying to improve behavioral health. We take e-health to be the use of computer technologies to pursue some of the typical goals associated with healthcare, i.e., the prevention, detection, assessment, and treatment of health problems.

E-health becomes an interesting set of possibilities because of the following challenges to healthcare systems:

- There are access problems such that some groups of individuals (rural, frontier, poor) do not have any or adequate access to care for their problems.
- There are problems with stigma. Unfortunately, it is often the case that seeing a mental health professional has a cost: People are embarrassed and worried that they may suffer negative reactions to them because of their client status.

- There are problems of such high prevalence that expanding existing delivery paradigms to address these is not feasible. Given current prevalence rates of problems such as depression or obesity or dementia, one needs new delivery paradigms because of the impracticalities of training and funding expansions of the existing paradigms. When one projects trends in these, there is reason to be more pessimistic about existing treatment delivery paradigms.
- There are quality problems such that healthcare (especially behavioral health) varies in ways that are undesirable. We all want excellent quality healthcare and often this standard is not widely available.
- There are cost problems. We all want value for our dollar. Healthcare is escalating at more than the general rate of inflation. Currently, healthcare utilizes about 16% of the GDP (in 1960 it was 5%). Individuals are looking for more cost-effective ways of treating problems.

E-health allows avenues to address these problems.

- E-mail and the web allow access to many who might not be near or able to afford traditional psychotherapy services. Increasingly, our population is becoming computer literate (trends would suggest that soon nearly all will be), and the price of web access is relatively cheap and sometimes free (public libraries).
- The web allows anonymity and thus decreased stigma.
- The web allows increased accountability. Web pages are open for all to inspect (vs what occurs behind the doors of a psychotherapist's office). Moreover, it is relatively easy to update content (vs books or practice guidelines).
- The web can allow inexpensive treatment. Some sites are free, others charge a fraction of what an hour of a psychotherapist's time.

Of course, there are limitations to the web and e-health. It is reasonable to hypothesize that humans have evolved to prefer face-to-face human contact, at least in times. An e-mail message may not be able to comfort us in times of grief or stress as a real human sitting a few feet from us. Although there are models of e-health in which video can be used, it still may be the case that at times being in the room with a client allows the therapist to pick up information that is missed in video.

However, these limitations do not imply that e-health is useless. Our view is that it is a useful tool, particularly in a stepped care model. Individuals who need information, skills training, and who may have lower levels of problems may attempt e-health before moving to more intense levels of intervention. This is consistent with the ethical prescription of using the least intrusive intervention for a problem.

However, it is important to note that just because the technology is "cool" and because it shares a resemblance to traditional psychotherapy, the e-health application cannot be assumed to share the evidence base of the traditional psychotherapy. E-health interventions need to be individually assessed for the safety and efficacy. However, when compared to traditional psychotherapy their cost-effectiveness should be assessed. It is interesting to calculate per unit costs of improvement. For example, let us say a traditional face-to-face individual psychotherapy reduces Beck Depression Inventory (BDI) scores 10 points on average, but costs $1000 to deliver. Let us say an e-health intervention reduces BDI scores by 7 points, but costs $210 to implement. The cost of the first is $100/BDI point, whereas the cost of the second is $30. This has to be taken into account, given the enormous numbers of individuals who are depressed. In addition, the ceiling of the two interventions has to be debated: Traditional psychotherapy, in this example, has a higher magnitude of effect. Of course, we should not assume that traditional psychotherapy will always be superior just because it is more "personal," "idiographic," or expensive. Seligman, for example, is claiming his "authentichappiness.com" Internet intervention for depression using positive psychology has equivalent results to face-to-face cognitive therapy.

We turn now to some special considerations regarding e-health.

INFORMED CONSENT

Providing comprehensive information regarding the nature, course, risks, benefits, and limitations of behavioral health treatment can be accomplished more efficiently by directing patients to treatment information online. Several websites are devoted to outlining the most empirically supported interventions for specific clinical problems and disorders, while describing alternative treatments. Providers can direct patients to these online resources as a regular part of the informed consent process in order to ensure that patients have a thorough understanding of the treatment offered by the provider. Patients can also learn about alternative treatments they may wish to pursue. Utilizing treatment information online to supplement informed consent promotes the transparency of behavioral healthcare, which enhances quality improvement efforts and helps clients make informed choices about their care. The following list of resources represents only a sample of websites that provide comprehensive explanations of treatments for specific clinical disorders, as well as descriptions of general approaches to treatment (i.e., behavioral, cognitive-behavioral, family systems). Other sites on the Internet are dedicated to specific clinical disorders, and offer both treatment information and psychoeducational materials related to that topic. Many general mental health resources provide links to the websites of national centers and/or academies that are disorder-specific.

- American Psychological Association (www.apa.org)
  - http://www.apa.org/divisions/div12/rev_est/
  - American Psychological Association Help Center (www.apahelpcenter.org)

  - http://apahelpcenter.org/articles/article.php?id=51
  - http://apahelpcenter.org/articles/article.php?id=52
- Association for Behavioral and Cognitive Therapies (www.aabt.org)
  - http://www.aabt.org/public/
- Evidence-Based Treatment for Children and Adolescents (www.effectivechildtherapy.com)
- Therapy Advisor (www.therapyadvisor.org)
- TriWest Healthcare Alliance (www.triwest.com)
  - https://www.triwest.com/triwest/unauth/newContent/newPDF/behavioralHealth/serv_nav_bh_treat.pdf
  - https://www.triwest.com/triwest/unauth/newContent/newPDF/behavioralHealth/Behavior_Therapy_Interventions.pdf

PSYCHOEDUCATION

Transparency in behavioral healthcare also includes educating patients about the symptoms, etiology, and myths associated with clinical disorders. This not only helps in informed consent, but education is incorporated in the initial phases of many behavioral health treatments. Providers can supplement brief psychoeducation in session by utilizing online resources that have already compiled information on a variety of clinical problems. Providers can download and print relevant pamphlets, handouts, and fact sheets for patients to review outside of session. Providers may also direct patients to specific websites to provide more in-depth explanations of clinical problems. Making use of reputable online resources for psychoeducation can minimize patient exposure to erroneous information gained through their own online research, and allows providers to offer patients comprehensive educational material more efficiently. The following websites provide educational information on a variety of clinical disorders; many of the sites offer handouts that can be downloaded and printed for patient use.

- American Academy of Child and Adolescent Psychiatry (www.aacap.org)
- American Psychological Association Help Center (www.apahelpcenter.org)
- Internet Mental Health (www.mentalhealth.com)
- Help Guide (www.helpguide.org)
- Kids Health (www.kidshealth.org)
- Mayo Clinic (www.mayoclinic.com)
- Medline Plus Mental Health (www.nlm.nih.gov/medlineplus/mentalhealth.html)
- Mental Health Matters (www.mental-health-matters.com)
- Mental Help Net (www.mentalhelp.net)
- National Center for Posttraumatic Stress Disorder (www.ncptsd.va.gov)
- SAMHSA's National Mental Health Information Center (http://mentalhealth.samhsa.gov)

- TriWest Healthcare Alliance (www.triwest.com)
- WHO Guide to Mental and Neurological Health in Primary Care (www.mentalneurologicalprimarycare.org)

SKILLS TRAINING

Relaxation, meditation, mindfulness, stress-management, and other coping skills are the foundation of many behavioral health treatments. Providers can utilize online resources to supplement skills training in session and then direct patients to specific websites for ongoing skills review and practice between appointments. The following websites provide explanations, rationales, and step-by-step training for a variety of coping skills that go beyond psychoeducation.

- General Coping
  - www.mentalneurologicalprimarycare.org/downloads.asp
  - www.mindtools.com
- Relaxation (www.shuteye.com/solutions_relax.asp)
- Stress (www.hooah4health.com/toolbox/stress/default.htm)
- Validation (http://eqi.org/valid.htm)
- Assertiveness (www.coping.org/relations/assert.htm)
- Depression and Suicidal Ideation (www.carmha.ca/publications/index.cfm?fuseaction=publications.showByClass&topic=1)
- Dialectical Behavior Therapy Self-Help (www.dbtselfhelp.com)
- Attention-Deficit/Hyperactivity Disorder (www.valueoptions.com/members/education/adhd/adhdsupport/adhdworkbook.pdf)
- Relapse Prevention (http://dmu.trc.upenn.edu/patientfeedback/pfweb2/clinresources.asp)
- Drinking (http://pubs.niaaa.nih.gov/publications/handout.htm)
- Smoking (www.cancer.org)
- Self-Help Programs
  - General (www.myselfhelp.com or www.authentichappiness.sas.upenn.edu)
  - Panic (www.panic-attacks.co.uk/panic_course_contents.htm)
  - Parenting (www.directiveparenting.com/index.aspx)

SELF-HELP

Using self-help in conjunction with traditional, face-to-face practice can help to free up practitioner resources and provides an economically viable practice. Self-help has been widely found to be an empirically supported adjunct to face-to-face therapy (see Chapters 2 and 4). The Internet can take this to a new level, in that it can provide interactivity and personalization in a way that other forms of self-help, such as books, cannot. Many of the studied self-help resources have used face-to-face as the adjunctive portion of the treatment, and have instead focused on the Internet-based self-help as the primary treatment. Whereas the majority of self-help resources available on the Internet have not been studied, those tested have proven effective (Marks et al., 2003; Mouton-Odum et al., 2006). Some examples of evidence-based sites include:

- StopPulling.com is an interactive computer program to help treat trichotillomania
  - www.stoppulling.com
- FearFighter is a computer-aided cognitive-behavioral therapy (CBT) program
  - www.fearfighter.com
- Fit and Healthy Kids is an online program that helps to treat child overweight
  - www.fitandhealthykids.com
- Selfhelp Magazine provides in-depth self-help resources
  - www.Selfhelpmagazine.com

SOCIAL SUPPORT

Social support groups are generally seen in the e-health world by way of asynchronous message boards. These boards may be used either with peers-only in conjunction to face-to-face therapy, or with a therapist-mediated board, such as Dr Robert Hsiung's Psycho-Babble board (Hsiung, 2000). Message boards allow a forum for people with similar problems to join together and form alliances that may not be possible within one's own social group, or possibly even city. The Internet knows no geological boundaries and allows people to find social support from all over the world.

Message boards also assist with information-seeking and this aspect of message boards is generally self-correcting, in that many users will correct any false information given by other users. It is preferable, albeit less feasible economically, to have professionals available to correct misinformation. Therapist or not, some form of mediator is necessary for such sites, to control for problems such as users providing maladaptive coping information. For example, an individual on a self-injury forum may begin to share cutting techniques, and a mediator is necessary to monitor and remove such posts. Instances of "Virtual Munchausen Syndrome" (Hsiung, 2000) may also occur, in which people feign suicidality or other extreme behaviors in hopes of receiving more attention.

- PsychoBabble is a message board moderated by professional therapist Dr Robert Hsiung.
  - www.dr-bob.com/babble

- Carepages.com provides a different form of social support, in which families or groups can be informed of an individual's illness.
  - www.carepages.com
- Selfhelp Magazine offers an extensive, supervised message board for a variety of issues.
  - www.selfhelpmagazine.com

TREATMENT COMPLIANCE

Patient compliance with clinical homework assignments, self-monitoring, and skills practice is critical to positive treatment outcomes. A variety of electronic strategies may help increase patient compliance. Providers can arrange scheduled e-mail messages that prompt patients to report on homework progress or skills practice. Providers may also create their own secure website where patients can access homework assignments, review skills, and submit self-monitoring data. Although these strategies require additional electronic capabilities and consideration of privacy and confidentiality issues, they may increase overall efficiency and treatment outcomes. The following books offer guidelines for providers who wish to incorporate electronic and Internet resources into their practices:

- Derrig-Palumbo & Zeine (2005). *Online Therapy: A Therapist's Guide to Expanding Your Practice*
- Hsiung (2002). *E-Therapy: Case Studies, Guiding Principles, and the Clinical Potential of the Internet*

Treatment compliance may also be enhanced by addressing patients' motivation to change. Handouts, fact sheets, and other self-help resources are available online to help patients understand how to handle the fear, frustration, and difficulties of making important behavior changes. Therapeutic techniques for increasing patient motivation are also available for providers. The following websites are good examples of these resources:

- TriWest Health Care Alliance—Motivation: Emotional Well-Being (www.triwest.com/triwest/default.html?/triwest/unauth/newContent/newBehavioralHealth/serv_emo_mot_self.asp)
- Motivational Interviewing (www.motivationalinterviewing.org)

ASSESSMENT

Providers who are interested in quality improvement can measure treatment outcomes by electronic means. Online questionnaires may be provided on a secure website, with scheduled e-mail prompts for patients to complete assessments at various intervals. A clinic website could also provide feedback to patients about their treatment progress by using graphs to display changes over time in self-reported symptoms and treatment goals. Many of the websites presented in this chapter provide specific assessment tools that can be downloaded free of charge and incorporated into a provider's clinic or practice. For example, Tri West Health Care Alliance (www.triwest.com) recommends various assessment tools for specific disorders under their Behavioral Health link for providers. A wide range of assessment instruments can also be found through the Center for HIV Identification, Prevention, and Treatment Services (CHIPTS) at http://chipts.ucla.edu/assessment/IB/Main_Pages/category2.asp.

CLINICIAN TRAINING

Dissemination of empirically supported treatments has increased through online resources. Quality training in specific treatment protocols is available through the Internet, and studies indicate that such online learning is effective. Providers can now utilize these training opportunities to increase their knowledge of best practices in behavioral health more efficiently and cost-effectively.

- APA Online Academy (www.apa.org/ce)
- Empirically Supported Treatment Manuals (http://www.apa.org/divisions/div12/journals.html)
- Motivational Interviewing (www.motivationalinterviewing.org)
- Trauma-Focused Cognitive-Behavioral Therapy (http://tfcbt.musc.edu)

OUTCOME DATA

The idea of combining technology and therapy is often unpalatable for practitioners. However, there is ample research to show that the combination could prove an efficient, effective, and resourceful supplement to traditional therapy. Much resistance seems to be due to the idea that online therapy would change the therapeutic alliance; but "it does appear that individuals are capable of establishing a warm and caring environment even without the assistance of f2f [face-to-face] cues, indicating that it may be possible to establish a working alliance through computer-mediated communication." (Kraus et al., 2004, p. 73)

The computer provides a medium in which clients have been repeatedly shown to disclose greater amounts of more clinically relevant information than they otherwise would in a face-to-face setting (Erdman et al., 1985; Ferriter, 1993). The computer also provides a means to obtain more objective and accurate assessment data (Carlbring et al., 2007; Erdman et al., 1985; Horesh, 2001; Wijndaele et al., 2007). Additionally, the Internet is always "on call." Winzelberg (1997) noted that, in his research on an online social support forum, two-thirds of the messages were posted between 6 pm and 7 am. In a purely face-to-face condition, a client seeking help or having a hard time at such hours would generally have to wait until normal office hours to seek therapeutic support.

The field of e-health is relatively new, but several areas have been researched extensively, and the data have largely supported e-health as an adjunctive (as well as primary) therapy. Outcome data supports both the effectiveness of treatment, and client satisfaction (Leibert et al., 2006).

Instead of considering e-therapy as the adjunctive piece of therapy, some of the research regarding e-health has based the majority of treatment on the Internet, and the adjunctive piece instead is face-to-face therapy or over the phone. These programs can still be used adjunctively, however, when dealing with issues such as comorbidity, or in order to reduce the time needed in face-to-face sessions.

Treating anxiety and depression over the Internet has been studied extensively, considering the relative newness of the field (Carlbring et al., 2006; Kenardy et al., 2003; Mataix-Cols & Marks, 2006; Przeworski & Newman, 2006). Marks et al. (2003) noted clinically meaningful results with three of four computer-mediated systems that were intended to act as " 'clinician extenders' and not 'clinician replacers'." The study set up a "computer-aided self-help clinic," which used several previously researched computer-aided treatment programs that would be available to individuals with a broad range of depressive and anxiety disorders. The systems included four programs: FearFighter, Cope, Balance, and BTSteps. FearFighter is an online phobia treatment program that walks clients through a 9-step exposure-based program. Cope and BTSteps both assisted clients through interactive voice response phone calls, which were available 24 hours daily. Balance was an interactive CD-ROM program. Of the four programs, only the BTSteps program was not found to be significant, and of the 108 subjects who completed the posttreatment data phase of all four programs combined, 80% of patients reported positive results, 10% unchanged, and only 9% reported worsening to some degree. Additionally, patients reported that they "told the computer sensitive things they would not tell a human" (Marks et al., 2003, p. 57). Although the programs were largely autonomous, it was run through a clinic that offered live help when needed (which was available both through phone or in-person at the clinic), although the clinical work for the 139 patients who completed treatment was completed within the equivalent of one full-time position.

One way the Internet can aid a practitioner is by providing expertise with specialized and relatively rare problems that the practitioner might not have the training to effectively treat. The literature is extensive regarding the use of the Internet to treat specific problems including an Internet intervention for pediatric encopresis (Ritterband et al., 2003), intervention for male sexual dysfunctions (Van Diest et al., 2007, Leusink & Aarts, 2006), and interventions for pediatric recurrent pain (Hicks et al., 2006). One study with minimal face-to-face contact provided an interactive self-help program— www.stoppulling.com—to clients suffering from trichotillomania (Mouton-Odum et al., 2006). The program included three phases: Assessment, intervention, and maintenance, and asked subjects to track hair-pulling as well as urges through each phase. The intervention phase personalized treatment by identifying specific triggers and teaching coping strategies surrounding these triggers. The subjects were also asked to set goals at this phase as well. The program provided a significant reduction in symptoms. The duration of interaction tended toward significance, suggesting that extended use of the program may lead to a bigger change in behavior. Additionally, it should be noted that some measures improved most significantly during the assessment phase, implying that self-monitoring may be an active component of treatment. Although these responses were less than ideal (only 31.7% responded to treatment), the response rates were comparable to those found in a face-to-face cognitive-behavioral approach (Lerner et al., 1998), and because of the economical benefits of the self-help program, these results are notable. However, the research team notes that, while not tested as such, stop-pulling.com "may provide a potentially useful self-help alternative or adjunctive approach for reducing repetitive hair pulling."

Some programs have also been developed specifically using computers as a supplement to face-to-face treatment (Connelly, 2005; Whitfield et al., 2006). Several other studies have shown the benefit of using technology for self-monitoring (Adachi et al., 2007; Glanz et al., 2006; Shiffman & Paty, 2000). Newman et al. ran a large-scale, international multisite effectiveness study for the treatment of Panic Disorder in which they compared a waitlist with brief therapy (6 sessions of CBT), brief therapy aided by handheld computers (6 sessions of CBT plus the use of a CBT program loaded into a portable computer), and traditional therapy (12 sessions of CBT). The computer provided diary and treatment functions. The diary function set alarm reminders for the client to input both levels of anxiety and number of panic attacks in the last 24 hours. The treatment components of the handheld computers included assistance with cognitive restructuring, exposure, and breathing tasks, which all started automatically at different points in the day. The client would also have the option to turn on the computer any time he or she is feeling anxious or simply wants to practice techniques. All interventions were found to be significantly more effective than the waitlist. The data provided evidence that the computer-based assistance is a viable option to shorten treatment length and minimized therapist interaction, while maximizing treatment outcomes. Many other studies have shown the effectiveness of treating panic disorder over the Internet, although few have been as large in scale (Carlbring et al., 2001; Klein & Richards, 2001; Richards & Alvarenga, 2002; Richards et al., 2003).

Perhaps the most intuitive transition from traditional psychotherapy to computer-based technology is psychoeducation. The Internet can act as a cheap and unrestrictive publisher, allowing for mental health professionals to make any handouts, homework, or general information available from home to clients. Practitioners could create their own sites with specialized information pertaining to their own practice, or simply direct clients to generalized psychoeducation sites, such as WebMD. Research on specialized psychoeducation sites has shown it to be an effective tool, both for practice and prevention (Robertson et al., 2006; Zabinski et al. 2003). One CBT-based computer psychoeducation program—Student Bodies—was found to be more effective in reducing risk factors for eating disorders than a similar program delivered by a live person in the classroom (Celio et al., 2000), although the high dropout rate may have affected results. Another example of promising psychoeducation in e-health is in a computer-based intervention for the families of children facing depression. The program, called Depression Experience Journal (www.experiencejournal.com/depression), allowed families of depressed children to read stories, poems, and hear songs about others who had been through similar circumstances. The overall participant satisfaction was quite high, and they reported "a strong sense that there are others facing the same issues" (Demaso et al., 2006, p. 162). The program also showed positive data on coping responses and attitude change.

FUTURE DIRECTIONS/ISSUES

Adjunctive e-health may come up in the context of considering a transition from face-to-face, toward online therapy (for example, if the client is going on an extended vacation or has become too busy to keep appointments); however, it has been noted that "it appears that suddenly shifting an existing f2f [face-to-face] therapeutic relationship to a computer-mediated environment is not ideal for therapeutic outcomes. If the mode of therapy is to be changed, the client should be made aware of the possible shortcomings ahead of time" (Kraus et al., 2004). In such a situation, it would be optimal to begin the therapy as adjunctive, instead of moving toward a new kind of relationship later in therapy.

RESEARCH

Although there is an ever-growing world of data regarding the adjunctive use of e-health, the majority of research tends to rely on testing at the level of technology, and lies on a foundation of untested assumptions. Further research should focus on effectiveness trials, to evaluate whether adjunctive e-health is a viable option for general and large populations. These studies could focus on which populations do not seem to benefit and whether it is due to dropout, unwillingness to use the Internet, or treatment ineffectiveness. Additionally, the assumption that e-health could assist with rural and stigmatized populations is one that has never been tested. Research suggests that the Internet is effective in dealing with some populations, such as disturbed adolescents (Zimmerman, 1987a, 1987b, 1989), but what we do not know is whether similar effects will be found in other untested populations so often discussed in the e-health literature.

Research should also look deeper into client satisfaction, client expectations, and alliances as they relate to adjunctive e-health therapy.

Video games have been used to promote psychoeducation, especially to children, although there does not appear to be any research thus far regarding its validity. In one study, a video game was designed as a psychoeducation tool for children with cancer, who were then asked about their preferences regarding information about the disease. The study reported that most children would want to play the game and found video games to be a preferable medium for learning about the disease. Several games have added treatment components to promote healthy living (such as Escape From Obeez City and Squire's Quest) and could in theory be used as adjunctive tools for overweight children. Further research should be done to test the effectiveness of such tools.

E-mail can also be an effective form of adjunctive therapy, although the research in this area is greatly lacking. In treating adolescents with eating disorders, Yager (2001) has found that e-mail allows for increased contact with clients, and allows for clients to gather thoughts and communicate when they are inspired to do so instead of when they have scheduled appointments. Yager (2001) has also found that some patients tend to express themselves more freely and less formally, in a way that he has found to be clinically relevant. Finally, Yager (2001) provides discussion on the idea that correspondence regarding things such as homework through e-mail frees up office visits for more "meaningful" issues. Although these are all worthy observations, there is no data to support whether this is an effective tool.

The general consensus among e-health providers is that e-therapy is not appropriate for suicidal patients. Many studies used suicidality as an exclusion criterion; however, the Israeli online crisis support, which specifically offered support for suicidal individuals, center SAHAR has been widely used, and is said to have successful feedback by users (Barak, 2007). Additionally, Fenichel et al. (2002) concluded that there is no evidence to support that online therapy for suicidal or crisis patients would not be suitable, and that it is instead comparable to the widely accepted telephone crisis call program.

TECHNOLOGY

Virtual reality exposure has been found to be effective as primary therapy for specific phobias (such as spiders and heights) and posttraumatic stress syndrome; however, the technology has not yet made it possible to integrate virtual reality exposure in a self-help format (Rothbaum et al., 2002; Carlin et al., 1997). As online technology continues to expand, it seems a likely possibility that the future will hold a "create-your-own-fear" exposure site, in which realistic exposure would be possible from a computer screen, which could be supplemented with therapist interaction.

Technology can be a great tool, but then again it does face Murphy's Law—anything that can go wrong with a given technology, will. Extensive storage backups should be in place when dealing with any therapy-related computer data, and a backup plan should be present for when the technology goes wrong. Also, troubleshooting information (or a contact phone number to provide troubleshooting information) should be made available to clients interacting with e-health technologies, even if it is as simple as informing them to wait for some time in the event of a server crash. (Kraus et al., 2004)

PRIVACY/ETHICS

As noted earlier in this chapter, some forms of adjunctive e-health tend to see online or computer counseling as the primary therapy, with telephone or face-to-face sessions supplementing these computer sessions. In this case, it would be feasible to see a client in a different state or country, at which point jurisdictional lines in licensing can be an issue (Hsiung, 2003).

The potential for computers to keep client and user data safe surpasses that of paper storage, but only with sufficient understanding and precaution (Grohol, 1999). Any therapist participating in adjunctive e-health should have a thorough understanding of encryption and data security to keep all client communications safe. As would be expected, a thorough consent should be provided with specific costs and risks to participating in any Internet or technological interactions, and therapists should only practice that in which they are competent.

Although several ethics codes exist pertaining to e-health, they tend to be generic and intuitive [ISMHO: Society for Mental Health Online (received July 2007). www.ismho.com; HONCOD: HON Code of Conduct for medical and health Web sites. (received July 2007). Kraus et al., 1999 www.hon.ch/honcode/conduct.html, ethicscode.com]. Following these codes is necessary, but not sufficient—it is up to the practitioner to realize what specific risks and ethical issues exist when dealing with specific technologies. For example, when exchanging client e-mails, the client must be informed that he or she holds the burden to keep her own e-mail safe from others sharing a computer. Many authorities in the field suggest that clinicians using e-mail or other digital interactions should ask the client to sign a separate consent form, informing the client specifically of the added risks to confidentiality (Yager, 2001).

The newness of the e-health field leaves many questions unanswered in terms of what is possible, what should be expected, and what precautions should be taken; this leaves the specific ethical decisions largely in the hands of the individual practitioners until the field is more widely recognized.

However, it is hoped that the therapist can consider augmenting their effectiveness by the use of computer technology. Perhaps they should assess client's adeptness at computers as well as their access to computers. If this is acceptable, they can then consider strategies that would allow them to either augment or replace face-to-face sessions with evidence-based e-health interventions. In addition, organizations responsible for prevention (see, for example, unr.sapac.edu) may use e-health to attempt to implement cost-effective prevention programs.

REFERENCES

Adachi, Y., Sato, C., Yamatsu, K., et al. (2007). A randomized controlled trial on the long-term effects of a 1-month behavioral weight control program assisted by computer tailored advice. *Behaviour Research & Therapy*, *45*(3), 459–470.

Barak, A. (2007). Emotional support and suicide prevention through the Internet: A field project report. *Computers in Human Behavior*, *10*(3), 407–417.

Carlbring, P., Brunt, S., Bohman, S., et al. (2007). Internet vs. paper and pencil administration of questionnaires commonly used in panic/agoraphobia research. *Computers in Human Behavior*, *23*(3), 1421–1434.

Carlbring, P., Gunnarsdottir, M., & Hedensjo, L. (2007). Treatment of social phobia: Randomised trial of internet-delivered cognitive-behavioral therapy with telephone support. *British Journal of Psychiatry*, *190*(2), 123–128.

Carlbring, P., Bohman, S., Brunt, S., et al. (2006). Remote treatment of Panic Disorder: A Randomized Trial of Internet-Based Cognitive Behavior Therapy Supplemented with Telephone Calls.

Carlbring, P., Westling, B.E., Ljungstrand, et al. (2001). Treatment of panic disorder via the Internet: A randomized trial of a self-help program. *Behavior Therapy*, *32*(4), 751–765.

Carlin, A.S., Hoffman, H.G. & Weghorst, S. (1997). Virtual reality and tactile augmentation in the treatment of spider phobia: A case report. *Behaviour Research & Therapy*, *35*(2), 153–158.

Celio, A.A., Winzelberg, A.J., & Wilfley, D.E. (2000). Reducing risk factors for eating disorders: Comparison of an Internet- and a classroom-delivered psychoeducational program. *Journal of Consulting and Clinical Psychology*, *68*(4), 650–657.

Connelly, M.A. (2005). 'Headstrong': A computer-based cognitive-behavioral intervention for recurrent pediatric headache. *Abstracts International: Section B: The Sciences and Engineering*, *65*(11-B), 6040.

Demaso, D.R., Marcus, N.E., Kinnamon, C., & Gonzalez-Heydrich, J. (2006). Depression experience journal: A computer-based intervention for families facing childhood depression. *Journal of the American Academy of Child & Adolescent Psychiatry*, *45*(2), 156–165.

Derrig-Palumbo, K. & Zeine, F. (2005). *Online Therapy: A Therapist's Guide to Expanding Your Practice*. New York: W.W. Norton & Company, Inc.

Erdman, H.P., Klein, M.H., Greist, J.H. (1985). Direct patient computer interviewing. *Journal of Consulting and Clinical Psychology*, *53*(6), 760–773.

Fenichel, M., Suler, J., Barak, A., et al. (2002). Myths and realities of online clinical work. *Cyber Psychology & Behavior*, *5*(5), 481–497.

Ferriter, M. (1993). Computer aided interviewing and the psychiatric social history. *Social Work and Social Sciences Review*, *4*(3), 255–263.

Glanz, K., Murphy, S. Moylan, J., et al. (2006). Improving dietary self-monitoring and adherence with hand-held computers: A pilot study. *American Journal of Health Promotion*, *20*(3), 165–170.

Grohol, J.M. (1999). *The Insider's Guide to Mental Health Resources Online* (p. 309). New York: Guilford Press.

Hicks, C.L., von Baeyer, C.L., & McGrath, P.J. (2006). Online psychological treatment for pediatric recurrent pain: A randomized evaluation. *Journal of Pediatric Psychology*, *31*(7), 724–736.

Horesh, N. (2001). Self-report vs. computerized measures of impulsivity as a correlate of suicidal behavior. *The Journal of Crisis Intervention and Suicide Prevention*, *22*(1), 2001.

Hsiung, R.C. (2000). The best of both worlds: An online self-help group hosted by a mental health professional. *CyberPsychology & Behavior*, *3*(6), 935–950.

Hsiung, R.C. (2002). *E-Therapy: Case Studies, Guiding Principles, and the Clinical Potential of the Internet*. New York: W.W. Norton & Company, Inc.

Hsiung, R.C. (2003). E-therapy: Opportunities, dangers and ethics to guide practice. In R. Wooten, P. Yellowlees, & P. McLaren (Eds.), *Telepsychiatry and e-Mental Health*. London: The Royal Society of Medicine Press Ltd.

Kenardy, J.A., Dow, M.G.T., & Johnston, D.W. (2003). A comparison of delivery methods of cognitive-behavioral therapy for panic disorder: An international multicenter trial. *Journal of Consulting and Clinical Psychology*, *71*(6), 1068–1075.

Klein, B. & Richards, J.C. (2001). A brief Internet-based treatment for panic disorder. *Behavioral and Cognitive Psychotherapy*, *29* (1), 113–117.

Kraus, R., Stricker, G., Hillowe, B.V., & Hall, J.E. (1999). Guidelines for mental Health and Healthcare Practice Online. *ethicscode.com*

Kraus, R., Zack, J.S., & Stricker, G. (2004). *Online counseling: A handbook for mental health professionals*. New York: Elsevier Science.

Leibert, T., Archer, J. Jr., Munson, J., & York, G. (2006). An exploratory study of client perceptions of internet counseling and the therapeutic alliance. *Journal of Mental Health Counseling*, *28*(1), 69–83.

Lerner, J., Franklin, M.E., & Meadows, E.A. (1998). Effectiveness of a cognitive behavioral treatment program for trichotillomania: An uncontrolled evaluation. *Behavior Therapy*, *29*(1), 157–171.

Leusink, P.M. & Aarts, E. (2006). Treating erectile dysfunction through electronic consultation: A pilot study. *Journal of Sex & Marital Therapy*, *32*(5), 401–407.

Marks, I.M., Mataix-Cols, D., & Kenwright, M. (2003). Pragmatic evaluation of computer-aided self-help for anxiety and depression. *Journal of Psychiatry*, *183*(1), 57–65.

Mataix-Cols, D. & Marks, I.M. (2006). Self-help with minimal therapist contact for obsessive-compulsive disorder: A review. *European Psychiatry*, *21*(2), 75–80.

Mouton-Odum, S., Keuthen, N.J., & Wagener, P.D. (2006). StopPulling.com: An interactive, self-help program for trichotillomania. *Cognitive and Behavioral Practice*, *13*(3), 215–226.

Przeworski, A. & Newman, M.G. (2006). Efficacy and utility of computer-assisted cognitive behavioral therapy for anxiety disorders. *Clinical Psychologist*, *10*(2), 43–53.

Richards, J.C. & Alvarenga, M.E. (2002). Extension and replication of an Internet-based treatment program for panic disorder. *Cognitive Behaviour Therapy*, *31*(1), 41–47.

Richards, J.C., Richardson, V., & Pier, C. (2003). The relative contributions of negative cognitions and self-efficacy to severity of panic attacks in panic disorder. *Behaviour Change*, *19*(2), 2002.

Ritterband, L.M., Cox, D.J., & Walker, L.S. (2003). An Internet intervention as adjunctive therapy for pediatric encopresis. *Journal of Consulting and Clinical Psychology*, *71*(5), 910–917.

Robertson, L., Smith, M., Castle, D., & Tannenbaum, D. (2006). Using the Internet to enhance the treatment of depression. *Australasian Psychiatry*, *14*(4), 413–417.

Rothbaum, B.O., Hodges, L., & Anderson, P.L. (2002). Twelve-month follow-up of virtual reality and standard exposure therapies for the fear of flying. *Journal of Consulting and Clinical Psychology*, *70*(2), 428–432.

Shiffman, S. & Paty, J.A. (2000). The efficacy of computer-tailored smoking cessation material as a supplement. *Archives of Internal Medicine*, *160*(11), 1675–1682.

Van Diest, S.L., Van Lankveld, J.J., & Leusink, P.M. (2007). Sex therapy through the Internet for men with sexual dysfunctions: A pilot study. *Journal of Sex & Marital Therapy*, *33*(2), 115–133.

Wijndaele, K., Matton, L., Duvigneaud, N., et al. (2007). Reliability, equivance and respondent preference of computerized versus paper-an-pencil mental health questionnaires. *Computers in Human Behavior*, *23*(4), 1958–1973.

Winzelberg, A. (1997). The analysis of an electronic support group for individuals with eating disorders. *Computers in Human Behavior*, *13*(3), 393–407.

Whitfield, G., Hinshelwood, R., & Pashely, A. (2006). The impact of a novel computerized CBT CD rom (overcoming depression) offered to patients referred to clinical psychology. *Behavioral and Cognitive Psychotherapy*, *34*(1), 1–11.

Yager, J. (2001). E-mail as a therapeutic adjunct in the outpatient treatment of anorexia nervosa: Illustrative case material and discussion of the issues. *International Journal of Eating Disorders*, *29*, 125–138.

Zabinski, M.F., Celio, A.A., Wilfley, D.E., et al. (2003). Prevention of eating disorders and Obesity via the Internet. *Cognitive Behavioral Therapy*, *32*(3), 137–150.

Zimmerman, D.P. (1987a). A psychological comparison of computer-mediated and face-to-face language use among severely disturbed adolescents. *Adolescence*, *22*, 827–840.

Zimmerman, D.P. (1987b). Effects of computer conferencing on the language use of emotionally disturbed adolescents. *Behavior Research Methods, Instruments & Computers*, *19*, 224–230.

Zimmerman, D.P. (1989). Electronic language: A study of word processing by the emotionally disturbed children and adolescents in residential treatment. *Behavior Research Methods, Instruments & Computers*, *21*, 181–186.

6

SUPPORT GROUPS

MICHAEL A. CUCCIARE

Veterans Affairs Palo Alto Health Care System and Stanford University School of Medicine

INTRODUCTION

WHAT IS SOCIAL SUPPORT?

The phrase "social support" most commonly refers to interpersonal transactions that express emotional concern, provide instrumental assistance and information relevant to a particular topic, or enhance the process of self-evaluation or problem solving (Taylor et al., 1986). It also includes the perception, by those involved in the transaction, that some kind of assistance is being provided and that it has the consequence of being helpful (Reif et al., 1995).

Social support can be divided into two general types—emotional and instrumental support. Emotional support consists of a wide variety of behaviors that have the consequence of reducing or alleviating uncomfortable emotions such as anxiety, uncertainty, or stress (Sandstrom, 1996). Emotional support commonly contains some type of verbal expression that may take the form of positive affirmations, words of reassurance, empathy, whereas nonverbal expressions can involve tangible items such as flowers or cards. In contrast, instrumental support includes the provision of tangible items or goods such as food or groceries, transportation, assistance with household tasks, money, or shelter (Finfgeld-Connett, 2005). Social support can be provided by a person who is physically present or by simply knowing that someone is available to provide support when needed, or by receiving tangible items such as cards or flowers (Gurowka & Lightman, 1995; Hupcey, 2001). Social support can come from many sources including family members, friends, or support groups (SGs) (Finfgeld-Connett, 2005; McLean, 1995; Taylor et al., 1986).

WHAT ARE SUPPORT GROUPS?

SGs are perhaps the most commonly discussed organized method for delivering social support and are used throughout the fields of mental health, social services, and medicine to address a wide variety of concerns and problems. For example, research supports the use of SGs for families of persons diagnosed with schizophrenia (Chien et al., 2004) and other severe mental illnesses (Heller et al., 1997), persons diagnosed with Alzheimer's disease (Snyder et al., 2007) and their caregivers (Bank et al., 2006), persons with cancer (Docherty, 2004; McLean, 1995; Spiegel et al., 1989) and their partners (Bultz et al., 2000), persons with diabetes (Oren et al., 1996), HIV/AIDS (Funck-Brentano et al., 2005), as well as persons experiencing stress and bereavement (Reif et al., 1995), and the consequences of suicidal behavior (Clark & Goldney, 1996).

SGs typically involve two or more people coming together to share mutual experiences with the purpose of better managing uncomfortable emotions such as depression, isolation, and/or alienation. SGs range from those developed by a few individuals from grass roots organizations to professionally developed SGs run by hospitals and clinics, and professional organizations (e.g., Alzheimer's Association and American Cancer Society). The main differences between SGs developed by grass roots and professional organizations is in the "ownership" of the program, how they are funded (e.g., member donations or by private organizations), and level of resources that can greatly impact their availability to potential members (McLean, 1995). For example, well-funded SGs like those offered by the professional organizations such as the Alzheimer's Association are widely available to persons in the community in terms of the number and frequency of meetings.

There are numerous organizations that provide SGs for individuals experiencing particular psychologically or medically related stressors. Some of the most widely known organizations that provide SGs include: The American Cancer Society (www.cancer.org); American Diabetes Association (www.diabetes.org); Depression and Bipolar Alliance (www.dbsalliance.org/); Alzheimer's Association (www.alz.org); National Alliance for the Mentally Ill (www.nami.org); and American Association of Suicidology (http://www.suicidology.org/).

Most, if not all, SGs have a particular content focus such as providing support to families of persons with serious mental illness or caregivers of persons with Alzheimer's disease. Despite having various foci, the structure of SGs is quite similar. SGs typically have between three and ten members (although larger groups have been reported, see Heller et al., 1997) who meet regularly (e.g., weekly or monthly) to share their experiences, thoughts, and feelings regarding a specific issue with the other members in the group (including the group leader). The groups are commonly open meaning that members can come and go as they please. Group meetings are often unstructured and follow the needs of the specific members. Despite the relatively unstructured nature, the primary purpose of SG meetings is to receive and provide emotional and instrumental support in an attempt to minimize the impact of distressing affect such as depression, hopelessness, and fear.

SGs can be led by both professionals and consumers. In many cases, professionals who run SGs have had some experience with the particular topic (e.g., had a family diagnosed with cancer), but this is not always the case. Group leaders serve a variety of purposes such as providing guidance, advice, and to serve as a moderator to group discussions. Consumers who lead SGs may have once been members and commonly have some experience with the content of interest (e.g., was once or currently a dementia caregiver). Professionals in various fields including psychology, social work, and medicine can also serve as leaders of SGs. SGs are usually free of charge and are located throughout the community, making them widely accessible to interested individuals. Large organizations such as the Alzheimer's Association provide a listing of ongoing SGs that allows users to conveniently search for SGs that occur on specific days and times in their community. In contrast, groups run by consumers or grass roots organizations often have limited financial resources and "person power" and therefore may offer SGs at limited days/times. Due to the proliferation of the Internet, many organizations are now offering SGs on the web using chat rooms, blogs, and telephone support. This method of delivering SGs can be particularly useful to individuals who experience geographical or other limitations to accessing SGs in person.

HOW COMMON ARE SUPPORT GROUPS?

It is difficult to determine just how many SGs are available in the United States at any one time and how many individuals are utilizing these services. This is partly the case because new SGs are constantly emerging and many individuals attending SGs do so irregularly. It is also important to point out that an additional difficulty in tracking the number of SGs and the number of attendees is due to many SGs now being available on the web. A review of the literature reveals a lack of research estimating both how many SGs exist physically and on the web in the United States, and the number of individuals utilizing such services. An additional reason for this finding may be that the phrase "support group" is sometimes used interchangeably with phrases such as "peer support," "group therapy," "mutual self-help" (e.g., Alcoholics Anonymous), and "psychoeducational" groups. Therefore, to limit the focus of this chapter, an emphasis will be placed on groups that emphasize the provision of emotional and other types of support, e.g., instrumental. This focus is an attempt to make a distinction between groups that are supportive in nature and those that are primarily and directly focused on behavior change. It is important to note that SGs can impact the ways members think, feel, and behave through group processes (e.g., emotional support); however, the alteration of behavior is not generally the primary objective of such groups (Finfgeld-Connett, 2005).

The rest of this chapter will focus on describing key process variables hypothesized to contribute to the effectiveness of SGs. Key process variables for SGs with a wide variety of content foci will be presented along with a discussion of outcomes related to these variables. Next, this chapter will discuss how SGs fit into the larger picture of treatment plan development. This discussion will focus primarily on how providers might integrate SG into the stepped care model of treatment planning. This chapter concludes with a general discussion of further research endeavors that may help facilitate the integration of SG into comprehensive treatment plans, and current efforts of disseminating and implementing SGs into practice.

SUPPORT GROUPS AND KEY PROCESS VARIABLES

SGs vary widely in terms of the specific problems they are designed to address, e.g., provide support to persons with severe mental illness or physical health problems such as HIV/AIDS. Despite these apparent differences in content, the processes thought to contribute to the effectiveness of SGs are presumed to be similar aside from the particular content focus of the group. SGs have the broad primary focus of providing a group context in which individuals with a common condition or who share a set of similar life circumstances can receive and share emotional support. The purpose of providing emotional support in the group context is to help members minimize the impact of affective distress, and normalize emotional experiences (Oren et al., 2007), i.e., to send the message "there are others who share your experiences." This broad therapeutic target is addressed by allowing member's to discuss their experiences with one another in an effort not only to reduce the impact of emotional stress but also to improve members' understanding of themselves, their emotional reactions to a wide variety of stressful situations, and improve self-care (Oren et al., 2007). Oren and colleagues suggest that Yalom's (1995) 11 factors that encompass an effective group therapy experience also pertain to the effectiveness of SGs. Dr Yalom's 11 factors are

- the instillation of hope;
- universality (e.g., "I'm not the only person experiencing this distress");
- imparting of information;
- altruism;
- the corrective recapitulation of the primary family group (the reworking of family dynamics in the group);
- development of socialization skills (learning how to communicate effectively);
- imitative behavior (modeling others behavior);
- interpersonal learning;
- group cohesiveness;
- catharsis/insight;
- existential factors.

Researchers have argued that these factors play a key role in the effectiveness of SGs despite the fact that SGs can vary widely in terms of their specific content focus (e.g., severe mental illness or cancer). Furthermore, these group processes can be subsumed into general "support factors" that include emotional and instrumental support, and information and education that have been shown to contribute to positive health outcomes in SG participants (Brentano et al., 2005). Unfortunately, space limitations of this chapter prevent a thorough review of the many SGs (and their varying content) presented and researched in the literature. However, the following section provides several notable and representative examples of SGs, and discusses recent research that highlights both the key processes involved in SGs and their impact on various psychosocial and health-related outcomes.

KEY PROCESS AND OUTCOMES VARIABLES ORGANIZED BY CONTENT FOCUS

FAMILIES OF ADULTS WITH SEVERE MENTAL ILLNESS

The phrase "severe mental illness" often refers to persons with psychological problems that are so debilitating that the person's ability to engage functional and occupational activities is severely impaired. Schizophrenia and bipolar disorder are often referred to as severe mental illnesses (Heller et al., 1997). Research has shown that several key process variables occur within the context of SGs for family members of adults with severe mental illness that contribute to positive outcomes. Heller and colleagues (1997) studied SGs that were led by both professionals and family members, with some occurring once a month, while others occurring more frequently (once a week). The most common severe mental illnesses reported by members were schizophrenia and bipolar disorder. Findings showed two beneficial general group processes reported by those attending the group—informational and relationship benefits. Informational benefits were characterized as an increase in members' understanding of severe mental illness, which resulted in such outcomes as (1) knowing how to better advocate for a family member with a severe mental illness and (2) coping more effectively with affective distress. Members demonstrating this benefit also showed increased knowledge of their family member's diagnosis and resources available in the community, as well as a better understanding of treatments for the diagnosis. SG participants reported relationship benefits, which included an improved ability to cope with the social stigma attached to having a family member with a severe mental illness, manage anger toward that family member, and improved overall relationships with all members of the family.

FAMILIES OF ADULTS WITH SCHIZOPHRENIA

Similarly, research on SGs for families of adults with schizophrenia suggests that the effectiveness of such services is dependent on the extent to which they provide emotional and informational support to members (Cuijpers, 1999). When achieved, these processes can result in many positive outcomes for families.

A recent randomized controlled trial (RCT) investigating the effectiveness of a 12-week SG for families of adults with schizophrenia found that upon completion of an SG group, family members reported significant reductions in their experience of burden associated with providing care to their family member and improvements in overall family functioning (Chien et al., 2004). Family members in the SG condition showed significant improvements in their ability to communicate with one another, participate in their respective roles, and engage in and listen to affective content when compared with a treatment-as-usual control condition receiving outpatient services. Researchers hypothesized that these outcomes were related to increased understanding and knowledge about schizophrenia, the ways in which it can impact a person's life, and improvements in coping with the emotional demands of providing care to an individual with a severe mental health problem (Chien et al., 2004). These findings provide further support to the notion that emotional and information-based support is key to the effectiveness of SGs.

BEREAVED PERSONS

Discussion of death and dying is a common component of many SGs, particularly those focused on potential terminal illnesses such as cancer; and certainly SGs focused on bereavement. SGs with this content focus allow bereaved persons to share their emotional struggles with persons who have also experienced a loss. It is also thought that the emotional expression of such struggles serves as a key cathartic process in helping bereaved persons learn how to better manage affective distress. A recent study conducted by Reif et al. (1995) provides empirical support for this assumption, while further elucidating other important processes that contribute to positive outcomes in participants. Group process factors such as number of participants, attitude toward the helpfulness of others, amount of help seeking, and degree of satisfaction with the emotional support provided by other members was shown to play a significant role in the effectiveness of these services. Specific findings indicated that as the number of members decreased and attitudes toward their helpfulness declined, the extent to which group participants sought out help from remaining members and their satisfaction with their help decreased. These findings demonstrate that group size and members' attitude toward the helpfulness of other members are related and play an important role in determining participants' satisfaction with the group process and the degree to which they will engage in emotional and/or instrumental support seeking.

In summary, research shows that two important processes are involved in an effective SG—emotional and instrumental (including the provision of information and education) support. Specific relationships between group size and attitudes toward group members' helpfulness contribute to the satisfaction and frequency of participants' help-seeking behavior have also been identified.

FAMILIES IMPACTED BY SUICIDE

SGs designed for survivors of parental suicide have similar therapeutic processes as those developed for bereaved persons. Of course, this makes sense as these two groups create a context in which members can provide and receive emotional support surrounding the death of a family member. The empirical literature on SGs for persons who have lost a family to suicide is small; however, a recent article by Mitchell et al. (2007) provides a theoretical framework for supportive interventions for this population of individuals. They suggest that supportive interventions may be useful particularly for children who have lost a parent to suicide. They argue that the Yalom's (1995) 11 curative factors for group therapy may also apply to children, especially the instillation of hope, emphasizing universality (e.g., "other people have also lost a parent") and interpersonal learning, facilitating group cohesion and catharsis, and imparting information. The instillation of hope in a group context may have particular importance in that it can allow bereaved children to begin trying out new ways of interacting with group members and the world around them (Mitchell et al., 2007).

Mitchell and colleagues developed an 8-week SG for bereaved children called the "Children's SOS Bereavement Support Group" (see Mitchell et al., 2007, for an outline of the SG). It is facilitated by a registered nurse and welcomes children between the ages of 7 and 13 years. Roughly 6–8 children attend the group weekly over an 8-week period. The SG generally follows Yalom's (1995) 11 factors and includes (1) an information/education component that centers on a discussion of suicide and why it happens, (2) the sharing of emotions regarding their parent's suicide, and a focus on developing hope and an appreciation for what other members have gone through, (3) a discussion of grief, and (4) a discussing of how other people react to them. The authors of this particular SG did not report any outcomes related to this specific SG. Other researchers have shown that SGs for suicide survivors can result in lessening the stigma of suicide (Clark & Goldney, 1995); however, in general, outcome data are lacking.

DEMENTIA CAREGIVERS

SGs for caregivers of persons with dementia are common in many communities throughout the United States, and this is mostly attributed to the proliferation of such agencies as the Alzheimer's Association. These SGs, like most, are conducted by having interested dementia caregivers come to a local chapter of the Alzheimer's Association, which allows them to participate in person with other caregivers. However, despite the effectiveness supportive interventions for reducing the negative health outcomes associated with dementia caregiving (e.g., high rates of depression, compromised immune system), many caregivers are often unable to seek out these services due to a wide variety of barriers (Wright et al., 1987). Some of the barriers found by Wright and Colleagues include difficulties arranging respite for carereceivers and scheduling conflicts with multiple healthcare visits.

Recent research has found that SGs for dementia caregivers can be effectively delivered through telephone. Bank and colleagues (2006) developed an SG that dementia caregivers could access at home through telephone. Participants were ethnically diverse and included Cuban and White Americans. The content of the SG was chosen by the participants and included an educational (i.e., medication management, respite, dealing with problem behaviors) and supportive component (i.e., instrumental and emotional support). The SG was conducted by a clinician with at least a master's degree in psychology. Each session lasted an hour and was held roughly once every month. Results of the evaluation found that participants reported the group to be helpful in increasing their knowledge and skills related to caregiving. SG participants tended to attribute any benefit from attending the SG to the supportive and educational focus. This is a particularly interesting study in that the findings show that the benefits of attending SGs can be obtained through the use of information technology.

FAMILIES OF PERSONS (AND PERSONS) WITH CANCER

Persons with cancer

Group-based supportive services have been shown to lead to important health benefits for persons with cancer and their families (Bultz et al., 2000; Spiegel, 1979; Spiegel et al., 1989). Research findings show that these services effectively tend to focus on helping group members deal with death and dying, communicate more effectively with their oncologists and treatment team, establish more collaborative working relationship with their treatment team, and increase family involvement in all aspects of the treatment process (e.g., improving communication among family members) (Spiegel, 1979). Dr Spiegel and colleagues' (1989) research in this area shows that supportive interventions that have their primary focus to help members better deal with death and dying, can lead to an increased lifespan in persons with cancer. In a classic study, Dr Spiegel and colleagues (1989) showed that women diagnosed with metastatic breast cancer assigned to a group-based support intervention had an average increased lifespan of 18 months when compared with similar individuals assigned to control condition. Furthermore, the researcher hypothesized that social support played a key role in this outcome. Specifically, the researchers noted that the group provided a safe context for members to express and receive emotional support. This was at least partially based on the observation that the members in the group developed an intense emotional bond with each other and exhibited a strong sense of acceptance with respect to their diagnosis. It was also stated that the increased lifespan observed in the experimental condition may have been associated with members' ability to mobilize resources more efficiently, better adhere to medication and treatment recommendations, and/or by improving dietary habits—all thought to be a consequence of reducing affective distress (Spiegel et al., 1989).

Partners of women with breast cancer

SGs developed for partners of women with breast cancer typical involve two key processes, education and emotional support, and research shows that these processes lead to improvements in psychosocial functioning for both women with breast cancer and their partners (Bultz et al., 2000). The SG developed by Bultz and colleagues met once a week for 1.5–2 hours over 6 weeks. It was lead by two psychologists and consisted of the two primary processes—education and support. Sessions 1 and 2 were focused on educating partners on the medical and psychosocial aspects of cancer. For example, in session 2, researchers invited an oncologist specializing in breast cancer to discuss the staging, treatment, and other relevant medical aspects of breast cancer. This allowed the partners of women with breast cancer to ask questions concerning the patient's illness. Session 3 through 6 were focused on providing emotional support and were less structured and focused. These sessions tended to focus on helping partners deal with the emotional aspects of their patient's illness such as allowing partners to explore their feelings, fears, and anxieties about the illness, as well as discuss particular challenges such as how to communicate and provide support with their partner about cancer, sexuality, and discuss fears concerning recurrence and death. These two processes were shown to result in partners reporting less mood disturbance upon completion of the SG when compared with control condition. In addition, results of the postassessment showed that patients whose partners received the SG reported less mood disturbance and also greater support from their partner and increased satisfaction with their marriage.

PERSONS WITH HIV/AIDS

Adolescents with HIV

Psychodynamically oriented SGs have been shown to improve psychosocial and medical outcomes in HIV-positive adolescents. Funck-Brentano et al. (2005) developed and evaluated an SG that met for 90 minutes once every 6 weeks for 1 year. The SG was led by two therapists trained in psychodynamic and family therapy. The groups were unstructured, which allowed members to develop their own discussions and share their feelings whenever they chose to do so. The therapeutic processes involved in this SG includes (see Funck-Brentano et al., 2005)

- fostering group cohesiveness and trust;
- providing a group context for members to share feelings and individual experiences;
- fostering individuality and safety when expressing emotions; and helping members be both a giver and a receiver of emotional support;
- promoting change and helping members identify and reach goals;
- working with group processes and managing a productive termination.

Researchers followed the adolescents participating in these SGs for 2 years to examine the impact on their psychosocial and medical well-being. They found that adolescents in the SG worried less and reported a decrease in negative perceptions about their illness at follow-up when compared with those in the control group. In addition, the percentage of adolescents showing an undetectable viral load dramatically increased from baseline to follow-up (30–80%), and this was not unchanged for participants in the control condition.

Adults with HIV/AIDS

Turner (2003) provides a historical overview of the development of SGs for adults with HIV/AIDS. The overview discusses processes involved in developing a group, its facilitation, and covers some of the basic themes and issues that arise throughout the lifespan of the SG. Turner suggests that group processes' purposes involved in SGs for persons with HIV/AIDS should center on

- increasing members' awareness of themselves and their illness;
- helping members adjust to their illness and its impact on their life;
- providing emotional and practical support for living with HIV;
- developing a supportive context for positive interactions to occur between members.

It is suggested that these groups cover a wide variety of issues relevant to having HIV/AIDS as well as issues relevant to the lifestyle of its members. For example, members provide each other with emotional support around family issues such as acceptance or non-acceptance of their gay lifestyle. Concerns about passing on the virus are often prevalent, particularly in the context of members deciding whether or not to seek companionship. Additional concerns about suffering and being dependent on others for care as the illness progresses are also frequently discussed.

PERSONS WITH DIABETES

SGs can positively influence medical outcomes in persons with diabetes. Oren et al. (1996) developed an SG that met for 10-week 90-minute meetings. The group was designed to focus on processes such as gaining a sense of community and personal insight into how diabetes impacts members' life, identifying and sharing emotions associated with having diabetes. Findings from the study showed that group members demonstrated decreased blood glucose levels at posttest when compared with baseline laboratory tests.

The group processes involved in this SG are outlined in their 10-week course schedule (see Oren et al., 1996 for a more thorough description):

- Week 1: Introductions of each member in which concerns, hopes, and goals are shared.
- Weeks 2–3: Identification of emotions and myths about diabetes.

- Weeks 4–5: Identification of stages of adaptation and emotions with respect to having diabetes; discussion of the risks of moralizing about "good" and "bad" blood glucose levels.
- Weeks 6–8: Members work on asserting themselves in ways that are consistent with their needs and feelings.
- Week 9: Information/education about diabetes is provided; members have an opportunity to ask a physician questions about diabetes.
- Week 10: Final meeting; provide emotional support and encouragement to members engaging in behavior change; goodbyes and telephone number exchange.

COST-EFFECTIVENESS OF SUPPORT GROUPS

Despite the relatively few studies directly examining the cost-effectiveness of SGs, their widespread usage is likely a consequence of them being relatively inexpensive to conduct. SGs often occur in community settings such as senior centers and churches, hospitals, and nonprofit agencies (Alzheimer's Association). SGs also tend to utilize volunteers to organize and commonly serve as facilitates of SGs, which reduce the cost of offering these services to the public.

Research directly examining the cost of conducting SGs is scarce. However, one relatively recent study conducted by Peak et al. (1995) provides an excellent example of how to conduct a cost-effectiveness analysis for psychosocial interventions. They found healthcare savings associated with attending an SG for spouses of frail elderly veterans. Spouses of frail elderly veterans were randomly assigned to an SG or usual care condition. Participants in the former condition agreed to attend SG meetings once a week for 8 weeks and then once a month for 10 months. The most common health problems identified by the care-giving spouse were diabetes, stroke, Parkinson's disease, and a variety of heart problems. A wide variety of outpatient and inpatient cost data were also collected from baseline to 1-year follow-up to estimate a total healthcare cost during that period of time. The researchers also conducted a thorough cost-analysis of the SG by estimating all costs associated with implementing the group including the cost of hiring a social worker to facilitate the group, time to arrange the group and handle phone calls, cost of refreshments, charges associated with a meeting room, secretarial support, telephone and utilities, and other various supplies. Their estimates revealed a total cost of $700 per participant to conduct the group. However, in their estimates of healthcare costs for the duration of the study and 1-year follow-up, researchers found that total (both outpatient and inpatient) care recipient costs were $7152 and $14 764 for the support and control condition, respectively. As can be seen, a difference in total healthcare costs of $7612 was found in the support condition lending support to the cost-effectiveness of SG for spouses providing care for a wide variety of health problems.

FOR WHOM ARE SUPPORT GROUPS PARTICULARLY BENEFICIAL?

As evident by the literature reviewed in this chapter, SGs can be used effectively to provide information/education, and emotional and instrumental support to a wide variety of populations, ethnicities, and age groups. This is especially important as SGs are a relatively inexpensive service to provide, as they can make use of volunteers and can be conducted conveniently in a wide variety of settings (e.g., community centers, churches, homes) (Sabir et al., 2003).

Although the empirical literature suggests that SGs can be helpful for many individuals, it is clear that SG participants vary in the extent to which they benefit from this type of service (Heller et al., 1997). Research has begun to work on identifying factors that can serve as predictors for determining which individuals might most benefit from attending SGs. Specifically, researchers are beginning to investigate specific participant characteristics (i.e., coping skills, health status, and demographic variables) that may play a role in predicating not only *who* will likely benefit, but *how* they might benefit (Docherty, 2004; Funck-Brentano et al., 2005; Heller et al., 1997; Sabir et al., 2003). The following section provides a review of this literature.

SUPPORT AND PHYSICAL HEALTH

One recent study by Heller and colleagues found demographic and health-related factors to be useful in predicting individuals who benefit most from attending an SG for families with severe mental illness. Specifically, family members who benefited most from the educational/information components of the group were those individuals who tended to (1) have less unmet service needs and informal support from relatives and friends outside of the SG, and (2) be very active in the group in terms of both the support they provided to others and the amount of support they received from the group. Heller's research group also found the physical health status of participants to be helpful in predicting participants receiving the greatest improvements in their interpersonal relationships as a result of attending the SG. Healthy individuals tended to show the greatest relationship benefits with respect to both their interactions with the family member diagnosed with the severe mental illness and the other members of the family.

COPING STYLES

Coping styles of persons diagnosed with cancer have been found to be associated with the benefits gained from supportive services. Docherty (2004) has found that the coping styles of "denial" and "shock," in response to a cancer diagnosis, are linked to the use of supportive and informational services. For example, patients reporting the use of denial as an initial response to receiving a cancer diagnosis tended to prefer reduced information about their care and an increased desire to have the responsibility of their care to remain with health-care professionals. In contrast, patients who responded to receiving a cancer diagnosis with shock gradually replaced this initial reaction with a more proactive style of coping as illustrated by an increased desire to acquire information about their illness. Both coping styles may have important implications for the design of SGs and which patients may benefit, at least initially after a diagnosis, from the informational/educational components. Accordingly, patients reacting to learning of their diagnosis might benefit, at least initially, from a larger proportion of emotional support and low levels of information. On the other hand, patients initially responding to such news with shock may be better suited to absorb a greater degree of information than individuals engaging in the former coping style.

ANXIETY

In their evaluation of SGs for adolescents diagnosed with HIV, Funck-Brentano et al. (2005) found that degree of conflict occurring between adolescents and parents was associated with SG participation. Their findings indicated that HIV-infected adolescents joining their SG were more likely to report significantly higher amounts of conflict with their parents. The type of conflict assessed centered on the extent to which parents had engaged in overprotective behaviors toward the adolescent. Researchers hypothesized that high levels of conflict may heighten preexisting levels of anxiety (most likely related to being infected with HIV) and thus increase adolescents' motivation for seeking support and subsequently attending an SG.

SIMILARITIES AMONG SUPPORT GROUP MEMBERS

Researchers have recently examined the role of similarity among group members in attempt to better predict the success of SGs for Alzheimer's caregivers (Sabir et al., 2003). The variables focused on included demographic (i.e., age and education), appraisal (e.g., satisfaction with caregiving responsibilities and day-to-day support,) and situational similarities (i.e., similarities in caregiving situation) among group members. It was predicted that similarities among group members on these variables would be positively associated with quality of relationships that developed in the group. However, the results did not support this hypothesis, and in fact, the only variable that seemed to enhance the relationship among caregivers was the shared experience of being a caregiver. The findings of this study have important implications for the design of SGs in that the matching of members on such characteristics as age, education, and various aspects of the caregiving situation seems unimportant in terms of predicting the quality of relationships among group members.

THE ROLE OF SUPPORT GROUPS IN STEPPED CARE TREATMENT PLANNING

SGs have an important role in treatment-planning process and, in particular, the stepped care model of treatment delivery. The low cost of delivering SGs makes them a useful service to have in the repertoire of healthcare organizations that utilize the stepped care model of treatment delivery. In the stepped care model, patients receive interventions along a continuum of care from least to most intensive (see O'Donohue et al., 2006). For example, psychological problems such as depression might be first addressed through relatively low-intensity intervention such as self-help books, SGs, and other interventions that do not necessarily require the presence of a licensed healthcare professional. These types of low-intensity interventions are considered *first level* care and are typically low-cost, and easily disseminated and implemented into healthcare settings. SGs are perhaps most appropriately administered as first level care as they are relatively inexpensive and can utilize nonprofessionals to facilitate and lead groups. In addition, SGs can consist of many members making them an efficient method for delivering emotional and instrumental support to persons in a wide variety of life circumstances, and suffering from various psychological and physical health problems. *Second level* care addresses clinical problems with nurses or social workers who may contact patients through phone or e-mail, conduct home visits, and utilize interventions that focus on problem solving and skills development. The second level utilizes skilled professionals that administer interventions that require both more time and skill to deliver than first level care. The *third level* of the stepped care model is designed to address the specific, individual needs of the patients (e.g., suicidal ideation, severe depression, lack of motivation). Third level care is the most time intensive and typically requires healthcare professionals with very specialized, highly skilled training. Using more than one level of care to address a patient's psychological problem is also quite common.

There are also several steps providers can take to maximize the effectiveness of SG (see Chapter 4 for a more thorough discussion of these factors). Some of the steps include becoming aware of local SGs for common patient problems and understanding which patients are particularly likely to benefit from such groups. Providers can familiarize themselves with local SGs by searching the Internet, talking with other providers (e.g., nurses and social workers) and nonprofit agencies that are commonly involved in organizing, and facilitating these groups. It is also suggested that providers read and understand the literature positing factors related to the effectiveness of SGs for individuals with certain characteristics.

As discussed earlier in this chapter, patients can benefit from SGs in a wide variety of ways and therefore might be matched to SG based on characteristics such as baseline coping skills, symptom severity, and degree of support outside of SG.

RESEARCH AGENDA

The prevalence and relative ease of organizing and facilitating SGs will no doubt contribute to the increase in the inclusion of SGs as an important component of comprehensive treatment plans. Thus, it is my opinion that future research should focus on better understanding both (1) which individuals might benefit most from SGs and (2) the cost-effectiveness of conducting such services in various healthcare settings. First, although there is a research literature investigating the various ways in which individuals might benefit from SGs, many of the studies are qualitative in nature and/or have small sample sizes (e.g., Docherty, 2004). Future research might incorporate the findings of studies, such as those reviewed earlier in this chapter, by examining factors that predict differential treatment effects using RCTs. For example, persons eligible for a particular SG might be assigned to conditions based on pretreatment assessment indicating a particular coping style or repertoire of skills. This would not only provide the field with more rigorous scientific evidence for understanding the differential treatment effects of SGs based on member skills or characteristics, but perhaps also provide implications for the pretreatment screening of such factors to match individuals to SGs with a particular emphasis (e.g., emotional and instrumental support vs education and information). Second, understanding the cost-effectiveness of SGs will become more important as healthcare organizations and providers begin to incorporate such support services into the treatment-planning process. Research in this area might focus on investigating the relative cost–benefit of using various providers (e.g., volunteers and licensed providers) as group facilitators, practical costs of conducting SGs in various settings (e.g., hospitals and community centers), and the cost–benefit of using SG for various time periods (i.e., the development of dose–response curves for SGs). It is also important to understand how SGs compare with other treatment components such as bibliotherapy or group therapies as these interventions are typically shorter in duration and in some cases perhaps less costly (as in the case of bibliotherapy).

DISSEMINATION AGENDA

Healthcare managers and providers would certainly benefit from research that further clarifies patient factors that predict the benefits of attending SGs; however, this does not mean that we should wait for this evidence to emerge before disseminating such services. As discussed earlier in this chapter, there are several studies that show that patients with a wide variety of psychological and physical health problems can benefit from attending an SG. Now, dissemination of these services appears to occur by either training of group facilitators (as in the case of many nonprofit agencies) or publishing protocols in scientific journals (e.g., Funck-Brentano et al., 2005; Oren et al., 1996).

Healthcare managers and providers interested in developing and/or implementing SGs into their setting might consult with nonprofit agencies delivering such services. Information on how to structure a group to maximize the exchange of support, practical group structure issues (e.g., number of participants, the use of a closed or open group, who to use as an ideal facilitator), and specific educational information on a particular topic might be gathered from talking with local or National agencies (see above for links to web addresses). In addition, this chapter provides a rough outline of the components involved in at least two SGs and additional components can be found in the references provided.

Information technology is also increasingly being used to disseminate SGs. Recent research published by Bank and colleagues (2006) is an excellent example of how an SG for dementia caregivers can be disseminated through telephone. There are also numerous examples of SGs on the World Wide Web. Searching the term "online support groups" in Google™ yields many websites that offer online SGs for persons with various life circumstances and health problems. For example, www.caregiving.com provides online SGs for dementia caregivers and cancercare.org (or http://supportgroups.cancercare.org/) provides SGs for persons with a wide variety of cancer diagnoses. As the use of the Internet continues to grow, we will almost surely see a parallel increase in the number of persons using the web as a method for accessing support services such as SGs.

CONCLUSION

SGs provide members with emotional and instrumental support as well as education and information about a wide variety of psychological and medical health problems. SGs have been found to be useful for both patients and caregiving family members, and may prove to be a useful adjunct to treatment plans utilizing evidence-based practices. As healthcare costs continue to rise and healthcare resources become scarcer, low-cost adjunctive services such as SGs will surely grow in demand among both patients and providers. A main goal of this chapter is to educate health care providers on the key process variables and related outcomes, and to provide a general overview of common health problems for which SGs have been developed. Furthermore, it is recommended that providers become aware of the various National and local agencies that provide SGs and health problems for which SGs have been developed so that they are better able to inform patients of the potential merits of participating in such services.

ACKNOWLEDGMENTS

The writing of this chapter was supported by the Health Services Research & Development Service of the U.S. Department of Veterans Affairs, Stanford University School of Medicine's Postdoctoral Research Fellowship in Health Services Research to M.A. Cucciare.

REFERENCES

Bank, A.L., Arguelles, S., Rubert, M., et al. (2006). The value of telephone support groups among ethnically diverse caregivers of persons with dementia. *The Gerontologist*, *46*(1), 134–138.

Bultz, B.D., Speca, M., Brasher, P.M., et al. (2000). A randomized controlled trial of a brief psychoeducational support group for partners of early stage breast cancer. *Psycho-Oncology*, *9*, 303–313.

Chien, W.T., Norman, I., & Thompson, D.R. (2004). A randomized controlled trial of a mutual support group for family caregivers of patients with schizophrenia. *International Journal of Nursing Studies*, *41*, 637–649.

Clark, S.E. & Goldney, R.D. (1995). Grief reactions and recovery in a support group for people bereaved by suicide. *Crisis: The Journal of Crisis Intervention and Suicide Prevention*, *16*(1), 27–33.

Cuijpers, P. (1999). The effects of family interventions on relative's burden: Meta-analysis. *Journal of Mental Health*, *8*, 275–285.

Docherty, A. (2004). Experience, functions and benefits of a cancer support group. *Patient Education and Counseling*, *55*, 87–93.

Finfgeld-Connett, D. (2005). Clarification of social support. *Journal of Nursing Scholarship*, *37*(1), 4–9.

Funck-Brentano, I., Dalban, C., Veber, C., et al. (2005). Evaluation of a peer support group therapy for HIV infected adolescents. *AIDS*, *19*(4), 1501–1508.

Gurowka, K.J. & Lightman, E.S. (1995). Supportive and unsupportive interactions as perceived by cancer patients. *Social Work in Health Care*, *21*, 71–88.

Heller, T., Roccoforte, J.A., Hsieh, K., et al. (1997). Benefits of support groups for families of adults with severe mental illness. *American Journal of Orthopsychiatry*, *67*(2), 187–198.

Hupcey, J.E. (2001). The meaning of social support for the critically ill patient. *Intensive and Critical Care Nursing*, *17*(4), 206–212.

McLean, B. (1995). Social support, support groups, and breast cancer: A literature review. *Canadian Journal of Community Mental Health*, *14*(2), 207–227.

Mitchell, A.M., Wesner, S., Garand, L., et al. (2007). A support group intervention for children bereaved by parental suicide. *Journal of Child and Adolescent Psychiatric Nursing*, *20*(1), 3–11.

O'Donohue, W.T., Cummings, N.A., Cucciare, M.A., et al. (2006). *Integrated behavioral health care: A guide to effective intervention*. New York: Prometheus Books.

Oren, M.L., Carella, M., & Helma, T. (1996). Diabetes support groups – study results and implications. *Employee Assistance Quarterly*, *11*(3), 1–20.

Peak, T., Toseland, R.W., & Banks, S.M. (1995). The impact of a souse-caregiver support group on care recipient health care costs. *Journal of Aging and Health*, *7*(3), 427–449.

Reif, L.V., Patton, M.J., & Gold, P.B. (1995). Bereavement, stress, and social support in members of a self-help group. *Journal of Community Psychology*, *23*, 292–306.

Sabir, M., Pillemer, K., Suitor, J., & Patterson, M. (2003). Predictors of successful relationships in a peer support program for Alzheimer's caregivers. *American Journal of Alzheimer's Disease and Other Dementias*, *18*(2), 115–122.

Sandstrom, K.I. (1996). Searching or information, understanding, and self-value: The utilization of peer support groups by gay men with HIV/AIDS. *Social Work in Health Care*, *23*, 51–74.

Snyder, L., Jenkins, C., & Joosten, L. (2007). Effectiveness of support groups for people with mild to moderate Alzheimer's disease: An evaluation survey. *American Journal of Alzheimer's Disease and Other Dementias*, *22*(1), 1–14.

Spiegel, D. (1979). Psychological support for women with metastatic carcinoma. *Psychosomatics*, *20*(11), 780–783.

Spiegel, D., Bloom, J.R., Kraemer, H.C., & Gottheil, E. (1989). Effect of psychosocial treatment on survival of patients with metastatic breast cancer. *The Lancet*, *2*(8668), 888–891.

Taylor, S.E., Falke, R.L., Shoptaw, S.J., & Lichtman, R.R. (1986). Social support, support groups, and the cancer patient. *Journal of Consulting and Clinical Psychology*, *54*(5), 608–615.

Turner, C. (2003). HIV support groups in a hospital setting. In B. Willinger & R. Alan (Eds.), *A History of Aids Social Work in Hospitals: A Daring Response to An Epidemic* (pp. 133–141). New York: Haworth Press.

Wright, S.D., Lund, D.A., Pett, M.A., & Casserta, M.S. (1987). The assessment of support group experiences by caregivers of dementia patients. *Clinical Gerontologist*, *6*, 35–39.

Yalom, I.D. (1995). *The theory and practice of group psychotherapy* (4th Ed.). New York: Basic Books (Perseus Books Group).

7

The Addiction Severity Index Multimedia Version

An Innovative Computerized Assessment Tool for Substance Abuse Treatment

Simon H. Budman,[*†] Stephen F. Butler,[*] and Albert J. Villapiano[*]

[*] *Inflexxion, Inc. and* [†] *Harvard Medical School*

The Addiction Severity Index (ASI) was first developed in 1980 by A. Thomas McLellan, the well-known addictionologist and his colleagues (1980, 1985, 1994, 1997). The ASI was designed as a structured clinical interview focusing on many key aspects of a substance abuser's life. Although the ASI assesses addiction problems, it also includes sections pertaining to medical problems, legal status, employment issues, family and social relationships, and psychiatric issues.

At the time that McLellan developed the ASI, clinical care for addictions was plagued by a myopic perspective that substance abusers in treatment should and could only deal with their drug or alcohol problems. Focusing on anything else was considered treatment resistance. Clinicians were taught never to trust substance abusers. Moreover, clinicians learned to be alert to abuser's denial or their ability to fool others and themselves by "changing the topic" from their *real* problems of drug or alcohol abuse. Furthermore, nothing could change unless or until the substance problem was addressed. Although it is clear that substance abusers may directly or indirectly obfuscate their addiction problems, McLellan perceived of the substance abuser with the respectful attitude that he or she is a "whole person" and that effective drug and alcohol treatment entails examining many aspects of the person's functioning.

The ASI was designed to provide a broad set of metrics regarding a client's functioning in many areas of life commonly associated with substance abuse problems. The ASI can also be administered on more than one occasion to measure outcomes in an individual client, or many clients' data can be aggregated and used to learn about the population of clients being seen at a given clinic, in a given region, and so on.

Since its initial development, it has been used worldwide and translated into 14 languages[1] including Spanish and Chinese. Many state and county systems in the United States use the ASI and the Federal Department of Veterans Affairs uses it as well. At present, it is the most widely used, standard measure for examining problem severity within and across substance abusers in treatment. It is also a very effective treatment-planning tool since McLellan and his colleagues (1994, 1997) demonstrated that if ASI severity scores are used to inform treatment interventions, clients stay in treatment longer, have more positive attitudes about treatment, and have better outcomes.

Because of the nature of the interview, McLellan has also maintained that the ASI needs to remain an interview rather than a paper and pencil self-report. Many questions included in the ASI are very personal and pertain to sensitive issues such as illegal activities and socially unacceptable behaviors. Therefore, the interview progresses from basic questions to more delicate and sensitive topics as the client's level of comfort with the interviewer increases. Because many individuals interviewed using the ASI have literacy problems or are functionally illiterate, they cannot be expected to read through a lengthy, complex interview and accurately rate their selections.

Our computerized version of the ASI, called the Addiction Severity Index Multimedia Version (ASI-MV®) will be the focus of this chapter. We have written previously about dissemination strategies for the ASI-MV® (Budman et al., 2003), but this presentation is the most broad-based, comprehensive elucidation regarding this powerful clinical tool.

PROBLEMS WITH THE ADDICTION SEVERITY INDEX

Although the ASI is very useful in a variety of ways, it is plagued by a number of important problems. Most of the issues associated with the ASI pertain to the fact that it is a lengthy, structured interview that requires extensive and repeated interviewer training to achieve and maintain reliability. To administer the ASI

[1] The European Monitoring Center for Drugs and Drug Addiction Website (http://eib.emcdda.europa.eu/index.cfm?fuseaction=public.Content&nNodeID=3538&sLanguageISO=EN) provides access to the ASI tool in 12 languages (English, Czech, Danish, French, Italian, Lithuanian, Hungarian, Dutch, Polish, Portuguese, Swedish, and Russian).

properly, a clinician requires many hours of preparation to achieve proficiency. There is also the problem of "rater drift," which means that human raters, after training on any standardized rating system, tend to drift away from the norm to which they were trained. These problems are further exacerbated by the fact that staff turnover at substance abuse treatment facilities is extremely high and job satisfaction is often very low. Substance abuse treatment facilities have employee turnover rates that average 50% per year (Carise et al., 2003). The ASI is also costly to administer; the administration of one ASI, even by an entry-level clinician costs at least $25, with fringe benefits (including scoring and report writing). For the most part, clinicians do not enjoy administering the ASI and view it as a hoop to jump through before "really getting down to treatment." Administering the ASI is even used as a "punishment" or remedy for bad clinicians in some settings. (Presumably, the structured interview helps mitigate the potential for damage.)

The ASI also requires the interviewer to contribute a number of subjective judgments that are intended to be rationalized through the training process. However, when the ASI is used for treatment placement and reimbursement decisions, the likelihood of biases influencing the process appears to be substantial. For example, if a certain threshold ASI severity score warrants a higher level of reimbursement, consciously or unconsciously, interviewers may tend to score clients as more severe.

THE ADDICTION SEVERITY INDEX-MULTIMEDIA VERSION

With these ASI problems in mind, the research and development team at Inflexxion began to work on a technological solution in the mid-1990s. With support from National Institute on Drug Abuse (NIDA), the Inflexxion team developed a computerized, client self-administered version of the ASI, with audio and video, entitled the Addiction Severity Index-Multimedia Version (ASI-MV®). Because minimal staff time (completion of a basic information screen) is necessary to administer the program, the ASI-MV® can be used for a fraction of the cost of a face-to-face ASI interview. Additionally, staff can focus on developing effective treatment plans rather than administering the ASI.

The ASI-MV® is offered in English, Spanish, and now Chinese (Mandarin and Cantonese). It is currently used in over 800 sites in the United States, Canada, and Australia. An online version, ASI-MV® Connect, was launched in the spring of 2007 and an adolescent version will be released in mid 2008. Although the online version actually resides on the user's desktop, it (like antivirus software) can be updated from the Internet on a regular basis and, in turn, can upload relevant information to the Internet automatically, in full compliance with HIPAA security and confidentiality requirements.

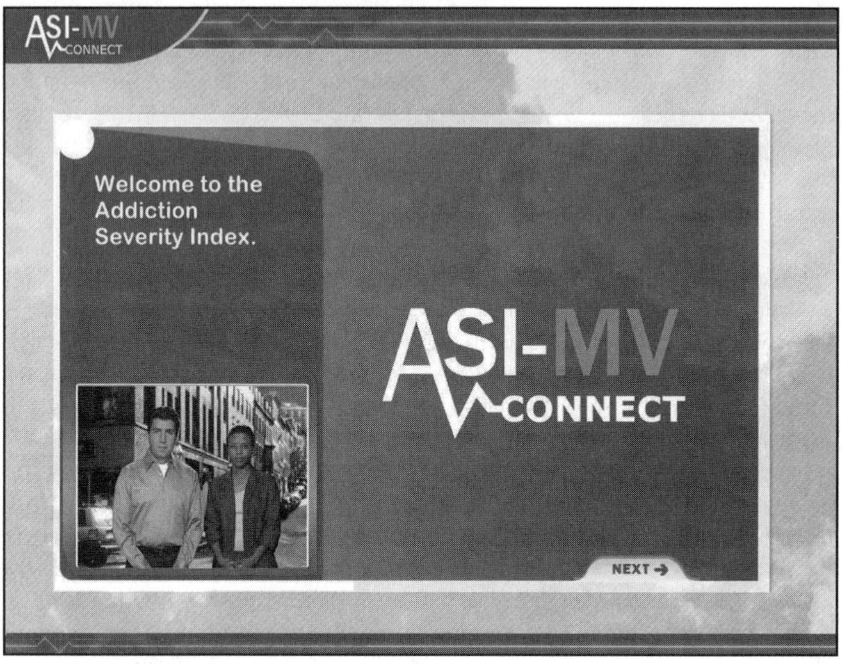

The ASI-MV® uses the metaphor of a virtual city to take users through the ASI questions. At the beginning of the program, the user is greeted by two "guides," George and Angela, who introduce the ASI-MV® (see screen shot above) and then "escort" the user to different offices within the city. The user "meets" on screen video interviewers at the offices representing various sections of the ASI (e.g., Medical, Legal, Family). For example, in the Medical section, the user meets a physician who asks medical-related questions. In the Legal section questions are asked by an attorney. Between sections, George or Angela return and escort the user to his or her next interview and offer encouragement, such as "You're halfway through." Interviewers in the program read the questions to users, but if an individual can read well and does not wish to wait for material to be read to them, he or she can navigate more quickly. The interviewee responds to questions by clicking the appropriate buttons that are highlighted as that response is read. Like a human interviewer, the ASI-MV® uses prior question responses to skip those items that are irrelevant to a particular interviewee. Thus, an individual who does not use heroin will not be asked any further questions about his or her heroin use.

The ASI-MV® screens are designed for use by clients with no prior computer experience. The large screen buttons are easy targets for the mouse (there is no fine scrolling, menu selection, or skillful manipulation of the mouse required). Users with no computer experience learn quickly to operate the mouse and appear to enjoy the experience as well. McLellan and his colleagues at Treatment Research Institute (TRI), conducted a small independent pilot study in November 2001, examining clients' responses to the ASI-MV® compared with the clinician-administered ASI. They found that 96% of the clients reported the ASI-MV® was "very" to "extremely" easy to use and clients preferred the ASI-MV® over the original ASI, 12 to 1 (Gurel & Carise, 2001). Additionally, the researchers found that clients with no computer experience said it was user-friendly, those with reading difficulty preferred the audio component of the ASI-MV®, and many clients reported feeling more comfortable and less threatened taking ASI-MV® by themselves. Also, Marsh Mathews, Program Manager for Mental Health Services—Options for Recovery in Vista, CA, reported that "Clients with no computer experience have no problem completing the ASI-MV®. They were more honest than with the interviewer and even counselors who were initially resistant to using the program, now like it." Clients quickly master the ASI-MV® regardless of education level, reading ability, and computer experience.

Because the original ASI provides the interview format but not necessarily the precise wording of questions, we needed to derive the exact wording for the ASI-MV® by observing experienced interviewers. The question format within the ASI-MV® was developed by working closely with expert ASI interviewers from TRI in Philadelphia. During observation we took note how interviewers asked particular questions, and responded to interviewee misunderstandings, etc. The current ASI-MV® wording was developed through an intense, iterative process.

Developing a computer-generated formula for the ASI Severity Ratings was even more difficult than wording the questions correctly. Because the Severity Ratings are derived from the interviewer's clinical judgment of interviewee severity based on responses to all questions within a section and not by an arithmetic formula, this was a significant challenge. Our initial approach to this challenge was to develop an algorithm (Butler et al., 1998) using data from over 1000 expert interviewer-administered ASIs. Repeated resampling of the dataset permitted derivation of stable regression equations predicting the Severity Ratings for each ASI domain from clients' answers to preselected interview items. This algorithm, dubbed the Predicted Severity Ratings (PSR), when tested with a new dataset proved a very accurate representation of expert interviewer Severity Ratings. Since the ASI-MV® was first developed, we have continued to refine the PSR algorithms and have sharpened them even further with new data.

OUTCOME DATA

In modifying the ASI for computer administration, it was most important that the scale not lose reliability and validity. For all the reasons described above, it is unlikely that the ASI "in the wild" is nearly as valid or reliable as when it is administered by experts in the carefully controlled and rarified environment of a research project. However, our goal was to develop the ASI-MV® into the "world's best" ASI interviewer, maintaining reliability and validity without being subject to the inconsistencies that occur with human interviewers. The research that we have conducted on the ASI-MV® strongly supports this contention.

A comprehensive psychometric test of the ASI-MV® established strong evidence of reliability and validity. A NIDA-funded study by Butler and colleagues (2001) found that the ASI-MV® was acceptable to client volunteers, required about the same amount of client time to administer (a mean of 43 minutes compared with 45–60 minutes for the interview), and minimal staff time. Once completed, the program automatically calculates Composite Scores as well as the mathematical prediction of the Interviewer Severity Rating (Butler et al., 1998). Test–retest reliability was tested over a 3-day period based on reasoning by McLellan and colleagues (1985) that this is a long enough interval to reduce likelihood of simply repeating answers from memory, but short enough to reduce the possibility of real changes in patients' situations. Furthermore, the IntraClass Correlation statistic was used to evaluate test–retest reliability. The interrater correlation coefficient (ICC) is recommended when the variables to be correlated belong to a common class, meaning that the variables share both their metric and variance (McGraw & Wong, 1996), as opposed to the Pearson *r*, which is used when measures have different scales (e.g., weight and height). Thus, the ICC is commonly used for examining reliability. Traditionally, interpretations of the magnitude of ICCs assume that values >0.80 represent "perfect" agreement; 0.61–0.80 is substantial; 0.41–0.60 is moderate; and 0.21–0.40 is fair reliability (McGraw & Wong, 1996). On the basis of these principles, the ASI-MV® was found to have excellent test–retest reliability (ICCs, between 0.81 and 0.97 for Composite Scores/0.76 to 0.90 for Severity Ratings).

Validity was examined in two ways. First, it was important to establish that the scores generated by the ASI-MV® are similar to some "gold standard." This is referred to as criterion validity. In this instance, the "gold standard" was considered to be to the traditional interviewer-administered ASI. Thus, we calculated agreement of the ASI-MV® assessment with an interviewer-administered ASI at a time 3 days before or after (in counterbalanced order) from the ASI-MV® assessment. In this context, the ASI-MV® yielded good criterion validity for the Composite Scores (ICCs between 0.54 and 0.95). Agreement with interviewers' judgments for Severity Ratings, however, was problematic, ranging from ICCs of –0.12 to 0.64. Exploration revealed considerable variability for each of the interviewers. That is, for each domain, some interviewers appeared to agree with the ASI-MV®, and some appeared to disagree. There were no domains for which all interviewers disagreed with the ASI-MV®. This state of affairs suggested a lack of interrater reliability among the interviewers. This could not be ruled out, because standard ASI training does not involve establishing interrater reliability of Severity Ratings. To further explore this situation, the PSR equations were applied to the interview data. This analysis yielded IntraClass correlations of acceptable levels (Medical 0.76; Employment 0.64; Alcohol 0.69; Drug 0.49; Legal 0.84; Family/Social 0.74; and Psychiatric 0.81). Thus, the data given to the interviewers by clients were not so different from the data the clients were reporting to the ASI-MV®; certainly not different enough to account for the disagreement in the Severity Ratings. Rather, the disagreement on Severity Ratings may be due to inconsistencies in the interviewers' judgments.[2]

Finally, convergent/discriminant validity was evaluated comparing the ASI-MV® scores on each domain with comparison measures for each of the domains. Convergent/ discriminant validity, a conservative assessment of validity, requires three conditions be met (Campbell & Fiske, 1959). First, each ASI-MV® domain score (Composite Score or Severity Rating) should be correlated in the appropriate direction with its designated comparison test. Second, each domain score should be more highly correlated with its designated comparison than with any of the other tests. Finally, a comparison test should be more highly correlated with its paired ASI domain score than with any of the other ASI domain scores. Correlations among all the ASI-MV® domain scores and their comparison measures are arranged as a matrix with the ASI-MV® scores on the rows and comparison measures across the columns. In this analysis, correlations on the diagonal represent convergent validity (correlation between a domain score and its comparison). Off-diagonal correlations reflect discriminant validity (correlations with a domain score and the comparison measures for the other domains). For the Composite Scores, the average on-diagonal correlation ($r = 0.37$) was significantly higher than the average off-diagonal correlation ($r = 0.17$) for the ASI-MV® ($t = 3.92$; $df = 47$, $p < 0.001$). Interestingly, the convergent/discriminant validity of the Composite Scores for the interviewer-administered ASI was less in evidence. The average on-diagonal correlation ($r = 0.28$) for the interviewer version was not significantly different from the average off-diagonal correlation ($r = 0.17$; $t = 1.82$; $df = 47$, NS), although the basic pattern of relationships was similar for the interviewer and ASI-MV® administered version (i.e., on-diagonal correlations tended to be larger than off-diagonal correlations). It should be noted that discriminant validity results reported by McLellan and colleagues (1985), conducted with the interviewers who helped to create the original ASI, did find significantly greater on-diagonal correlations than off-diagonal ones.

Similar results were obtained for the Severity Ratings. Again, there was support for the discriminant validity of the ASI-MV® Severity Ratings, with the

[2] It is interesting to note that the research interviewers who administered the interview ASI in this study were trained using standard ASI training procedures, which do not require establishing interrater reliability. On the basis of our experience in this study, a subsequent study examining the psychometric properties of a Spanish language ASI-MV®, considerable effort was made to establish interrater reliability among the interviewers. In this study (Butler et al., 2007a, MS in preparation), the range of ICCs for the Severity Ratings between the computerized version and the interviewers was –0.12 to 0.64 when interviewers were not trained to be reliable and 0.64–0.78 when they were. This finding further supports our contention that the relationship between interviewers' judgments and the ASI-MV® Severity Ratings were adversely affected by the lack of interviewer training. Implications seem clear for the clinical setting, where such intensive training and supervision are not present.

average on-diagonal correlation ($r = 0.44$) significantly higher than the average off-diagonal correlation ($r = 0.18$; $t = 5.85$; $df = 47$, $p < 0.001$). And again, the average correlations for the interviewer-generated Severity Ratings were not significantly different (on-diagonal mean $r = 0.24$; off-diagonal mean $r = 0.15$, $t = 1.78$; $df = 47$, NS). This was particularly true for the Severity Ratings. In every case where agreement with interviewers' judgments was poor, the ASI-MV® demonstrated superior convergent/discriminant validity.

These psychometric results suggest that part of what the ASI-MV® brings to an ASI assessment is consistency. The careful construction of the ASI-MV® has led to a system that has been shown to be reliable and valid. When discrepancies are found with human interviewers, the ASI-MV® appears to perform in a manner that is more consistent. Indeed, a direct comparison of Severity Ratings generated by the ASI-MV® and by *expert* ASI interviewers (Butler et al., 1998) revealed correlations above 0.84 for five of the seven domains, with legal at 0.66 and family/social at 0.75. Given the importance of training and consistency in achieving reliable and valid ASI assessments, the expense of training and recalibrating clinical interviewer, and the frequent turnover of counseling staff at treatment centers (Carise et al., 2003), the relevance of an automated tool like the ASI-MV® is evident for settings where training and maintaining *expert* ASI interviewers is impractical or impossible. Furthermore, such consistency makes results directly comparable across treatment and research settings.

In addition to these psychometric advantages, clients are unanimously enthusiastic about using the program. After several thousand research and commercial administrations, we have encountered (or heard about) only one client who could not complete the program after a brief, initial introduction. This user had severe multiple sclerosis, who became fatigued easily and had extremely poor eye/hand coordination and muscle control. Spontaneous comments by clients in both research and commercial settings suggest that they consider the ASI-MV® interesting, attractive, and engaging. Moreover, the time required for completing the ASI-MV® is comparable to the amount of time estimated for the ASI interview. Client experiences using a computer mouse with the ASI-MV® for the first time have been quite satisfactory as well. Inexperienced users have quickly learned how to use the mouse.

HOW COST-EFFECTIVE IS THE ADDICTION SEVERITY INDEX-MULTIMEDIA VERSION

The ASI-MV® has proven to be both a cost-effective and a time-saving tool for commercial customers of Inflexxion. The average cost to administer, score, and generate a full narrative report of ASI-MV® is about $7. As stated earlier, the cost to have a staff person administer the ASI, including the scoring and write-up, is at least $25, with fringe benefits. Utilization of the ASI-MV® represents a potential 72% savings in assessment costs.

Within the first year of ASI-MV® implementation among 30 provider groups, contracted with a large regional coordinating agency in Michigan, the coordinating agency's management reported that providers were saving about $45 per assessment. They also reported average staff assessment time decreased from 2 to 1 hour. Annually, this is saving the region about $225 000 and, as a result, they have increased the number of counseling sessions initially authorized from 10 to 11.

Many ASI-MV® sites report similar major savings and reallocation of resources accordingly.

WHERE CAN THE ASI-MV® BE USED?

There are currently about 80 000 administrations of the ASI-MV® per year, and this number is expected to accelerate dramatically once the ASI-MV® Connect is widely adopted. ASI-MV® Connect is a clinical and research tool with an impressive range of application in settings such as substance abuse, mental health, behavioral healthcare, dual diagnosis, and methadone maintenance programs; drug courts; probation departments; correctional facilities; Treatment Accountability for Safer Communities (TASC) organizations; driving under the influence (DUI) programs; and welfare (TANF) organizations.

The Oklahoma Department of Mental Health and Substance Abuse Services (ODMHSAS) has approved the use of the ASI-MV®, and it is being used in its substance abuse settings, drug courts, and DUI assessments. In 2004, at the request of the ODMHSAS, we were able to add an electronically generated report to the ASI-MV® program that extracted 20 of the ASI questions that the state uses as a screen for victims of domestic violence and sexual assault. A positive screen results in a referral for a full assessment. Also, the City of Oklahoma City Municipal Courts' Probation Department established an on-site testing and assessment center where the ASI-MV® helped improve the efficiency of their Probation Officers. According to Lashawn Thompson, Chief Probation Officer

> "the ASI-MV has tremendously enhanced our program. The ASI-MV allows the probation officer to focus on the defendant and their current issues rather than spending an enormous amount of time on paperwork, thereby, increasing productivity and services. Prior to establishing an on-site testing and assessment center, only two assessments per officer could be completed daily. Probation Services can now complete eight assessments daily. This testing center only requires the supervision of one office."

The New Mexico Department of Health, Behavioral Health Services Division, has approved the statewide use of the ASI-MV® and made it available to contracted substance abuse providers. In 2005, Inflexxion helped New Mexico analyze their ASI and ASI-MV® data to measure outcome, as defined by change in Composite Scores, and to better understand their population in treatment.

Now, through Value Options New Mexico, they have "real-time" access to their aggregate data on the new Web-based ASI-MV® Connect Data Center.

Louisiana's Office of Addictive Disorders (OAD) and the Department of Social Services are using the ASI-MV® statewide to screen their TANF(welfare) population. Although the ASI-MV® is generally not used as screening tool, the OAD realized that the information generated in the seven ASI domains would assist them in better understanding their population's needs, improving services delivered, and in helping TANF recipients overcome barriers to finding work. According to Quinetta Rowley, TANF Liaison for the OAD in Baton Rouge, LA, "I think the ASI-MV is an excellent guide for the clinicians that have trouble administering a thorough assessment. I like the different domains it addresses and it addresses the whole person." And, Angel D. Lechtenberg, a Social Services Counselor for the OAD in Lake Charles, LA, found that

> "Comparing previous monthly reports of clients referred, the number of clients referred for substance abuse issues has increased. The assessment is ready to be shared with client's substance abuse counselor. Also, other opportunity areas in client's life are identified and services can be recommended and/or provided for client, including mental health, family counseling, smoking cessation, anger management, etc."

The ASI-MV® also has great utility for the average clinician who sees substance abuse clients. It is an ideal way to look at standardized data and have that data organized in a report (which can be used for documentation and insurance purposes). The data and the report also have direct implications for good treatment planning. One solo practitioner in Texas, Julie West, has dramatically increased her practice doing drug and alcohol evaluations using the ASI-MV® as a core component of those evaluations. Her practice increased so greatly that she needed to bring on more clinicians.

ROLE IN A COMPREHENSIVE TREATMENT PROGRAM

In a study of inpatient and outpatient/day treatment programs, McLellan et al. (1994) investigated the effects of matching services to three functional areas of concern for chemically dependent clients: Employment, family/social, and psychiatric problems. A randomized clinical trial examined outcomes for clients who received services that were matched to their problem areas versus control clients who received unmatched services. In the targeted areas, the matched clients achieved better outcomes than unmatched controls, with employment and psychiatric improvements achieving statistical significance. This research suggests that significant therapeutic gains can be obtained by matching the client's needs to the services that he or she receives. These findings support the importance of substance abuse programs to address ancillary areas, which are known to be major predictors of outcome (McLellan et al., 1994). An effort by McLellan and colleagues (1997) to follow-up on this work in a more practical, nonresearch setting found that the effects were difficult to implement across programs. However, they concluded that within a program, it is possible to match treatment to problems and that such matching increases the effectiveness of substance abuse treatment systems.

RESEARCH AGENDA

The Inflexxion team has been working on the ASI-MV® and now the ASI-MV® Connect in a comprehensive set of studies since 1996. Much of this NIDA-funded research has involved extending the ASI-MV® to other languages, especially Spanish and Chinese (Mandarin and Cantonese), using state-of-the-art procedures for adapting psychological measures to other languages and cultures (e.g., Geisinger, 1994; Rogler, 1999). These procedures reflect attempts to deal with the effects of cultural misunderstandings on content validity of adapted psychological assessments. The primary focus of these concerns is that satisfactory content validity of a measure cannot be assumed to transfer to another language and culture. Although translations of the ASI exist, according to bilingual counselors, some are not adequate for use with substance abuse populations in the US. For instance, the existing Spanish translation is done in formal Castilian Spanish. Counselors who work with Spanish-speaking clients reported that they usually translated the English version themselves "on the fly" as they worked with a client. Our efforts involved adapting the ASI-MV® wording with bilingual counselors from Mexican-American, Cuban-American, and Puerto Rican backgrounds. These efforts resulted in a Spanish language ASI-MV® with the same advantages of the English version. Indeed, recently collected psychometric data with clients in substance abuse treatment from the three predominant Spanish-speaking cultures in the US are excellent (Butler et al., 2007a ms in preparation). For example, 3-day, test–retest correlations range from 0.60 to 0.93 for the Composite Scores and from 0.69 to 0.89 for Severity Ratings. Criterion validity (comparison with an interviewer) achieved ICCs between 0.81 and 0.93 for Composite Scores and between 0.64 and 0.78 for Severity Ratings, which are in the range of "substantial" to "perfect" agreement (McGraw & Wong, 1996). Using the same procedures described above for the English version, discriminant validity was demonstrated. For composite scores, the average on-diagonal correlation for the Spanish ASI-MV® domains was $r = 0.50$ and was significantly greater than the average off-diagonal correlation of $r = 0.17$ ($t = 6.80$, $df = 47$, $p < 0.001$). Similarly, the Severity Ratings of the Spanish ASI-MV® yielded a significant difference between the on- and off-diagonal correlations (average on-diagonal $r = 0.52$; average off-diagonal $r = 0.20$; $t = 5.70$, $df = 47$, $p < 0.001$). This compares well with the same correlations obtained for the interview version. That is, for composite scores from the interview, the average on-diagonal correlation was $r = 0.43$, and the average off-diagonal r was 0.16 ($t = 5.13$, $df = 47$, $p < 0.001$). For the Severity Ratings, the figures for interviewers were for the on-diagonal $r = 0.27$ and for the off-diagonal $r = 0.14$, which was not a significant difference. Finally, there was good evidence for structural invariance between the Spanish adaptation of the ASI-MV® and the English ASI. A similar approach was used to adapt the ASI-MV® to two Chinese languages, Mandarin and Cantonese. Psychometric data have been collected on this adaptation and the analyses are currently underway. In both the Spanish and the Chinese projects, special attention was given to achieving a culturally and linguistically appropriate adaptation that results in a reliable and valid assessment.

Another interesting project that was completed in early 2007 is called the ASI-MV® Connect Data Center (originally titled Addiction Resources.com). This project, also funded by NIDA, is an enhancement of the ASI-MV® that provides clinic administrators access to a robust online data-reporting portal. The purpose of this website is to increase efficiency for the "typical" clinic administrator to begin use of actual ASI data in clinical practice. After uploading aggregate, deidentified ASI-MV® data from a clinical setting, administrators can use the portal to easily manipulate data and create tables and graphs. Straightforward tools allow even novice users to construct simple descriptive analyses with various demographic breakdowns. The commands to manipulate data are in English and require no previous statistical knowledge; the tables and graphs can even be copied into word processors for report creation. Designed for people with little or no statistical background, the portal also includes a brief online tutorial about basic statistical principles and use of the reporting features.

A field trial of the website prototype (Butler et al., 2007b ms in preparation). Examined the effect of the training program on the acquisition of statistical knowledge by clinic administrators exposed to the ASI-MV® Connect Data Center online training program as compared with clinic administrators exposed only to written materials or no training at all. Results suggest that the clinic administrators exposed to the training program performed significantly better on a statistics knowledge test than individuals exposed only to written materials or no training at all. In addition, those exposed to the training were significantly more confident than controls in their ability to use clinical data. Finally, satisfaction ratings on the entire program were extraordinarily positive. Respondents indicated "good" or "very good" satisfaction on the overall concept of the program (96%) and the potential usefulness of the program to impact quality (92%). Comments about the website were similar to this: "I liked being able to flip the variables, the color graphics, and easy to understand directions. [It] even helped to simplify stats (with which I ALWAYS had some trouble." Given these findings, we believe that ASI-MV® Connect Data Center will help clinical administrators develop the skills they need to use clinical data and improve the quality of substance abuse treatment. ASI-MV® Connect Data Center along with the ASI-MV® line of assessments are all consistent with Inflexxion's ultimate goal: Enhance substance abuse assessment and treatment by integrating systematic and data-driven processes into ongoing, real-world treatment settings.

A note is warranted here regarding the ASI-MV® and ASI-MV® Connect as an Internet-based application. In 2004, the American Psychological Association

(APA) published the results of a task force on issues related to psychological testing and assessment on the Internet (Naglieri et al., 2004). It is important to remember, however, that ASI-MV® Connect, while connected to an Internet database, is not, strictly speaking, Internet-based testing. This means that individuals surfing the web will never encounter and take the ASI-MV® on their own. Rather, with ASI-MV® Connect, the client is administered the assessment only in a controlled clinical setting. The person's clinician must be a customer of Inflexxion and sign onto the site before the client sits down at the computer. In actuality, the ASI-MV® program is resident on the clinician's computer, and only data exchanges, updates of special-interest items, and aggregate analysis reporting (i.e., ASI-MV® Connect Data Center) comprise ASI-MV® Connect. Hence, many concerns addressed by Naglieri's task force (e.g., concerns about who is "really" taking the test, under what conditions, and who is interpreting the results to the test-taker) do not really apply. The other issues remarked on by the task force reflect concerns that any assessment needs to consider, such as establishing appropriate psychometric properties of an assessment, empirically demonstrating equivalence of a computerized version of an assessment with its traditional version, and ensuring appropriate consideration of culturally and linguistically diverse groups, are all well accounted for and documented for the ASI-MV®.

DISSEMINATION AGENDA

Regardless of the quality of an innovation, it may still be difficult to get that innovation adopted (Budman et al., 2003). Currently, the ASI-MV® is used in over 800 sites among 49 states, in addition to Puerto Rico, Canada, and Australia. With the introduction of the Internet-based program, the ASI-MV® Connect, and a focused internal sales and marketing staff, we anticipate increased sales and a rapid increase in use of this program. To date, the ASI-MV® has achieved broad dissemination through promotion at conferences, online advertising, and word of mouth. In considering how to enable new technologies (such as the ASI-MV® and ASI-MV® Connect) to achieve widespread use, we draw heavily from Everett Rogers' (1995) Diffusion of Innovations theory. Rogers maintains that there are ten important elements that help to determine whether an innovation will achieve widespread adoption and how quickly such adoption occurs. These include issues such as Relative Advantage compared with other approaches to the same problem; Trialability, whether the innovation can be tested before making a major commitment to the new approach; and Observability of the innovation, meaning the degree to which the innovation leads to observable impact for the user and/or other users.

Berwick (2003), in an important article applying this work to healthcare, has taken Rogers' concepts and consolidated them into three major "clusters of influence" that contribute to diffusion. These are (1) perceptions of the innovation; (2) characteristics of those who adopt the innovation or fail to do so; (3) and contextual factors such as management and organizational elements.

PERCEPTIONS OF THE INNOVATION

How users perceive an innovation and its potential benefits is pivotal in determining whether the innovation is adopted. Benefit, however, is a complex concept. The benefit that a user derives is generally weighed against what he or she is risking by making the change in question. Most people are risk averse and more comfortable with the "tried and true." Furthermore, they may be fearful that an innovation may put extra demands on them, require them to do something new, or give up the familiar. When we first began to sell the ASI-MV® to substance abuse treatment centers in the late 1990s, some clinicians were so uncomfortable with the data they received from the computerized interview that they repeated the entire ASI interview again verbally. Clinicians wanted to see whether their clients were "really being honest" with the computer and believed that this would not be the case. Certainly, treatment center managers were not pleased to have the ASI being done twice on each client; the clients were not pleased either. With time, these perceptions changed particularly as clinicians and administrators saw that data from the ASI-MV® appeared to "make sense" clinically.

Furthermore, there is reason to believe that clients may be more self-disclosing to computer-administered assessments than to live interviewers. Several recent studies have sought to compare the relative accuracy of a computer-assisted ASI assessment modality with a human-facilitated version (Flynn et al., 2005). Research teams have also observed that substance abusers tend to have more honest responses with a computer-prompted assessment aid (Turner et al., 2005). Our own work (e.g., Butler & Villapiano, 2007c) supports the contention that substance abuse clients entering treatment respond with equal or greater honesty to a computer-based interview than with a human interviewer. For example, we compared client responses on the ASI-MV® with responses of the same clients during an ASI interview approximately 3 days apart (order of administration counterbalanced). Although the self-report responses given to the ASI-MV® were in good agreement with responses given to a live interviewer, the question examined was whether some kind of response bias (e.g., denial) would result in clients reporting less severity or otherwise minimizing their problems. In fact, comparisons of the Composite Scores revealed that five of the seven ASI domain Composite Scores (Medical, Drug, Legal, Family and Social, and Psychiatric) were significantly higher (indicating greater problem severity) on the ASI-MV® than when administered by a human interviewer. Composite Scores for the Employment and Alcohol domains were not significantly different. Item by item comparisons revealed the same pattern, namely that there was either no difference between the computer and interviewer-administered ASI responses or, when there was a difference, the computer administration generally reported greater problem severity, not less. Taken together, these findings argue against the hypothesis that a response bias such as denial adversely affects the results of computer-administered assessments.

A second element of perceptions that contributes or detracts from diffusion of an innovation is its compatibility with the "values, beliefs and past history and current needs of the individuals" (Berwick, 2003, p. 1971). If a counselor believes that he or she "must get a feel for every incoming client" by administering the intake and ASI personally, it is unlikely that that individual will allow the ASI component to be automated. However, if he or she feels that ASI and other structured aspects of the intake are impediments that prevent the clinician from getting down to the "the real business of treatment," the ASI-MV® may be viewed as highly facilitative. In most cases, clinicians have viewed the ASI-MV® as simplifying their work and eliminating a burdensome task.

Third is the complexity of the innovation. The more complicated and difficult the innovation, the more unlikely rapid adoption becomes. Fortunately, the ASI-MV® from the clinician's perspective is quite easy to implement and requires little actual work once the software has been properly installed. Two other important aspects of perception of the innovation that contribute to rapid dissemination are trialability and observability. Trialability pertains to whether an individual who is trying out the innovation can do so with minimal cost and disruption to what they are currently doing. Observability is the ability of interested potential users to watch and learn from others who are already using the innovation. At present, ASI-MV® trialability is achieved by allowing interested individuals to actually try out the program for free without having to commit to its long-term use. This trial period can occur without making any major changes in other processes and/or systems. Observability comes from our satisfied customers who can provide examples and testimonials about how they are using the program and how it impacts their facility.

INDIVIDUAL CHARACTERISTICS

A second cluster of factors relevant to the speed of dissemination are the characteristics of individuals who may adopt the change. According to Rogers, there is an "S" curve of adoption with progressively more of the target population adopting an innovation over time.

Characteristically, the "S" curve has different types of individuals adopting an innovation at different points after its introduction. The first population to adopt an innovation is called "Innovators". These individuals tend to be less concerned about risk, knowledgeable about innovations, and are more adventuresome than their counterparts who adopt at a later point. Berwick (2003) describes Innovators in healthcare as "mavericks" who may be somewhat disconnected from their more cautious colleagues. The next segment to adopt an innovation is called "Early Adopters." These individuals are better positioned than the Innovators

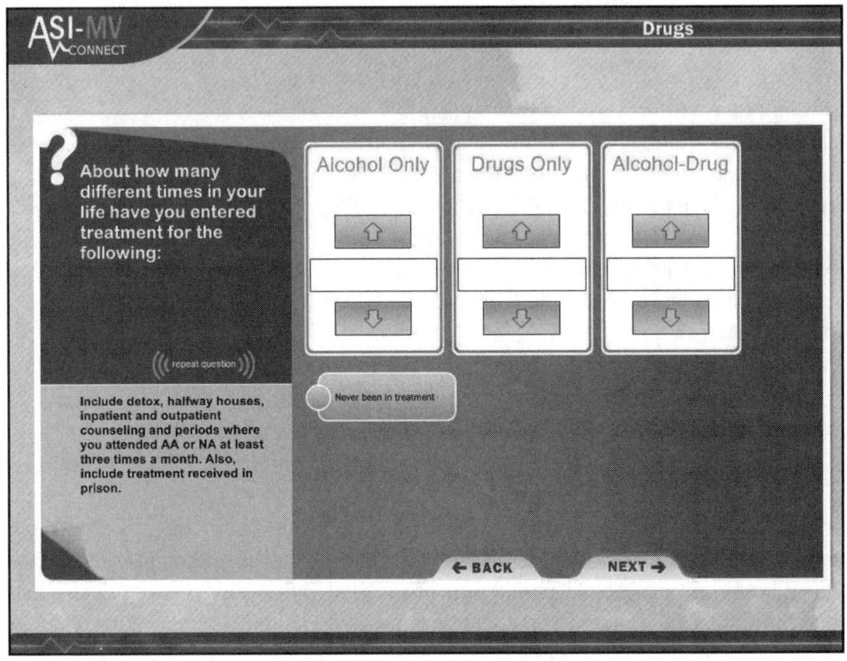

because they are generally well-connected opinion leaders in the healthcare community. They routinely experiment with new innovations and share their experiences with others. Although Early Adopters tend to have broad and/or national connections, the Early Majority describes a more locally based group. Members of the Early Majority are more risk averse than Early Adopters but will try new things based on input from their local colleagues. The next group, the "Late Majority," will adopt innovations based on input from the Early Adopters. They are highly risk averse and cautious. The final segment is the "Laggards." This segment is most likely to be very traditional and very cautious about adopting a technology. They are reluctant to move away from an approach they have used for many years.

In general, we have encountered many of these types of individuals in our attempt to disseminate the ASI-MV®. From the clinicians who viewed ASI-MV® as a key innovation in the late 1990s, to the regional advocates who have helped champion the ASI-MV® in a number of states, to those who indicate that they will never use computerized programs in their clinical practices, we have seen all the characteristic groups that Rogers identified. Because a few influential early users have proven to be crucial advocates in many states, we have plans to foster "user groups" and utilize peer marketing approaches, which appear to be highly effective.

CONTEXTUAL CHARACTERISTICS

Refers to the fact that innovation is harder to come by within some organizations than others. This often relates to the organizational climate and leadership issues. Some organizations are typified by low tolerance of innovation and a desire to remain the same or a contrasting situation with a dogmatic and autocratic style of introducing innovation, which does not accept processes that move people to innovate. On the other hand, some organizations encourage and bless innovation and can tolerate the frustrations and growing pains that often accompany new approaches. In any situation or change, agents introducing innovation must be prepared to examine the context into which the innovation is being introduced. Without such contextual awareness, innovation can fail.

It has been our experience that innovation-friendly leadership at a high level of administration is almost always essential for the ASI-MV® to be implemented. We work with several large organizations that have been using the ASI-MV® for 5 or more years. These organizations have had strong leadership advocates for ASI-MV®. Such support has been essential to sustaining the use of the program even when unexpected problems arose.

DIFFUSION OF INNOVATION AND THE ASI-MV®: LESSONS LEARNED

We make no claims that our dissemination of the ASI-MV® has been as rapid or effective as we would like. Our efforts in this area remain a work in progress. However, there are several important lessons that we have learned. (1) *Build a product that serves a significant need.* The ASI is required in many places and the availability of the ASI-MV® makes clinical practice and administration of substance abuse treatment programs easier than it would be without this program; (2) *Get the word out and keep the word out.* We put a great deal of time, effort, and money into letting potential users know about the program, how it works, and what it can do for them; (3) *Understand the motivation to use your product.* If you are not meeting customer needs in very specific ways that are useful to them, they will not use your product. Our original ASI-MV® had a minimal clinical report associated with it. Customers told us that the report was enormously important to them and without a good reporting mechanism, the program would not meet their needs. We have spent years building and modifying different types of reports that can be placed in the clients' charts. Without these reports, treatment centers would not be getting what they need to make a purchase worthwhile; (4) *Continue to benefit your customers.* Frequently add useful features that speak directly to customer needs. For example, the Spanish version of our program was developed in response to customer feedback, and we are currently engaged in working on an adolescent version of the ASI-MV®. "Listening to the voice of the customer" is critical to remaining at the forefront of innovation and keeping our product visible and fresh.

We believe that our overall approach to computerized assessment in substance abuse treatment can help to significantly improve the quality of drug and alcohol treatment in this country. We also have begun to consider a next generation of computerized programs that can gather clinical data, make treatment recommendations, and "learn" about which of those recommendations work best through the process of neural networking and case-based reasoning. The ultimate goal of such programs would be to provide clinicians with outstanding computerized tools that scientifically improve treatment. We believe that the clinician will remain essential to treatment, however, the clinicans' traditional role will change in the future. By combining their clinical acumen with advancements in science and technology they will have numerous resources available that will become integral parts of good behavioral care.

REFERENCES

Berwick, D.M. (2003). Disseminating innovations in health care. *JAMA*, *289*, 1969–1975.

Budman, S.H., Portnoy, D. & Villapiano, A.J. (2003). *How to Get Technological Innovation Used in Behavioral Health Care: Build it and They Still Might not Come. Psychotherapy: Theory/ Research/ Practice/Training*, *40*(12), 45–54.

Butler, S.F., Budman, S.H., Goldman, R.J., et al. (2001). Initial validation of a computer-administered addiction severity index: The ASI–MV. *Psychology of Addictive Behaviors*, *15*, 4–12.

Butler, S.F., Newman, F.L., Cacciola, J.S., et al. (1998). Predicting ASI interviewer severity ratings for a computer-administered Addiction Severity Index. *Psychological Assessment*, *10*, 399–407.

Butler, S.F., Licari, A., & Cunningham, J.A. (2007b ms in preparation). *Addictionresources.com: A New Concept for Facilitating Use of Clinical Data in the Clinical Management of Substance Abuse Treatment.*

Butler, S.F., Redondo, J.P., Cunningham, J.A., & Villapiano, A.J. (2007a ms in preparation). *Validation of the Spanish Addiction Severity Index Multimedia Version (S–ASI–MV).*

Butler, S.F. & Villapiano, A.J (2007c ms in preparation). *Impact of computer-administration of the Addiction Severity Index on respondents' honesty in answering questions.*

Campbell, D.T. & Fiske, D. (1959). Convergent and discriminant validity by the multi-trait multi-method matrix. *Psychological Bulletin*, *56*, 81–105.

Carise, D., McLellan, A.T., & Gifford, L.S. (2003). *Developing A National Addiction Treatment Information System.* Accessed online 12/2/03 at http://www.densonline.org/DENSArt1update-040101.pdf

Flynn, P., Beaston-Blaakman, A., Broome, K., et al. (October, 2005). *Drug Abuse Treatment Provider Estimates of Accounting and Economic Costs of Treatment Using the Treatment Cost Analysis Tool (TCAT).* Paper presented at Addiction Health Services Research conference, Santa Monica, CA.

Geisinger, K.F. (1994). Cross-cultural normative assessment: Translation and adaptation issues influencing the normative interpretation of assessment instruments. *Psychological Assessments*, *6*, 304–312.

Gurel, O. & Carise, D. (2001). *ASI-MV Pilot Study* (Unpublished report). Philadelphia: Treatment Research Institute.

McGraw, K.O. & Wong, S.P. (1996). Forming inferences about some intraclass correlation coefficients. *Psychological Methods*, *1*, 30–46.

McLellan, A.T., Alterman, A.I., Metzger, D.S., et al. (1994). Similarity of outcome predictors across opiate, cocaine, and alcohol treatments: Role of treatment services. *Journal of Consulting and Clinical Psychology*, *62*, 1141–1158.

McLellan, A.T., Grissom, G.R., Zanis, D., et al. (1997). Problem-service "matching" in addiction treatment: A prospective study in 4 programs. *Archives of General Psychiatry*, *54*, 730–735.

McLellan, A.T., Luborsky, L., Cacciola, J., et al. (1985). New data from the Addiction Severity Index: Reliability and validity in three centers. *Journal of Nervous and Mental Disease, 173,* 412–423.

McLellan, A.T., Luborsky, L., Woody, G.E., & O'Brien, C.P. (1980). An improved evaluation instrument for substance abuse patients: The addiction severity index. *Journal of Nervous and Mental Disease, 168,* 26–33.

Naglieri, J.A., Drasgow, F., Schmit, M., et al. (2004). Psychological testing on the Internet: New problems, old issues. *American Psychologist, 59,* 150–162.

Rogers, E.M. (1995). *Diffusion of Innovations* (4th Ed.). New York: Free Press.

Rogler, L.H. (1999). Methodological sources of cultural insensitivity in mental health research. *American Psychologist, 54,* 424–433.

Turner, C.F., Villarroel, M.A., Rogers, S.M., et al. (2005). Reducing bias in telephone survey estimates of the prevalence of drug use: a randomized trial of telephone audio-CASI. *Addiction, 100,* 1432–1444.

8

EXERCISE AS AN ADJUNCTIVE EVIDENCE-BASED TREATMENT

BRIE A. MOORE* AND AMANDA ADAMS†

*University of Nevada, Reno, Department of Psychology and UCLA Semel Institute for Neuroscience and Human Behavior
†California State University, Fresno, Department of Psychology

INTRODUCTION

In the changing healthcare delivery and reimbursement environment, cost-effective, short-term, and self-help therapies are being strongly encouraged. To this end, adjunct treatments have become increasingly important. According to the US Department of Health and Human Services (2002), over $84 million is spent annually on chronic diseases that can be prevented or considerably improved through increased physical activity. Exercise is one example of a safe and cost-effective, therapeutic adjunct in the treatment of a variety of behavioral health concerns. When used in combination with empirically validated treatments such as cognitive-behavioral therapy (CBT), exercise has been found to improve pain and functional capacity in patients with chronic pain conditions such as fibromyalgia (Redondo et al., 2004), increased health-related behavior, including smoking cessation (Albrecht et al., 1998; Faulkner et al., 2007), obesity (Epstein et al. 2006), body image disturbance (McAulay et al., 2002), alcohol dependence (Ermalinski et al., 1997), and improving quality of life in HIV/AIDS treatment (Ciccolo et al., 2004). Exercise has also been found to help remediate depression (Craft & Perna, 2004), particularly in older adult populations (Palmer 2004). In this chapter, we highlight the benefits of exercise as a safe, low-cost, and effective adjunctive intervention for the treatment of (1) health behavior change; (2) depression; and (3) fibromyalgia.

DOSAGE

Before we review the extant literature, it is important to operationalize "exercise." Current physiologic guidelines support that 20–60 minutes of cardiovascular activity, 3–5 days per week, at 60–80% of the age-adjusted maximal heart rate (or a weekly caloric cost of 2000 kcal), represents an effective dose with minimal medical risk (Haskell et al., 2007). However, not only do therapeutic dosages vary considerably across studies, it remains unclear whether a physiological, metabolic, or endocrine response is necessary for psychological outcomes to occur.

HEALTH BEHAVIOR CHANGE

Obesity, smoking, alcohol addiction, and unsafe behaviors leading to HIV and AIDS all are characterized by a pattern of behaviors that contribute to (or cause) an undesired physical condition. Behavior change is required to eliminate or reduce the primary problem in each case and often remediate the physiological sequelae. Physical activity has been used successfully as an adjunctive treatment and sometimes as a primary treatment for a variety of conditions associated with health behavior change. In the following section, we will briefly review the data supporting exercise as an effective adjunctive treatment in health behavior change. Because physical activity has been so widely studied in association with weight management, various behavioral strategies will first be discussed in detail. Following this review, we will briefly present the empirical literature supporting exercise as an adjunctive treatment for smoking, alcohol use, and chronic conditions including HIV/AIDS.

OBESITY

Physical activity and exercise are sometimes used adjunctively to other treatments, such as medical procedures or cognitive-behavioral techniques for weight loss and obesity management or prevention. However, exercise is often the primary treatment for these conditions. Behavioral science has supplied a foundation for understanding physical activity and has been used to establish conceptual and empirical groundwork for designing and implementing physical activity programs. Several reviews of the literature spanning nearly 30 years agree that the majority of effective interventions have used a combination of cognitive-behavioral and behavioral strategies (Baranowski et al., 1998; Brawley et al., 2000; Dishman, 1991; Leith & Taylor, 1992; Robinson & Rogers, 1994; van der Bij et al., 2002). Behavioral science models are characterized by a focus on analysis that allows some predictive quality and principle-based procedures that promote behavior change (Baranowski et al., 1998).

Several behavioral strategies have over time accumulated considerable empirical support. Reinforcement (i.e., feedback), prompting, stimulus control, self-monitoring, and contracting are all behavioral techniques that have been extensively studied as applied to areas of complex behavior change including physical activity. In some studies, one behavioral strategy is used in isolation, but more commonly, two or more behavioral techniques are used together in a behavioral treatment package, possibly along with cognitive-behavioral or other nonbehavioral techniques. Although treatment packages are the norm, the combinations of components in different packages vary greatly. Most studies use behavioral treatment strategies as components in a broader treatment package (Martin et al., 1984).

REINFORCEMENT AND FEEDBACK (CONSEQUENCE CONTROL)

Reinforcement may be the most easily generalized behavioral principle and is a cornerstone of any effective behavioral change program. The procedure of reinforcement is appropriately regarded as providing praise, or another reward to the participant after a desirable behavior occurs. This procedure is commonly referred to as "feedback" in intervention studies. Feedback in the form of positive reinforcement has most often been administered by delivering statements of praise after reaching a predetermined goal (positive reinforcement). The overt verbal reinforcement may be accompanied by a nonverbal or intrinsic reinforcer that increases its value (i.e., the feeling of accomplishment). In this way, both extrinsic/overt reinforcers and covert/intrinsic reinforcers are likely at work, but only the overt reinforcers are observable direct measures of a treatment component. Feedback and/or reinforcement has been listed as a successful intervention strategy most often used in studies aimed at increasing physical activity for the primary purposes of weight loss and the health benefits associated with weight loss (Gillet et al., 1996; Kau & Fisher, 1974; Taggart et al., 1986; Wallace et al., 1998).

PROMPTING

Prompting can take many forms, including textual prompts, as in written guidelines or leaflets, verbal prompts from interventionists, and within stimulus prompts that are inherently a part of many self-management techniques. Phone calls are one of the most prevalent ways to deliver prompts to research participants (Nicolson, 2000). A prompt is administered after the antecedent for a particular behavioral response has occurred, but before the behavior has occurred with the intended effect of increasing the chances that the behavior will indeed occur as intended (Cooper et al., 1987). Thus, a prompt is a form of assistance for completing a behavioral response that has not occurred at a high rate in the past. Prompting often is used in conjunction with stimulus control, another antecedent technique, and has been listed as an effect component of behavioral intervention in several studies including Fitterling et al., 1988; King et al., 2000; Kriska et al., 1986; Lombard et al., 1995; Martin et al., 1984; Wallace et al., 1998.

STIMULUS CONTROL

Stimulus control procedures vary widely. In this antecedent procedure, the stimulus that is intended to evoke the desired behavior is manipulated in some way to make it more salient thus increasing the likelihood that the behavior will occur (Cooper et al., 1987). These techniques can include instructions from a therapist, such as cleaning out the fridge to remove unwanted food choices or throwing away any available alcohol or cigarettes. A less direct use of stimulus control can be considered an environmental stimulus control strategy (sometimes conceptualized as a setting event or establishing operation) and involves changing the actual physical environment that was associated with the past undesirable behavior. An example is removing oneself from the environment in which past behaviors have occurred, such as not going to a nightclub associated with past drinking binges. Stimulus control procedures may have a secondary unintended, but beneficial effect as they are likely to become part of a successful participants changing behavioral repertoire. That is, instead of being something that is added and then faded away, like a prompt, the individual learns to incorporate new lifestyle habits into his or her existing behavioral repertoire, thus setting his or her own stimulus cues (having shoes and clothes laid out for a morning walk or facilitating the consumption of healthy meals by shopping in advance and menu planning). This new behavioral pattern becomes an enduring part of a new behavioral repertoire that is supportive of maintaining the new healthy pattern of physical activity.

Studies that have successfully included stimulus control as an intervention component include Brownell et al., 1980; Kau & Fisher, 1974; Martin et al., 1984; Owen et al., 1987.

SELF-MONITORING

Self-monitoring has been shown to have robust behavior change effects. Being aware of one's own behavior is sometimes all that is required for behavior changes. Self-monitoring can be done in many ways: keeping a detailed journal that involves writing down all food consumed, physical activity, or number of cigarettes smoked. Self-monitoring can give information about the behavior itself and how it may most effectively be changed by indicating where and when offending behaviors most often occur. Self-monitoring may be faded over time; however, a simple form of record keeping is a common practice for many adults and can easily become part of one's everyday routine on a permanent basis.

Studies that have successfully included self-monitoring as a component of physical activity intervention include King, et al., 1992; Martin, et al., 1984; Oldridge & Jones, 1983; Owen et al., 1987.

BEHAVIORAL CONTRACTS

Behavioral contracting involves a written document stating goals and the reward or other outcome for meeting (or failing to meet) the stated goals. Usually, guidelines for goal writing include keeping the goal realistic (usually small), measurable, observable (recordable), and on a proposed timeline. The other part of the contract involves rewards for achieving the goals that are agreed upon and sometimes facilitated by another party. A monetary reward or cost is a common consequence in many behavioral contracts for physical activity. Often, the consequence is the loss of money already put forth for this purpose by the participant. Contracts have many benefits to the practitioner in that they have inherent flexibility and can be written to state appropriate goals for any individual. Furthermore, the contract can incorporate a number of health goals with consequences that are individualized to incorporate meaningful outcomes for the unique participant. An additional benefit of contracts is that they can be mediated by a number of people other than a professional, including a significant other or a family member.

Behavioral contracting is one of the more widely used methods for establishing a change in physical activity and has been used successfully in a number of studies including Epstein et al., 1980; Neale et al., 1990; Singleton et al., 1987; Wysocki et al., 1979.

SMOKING

A large body of literature has supported physical activity/exercise as a primary or adjunctive treatment in smoking cessation. Marcus, Albrecht and colleagues have shown repeated favorable results when using exercise as a primary or as an adjunctive treatment for smoking cessation. A 1995 study with 20 previously sedentary female smokers used exercise training as the primary intervention and showed improved short-term quit rates (Marcus et al., 1995). A larger study involving a sample of 281 female smokers randomly assigned to a cognitive-behavioral smoking cessation program with or without vigorous exercise revealed that participating in vigorous exercise facilitates short- and longer-term smoking cessation in women combined with a cognitive-behavioral program (Marcus et al., 1999). Thus, used adjunctively to cognitive-behavioral techniques, Marcus and Albrecht have consistently shown positive effects for the use of physical activity as a treatment for smoking cessation.

In an effort to improve on methodological shortcomings from pat research, the same group of researchers developed a large-scale study called the "Commit to Quit" trial evaluated the contribution of exercise to smoking cessation (Marcus et al., 1997). Among the variables examined in this study was the relationship between motivational readiness for exercise adoption and high levels of concerns of weight gain after ceasing smoking. This was a large clinical trial comparing the relative efficacy of cognitive-behavioral smoking cessation programs plus vigorous exercise with the same treatment plus a control contact group using breath monitors to measure physiological levels of nicotine in one's system (Marcus, et al., 1997). With growing empirical support from large randomized studies, the use of exercise as an adjunctive treatment for smoking cessation is growing and becoming more conclusive in its support for choosing to include exercise in treatment; however, there is much needed work in this particular area of research.

Ussher et al. examined literature on exercise as an aid to smoking cessation in a 2000 review. They found eight randomized controlled trials (RCTs) published between 1980 and 1999 specifically examining the effect of exercise on smoking cessation. Of the eight trials, only two found a positive effect and the others showed no effect. They concluded that although there is some evidence for exercise aiding smoking cessation, there is a need for more rigorously designed studies. In an effort to address this need, Faulkner and colleagues have published a recent article addressing some of the limitations of past research and considering the importance of addressing the issues of effectiveness and practical concerns has aimed for a "Better Practices" model that may provide a framework for furthering work in this area (Faulkner et al., 2006).

ALCOHOL

The use of exercise as an adjunctive treatment for alcoholism may be growing in practice, but, to this point, there is scarce empirical evidence for the use of exercise as a treatment. The vast majority of available research, when considering the interaction between exercise and alcohol, examines how exercise alters the effects of alcohol on various metabolic and physiological mechanisms in the human body. Although the research on how exercise may be used as an effective treatment for alcoholism is limited, initial studies show promising results. Ermaliski and colleagues (1997) investigated the effects of a physical fitness program as an adjunct to the typical treatment program for a group of alcoholic patients. Those who participated in the exercise program showed significantly less craving for alcohol than members in the standard treatment group. Additionally, the group treated with physical activity saw themselves as having more internal locus of control (Ermalinski et al., 1997). Including measures such as report of locus of control offers some insight as to why exercise may be an effective adjunctive treatment for so many different types of problems.

HIV/AIDS AND CHRONIC CONDITIONS

Another developing area of research is in using exercise as part of a treatment package for chronic conditions such as HIV and AIDS. A common treatment for HIV-infected persons is the use of highly active antiretroviral therapy (HAART) that reduces the mortality of HIV-infected person, but also leaves patients with fatigue, nausea, pain, anxiety, and depression. In a 2004 publication, Ciccolo and colleagues discussed the use of exercise as an adjunctive treatment instead of the more commonly used pharmacological treatments aimed at improving the quality of life for patients undergoing treatment (Ciccolo et al., 2004). They conclude that while results are generally positive, existing studies have utilized small samples with high attrition rates, and many studies were conducted before the use of HAART, now standard, which limits the ability to generalize findings. Data from other chronic conditions and healthy samples suggest that exercise has the potential to be a beneficial treatment across the range of symptoms experienced by HIV-infected individuals (Ciccolo et al., 2004). Support for this position can be found in a 2003 review on patients with chronic diseases and in particular focuses on counteracting protein wasting (Zinna & Yarasheski, 2003). This piece summarizes the findings from studies that have examined the potential benefits of exercise training for the treatment of wasting associated with sarcopenia, cancer, chronic renal insufficiency, rheumatoid arthritis, osteoarthritis, and HIV. These conditions share a fundamental mechanism that causes an imbalance between muscle protein synthetic and proteolytic processes (Zinna & Yarasheski, 2003). Findings from studies have shown that even a modest increase in physical activity can mitigate muscle protein wasting and that participants in an exercise training program can gain muscle protein mass, strength, endurance and in some cases, are more capable of performing daily living activities (Zinna & Yarasheski, 2003).

DEPRESSION

Depression has been ranked as the leading cause of disability in the United States and affects approximately 121 million people worldwide (WHO, 2007). It ranks second only to heart disease in terms of disease burden and is projected to be the leading cause of disease burden by the year 2020 (Apeldorf & Alexopoulous, 2003; Goodwin, 2003). Depression has deleterious effects on health and is associated with increased healthcare costs, worse outcomes after acute medical events, decreased physical functioning, and decreased overall mortality rates (Crystal et al., 2002; Palmer, 2005). In the United States alone, over $44 billion is spent each year on lost work productivity related to depression (Stewart et al., 2003). However, only 25% of those affected have access to effective treatments (WHO, 2007).

Primary care providers are uniquely positioned to promote behavioral approaches, such as exercise. Currently, depressed patients treated in primary care settings receive predominately pharmacotherapy (Craft & Perna, 2004). However, due to adverse side-effect profiles, low response rates (e.g., 50%), even lower remission rates (30–35%), poor adherence, and persistent impairments in functioning, safe, low-cost, and effective treatments for depression are sorely needed in primary care. Treatment can be improved by providing education regarding safe, well-established, and effective nonpharmacologic treatments such as CBT (Young et al., 2001) and strategies such as exercise (Craft & Perna, 2004). Exercise alone has been shown to alleviate symptoms in both clinical and subclinical depression (Dunn et al., 2001, 2002, 2005; O'Neal et al., 2000) and in some studies, to be as effective as treatment with sertraline or a combination of sertraline and aerobic exercise (Blumenthal et al., 1999). When used adjunctively with other treatments for depression, exercise has received empirical support for use as an augmentation strategy and has been associated with improved quality of life (Dimeo et al., 2001; Veale et al., 1992). Meta-analytic findings suggest that exercise is an effective intervention for the short-term management of depressive symptoms (Lawlor & Hopker, 2001). Together, empirical data suggest that exercise has numerous physical and psychological benefits and is a safe adjunct or alternative treatment to medication for the treatment of depression (Palmer, 2005).

Depression is typically underdiagnosed in at least half of all older adults, oftentimes because of the presence of comorbid medical conditions and a greater reliance on the report of physical symptoms such as lack of sleep or energy and weight loss as opposed to sadness, feelings of guilt, suicidal ideation, or worthlessness (Apeldorf & Alexopoulous, 2003; Dantz et al., 2003; Kaplan et al., 1999). However, the prevalence of depressive symptoms in older adults can be as high as 30% in community populations and as high as 40% in hospitalized and nursing home residents (Leon et al., 2003). Currently, only 30% of adults over 65 years and 12% of those aged 75 years and above engage in regular physical activity (Heath & Stuart, 2002). Exercise is not often prescribed to older adults, despite the vast amount of current research available demonstrating its efficacy (Palmer, 2005).

The relationship between increased physical activity and depression has received the most empirical attention in the treatment of older adults. Many RCTs have demonstrated the effectiveness of exercise as a treatment for depression, with some studies indicating that exercise can be as successful a treatment alternative as medication (Goodwin, 2003; Lawlor & Hopker, 2001). Exercise has been particularly effective in treating depressive symptoms in older adults who respond poorly to traditional treatments alone (Mather et al., 2002). In fact, when older adults were randomized to a 10-week exercise class or health education class, a greater proportion of those who attended the exercise class demonstrated 30% or more reductions in depressive symptoms on the Hamilton Rating Scale for Depression (Mather et al., 2002). Research indicates that exercise significantly decreases depression scores for persons with high and low measured symptomatology, decreases pain and disability (Penninx et al., 2002), improves subjective well-being (Stathi et al., 2002), has a positive effect on meaning in life and self-rated health and functioning (Takkin et al., 2001), increases self-efficacy (McAulay et al., 2002), and is associated with decreased rates of depressive and anxiety disorders (Goodwin, 2003). Some researchers hypothesize that improvements in pain and perceived health status, increased social connectedness, reductions in stress, distraction from negative thoughts, and increased cognitive functioning may account for the effects of exercise in the prevention and treatment of depression in older adults (Goodwin, 2003). Together, reviews of medical and gerontological studies have found that exercise markedly reduces depressive symptoms and is a safe adjunct or alternative to pharmacotherapy for depression (Palmer, 2005).

FUNCTIONAL PAIN SYNDROMES: FIBROMYALGIA

In addition to its role in mood regulation, for at least a subset of the population, exercise has also been found to play a key role in the management of pain and fatigue in response to stress (Glass et al., 2004). Exercise has been investigated as an adjunctive treatment in the care of patients with a wide variety of functional pain conditions including fibromyalgia, chronic fatigue syndrome, and other conditions that are thought to involve a biological stress response. Primary treatment approaches vary by disorder and complexity of presentation, but typically include a combination of symptomatic relief through physiological means (i.e., pharmacotherapy) and CBT (Goldenberg et al., 2004). Given the dearth of well-controlled clinical trials evaluating the efficacy of exercise as an adjunctive treatment across functional pain syndromes, we will briefly summarize the available data supporting exercise in the treatment of fibromyalgia.

Fibromyalgia is a syndrome of unknown etiology characterized by chronic widespread pain, increased tenderness to palpation, and additional symptoms such as disturbed sleep, stiffness, fatigue, and psychological distress (Offenbacher & Stucki, 2000). It is diagnosed based on a patient's report of widespread pain of 3 months' duration or longer and identification of 11 of 18 possible tender points (Wolfe et al., 1990). In community-based studies, approximately 2% of adults and 1.2–6.2% of school-age children screened positive for fibromyalgia (Quisel et al., 2004). Persons with fibromyalgia use an average of 2.7 drugs at any one time for related symptoms, make an average of 10 outpatient visits per year, and are hospitalized once every 3 years (Wolfe et al., 1997). Clearly, effective treatments are needed to address morbidity and associated medical utilization.

Despite the specific psychiatric condition targeted, the effects of exercise are most pronounced when they are used as one component in an integrated, multidisciplinary approach to pain management (Henningsen et al., 2007). Redondo and colleagues (2004) investigated the efficacy of a physical exercise-based program and CBT in decreasing the functional impact of fibromyalgia. After 8 weeks of treatment, participants in both groups reported reduced interference because of fibromyalgia and improved coping responses. These findings did not persist at 1-year follow-up, but participants who received the physical exercise intervention maintained significantly greater improvements in functional capacity as compared with CBT controls. These findings are consistent with those of other studies indicating that regular exercise improves pain, energy, work capacity, and physical and social activities in persons with fibromyalgia (Offenbacher & Stucki, 2000).

A 2003 Cochrane review identified 7 well-controlled clinical investigations of the impact of exercise on fibromyalgia-related pain and morbidity (Busch et al., 2002). Aerobic conditioning was defined as (1) 2 days per week; (2) at 55–90% of predicted maximum heart rate; (3) 20–60 minutes; and (4) for at least 6 weeks. In these studies, exercise resulted in improvements in global well-being, physical function, aerobic fitness, and pain threshold of tender points (2002). When evaluated in a primary care setting, adherence to a regular exercise program has been found to reduce consultations and prescriptions significantly (Peters et al., 2002). Exercise appears to hold considerable promise in reducing unnecessary medical utilization in persons with pain of unexplained etiology.

AVAILABILITY AND DISSEMINATION

The most effective strategies for increasing exercise include written exercise prescriptions, patient goal setting, individually tailored physical activity regimens, and scheduled follow-ups (Heath & Stuart, 2002). A number of Internet-based resources for writing exercise prescriptions exist (U.S Preventive Services Task Force, 2003). These include the American Academy of Orthopedic Surgeons (www.aaos.org), the American College of Sports Medicine (www.acsm.org), American Diabetes Association (www.diabetes.org), the American Heart Association (http://www.americanheart.org, 2007), American Physical Therapy Association (www.apta.org), Arthritis Foundation (www.arthritis.org), National Institute on Aging (www.nih.gov/nia), the National Osteoporosis Foundation (www.nof.org), and the National Heart, Lung and Blood Institute (www.nhlbi.nih.gov). Another excellent source of online information and support is the website for the Centers for Disease Control (CDC) (http://www.cdc.gov, 2007). The CDC physical activity page contains a great deal of information that includes education, techniques for getting started, and techniques for continuing a program http://www.cdc.gov/nccdphp/dnpa/physical/index.htm, 2007). The CDC includes links to research and further information including motivational strategies.

FUTURE DIRECTIONS

The benefits of exercise and increased physical activity has vast implication across a number of different problems and conditions. In some areas, such as weight management and obesity treatment, the research is vast and has enjoyed the benefit of numerous replications with different populations and package components. In fields such as smoking cessation, there is moderate to strong support for the use of physical activity programs in conjunction with traditional treatment programs, and empirical support is continuing to grow in this quickly developing area of research. In other areas, such as alcoholism and chronic disease conditions, evidence is just beginning to mount in support of exercise as an adjunctive treatment, but with promising results thus far. Additional research is warranted to further investigate the clinical implications of using exercise as a preventive and intervention strategy across a wide variety of conditions.

Professionals in a multitude of fields, including mental health professionals, counselors, program directors, psychologists, and, arguably the most influential professionals, physicians, are encouraged to consider the potential benefits of prescribing exercise as an adjunctive treatment. Medical doctors, especially in the early stages of diagnosis and prescription, have a large degree of influence over patient behavior. This influence is particularly important when discussing issues related to health behavior change, including smoking, dietary habits, and exercise. Winslow and colleagues suggest a three-step process when professionals are interacting with patients to encourage behavior change that includes explanation/education, goal setting, and ongoing monitoring (Winslow et al., 1996). Although the directed interaction with patients during routine office visits seems a reasonable endeavor, one recent study concludes that although physicians have the potential to impact health behaviors through simple discussion and routine follow-up, only about half are using this opportunity (Nawaz et al., 2000). In conclusion, the use of behavioral techniques in promoting health behavior change is well-supported and relatively easy to implement. The established and growing body of research supporting the inclusion of exercise to enhance the treatment effects across numerous areas should encourage health professionals to examine this simple yet powerful adjunctive treatment option.

REFERENCES

Albrecht, A.E., Marcus, B.H., Roberts, M., et al. (1998). Effect of smoking cessation on exercise performance in female smokers participating in exercise training. *American Journal of Cardiology, 82*, 950–955.

American Heart Association. (2007). Accessed on June 1, 2007 from: http://www.americanheart.org/presenter.jhtml?identifier=3040839

Apeldorf, W.J., & Alexopoulos, G. S. (2003). Late life mood disorders. In Principles of geriatric medicine and gerontology (5th Ed.) (pp. 1443–1458). York, PA: McGraw-Hill.

Baranowski, T., Anderson, C., & Carmack, C. (1998). Mediating variable framework in physical activity interventions: How are we doing? Might we do better? *American Journal of Preventative Medicine, 15*, 266–297.

Blumenthal, J.A., Babyak, M.A., Moore, K.A., et al. (1999). Effects of exercise training on older patients with major depression. *Archives of Internal Medicine, 159*, 2349–2356.

Brawley, L.R., Rejeski, W.J., & Lutes, L. (2000). A group-mediated cognitive-behavioral intervention for increasing adherence to physical activity in older adults. *Journal of Applied Biobehavioral Research, 5*, 47–65.

Brownell, K.D., Stunkard, A.J., & Albaum, J.M. (1980). Evaluation and modification of exercise patterns in the natural environment. *American Journal of Psychiatry, 137*, 1540–1545.

Busch, A., Schacter, C.L., Peloso, P.M., & Bombardier C. (2002). Exercise for treating fibromyalgia syndrome. *Cochrane Database Systematic Review, 3*: CD003786.

Centers for Disease Control (2007). Retrieved from the World Wide Wed, June 1, 2007 from: http://www.cdc.gov/nccdphp/dnpa/physical/index.htm

Ciccolo, J.T., Jowers, E.M., & Bartholomew, J.B. (2004). The benefits of exercise training for quality of life in HIV/AIDS in the post-HAART era. *Sports medicine, 34*, 487–499.

Cooper, J.C., Heron, T.E., & Heward, W.L. (1987). *Applied Behavior Analysis*. New York: Macmillan Publishing Company.

Craft, L.L., & Perna, F.M. (2004). The benefits of exercise for the clinically depressed. *Primary Care Companion Journal of Clinical Psychiatry, 6*(3), 104–111.

Crystal, S., Sambamoorthi, U., Walkup, J.T., & Akincigil, A. (2002). Diagnosis and treatment of depression in the elderly medicare population: Predictors, disparities and trends. *Journal of the American Geriatric Association, 51*, 1718–1728.

Dantz, B., Ashton, A.K., D'Mello, D.A., et al. (2003). The scope of the problem: Physical symptoms of depression. *The Journal of Family Practice, 12*(Suppl.), 6–7.

Dimeo, F., Bauer, M., Varahram, et al. (2001). Benefits from aerobic exercise in patients with major depression: A pilot study. *British Journal of Sports Medicine, 35*, 114–117.

Dishman, R.K. (1991). Increasing and maintaining exercise and physical activity. *Behavior Therapy, 22*, 345–378.

Dunn, A.L., Trivedi, M.H., Kampert, J.B., et al. (2005). Exercise treatment for depression efficacy and dose response. *American Journal of Preventive Medicine, 28*, 1–8.

Dunn, A.L., Trivedi, M.H., & O'Neal, H.A. (2001). Physical activity dose-response effects on outcomes of depression and anxiety. *Medicine, Science, Sports and Exercise, 33*(6), S587–S597.

Dunn, A.L., Trivedi, M.H., Kampert, J.B., et al. (2002). The DOSE study: A clinical trial to examine efficacy and dose response of exercise as treatment for depression. *Controlled Clinical Trials, 23*, 584–603.

Epstein, L.H., Roemmich, J.N. Paluch, R.A., & Raynor H.A. (2006). Physical activity as a substitute for sedentary behavior in youth. *Annuals of Behavioral Medicine, 29*(3), 200–209.

Epstein, L.H., Wing, R.R., Thompson, J.K, & Griffin, W. (1980). Attendance and fitness in aerobics exercise. The effects of contract and lottery procedures, *Behavior Modification, 4*, 465–479.

Ermalinski, R., Hanson, P.G., Lubin, B., et al. (1997). Impact of body-mind treatment component on alcoholic inpatients. *Journal of Psychosocial Nursing and Mental health Services, 35*, 39–45.

Faulkner, G., Taylor, A., Ferrence, R., et al. (2006). Exercise science and the development of evidence-based practice: A "better practices" framework. *European Journal of Sports Sciences, 6*, 117–128.

Faulkner, G., Taylor, A., Munro, S., et al. (2007). The acceptability of physical activity programming with a smoking cessation service for individuals with severe mental illness. *Patient Education and Counseling, 66*(1), 123–126.

Fitterling, J.M., Martin, J.E., Gramling, S., & Cole, P. (1988). Behavioral management of exercise training in vascular headache patients: An investigation of exercise adherence and headache activity. *Journal of Applied Behavior Analysis, 21*, 9–19.

Gillet, P.A., White, A.T., & Caserta, M.S. (1996). Effect of exercise and or fitness education on fitness in older sedentary obese women. *Journal of Aging and Physical Activity, 4*, 42–55.

Glass, J., Lyden, A., Petzke, F., et al. (2004). The effect of brief exercise cessation on pain, fatigue, and mood symptom development in healthy, fit individuals. *Journal of Psychosomatic Research, 57*(4), 391–398.

Goldenberg, D.L., Burckhardt, C., Crofford, L. (2004). Management of fibromyalgia syndrome. *Journal of the American Medical Association, 292*, 2388–2395.

Goodwin, R.D. (2003). Association between physical activity and mental disorders among adults in the United States. *Preventive Medicine, 36*, 698–703.

Heath, J.M., & Stuart, M.R. (2002). Prescribing exercise for frail elders. *Journal of American Board of Family Practice, 15*, 218–228.

Winslow, E., Bohannon, N., Brunton, S.A., & Mayhew, H.E. (1996). Lifestyle modification: Weight control, exercise, and smoking cessation. *American Journal of Medicine*, *101*, 25S–33S.

Wolfe, F. Anderson, J., Harkness, D., et al. (1997). A prospective, longitudinal, multicenter study of service utilization and costs in fibromyalgia. *Arthritis and Rheumatology*, *40*, 1560–1570.

Wolfe, F., Smythe, H.A., Yunus, M.B., et al. (1990). The American college of rheumatology 1990 criteria for the classification of fibromyalgia. *Arthritis and Rheumatology*, *33*, 160–172.

World Health Organization. Depression. Available at www.who.org/int/en/ Accessed on June 15, 2007.

Wysocki, T., Hall, G., Iwata, B., & Riordan, M. (1979). Behavioral management of exercise contracting for aerobic points. *Journal of Applied Behavior Analysis*, *12*, 55–64.

Young, J.E., Weinberger, A.D., Beck, A.T. (2001). Cognitive therapy for depression. In Barlow, D. H. (Ed.). Clinical Handbook of Psychological Disorders, Third Edition. New York, NY: Guilford Press.

Zinna, E.M., & Yarasheski, K.E. (2003). Exercise treatment to counteract protein wasting of chronic diseases. *Current Opinion in Clinical Nutrition & Metabolic Care*, *6*, 87–93.

9

Meditation and Relaxation

Kenneth Kushner* and Mark Marnocha†

*University of Wisconsin, School of Medicine and Public Health
†Fox Valley Family Medicine, School of Medicine and Public Health

DESCRIPTION OF THE INTERVENTIONS

There is clear logic in considering meditation and relaxation together in one chapter. First, both bridge the Cartesian duality and are often described as "mind/body" interventions. Extensive research has shown that meditation and relaxation impact psychological as well as physical well-being (Lehrer & Woolfolk, 1993; Murphy & Donovan, 2006). Second, both are often referred to as "self-regulation" techniques (Shapiro, 1980). As such, they are frequently described as ways that individuals can gain control of their own thoughts, emotions, and bodily processes. Yet another reason for considering meditation and relaxation together is that there is often a blurring of the boundaries between the two. Some, notably Benson (1975), have postulated that there are no fundamental differences among various types of meditation and relaxation techniques. Others have argued that different techniques have specific effects (see Lehrer & Woolfolk, 1993; and Lehrer et al., 1994 for reviews of this debate). Finally, both meditation and relaxation have the potential to be ideal adjuncts to other forms of psychotherapy. Because they typically consist of skills that a client presumably can learn in a brief time and practice on his/her own, these modalities can conveniently be added to other therapeutic interventions.

Although combining meditation and relaxation in a single chapter has a clear rationale, doing so creates some definite challenges. First, they have extensive literatures. The combined number of citations in Medline since 1966 using meditation or relaxation techniques as keywords is close to 5000 articles. Even when one considers that many of the articles are nonempirical in nature—and thus obviously not relevant to evidence-based standards—reviewing the literature can be a challenge. For a busy clinician looking into these techniques as potential adjuncts to psychotherapy, the sheer amount of literature can seem overwhelming.

A second challenge presented by the combined literatures stems from the variety of techniques that have been subsumed under the rubrics of meditation and relaxation. For example, meditative traditions from many religious traditions have been applied to clinical settings, often with great claims of effectiveness. The differences among various meditative traditions may seem subtle. Descriptions of the techniques may be cast in esoteric jargon unclear to clinicians without backgrounds in these traditions. Furthermore, some techniques have been applied to certain clinical problems but not to others. This raises the question of how specific is the therapeutic effectiveness of the various techniques to specific problems. Again, the size of the literature on meditation and relaxation can intimidate the busy clinician wishing to answer these questions in order to make an empirically sound recommendation for a client.

Yet another challenge presented to the clinician—let alone to the reviewer—by the size of the literature is the blurring of the boundaries between meditation and relaxation described above. In performing the literature search for this chapter, we found that the same clinical technique would sometimes have the keyword meditation, sometimes relaxation, and sometimes both. This is not surprising because some of the most researched relaxation techniques are modifications of centuries-old meditation techniques. It was often difficult to decide whether a technique should be referred to as meditation or relaxation.

MEDITATION

Most, if not all, religious traditions have some type of meditative discipline. In *The Meditative Mind: The Varieties of Meditative Experience*, Goleman (1988) describes meditative traditions from Hinduism [Bhakti, Transcendental Meditation (TM), Ashtanga Yoga, Kundalini Yoga], Buddhism (Vipassana, Tibetan, Tantrism, Zen), Judaism (Kabbalah), Christianity (Hesychasm, the Rosary), and Islam (Sufism). Typically, meditative traditions represent mystical branches of religions and are intended to induce transcendental experiences as defined by the particular religious tradition. As such, they were not intended to be psychotherapies in the Western sense of the word, although religious traditions have all participated in their cultures' healing methods, medical and psychological (Frank, 1973). However, because they are generally recognized as creating positive psychological and physiological states (i.e., a sense of well-being, relaxation), they became of interest to Western psychotherapists.

There have been attempts to arrive at a common definition of meditation that encompasses the variety of meditative techniques. For example, Shapiro and Walsh stated "meditation can be defined as a family of practices that train attention and awareness, usually with the aim of fostering psychological and spiritual well-being and maturity. Meditation does this by training and bringing mental processes under greater voluntary control, and directing them in beneficial ways" (2003). Several typologies of meditation have been attempted. A common one is to divide meditative disciplines into concentrative (focusing awareness on a single object or movement) or awareness (allowing attention to "move to a variety of objects and investigate them all") (Shapiro & Walsh, 2003) as well as types that combine both concentration and awareness (Shapiro, 1980). Although there may be many commonalities among the various forms of meditation, there is also tremendous diversity of techniques. As Shapiro pointed out, "some involve sitting quietly and produce a state of quiescence and restfulness. Some involve sitting quietly and produce a state of excitement and arousal. Some ... involve physical movement to a greater or lesser degree. Sometimes these 'movement meditations' result in a state of excitement, sometimes a state of relaxation." (Shapiro, 1982). Thus, although there may be theoretical and empirical reasons to assume that at least some types of meditation may have similar psychological and physiological effects (Benson, 1975), there is equal reason to believe that there may be significant differences among them as well, and physiological differences among different types of meditation have been demonstrated (Lehrer & Woolfolk, 1993). However, Walsh and Shapiro's recent (2006) caution stands, that Western psychology should avoid "assimilative integration in which much of the richness and uniqueness of meditation and its psychologies and philosophies have been overlooked."

There have been extensive reviews of the effects of various types of meditation on physiological and psychological parameters, including electrocortical activity, electrodermal activity, respiration, cardiovascular response, metabolism, cerebral blood flow, hemispheric lateralization, and blood pressure (see Shapiro and Walsh, 1984, 2003; Murphy and Donovan, 2006; and Walsh and Shapiro, 2006 for reviews). Recent research has found meditation to influence immune functioning (Davidson et al., 2003; Robinson et al., 2003). There have also been several reviews specifically on the use of meditation in psychotherapy (Bogart, 1991; Delmonte, 1986; La Torre, 2001; Smith, 1975; West, 1987). In spite of the plethora of meditative traditions and techniques, a relatively small subset has been the focus in the empirical psychotherapy literature. These will be discussed below.

HINDU TRADITIONS

YOGA[1]

Westerners probably associate yoga with physical postures and stretching, referred to as *asanas* in Sanskrit. However, *asanas* are only one aspect (translated as "limb" from the Sanskrit) of the practice of yoga. The other limbs involve moral precepts and other forms of meditation. There are numerous meditative techniques that come out of the yogic tradition. (Becker, 2000). Many of them, particularly those in the Kundalini Yoga tradition, emphasize breathing, referred

[1] Although there is some association between yoga and Buddhist traditions, it is primarily identified with Hinduism and will be discussed in that context accordingly.

to collectively as pranayama, one of the limbs of yoga. Reviews of the literature on Yoga in psychotherapy have been published by Becker (2000), Khalsa (2004), and Patel (1984).

While description of the many types of yoga practices is beyond the scope of this chapter, two in particular have special relevance to research on yoga as psychotherapy. Sudarshan Kriya Yoga (SKY), a form of *pranayama*, has been applied to the treatment of depression (Brown & Gerbarg, 2005a; Brown & Gerbarg, 2005b). Basic SKY is taught in a 22-hour course. It involves training in four different types of controlled breathing: 3-stage slow breathing *(ujjayi)*, rapid breathing *(bhastrika)*, chanting of "om," and cyclical breathing (*Sudarshan Kriya*). Shannahoff-Khalsa (2004b) modified Kundalini meditation techniques specifically for treatment of psychiatric patients.

TRANSCENDENTAL MEDITATION

TM is one of the most well-known and possibly the most popular form of meditation in the West. It was brought to the West by Maharishi Mahesh Yogi, a prolific teacher and writer. The fundamental technique of TM involves meditation on a *mantra*, a Sanskrit word or sound. A basic tenet of TM is that the selection of the *mantra* for a particular individual is extremely important. The *mantra* must be given to a student by a bona fide teacher of TM. and the manner in which *mantras* are selected is shrouded in considerable secrecy. The actual process of TM involves concentration on the *mantra* as the meditator repeats it in his/her mind. When the practitioner notices that his/her thoughts have wandered from the *mantra*, he/she gently refocuses attention on it. Both the concentration on the mantra and the refocusing should be done gently, rather than in a forced manner. In this way, effortful concentration is avoided (Goleman, 1988). No special postures or physical activities are necessary for the basic practice of TM; the student is told to sit comfortably in a chair and breathe naturally.

BUDDHIST TRADITIONS

VIPASSANA (INSIGHT) MEDITATION

Vipassana (Insight) and mindfulness often are used interchangeably. Insight has been defined in the context of Buddhism as "a clear awareness of exactly what is happening as it happens" (Gunaratana, 1991). Historically, mindfulness is a precursor to insight, when one can maintain mindfulness continuously (Goleman, 1988). Vipassana is associated with one of the oldest Buddhist traditions still in existence: Theraveda, which is primarily practiced in Sri Lanka and Southeast Asia.[2] The practice of mindfulness meditation involves observing one's thoughts

[2] "Mindfulness" is also associated with some later Buddhist traditions, including some forms of Zen.

and bodily sensations in a nonjudgmental, nonreactive manner. Typically, the practitioner begins a session of meditation by focusing awareness on his or her breath. The meditator does not try to control the breath; rather, he or she just observes the sensations of breathing. However, as the person relaxes, the breaths naturally get longer.

ZEN

The basis of Zen is meditative practice known as *zazen*, which literally means "seated Zen" in Japanese. Like mindfulness meditation, it is traditionally practiced in seated cross-legged positions; however, alternative postures can be used. There are two major traditions of Zen still in existence: The Rinzai Sect and the Soto Sect, which differ somewhat in the practice of zazen. Soto Zen bears similarity to mindfulness meditation in that the practitioner is taught to observe his or her thoughts and bodily sensations. Similarly, the breath is observed but not controlled. Zazen in the Rinzai tradition emphasizes concentration rather than mindfulness. Beginning practitioners are given the task of counting their breaths (typically exhalations only, from 1–10).[3] If the meditator reaches 10, he or she starts again with 1. If he or she notices that he or she has lost track of the count, the instruction is to start again at 1. Rather than observing the breath, the Rinzai practitioner explicitly regulates it through the use of a technique known as *tanden* or *hara* breathing (Kushner, 2000; Lehrer et al., 1999; Von Durckheim, 1977), which involves the use of purposefully slow, deep respirations using the muscles of the lower abdomen (*hara*, in Japanese). With practice students learn that *tanden* breathing fosters concentration and that proper posture is necessary for proper breathing.

RELAXATION

Progressive Relaxation

The development of modern clinical methods commonly referred to as "relaxation training techniques" is usually identified with Edmond Jacobson (Bernstein & Borkevec, 1973; Jacobson, 1929; Lehrer, 1982), who developed a technique to directly decrease muscular tension by alternatively tensing and relaxing different muscle groups. The original technique, called "progressive relaxation" (PR), was quite lengthy and involved as many as 50 or more sessions over a period of months to years (Bernstein & Borkevec, 1973). Over the years, abbreviated variations of Jacobson's procedures have been introduced (Bernstein & Given, 1984; Wolpe, 1969). Some believe that the shortened versions should be viewed as distinct from Jacobson's (Lehrer & Woolfolk, 1984), and perhaps less effective (Lehrer, 1982). However, these all utilize similar procedures of tensing and relaxing various muscle groups. Other procedures have

[3] Some Soto instructors also use breath counting, at least in the beginning.

added techniques to enable the subject to develop a relaxed state on cue in a very short time. A well-researched example of this is "Applied Relaxation" (AR) (Ost, 1987). After learning an abbreviated version of PR, the subject is taught to associate the sensation of relaxation induced by PR to the cue to taking a breath and subvocalizing "relax." With practice, subjects can learn to relax in 20–30 seconds.

A component that appears in both relaxation and meditation techniques is that of breathing, either as an outcome or as a primary technique. Although beyond the scope of this review, breathing training and regulation techniques appear in current treatment protocols for panic disorder (Meuret & Wilhelm, 2003), and current reviews (Gilbert, 2003; Ley, 1999) have provided evidence for breathing training having a beneficial effect on panic, anxiety, and physiological disorders.

THE RELAXATION RESPONSE

The technique commonly referred to as the "relaxation response" is a modification of TM. It was developed by Benson with the explicit purpose of "deculti-fying" the meditative experience and of applying it to clinical situations without the religious trappings of TM or other spirituality-based meditation techniques (1975). Benson originally used the term "relaxation response" to refer to what he viewed as a constellation of physiological effects induced by all forms of meditation. The actual technique he developed to induce the relaxation response is sometimes referred to as the "respiratory one method" (Carrington, 1993). However, the term relaxation response is commonly used to describe Benson's method. According to the technique, the subject uses the word "one" or other word or sound of his or her choice as one would use a mantra in TM. Similar mantra-based clinical techniques have also been report by Carrington (1993) and Murphy et al. (1986).

CONTEMPORARY MULTIMODAL THERAPY PROGRAMS BASED ON MEDITATION

Mindfulness-based Stress Reduction

Mindfulness-based stress reduction (MBSR) was developed by Kabat-Zinn at the University of Massachusetts. The development and structure of the program are thoroughly described in his book, *Full Catastrophe Living* (Kabat-Zinn, 1990). MBSR, as the name implies, incorporates mindfulness meditation as a central component. The original program involved eight consecutive weekly group sessions involving instruction and practice in Mindfulness meditation as well as Hatha yoga, and lectures and discussions about Mindfulness and the role of stress in health and illness. Participants are expected to practice both meditation and yoga *asanas* for 45 minutes a day, 6 days a week, and to record the results of awareness exercises in a book for 15 minutes a day. Participants are also required to attend a daylong silent retreat on a weekend toward the end of the program. This "Day of Mindfulness" consists of prolonged practice of meditation and yoga. MBSR was originally developed for medical patients with maladaptive health behaviors, stress-related conditions, and/or chronic pain. As originally practiced by Kabat-Zinn, the groups were diverse in terms of the types of patient problems. Programs modeled after Kabat-Zinn's have proliferated both nationally and internationally.

Mindfulness-based Cognitive Therapy

Mindfulness-based cognitive therapy (MBCT) can be viewed as a variation of MBSR. The evolution of the program is thoroughly discussed by its originators who are cognitive-behavioral therapists (Segal et al., 2002) and developed it as a way to prevent relapses of major depressive episodes. They came to believe that mindfulness meditation may be a particularly effective way for patients to recognize, through dispassionate observation of their thoughts, feelings, and bodily sensations, the early stages of relapse. After observing Kabat-Zinn and colleagues in action, they developed an eight-session group program that includes elements of MBSR, such as the practice of mindfulness meditation with other exercises and didactic content more specifically relevant to cognition and depression.

Dialectical and "Third Wave" Behavioral Therapy

The term "third wave behavioral therapy" has been used to refer collectively to a number of therapies that grew out of behavioral analysis. Often, they employ mindfulness as a way of teaching acceptance (Hayes et al., 2004). Dialectical Behavioral Therapy (DBT) is perhaps the best known representative of these therapies. It was developed by Linehan et al. (1991) to treat patients with borderline personality disorder (BPD). Mindfulness is one of four core skills emphasized in the program. The others are interpersonal skills, emotion regulation skills, and distress tolerance skills. Linehan describes mindfulness skills as "psychological and behavioral versions of meditation skills usually taught in Eastern spiritual practices" and drew heavily on her own experiences as a Zen student in including them in her program. The original version of DBT involves both weekly individual therapy and a skills training group. Typically, the treatment lasts 1 year.

OUTCOME DATA

In this section, we will discuss the outcome data on meditation and relaxation, with a particular eye toward their uses as adjuncts to psychotherapy. It should be clear from what we have written above that the size of the literature and the diversity of interventions subsumed makes this a challenging task. To make it manageable within the restrictions of one chapter, we will focus on the highest standard of clinical evidence: Randomized controlled trials (RCTs) with clinical populations. We feel that this focus will address the most basic question posed by the practicing clinician: What do we know about the efficacy of these methods with the types of clients most likely to seek help from a psychotherapist?

In reviewing the literature for this chapter, we adopted the following strategy. First, we searched the Medline, Cochrane, DARE, and PsychInfo databases for the following keywords: Meditation, mindfulness, TM, Zen, relaxation, relaxation techniques, and stress management. We then culled the results and extracted those that included randomized clinical trials (either by keyword or by perusal of the methodologies) or randomized trials with subjects who met interview or psychometric criteria of pathology (i.e., subjects recruited in the media who scored in clinical ranges of depression inventories). We then excluded studies of patients with primarily physical problems (i.e., interventions on pain in cancer patients). When relevant, we included studies referenced in articles that did not appear in our computer searches as long as they met the other inclusion requirements. This left us with a set of RCTs on patients or subjects primarily with DSM axis 1 diagnoses.

The fact that we are interested in meditation and relaxation as *adjuncts* to psychotherapy also posed some methodological issues. The basic research paradigm for study of an adjunctive measure is additive in nature, evaluating outcomes of a type of therapy, i.e., short-term psychodynamic therapy, with and without an adjunctive intervention, i.e., a form of meditation. Such research should also control for attention and time effects, i.e., a placebo control condition. Thus, there would be, at a minimum, a 2-group design: Psychodynamic therapy plus meditation versus psychodynamic therapy plus placebo. Few studies reviewed met this basic standard. For that reason, we will primarily review randomized controlled studies that considered meditation and relaxation as treatments in themselves, rather than as adjuncts to other forms of psychotherapy. When relevant, we will discuss a few less-controlled studies that we feel have particular usefulness. Our efforts were devoted primarily to the subset of meditation and relaxation interventions that have been relatively well-defined, replicated, and investigated as stand-alone interventions. Other reviews, i.e., Jorm et al. (2004), have looked at evidence pertaining to highly diverse relaxation or meditation techniques applied to a range of similar disorders, leaving the clinician unsure as to the evidence for a specific procedure for relaxation or meditation practice.

STUDIES OF MULTIPLE DIAGNOSTIC CATEGORIES

Kutz et al. (1985), in an uncontrolled study, used a multimodal relaxation program (relaxation response, mindfulness meditation, body awareness exercises, and mindfulness exercises) with 20 patients in psychodynamic therapy. They found substantial improvement on therapist and patient self-report measures of well-being. Weiss et al. (2005), in a nonrandomized and marginally controlled study, offered a variation of MBSR to patients in individual therapy with the senior author. The patients who opted into the adjunctive program had DSM-IV diagnoses of depression and anxiety. They found the MBSR patients roughly equivalent to patients who remained in individual therapy alone on measures of psychological distress. However, the MBSR patients terminated individual therapy at a significantly greater rate.

ANXIETY DISORDERS

Combined Groups of Anxiety Disorders

In an uncontrolled study, Kabat-Zinn et al. (1990) found that MBSR reduced therapist and self-ratings of anxiety for combined groups of patients with generalized anxiety disorder and/or panic disorder with or without agoraphobia. Analysis of a subset of subjects indicated that therapeutic gains were maintained after 3 years (Miller et al., 1995).

Generalized Anxiety Disorder

Benson et al. (1978) compared the Relaxation Response to self-hypnosis on a sample of patients diagnosed with "anxiety neurosis." They found substantial improvement in both groups. Remarkably, the instructions for both interventions were given in only one session; the subjects were then left on their own to practice it at home. Another study found TM, PR, and PR plus EMG biofeedback to all result in improvement in DSM-II anxiety neurotics. There were no differences among the various treatments (Raskin et al., 1980b).

Several studies involved trials of AR and cognitive therapy. Fisher and Durham (1999) reanalyzed four of them from the standpoint of clinically significant changes on the State-Trait Anxiety Inventory. They found essentially parity between AR and cognitive therapy, with recovery rates at 6-month follow-up between 50 and 60%. Both fared better than other treatments in other randomized clinical trials reviewed by Fisher and Durham. Ost and Breitholtz (2000) and Arntz (2003) also found equivalence between AR and cognitive therapy in the treatment of generalized anxiety.

Panic Disorder and Agoraphobia

Three studies compared PR to other treatments for panic disorder. Michelson et al. (1983) contrasted PR to other treatments commonly used in the cognitive-behavioral treatment of panic disorder: Graduated exposure and paradoxical intention. Although all three treatments produced significant improvements, both relaxation and exposure tended to lead to faster improvement. There were no differences between PR and graduated exposure. Barlow et al. (1989) compared four conditions: PR alone; exposure to somatic cues plus cognitive therapy; PR plus both exposure and cognitive therapy; and a wait-list control. Subjects in all three treatment conditions improved more than those in the control group. Both treatments with exposure had significantly more subjects who were panic free at the end of the study that those who had PR alone. Beck et al. (1994) compared PR to cognitive therapy without exposure and a minimal contact control for patients with panic disorder. Both treatments yielded significant improvements compared with the control. There was slightly more improvement in subjects given cognitive therapy compared to those given PR.

Five studies examined the use of AR in panic disorder. Significant improvement in symptomatology was found in all of them. Two of them (Ost, 1988; Ost et al., 1993) compared AR to more traditional PR. Both found slight advantages for AR. Two studies contrasted AR and cognitive therapy. Clark et al. (1994) found better outcomes for cognitive therapy than for either AR or treatment with imipramine. Arntz and Van Den Hout (1996) found cognitive therapy to be superior to AR in reducing panic frequency. In contrast, Ost et al. (1993) found no outcome differences between AR and cognitive behavioral therapy (CBT).

Other Phobias

Jorm et al. (2004) reviewed complementary and self-help treatments for anxiety disorders, including a number of studies involving relaxation techniques for a variety of phobias. They concluded that the family of relaxation techniques is effective for dental phobia and test anxiety. They did not differentiate among different types of relaxation techniques. When we reviewed the studies they cited pertaining to test anxiety, we found they overwhelmingly involved nonclinical samples or used diverse or poorly defined relaxation interventions. Ost and colleagues conducted a series of studies of the impact of AR or modifications of AR on a number of simple phobias. They found AR and active behavioral interventions to be effective treatments; they did not find differences in effectiveness between AR and the other interventions. These comparisons included AR and social skills training for social anxiety (Jerremalm et al., 1986a; Ost et al., 1981), self-instruction training for dental phobia (Jerremalm et al., 1986b), exposure for blood (Ost et al., 1984, 1989), and for claustrophobia (Ost et al., 1982).

Obsessive-Compulsive Disorder

Fals-Stewart et al. (1993) utilized PR as a control group for a study comparing individual versus group behavioral therapy. They found both behavioral treatments to be superior to relaxation at the conclusion of treatment. In one of the few studies that compared different types of meditation in a randomized clinical trial, Shannahoff-Khalsa et al. (1997) and Shannahoff-Khalsa (2003) found greater improvement for obsessive-compulsive disorder (OCD)-spectrum patients treated with a set of Kundalini Yoga exercises than for patients treated with a combination of Relaxation Response and mindfulness meditation.

Posttraumatic Stress Disorder

Echeburua et al. (1997) compared cognitive-behavioral therapy (CBT) (self-exposure and cognitive restructuring) to PR in the treatment of female sexual assault victims seeking treatment for posttraumatic stress disorder (PTSD). Most of the patients improved, but the success rates were higher in the CBT group. It should be noted, however, that the CBT patients had almost double the amount of in-therapy time than those receiving PR. Marks et al. (1998) found that relaxation training, without specific active coping skills and utilized as a placebo control, produced moderate benefit at 3-month follow-up, and that combinations of exposure and restructuring were "usually" better than relaxation alone. Taylor et al. (2003) found that a relaxation intervention for PTSD patients utilizing Marks et al.'s (1998) protocol was equivalent in efficacy and speed to EMDR, but less effective than combined imaginal and in vivo exposure, also based on Marks et al. (1998). Vaughan et al. (1994) compared AR with EMDR and imaginal exposure relative to waiting list control and found all three conditions to be equivalent in their superiority to waiting list control. Intriguing questions remain concerning the role and components of relaxation treatments for PTSD; Taylor et al. (2003) observe that such treatment is "potentially useful but understudied" and that successful relaxation skill acquisition may facilitate spontaneous exposure to trauma-related stimuli. Bradley et al.'s (2005) recent meta-analysis echoes this ambiguity about relaxation interventions for PTSD, finding that relaxation is generally treated as a "supportive control condition" not compared with waiting list control conditions. They observed that relaxation's and supportive therapy's roles as control conditions leave neither of them "intended (and presumably perceived by the research therapists conducting them) to succeed" (p. 226).

DEPRESSIVE DISORDERS

Several studies have compared relaxation or meditation to pharmacotherapy. McLean and Hakstian (1979) used an unspecified relaxation program as an attention placebo for a study comparing brief psychodynamic therapy, behavior therapy, and amitriptyline as treatments for unipolar depression. They found behavior therapy superior to both relaxation and amitriptyline, which were equivalent in terms of outcome. Psychodynamic therapy fared the worst. In a subsequent reanalysis of the data, McLean and Taylor (1992) found no relationship between severity of depression and relative efficacy of the various treatment modalities. Murphy et al. (1995) also used relaxation as an attention control. Mild to moderately depressed outpatients were treated with either imipramine, CBT, or PR. They found the outcomes for the two psychological interventions to be equivalent, but both were superior to imipramine. In a remarkable study that also employed a tricyclic antidepressant, Janakiramaiah et al. (2000) used as subjects inpatients diagnosed with melancholic depression. They were treated with either SKY, electroconvulsive therapy (ECT), or pharmacotherapy. Patients improved in all three groups, with most improvement in the ECT group. There were no significant differences in response between the yoga and pharmacotherapy groups.

Reynold and Coats (1986), in one of the few RCTs involving adolescents, compared CBT, PR, and a wait-list control on groups of high school students meeting psychometric criteria for depression. They found CBT and PR to be equivalent and superior to the control group. At the other end of the life cycle, Lynch et al. (2003) found that the addition of DBT skills group plus telephone case management to psychotropic medication management resulted in greater remission of depression in geriatric patients than medication management alone.

In a particularly well-designed series of studies, Teasdale, Segal, and colleagues have focused on the efficacy of MBCT in preventing relapse/recurrence of major depression. Teasdale et al. (2000) contrasted MBCT and treatment as usual (TAU) for patients in recovery from recurrent major depressive disorder. They found MBCT to be superior for patients with 3 or more previous major depressive episodes. No such advantage was found for patients with 2 or less previous episodes. This result was replicated in a later study (Ma & Teasdale, 2004).

EATING DISORDERS

Two studies have investigated the use of DBT in eating disorders. Telch et al. (2001) compared an abbreviated version of DBT adapted to women with binge-eating disorder to a wait-list control. The DBT group had a significant reduction in binge eating and eating pathology. Safer et al. (2001) found a shortened version of DBT resulted in significantly greater decrease in binging/purging behavior compared with a wait-list control for a group of women with bulimia nervosa.

SUBSTANCE ABUSE DISORDERS

Gelderloos et al. (1991) reviewed 24 studies that investigated the benefits of the TM program in treating and preventing the "misuse of chemical substances," including alcohol, cigarettes, and recreational drugs on a broad range of subjects. Although most of the studies are nonexperimental and uncontrolled, the authors conclude that "all studies showed positive effects of the TM program." Three of the studies were RCTs. Myers and Eisner (1974) assigned volunteer male college students to either TM, karate training, or a no-treatment control. Subjects in both intervention groups reported less usage of harmful drug use compared with controls. Brautigam (1977) compared the TM program to a wait-list control for young adult drug users recently treated for hepatitis. Reports of drug use decreased for the TM group and increased for the control group. Taub et al. (1994) compared the TM program to standard treatment or one of two relaxation programs for chronic "skid row" alcoholics recently released from detoxification centers. They reported that after 18 months, 65% in the TM group were completely abstinent versus 25% in the standard treatment group.

Murphy et al. (1986) compared a "mantra-based concentrative exercise" to running and a no-treatment control for a sample of "heavy" drinking college students. They found significantly greater reduction in self-reports of alcohol consumption in the running group than in either the meditation or the control groups. However, when they divided the meditators into high and low compliers, based on self-report, they found the high compliers to have reduction rates equivalent to the running group.

Shaffer et al. (1997) compared Hatha Yoga training to the conventional adjunctive treatment of psychodynamically oriented group psychotherapy for patients on methadone maintenance. They found that both treatments contributed to significantly reduced drug use and criminal activities. There were no differences between the two types of adjunctive treatments.

Several studies have investigated the effectiveness of DBT for excessive drinking in patients with BPD. These will be discussed below.

BORDERLINE PERSONALITY DISORDER

Linehan and colleagues, in a very well-designed series of studies, have found DBT to be superior to TAU for women with BPD. Because their TAU groups involved referral of subjects to community mental health practitioners, they thereby controlled for threats to external validity such as time and attention. Specifically, Linehan and colleagues found that DBT resulted in greater reduction in the number and severity of parasuicidal events, fewer hospital days, and greater improvement in interpersonal functioning (Linehan et al., 1991, 1993, 1994). Similar results have been reported more recently in the Netherlands (Verheul et al., 2003). Linehan and colleagues found DBT to be more effective than TAU in reducing substance abuse comorbid with BPD (Linehan et al., 1999) but equivalent to a combined 12-step and comprehensive validation program for a sample of heroin-addicted borderline subjects (Linehan et al., 2002). Van den Bosch et al. (2002) found no differences in effect between DBT and TAU on substance abuse in borderline patients. Double-blind, placebo-controlled studies have found that the addition of fluoxetine did not enhance the effectiveness of an abbreviated version of DBT (Simpson et al., 2004) whereas the addition of olanzapine did (Soler et al., 2005).

ATTENTION DEFICIT/HYPERACTIVITY DISORDER

Goldbeck and Schmid (2003) compared autogenic training to a wait-list control for a sample of "mildly disturbed" children, some of whom were diagnosed with attention deficit/hyperactivity disorder (ADHD). They found greater improvement in the intervention group, particularly for "externalizing" children. They did not provide separate analyses for those diagnosed with ADHD. Gonzalez and Sellers (2002) studied the effectiveness of a multimodal stress management program on children diagnosed with ADHD. The program involved PR, imagery, exercise, time management, assertiveness training, and anger management. They found a therapist-led version of the program to be superior to both a parent-led version and a wait-list control.

SUMMARY OF THE OUTCOME DATA

Using the criteria for empirically validated treatments delineated by Division 12 of the American Psychological Association on the Psychological Intervention Guidelines (Task Force on Promotion and Dissemination of Psychological

Procedures, 1995), only one of the interventions reviewed meets the criteria for well-established treatments. DBT, as a treatment for BPD, has been demonstrated in more than two well-designed between-group studies utilizing clearly defined subject groups to be superior on a number of outcome measures to traditional treatment. The treatment is thoroughly manualized, and the effects have been demonstrated by two investigatory teams (Linehan et al., 1991; Linehan, 1993a; Verheul et al., 2003). The use of DBT as a treatment of substance abuse comorbid with BPD has not been studied as thoroughly, and currently does not meet the standards of well-established treatments.

A number of treatments reviewed meet the criteria for probably efficacious treatments. A summary of those that meet this standard of evidence is displayed in Table 9.1.

We recognize the designation of "empirically supported treatment" is controversial (see Norcross et al., 2006, for a recent dialogue on the issues) and that establishment of an intervention as "empirically supported"* does not necessarily imply its superiority to others. We do believe, however, that the criteria for "probably efficacious"* constitute an appropriate minimum standard of evidence. That said, there is no clear evidence supporting any of the interventions reviewed over the others for the disorders in question. Similarly, there is no evidence from the randomized clinical trials of the superiority of relaxation over meditation or vice versa. By and large, such comparative trials have not been conducted, nor have trials that would examine specific adjunctive contributions to outcomes.

Given the proliferation of research on MBSR, it is worth commenting on why we excluded it from our list of probably efficacious treatments. Although recent reviews have referred to MBSR as meeting the criteria for a probably efficacious treatments (Baer, 2003; Walsh & Shapiro, 2006), most of the studies reviewed have involved patients with pain and/or other psychosomatic problems, which are not the focus of our review. Although patients with DSM diagnoses have been included in some studies on MBSR, these have typically been in heterogeneous diagnostic groups. As Baer points out, MBSR was not developed to treat any specific disorder. While we believe that MBSR has tremendous potential as a health-related intervention and as a treatment for a variety of psychological problems, we simply do not feel that studies have been conducted that meet the standards set by Division 12 for probably efficacious treatments for specific traditional DSM psychiatric disorders. More specifically, we could not identify a

* **Criteria for Empirically-Supported Treatments** (Paraphrased from Task Force on Promotion and Dissemination of Psychological Procedures, 1995)

Well-established: Manualized treatments researched by at least 2 different investigators, using well-specified client samples, with EITHER (A) 2 or more between group studies superiority to placebo or another treatment, and/or equivalence to an established treatment in an adequately-powered study OR (B) a large series of well-designed single case studies demonstrating efficacy compared to another intervention as in 'A' above.

Probably Efficacious: Two studies showing superiority to waiting-list control OR One or more studies meeting criteria for A above but only 1 investigator OR Two or more positive studies but heterogeneous samples OR A small series of well-designed single case studies.

TABLE 9.1 Summary of Treatments Meeting Criteria for Probably Efficacious Treatments

Condition	Intervention	Citation for evidence
Generalized anxiety disorder	AR	Borkovec & Costello, 1993; Ost & Breitholtz, 2000
Panic disorder with or without agoraphobia	AR	Ost, 1988; Ost et al., 1993
Dental phobia	AR	Jerremalm et al., 1986b; Willumsen et al., 2001
Obsessive-compulsive disorder	Specific Kundalini Yoga exercises	Shanahoff-Khalsa, 1997, 2003
Depressive disorders: Symptomatic	PR	Murphy et al., 1995; Reynolds & Coats, 1986
Major depressive disorder: Relapse prevention*	MBCT	Ma & Teasdale, 2004; Teasdale et al., 2000
Binge-eating disorder, bulimia nervosa	DBT	Safer et al., 2001; Telch et al., 2001
Alcohol abuse disorder	TM†	Taub et al., 1994
Substance abuse disorder, comorbid with borderline personality disorder	DBT	Linehan et al., 1999

* For patients with two or less previous major depressive episodes.

† Because of the highly structured nature of the TM program, we determined that it met the requirement for manualization.

AR, applied relaxation PR, progressive relaxation; MBCT, Mindfulness-based cognitive therapy; TM, Transcendental Meditation; DBT, Dialectical Behavioral Therapy.

single well-controlled study on a clinical population with a homogenous DSM-IV diagnosis. As noted above, we do feel that MBCT, a variation of MBSR, meets the criteria for probably efficacious treatment for the prevention of relapse from depression. We also anticipate that it will soon be established as an empirically validated treatment.

KEY PROCESS VARIABLES

By and large, process variables have not been studied, let alone linked to outcome, in randomized trials of meditation and relaxation in clinical samples. However, some key mediator variables can be discerned from the literature.

DROPOUT RATES

There is considerable variability of attrition rates of subjects (after randomization) in the studies we reviewed. For example, Benson et al. (1978)[4] reported a 54%

[4] They state that 37 of 69 subjects "did not complete the protocol;" they do not indicate whether they dropped out after the interventions began.

dropout rate whereas Arntz and Van Den Hout (1996) reported less than 3%. Although intention-to-treat analyses allow one to account for attrition rates when interpreting results, an intervention that many subjects will not complete will have less general utility than one with a lower dropout rate for the same population. On the basis of the literature reviewed, there is no compelling evidence of differential attrition rates among various types of interventions. The intervention that has the best-studied attrition rate to date is MBSR. Kabat-Zinn and Chapman-Waldrop (1988) found that 76% of 784 consecutive patients with a range of medical and psychological problems completed the 8-week program.

COMPLIANCE WITH PRACTICE

Meditation and relaxation are skills that can take considerable practice to master. For that reason, merely participating in a treatment for a set period of time (i.e., completion of study) does not guarantee proficiency in a given technique. Typically, subjects are given training by a professional with instructions to practice on their own. Clearly, the amount of practice theoretically should be related to therapeutic outcome. Yet few studies obtained internal measures of compliance with the instructions to practice and linked them to outcome. All such studies relied on self-reports, which are, of course, of questionable veracity. The best example of how practice can be related to outcome was reported by Murphy et al. (1995) in their study of problem drinkers. They found that, overall, their group of runners had significantly greater reduction of alcohol consumption than did either their meditation or no-treatment control groups. However, when they divided their meditators into high and low compliers, high compliers' outcomes were equivalent to those in the exercise group. Shapiro et al. (2003) found self-reports of practice positively related to outcome among breast cancer patients with insomnia. On the other hand, Davidson et al. (2003) found no relationship between reports of practice and biological or self-report measures of anxiety and affect in healthy normal subjects participating in MBSR in their workplace.

PROFICIENCY WITH TECHNIQUE

Completing a treatment protocol and practicing at home do not in themselves guarantee proficiency in technique. And, as noted above, self-reports of practice are not necessarily reliable. Yet, few of the outcome studies reviewed included internal measures of proficiency with the various therapeutic techniques. Raskin et al. (1980a) followed frontalis EMG changes—muscle tension indicators of decreased anxiety—in patients treated with either TM or PR. They found no association between muscle relaxation and clinical outcome. Recent research and theory about heart rate variability suggests it may be a strong candidate as a measure of proficiency, particularly for meditation or relaxation approaches that aim to alter respiration patterns as a means to achieve a relaxed state (Lehrer et al., 1999, 2000).

To be sure, physiological measures of proficiency may be easier to operationalize than are cognitive measures. However, the MBCT investigators have shown that this is possible. In attempts to determine the mechanisms behind the efficacy of MBCT, Teasdale and colleagues have examined mechanisms by which MBCT reduces relapses of depression. Williams et al. (2000) found that recovered patients given MBCT gave significantly fewer generic memories in response to cue words than did patients receiving TAU. Overly general memories have been associated with depression and other conditions. Teasdale et al. (2002) analyzed metacognitive awareness in patients in remission or recovery from recurrent major depression who had participated in either MBCT or TAU. Metacognitive awareness refers to "a cognitive set in which negative thoughts and feelings are seen as passing events in the mind rather than as inherent in the self or as necessarily valid reflections of reality" (Teasdale, 2002). From the standpoint of CBT, metacognitive awareness would thus give people "distance" from dysfunctional cognitions related to depression. As such, increased metacognitive awareness can be seen as a measure of proficiency with mindfulness. As predicted, patients in the MBCT treatment, in addition to having reduced relapse rates, demonstrated increased metacognitive awareness compared with the TAU group.

COST-EFFECTIVENESS

By definition, the use of meditation and relaxation as adjuncts to psychotherapy implies costs in addition to those of the primary psychotherapeutic treatment. There are several ways in which adjunctive measures can be cost-effective: (1) By shortening overall treatment time; (2) by shortening the length of a more expensive primary treatment; (3) by preventing relapse or comorbid disorders; (4) by preventing utilization of other medical services [as in the so-called "offset" phenomenon (Cummings & VandenBos, 1981)]; (5) by having fees so low that additional costs are not significant. By and large, the issue of cost-effectiveness has not been addressed in the randomized clinical trials of meditation and relaxation. However, there is indirect evidence that some of the interventions may be highly cost-effective.

In the study cited earlier, Benson et al. (1978) found substantial improvement in anxiety neurotics after one individual lesson in the Relaxation Response with instructions to practice at home. Although the study can be faulted for having an apparently large attrition rate, it does show that even minimal instruction in the technique can lead to therapeutic gains. If similar results could be obtained from group instruction, the overall costs of using the Relaxation Response as an adjunct would have been further reduced.

Orme-Johnson (1987) compared 5 years of insurance utilization of 2000 TM practitioners with normative data from the same insurance carrier. They found lower overall health care utilization in the TM group for inpatient mental health services, resulting in a difference of \$623 571 per 1000 subscribers over the

5 years. Although Orme-Johnson acknowledges that this was a nonrandomized study and that the results might have reflected preexisting differences in those who chose to practice TM versus those who did not, the study does suggest the possibility of significant cost-offset as a result of the meditative practice.

Cost-effectiveness claims have been made by the team of researchers that developed MBCT. Such claims are based on the program's relatively large group format (up to 12 participants) and its relationship with prevention of relapse/recurrence of depression in relatively well-controlled studies. Ma (2004) reported that the MBCT program required only 3 hours of therapist time per patient. The potential savings of health care expenses of MBCT is suggested in a study by Scott et al. (2003) that compared clinical management by a psychiatrist to clinical management plus 18 individual sessions of adjunctive cognitive therapy for subjects with partially recovered depression. They found cumulative relapse rates to be significantly lower in the cognitive therapy group. After analyzing total health care expenditures for both groups of patients, the cognitive therapy group, excluding the costs of providing the cognitive therapy, incurred significantly less incremental health care costs. However, when they considered the costs of providing cognitive therapy, the psychiatric management group had significantly lower overall health care costs. Because there is evidence that MBCT is probably efficacious in preventing relapse of depression and that the expenses of providing it are considerably less than that for cognitive therapy, it is reasonable to speculate that it is a cost-effective treatment.

The same issues of the economy of scale of the size of MBCT groups are also relevant to the MBSR program on which it was modeled. MBSR are usually conducted in groups of 15–20 individuals, for eight 2-hour sessions plus a daylong retreat (Beck et al., 1994; Gilbert, 2003; Goleman, 1977, 1988; Kabat-Zinn & Singer, 1981), making it a highly efficient program for the amount of clinical contact. The results of the uncontrolled studies of the effectiveness of the program—including measures of long-term reduction of symptoms—with a sample of patients with a variety of anxiety disorders suggest that the treatment may be cost-effective.

Although Linehan and her colleagues have not conducted cost–benefit analyses per se of DBT, there are data to suggest that the treatment may lead to reduced overall health care expenditures when contrasted with TAU. The reduction both in psychiatric hospital days and in parasuicidal events (which can lead to increased medical attention and emergency services) suggests that costs of DBT may be offset by other health care savings (Linehan et al., 1991, 1993, 1994).

ROLE IN COMPREHENSIVE TREATMENT PLAN OR STEPPED CARE AND COORDINATION ISSUES

Existing data give little empirical evidence of the role of meditation and relaxation in comprehensive treatment planning or in stepped care and coordination issues, and there is little existing evidence of the efficacy of these modalities as adjuncts to other types of treatment. Suggestions regarding their role in treatment planning must largely be based on extrapolation from the outcome data reviewed above. Nonetheless, we have identified three issues that merit consideration.

TIMING OF THE ADJUNCTIVE INTERVENTIONS

With one significant exception, the studies reviewed above introduced meditation and relaxation when the subjects were symptomatic, either acutely or chronically. Thus, whether the target condition was a type of anxiety disorder, eating disorder, or substance abuse disorder, the subjects had to be currently symptomatic (often meeting DSM criteria) to be included in the study. Thus, to the extent that these interventions have been shown to be beneficial, the evidence suggests that they are likely to be efficacious in acute or chronic but symptomatic stages and that they can be conducted simultaneously with primary interventions.

The exception alluded to above is depression. Although several trials demonstrated positive results during symptomatic phases, the best-designed and controlled series of studies—those on MBCT—were conducted on subjects in remission from major depressive disorder. MBCT was developed specifically as an adjunct to other interventions, notably cognitive therapy and/or psychopharmacological management, administered in the acute phase. Thus, although there is reasonable evidence that MBCT is probably efficacious in preventing relapse for patients with 2 or less previous episodes, its efficacy as a treatment in the acute phase has not been studied. Similarly, the efficacy of other forms of meditation and relaxation in preventing relapse of depression or other conditions has not been studied.

INPATIENT VERSUS OUTPATIENT TREATMENT

The question of the role of meditation and relaxation in inpatient versus outpatient treatment is closely related to the issue of the timing of the intervention because inpatient stays typically take place during the most acute and symptomatic phases. With one exception, all of the trials reviewed above were conducted on nonhospitalized subjects. Janakiramaiah et al.'s (2000) study showing efficacy of SKY on hospitalized patients with melancholic depression suggests that meditative techniques may have value as an adjunctive measure during hospitalization.

ADVERSE REACTIONS

Meditation and relaxation are typically viewed as benign interventions. However, there have been reports of adverse reactions to them (Epstein & Lieff, 1981; Heide & Borkevec, 1983; Otis, 1984). While such reactions seem to be uncommon, they do suggest the advisability of monitoring the effects of the adjunctive interventions and the need for communication between the primary therapist and the individual conducting the adjunctive intervention.

RESEARCH AGENDA

INCREASED USE OF RANDOMIZED CONTROLLED CLINICAL TRIALS

Despite the amount of research on meditation and relaxation, we were surprised at how few randomized controlled studies are published to say nothing of systematic reviews or meta-analyses. Because nonspecific factors can easily confound outcome data in research on any type of psychotherapeutic intervention, the RCT remains the highest standard of evidence. The use of active control groups is especially important in order to account for the effects of expectancy and attention. Linehan's research on DBT, in which TAU subjects were referred to practitioners, is a model in this regard.

THE USE OF MEDITATION AND RELAXATION AS ADJUNCTS TO OTHER FORMS OF THERAPY

There is little research specific to the use of meditation and relaxation as adjuncts to other types of psychotherapy. This is true despite the growing literature on the integration of Eastern philosophical and meditative traditions with conventional psychotherapy (i.e., Epstein, 1995; Mruk & Hartzell, 2003). Exploring the additive effects of meditation and relaxation when used in conjunction with other therapies should be a high priority for future research, along with identification of the added patient skills that predict improved outcomes.

COMPARISONS OF THE EFFICACY OF VARIOUS TYPES OF INTERVENTIONS FOR SPECIFIC PROBLEMS

The debate as to whether forms of relaxation and meditation are interchangeable or whether they have specific effects is longstanding and has been alluded to earlier in this chapter. Randomized controlled clinical trials comparing different interventions would be important in answering the questions of the relative clinical efficacy of the various forms and types of meditation and relaxation programs for specific problems. Continued research examining profiles of psychophysiological, cognitive, and behavioral responses to diverse meditation and relaxation techniques will be invaluable for the design of interventions and trials (Lehrer et al., 1999).

COST-EFFECTIVENESS STUDIES

The cost-effectiveness of any adjunctive interventions will be of interest to clients, health care plans, and other third-party carriers. There is reason to suspect that at least some of the interventions reviewed may result in overall reductions in health care expenses.

STUDIES LINKING MEDIATOR VARIABLES TO OUTCOME

Mediator variables such as compliance with instructions to practice and proficiency with the techniques taught in an intervention should be related to therapeutic outcome.

STUDIES OF THE RELATIVE CONTRIBUTIONS OF THE COMPONENTS OF COMBINED INTERVENTIONS

Several of the best-studied interventions entail combinations of various therapeutic elements. For example, MBCT combines the practice of mindfulness meditation with cognitive therapy and, presumably, support from group interaction. Thus, one cannot conclude with certainty—especially in the absence of mediator variables—that the therapeutic outcomes are due to the meditative components of the programs.

DISSEMINATION AGENDA

Information on meditation and relaxation is readily available. In fact, the challenge to the clinician is how to sift and winnow through the voluminous material in order to find techniques that are empirically based. For example searching for books on meditation and relaxation on Amazon.com resulted in over 9000 and 1531 hits, respectively. In this chapter, we have focused on randomized controlled clinical trials in order to examine the highest level of evidence for the use of meditation and relaxation as adjuncts to psychotherapy for common DSM conditions. In so doing, we have identified a set of techniques that are either empirically supported or probably effective for specific problems. We have highlighted, in the Table 9.2, key reviews and, when relevant and available, instructional materials, and additional resources for the techniques.

TABLE 9.2 Dissemination Agenda for Selected Treatments

Treatment	Selected reviews	Selected instructional literature	Other resources
Meditation, general	Delmonte, 1986; La Torre, 2001; Murphy & Donovan, 2006; Walsh & Shapiro, 2006	Dharmanet (http://www.dharmanet.org) serves as an online clearinghouse for information about meditation and meditation centers	
Yoga	Becker, 2000; Brown & Gerbarg, 2005a; Patel, 1984; Shannahoff-Khalsa, 2004a	Desikacher, 2006; Mehta & Mehta, 1990; Vaughan et al., 1994	The Art of Living Foundation (http://www.artofliving.org)

(*Continues*)

TABLE 9.2 (*Continued*)

Treatment	Selected reviews	Selected instructional literature	Other resources
Transcendental Meditation	Orme-Johnson, 1977	Provided through the Transcendental Meditation Program	http://www.tm.org/index.html
Zen	Austin, 1988	Kapleau, 1966; Omori, 1996	Dharmanet (http://www.dharmanent.org)
Vipassana/Mindfulness meditation	Gunaratana, 1991	Gunaratana, 1991; Kabat-Zinn, 2005	Insight Meditation Society (http://www.dharma.org/); The Institute for Meditation and Psychotherapy (http://www.meditation andpsycho-therapy.org)
Relaxation, general	Lehrer & Woolfolk, 1993		
Progressive relaxation	Bernstein & Given, 1984; McGuigan, 1984	Bernstein & Given, 1984	
Applied relaxation	Ost, 1987	Ost, 1987	
Relaxation response	Jacobs, 2001; Mandle et al., 1996	Benson, 1975	http://www.mbmi.org/
Mindfulness-based stress reduction	Bishop, 2002; Grossman et al., 2004	Kabat-Zinn, 1990	http://www.umassmed.edu/cfm/
Mindfulness-based cognitive therapy	Bishop, 2002	Segal et al., 2002	
Dialectic behavioral therapy	Rizvi & Linehan, 2001	Hayes et al., 2004; Linehan, 1993a, 1993b	

REFERENCES

Arntz, A. & Van Den Hout, M. (1996). Psychological treatments of panic disorder without agoraphobia: Cognitive therapy versus applied relaxation. *Behaviour Research & Therapy*, *34*, 113–121.

Arntz, A. (2003). Cognitive therapy versus applied relaxation as treatment of generalized anxiety disorder. *Behaviour Research & Therapy*, *41*, 633–646.

Austin, J.H. (1998). *Zen and the brain: Toward an understanding of meditation and consciousness*. Cambridge, Ma.: M.I.T. Press.

Baer, R. (2003). Mindfulness training as a clinical intervention: A conceptual and empirical review. *Clinical Psychology: Science and Practice*, *10*, 125–143.

Barlow, D.H., Craske, M.G., Cerny, J.A., & Klosko, J.S. (1989). Behavioral treatment of panic disorder. *Behavior Therapy, 20*, 261–282.

Beck, J.G., Stanley, M.A., Baldwin, L.E., et al. (1994). Comparison of cognitive therapy and relaxation training for panic disorder. *Journal of Consulting and Clinical Psychology, 62*, 818–826.

Becker, I. (2000). Uses of yoga in psychiatry and medicine. In P.R. Mushkin (Ed.), *Complementary and Alternative Medicine and Psychiatry* (pp. 107–145). Washington, DC: American Psychiatric Press.

Benson, H. (1975). *The Relaxation Response*. New York: Morrow.

Benson, H., Frankel, F.H., Apfel, R., et al. (1978). Treatment of anxiety: A comparison of the usefulness of self-hypnosis and a meditational relaxation technique. An overview. *Psychotherapy & Psychosomatics, 30*, 229–242.

Bernstein, D.A. & Borkevec, T.D. (1973). *Progressive Relaxation Training*. Champaign, IL: Research Press.

Bernstein, D.A., & Given, B.A. (1984). Progressive relaxation: Abbreviated methods. In R. Woolfolk & P.M. Lehrer (Eds.), *Principles and Practice of Stress Management* (pp. 43–68). New York: Guilford.

Bishop, S.R. (2002). What do we really know about mindfulness-based stress reduction? *Psychosomatic Medicine, 64*, 71–83.

Bogart, G. (1991). The use of meditation in psychotherapy: A review of the literature. *American Journal of Psychotherapy, 45*(3), 383–412.

Bradley, R., Greene, J., Russ, E., et al. (2005). A multidimensional meta-analysis of psychotherapy for PTSD. *American Journal of Psychiatry, 162*, 214–227.

Brautigam, E. (1977). Effects of the Transcendental Meditation program on drug abusers: A prospective study. In D. Orme-Johnson & J. Farrow (Eds.), *Scientific Research on the Transcendental Meditation Program: Collected Papers*. Rheinweiler, W. Germany: MERU Press.

Brown, R.P., & Gerbarg, P.L. (2005a). Sudarshan Kriya Yogic breathing in the treatment of stress, anxiety, and depression. Part II-clinical applications and guidelines. *Journal of Alternative & Complementary Medicine, 11*, 711–717.

Brown, R.P., & Gerbarg, P.L. (2005b). Sudarshan Kriya yogic breathing in the treatment of stress, anxiety, and depression: Part I-neurophysiologic model. *Journal of Alternative & Complementary Medicine, 11*, 189–201.

Carrington, P. (1993). Modern forms of meditation. In *Principles and practice of stress management* (2nd Ed., pp. 139–168). New York: Guilford.

Clark, D.M., Salkovskis, P.M., Hackmann, A., et al. (1994). A comparison of cognitive therapy, applied relaxation and imipramine in the treatment of panic disorder. The *British Journal of Psychiatry, 164*, 759–769.

Cummings, N.A., & VandenBos, G.R. (1981). The twenty years Kaiser-Permanente experience with psychotherapy and medical utilization: Implications for national health policy and national health insurance. *Health Policy Quarterly, 1*, 159–175.

Davidson, R.J., Kabat-Zinn, J., Schumacher, J., et al. (2003). Alterations in brain and immune function produced by mindfulness meditation. *Psychosomatic Medicine, 65*, 564–570.

Delmonte, M.M. (1986). Meditation as a clinical intervention strategy: A brief review. *International Journal of Psychosomatics, 33*, 9–12.

Desikacher, T.K.V. (2006). *Heart of Yoga: Developing a Personal Practice*. New York: Aperture.

Echeburua, E., de Corral, P., Zubizarreta, I., & Sarasua, B. (1997). Psychological treatment of chronic posttraumatic stress disorder in victims of sexual aggression. *Behavior Modification, 21*, 433–456.

Epstein, M. (1995). *Thoughts Without a Thinker*. New York: Basic Books.

Epstein, M.D. & Lieff, J.D. (1981). Psychiatric complications of meditation practice. *Journal of Transpersonal Psychology, 12*, 137–147.

Fals-Stewart, W., Marks, A.P., & Schafer, J. (1993). A comparison of behavioral group therapy and individual behavior therapy in treating obsessive-compulsive disorder. *Journal of Nervous and Mental Diseases, 181*, 189–193.

Fisher, P.L. & Durham, R.C. (1999). Recovery rates in generalized anxiety disorder following psychological therapy: An analysis of clinically significant change in the STAI-T across outcome studies since 1990. *Psychological Medicine, 29*, 1425–1434.

Frank, J. (1973). *Persuasion and Healing: A Comparative Study of Psychotherapy.* (Revised ed.) Baltimore, MD: Johns Hopkins University Press.

Gelderloos, P., Walton, K.G., Orme-Johnson, D.W., & Alexander, C.N. (1991). Effectiveness of the Transcendental Meditation program in preventing and treating substance misuse: A review. *International Journal of the Addictions, 26*(3), 293–325.

Gilbert, C. (2003). Clinical applications of breathing regulation: Beyond anxiety management. *Behavior Modification, 27*, 692–709.

Goldbeck, L. & Schmid, K. (2003). Effectiveness of autogenic relaxation training on children and adolescents with behavioral and emotional problems. *Journal of the American Academy of Adolescent Psychiatry, 42*, 1046–1054.

Goleman, D. (1977). *The Varieties of Meditative Experience.* New York: Dutton.

Goleman, D. (1988). *The Meditative Mind: The Varieties of Meditative Experience.* New York: Putnam.

Gonzalez, L.O. & Sellers, E.W. (2002). The effects of a stress-management program on self-concept, locus of control, and the acquisition of coping skills in school-age children diagnosed with attention deficit hyperactivity disorder. *Journal of Child Adolescent Psychiatric Nursing, 15*, 5–15.

Grossman, P., Niemann, L., Schmidt, S., & Walach, H. (2004). Mindfulness-based stress reduction and health benefits. A meta-analysis. *Journal of Psychosomatic Research, 57*(1), 35–43.

Gunaratana, H. (1991). *Mindfulness in Plain English.* Taipei, Taiwan: Buddha Educational Foundation.

Hayes, S.C., Follette, V.M., & Linehan, M.M. (2004). *Mindfulness and Acceptance: Expanding the Cognitive-Behavioral Tradition.* New York: Guilford.

Heide, F.J. & Borkevec, T.D. (1983). Relaxation-induced anxiety: Paradoxical anxiety enhancement due to relaxation training. *Journal of Consulting and Clinical Psychology, 51*, 171–182.

Jacobs, G.D. (2001). The physiology of mind-body interactions: The stress response and the relaxation response. *Journal of Alternative & Complementary Medicine, 7* (Suppl 92).

Jacobson, E. (1929). *Progressive Relaxation: A Physiological and Clinical Investigation of Muscular States and their Significance in Psychology and Medical Practice.* Chicago, IL: University of Chicago Press.

Janakiramaiah, N., Gangadhar, B.N., Naga Venkatesha Murthy, P.J., et al. (2000). Antidepressant efficacy of Sudarshan Kriya Yoga (SKY) in melancholia: A randomized comparison with electroconvulsive therapy (ECT) and imipramine. *Journal of Affective Disorders, 57*, 255–259.

Jerremalm, A., Jansson, L., & Ost, L.G. (1986a). Cognitive and physiological reactivity and the effects of different behavioral methods in the treatment of social phobia. *Behaviour Research & Therapy, 24*, 171–180.

Jerremalm, A., Jansson, L., & Ost, L.G. (1986b). Individual response patterns and the effects of different behavioral methods in the treatment of dental phobia. *Behaviour Research & Therapy, 24*, 587–596.

Jorm, A.F., Christensen, H., Griffiths, K. M., et al. (2004). Effectiveness of complementary and self-help treatments for anxiety disorders [Review]. *Medical Journal of Australia, 181* (Suppl 46).

Kabat-Zinn, J. (1990). *Full Catastrophe Living: Using the Wisdom of Your Body and Mind to Face Stress, Pain and Illness.* New York: Delta Publishing.

Kabat-Zinn, J. (2005). *Wherever You Go, There You Are: Mindfulness Meditation in Everyday Life.* New York: Hyperion.

Kabat-Zinn, J. & Chapman-Waldrop, A. (1988). Compliance with an outpatient stress reduction program: Rates and predictors of program completion. *Journal of Behavioral Medicine, 11*, 333–353.

Kabat-Zinn, J., Massion, A.O., Kristeller, J., et al. (1990). Effectiveness of a meditation-based stress reduction program in the treatment of anxiety disorders: Teaching risk-factor counseling skills to medical students, house staff, and fellows. *American Journal of Psychiatry*, *6* (Suppl), 35–42.

Kabat-Zinn, J. & Singer, R.H. (1981). An outpatient program in behavioral medicine for chronic pain patients based on the practice of mindfulness meditation: Theoretical considerations and preliminary results. *General Hospital Psychiatry*, *89*, 109–114.

Kapleau, P. (1966). *The three pillars of Zen: Teaching, practice and enlightenment.* New York: Harper and Row.

Khalsa, S.B. (2004). Yoga as a therapeutic intervention: A bibliometric analysis of published research studies. *Indian Journal of Physiology & Pharmacology*, *48*, 269–285.

Kushner, K. (2000). *One Arrow, One life: Zen, Archery and Enlightenment.* Boston: Tuttle.

Kutz, I., Leserman, J., Dorrington, C., et al. (1985). Meditation as an adjunct to psychotherapy: An outcome study. *Psychotherapy & Psychosomatics*, *43*, 209–218.

La Torre, M.A. (2001). Meditation and psychotherapy: An effective combination. *Perspectives in Psychiatric Care*, *37*, 103–106.

Lehrer, P., Sasaki, Y., & Saito, Y. (1999). Zazen and cardiac variability. *Psychosomatic Medicine*, *61*, 812–821.

Lehrer, P.M. (1982). How to relax and how not to relax: A re-evaluation of the work of Edmund Jacobson I. *Behaviour Research & Therapy*, *20*, 417–428.

Lehrer, P.M., Carr, R., Sargunaraj, D., & Woolfolk, R.L. (1994). Stress management techniques: Are they all equivalent, or do they have specific effects? *Biofeedback & Self Regulation*, *19*, 353–401.

Lehrer, P.M., Vaschillo, E., & Vaschillo, B. (2000). Resonant frequency biofeedback training to increase cardiac variability: Rationale and manual for training. *Applied Psychophysiology and Biofeedback*, *25*, 177–191.

Lehrer, P.M. & Woolfolk, R.L. (1984). Are stress reduction techniques interchangeable, or do they have specific effects: A review of the literature. In R. Woolfolk & P.M. Lehrer (Eds.), *Principles and Practice of Stress Management* (pp. 404–477). New York: Guilford.

Lehrer, P.M. & Woolfolk, R.L. (1993). *Principles and Practice of Stress Management.* (2nd Ed.) New York: Guilford.

Ley, R. (1999). The modification of breathing behavior. Pavlovian and operant control in emotion and cognition. *Behavior Modification*, *23*, 441–479.

Linehan, M.M. (1993a). *Cognitive-Behavioral Treatment of Borderline Personality Disorder.* New York: Guilford.

Linehan, M.M. (1993b). *Skills Training Manual for Treating Borderline Personality Disorder.* New York: Guilford.

Linehan, M.M., Armstrong, H.E., Suarez, A., et al. (1991). Cognitive-behavioral treatment of chronically parasuicidal borderline patients. *Archives of General Psychiatry*, *48*, 1060–1064.

Linehan, M.M., Dimeff, L.A., Reynolds, S.K., et al. (2002). Dialectical behavior therapy versus comprehensive validation therapy plus 12-step for the treatment of opioid dependent women meeting criteria for borderline personality disorder. *Drug & Alcohol Dependence*, *67*, 13–26.

Linehan, M.M., Heard, H.L., & Armstrong, H.E. (1993). Naturalistic follow-up of a behavioral treatment for chronically parasuicidal borderline patients. [erratum appears in Arch Gen Psychiatry 1994 May; 51(5): 422]. *Archives of General Psychiatry*, *50*, 971–974.

Linehan, M.M., Schmidt, H. III., Dimeff, L.A., et al. (1999). Dialectical behavior therapy for patients with borderline personality disorder and drug-dependence. *American Journal on Addictions*, *8*, 279–292.

Linehan, M.M., Tutek, D.A., Heard, H.L., & Armstrong, H.E. (1994). Interpersonal Outcome of Cognitive Behavioral Treatment for Chronically Suicidal Borderline Patients. *American Journal of Psychiatry*, *151*, 1771–1776.

Lynch, T.R., Morse, J.Q., Mendelson, T., & Robins, C.J. (2003). Dialectical behavior therapy for depressed older adults: A randomized pilot study. *American Journal of Geriatric Psychiatry*, *11*, 33–45.

Ma, S.H. & Teasdale, J.D. (2004). Mindfulness-based cognitive therapy for depression: Replication and exploration of differential relapse prevention effects. *Journal of Consulting & Clinical Psychology*, *72*(1), 31–40.

Mandle, C.L., Jacobs, S.C., Arcari, P.M., & Domar, A.D. (1996). The efficacy of relaxation response interventions with adult patients: A review of the literature. *Journal of Cardiovascular Nursing*, *10*, 4–26.

Marks, I., Lovell, K., Noshirvani, H., et al. (1998). Treatment of posttraumatic stress disorder by exposure and/or cognitive restructuring: A controlled study. *Archives of General Psychiatry*, *55*, 317–325.

McGuigan, F.J. (1984). Progressive relaxation: Origins, principles and clinical applications. In R.Woolfolk & P.M. Lehrer (Eds.), *Principles and Practice of Stress Management* (pp. 12–42). New York: Guilford.

McLean, P. & Taylor, S. (1992). Severity of unipolar depression and choice of treatment. *Behaviour Research & Therapy*, *30*, 443–451.

McLean, P.D. & Hakstian, A.R. (1979). Clinical depression: Comparative efficacy of outpatient treatments. *Journal of Consulting & Clinical Psychology*, *47*, 818–836.

Mehta, M. & Mehta, S. (1990). *Yoga: The Iyengar Way*. New York: Knopf.

Meuret, A.E. & Wilhelm, F.H. (2003). Breathing training for treating panic disorder. Useful intervention or impediment? *Behavior Modification*, *27*, 731–54.

Michelson, L., Mavissakalian, M., & Marchione, K. (1983). Cognitive and behavioral treatment of agoraphobia: Clinical, behavioral and psychophysiological Outcomes. *Journal of Consulting and Clinical Psychology*, *53*, 913–925.

Miller, J.J., Fletcher, K., Kabat-Zinn, J., et al. (1995). Three-year follow-up and clinical implications of a mindfulness meditation-based stress reduction intervention in the treatment of anxiety disorders. Meditation, melatonin and breast/prostate cancer: Hypothesis and preliminary data. *General Hospital Psychiatry*, *44*, 39–46.

Mruk, C.J. & Hartzell, J. (2003). *Zen and Psychotherapy: Integrating Traditional and Non-Traditional Approaches*. New York: Springer.

Murphy, G.E., Carney, R.M., Knesevich, M.A., et al. (1995). Cognitive behavior therapy, relaxation training, and tricyclic antidepressant medication in the treatment of depression. *Psychological Reports*, *77*, 403–420.

Murphy, M. & Donovan, S. (2006). *The Physical and Psychological Effects of Meditation: A Review of Contemporary Research with a Comprehensive Bibliography 1931–1996*. Sausalito, CA: Institute of Noetic Sciences.

Murphy, T.J., Pagano, R.R., & Marlatt, G.A. (1986). Lifestyle modification with heavy alcohol drinkers: Effects of aerobic exercise and meditation. *Addictive Behaviors*, *11*, 175–186.

Myers, T.I. & Eisner, E.J. (1974). *An Experimental Evaluation of the Effects of Karate and Meditation* (Rep. No. Final Report for the U.S. Army Institute for Behavioral and Social Sciences, Social Processes Technical Area). Washington, DC: American Institutes for Research.

Norcross, J., Beutler, L.E., & Levant, R.F. (2006). *Evidence-based Practices in Mental Health: Debate and Dialogue on the Fundamental Questions*. Washington, DC: American Psychological Association.

Omori, S. (1996). *Introduction to Zen training*. New York: Kegan Paul.

Orme-Johnson, D. (1977). *Scientific Research on the Transcendental Meditation Program*. Los Angeles: Mahirishi University Press.

Orme-Johnson, D. (1987). Medical care utilization and the Transcendental Meditation program [erratum appears in *Psychosom Med* 1987 Nov–Dec;49(6):637]. *Psychosomatic Medicine*, *49*, 493–507.

Ost, L.G. (1987). Applied relaxation: description of a coping technique and review of controlled studies. *Behaviour Research & Therapy*, *25*, 397–409.

Ost, L.G. (1988). Applied relaxation versus progressive relaxation in the treatment of panic disorder. *Behavior Research & Therapy*, *26*, 13–22.

Ost, L.G. & Breitholtz, E. (2000). Applied relaxation vs. cognitive therapy in the treatment of generalized anxiety disorder. *Behaviour Research & Therapy, 38*, 777–790.

Ost, L.G., Jerremalm, A., & Johansson, J. (1981). Individual response patterns and the effects of different behavioral methods in the treatment of social phobia. *Behaviour Research & Therapy, 19*, 1–16.

Ost, L.G., Johansson, J., & Jerremalm, A. (1982). Individual response patterns and the effects of different behavioral methods in the treatment of claustrophobia. *Behavior Research & Therapy, 20*, 445–460.

Ost, L.G., Lindahl, I.L., Sterner, U., & Jerremalm, A. (1984). Exposure in vivo vs applied relaxation in the treatment of blood phobia. *Behaviour Research & Therapy, 22*, 205–216.

Ost, L.G., Sterner, U., & Fellenius, J. (1989). Applied tension, applied relaxation, and the combination in the treatment of blood phobia. *Behaviour Research & Therapy, 27*, 109–121.

Ost, L.G., Westling, B.E., & Hellstrom, K. (1993). Applied relaxation, exposure in vivo and cognitive methods in the treatment of panic disorder with agoraphobia. *Behaviour Research & Therapy, 31*, 383–394.

Otis, L.S. (1984). Adverse Effects of Transcendental Meditation. In (pp. 201–208). New York: Aldine.

Patel, C. (1984). Yogic therapy. In R.L. Woolfolk & P.M. Lehrer (Eds.), *Principles and Practice of Stress Management* (pp. 70–103). New York: Guilford.

Raskin, M., Bali, L.R., & Peeke, H.V. (1980a). Muscle Biofeedback and Transcendental Meditation. *Archives of General Psychiatry, 37*, 93–97.

Raskin, M., Bali, L.R., & Peeke, H.V. (1980b). Muscle biofeedback and Transcendental Meditation: A controlled evaluation of efficacy in the treatment of chronic anxiety. *Archives of General Psychiatry, 37*, 93–97.

Reynolds, W.M. & Coats, K.I. (1986). A comparison of cognitive-behavioral therapy and relaxation training for the treatment of depression in adolescents. *Journal of Consulting and Clinical Psychology, 54*, 653–660.

Rizvi, S.L. & Linehan, M.M. (2001). Dialectical behavior therapy for personality disorders. *Current Psychiatry Reports, 3*, 64–69.

Robinson, F.P., Mathews, H.L., & Witek-Janusek, L. (2003). Psycho-endocrine-immune response to mindfulness-based stress reduction in individuals infected with the human immunodeficiency virus: A quasiexperimental study. *Journal of Alternative & Complementary Medicine, 9*(5), 683–694.

Safer, D.L., Telch, C.F., & Agras, W.S. (2001). Dialectical behavior therapy for bulimia nervosa. *American Journal of Psychiatry, 158*, 632–634.

Scott, J., Palmer, S., Paykel, E., et al. (2003). Use of cognitive therapy for relapse prevention in chronic depression. Cost-effectiveness study. *British Journal of Psychiatry, 182*, 221–227.

Segal, Z., Williams, J., & Teasdale, J. (2002). *Mindfulness-Based Cognitive Therapy for Depression: A New Approach to Preventing Relapse*. New York: Guilford.

Shaffer, H.J., LaSalvia, T.A., & Stein, J.P. (1997). Comparing Hatha yoga with dynamic group psychotherapy for enhancing methadone maintenance treatment: A randomized clinical trial. *Alternative Therapies in Health & Medicine, 3*, 57–66.

Shannahoff-Khalsa, D. (1997). Yogic meditation techniques are effective in the treatment of obsessive compulsive disorders. In E. Hollander & D. Stein (Eds.), *Obessive Compulsive Disorders: Etiology, Diagnosis and Treatment* (pp. 283–329). New York: Marcel Dekker, Inc.

Shannahoff-Khalsa, D.S. (2003). Kundalini yoga meditation techniques for the treatment of obsessive-compulsive and OC spectrum disorders. *Brief Treatment and Crisis Intervention, 3*, 369–382.

Shannahoff-Khalsa, D.S. (2004a). An introduction to Kundalini yoga meditation techniques that are specific for the treatment of psychiatric disorders. *Journal of Alternative & Complementary Medicine, 10*, 91–101.

Shannahoff-Khalsa, D.S. (2004b). An introduction to Kundalini yoga meditation techniques that are specific for the treatment of psychiatric disorders [Review]. *Journal of Alternative & Complementary Medicine, 10*, 91–101.

Shapiro, D.H. (1980). *Meditation: Self-Regulation Strategy and Altered State of Consciousness.* New York: Aldine.

Shapiro, D.H. (1982). Overview: Clinical and physiological comparison of meditation and other self-control strategies. *American Journal of Psychiatry, 139*, 267–274.

Shapiro, S.L., Bootzin, R.R., Figueredo, A.J., et al. (2003). The efficacy of mindfulness-based stress reduction in the treatment of sleep disturbance in women with breast cancer: An exploratory study. *Journal of Psychosomatic Research, 54*(1), 85–91.

Shapiro, D.H. & Walsh, R. (1984) (eds). *Meditation: Classic and Contemporary Perspectives.* New York: Aldine.

Shapiro, S.L. & Walsh, R. (2003). An analysis of recent meditation research. *Humanistic Psychologist, 31*, 86–114.

Simpson, E.B., Yen, S., Costello, E., et al. (2004). Combined dialectical behavior therapy and fluoxetine in the treatment of borderline personality disorder. *Journal of Clinical Psychiatry, 65*, 379–385.

Smith, J.C. (1975). Meditation as psychotherapy: A review of the literature. *Psychological Bulletin, 82*(4), 558–564.

Soler, J., Pascual, J.C., Campins, J., et al. (2005). Double-blind, placebo-controlled study of dialectical behavior therapy plus olanzapine for borderline personality disorder. *American Journal of Psychiatry, 162*, 1221–1224.

Task Force on Promotion and Dissemination of Psychological Procedures (1995). Training in and dissemination of empirically-validated psychological treatment: Report and recommendations. *The Clinical Psychologist, 48*, 2–23.

Taub, E., Steiner, S.S., Weingarten, E., & Walton, K.G. (1994). Effectiveness of broad spectrum approaches to relapse prevention in severe alcoholism: A long-term, randomized, controlled trial of transcendental meditation, EMG biofeedback and electronic neurotherapy. *Alcohol Treatment Quarterly, 11*, 187–220.

Taylor, S., Thordarson, D.S., Maxfield, L., et al. (2003). Comparative efficacy, speed, and adverse effects of three PTSD treatments: Exposure therapy, EMDR, and relaxation training. *Journal of Consulting and Clinical Psychology, 71*, 330–338.

Teasdale, J.D, Moore, R.G, Hayhurst, H., et al. (2002). Metacognitive awareness and prevention of relapse in depression: Empirical evidence. *Journal of Consulting and Clinical Psychology, 70*(2), 275–287.

Teasdale, J.D., Williams, J.M., Ridgeway, V.A., et al. (2000). Prevention of relapse/recurrence in major depression by mindfulness-based cognitive therapy. *Journal of Consulting and Clinical Psychology, 68*(4), 615–623.

Telch, C.F., Agras, W.S., & Linehan, M.M. (2001). Dialectical behavior therapy for binge eating disorder. *Journal of Consulting and Clinical Psychology, 69*, 1061–1065.

Van den Bosch, L.M., Verheul, R., Schippers, G.M., & van den, B.W. (2002). Dialectical Behavior Therapy of borderline patients with and without substance use problems: Implementation and long-term effects. *Addictive Behaviors, 27*, 911–923.

Vaughan, K., Armstrong, M.S., Gold, R., et al. (1994). A trial of eye movement desensitization compared to image habituation training and applied muscle relaxation in post-traumatic stress disorder. *Journal of Behavior Therapy & Experimental Psychiatry, 25*(4), 283–291.

Verheul, R., van den Bosch, L.M., Koeter, M.W., et al. (2003). Dialectical behaviour therapy for women with borderline personality disorder: 12-month, randomised clinical trial in The Netherlands [see comment]. *British Journal of Psychiatry, 182*, 135–140.

Von Durckheim, K.G. (1977). *Hara: The Vital Centre of Man.* London: Allen and Unwin.

Walsh, R. & Shapiro, S. (2006). The meeting of meditative disciplines and Western psychology. *The American Psychologist, 61*, 227–239.

Weiss, M., Nordlie, J.W., & Siegel, E.P. (2005). Mindfulness-based stress reduction as an adjunct to outpatient psychotherapy. *Psychotherapy & Psychosomatics*, *74*(2), 108–12.

West, M. (1987). *The Psychology of Meditation*. Oxford: Clarendon Press.

Williams, J.M., Teasdale, J.D., Segal, Z.V., & Soulsby, J. (2000). Mindfulness-based cognitive therapy reduces overgeneral autobiographical memory in formerly depressed patients. *Journal of Abnormal Psychology*, *109*(1), 150–155.

Willumsen, T., Vassend, O., & Hoffart, A. (2001). A comparison of cognitive therapy, applied relaxation, and nitrous oxide sedation in the treatment of dental fear. *Acta Odontologica Scandinavica*, *59*, 290–296.

Wolpe, J. (1969). *The Practice of Behavior Therapy*. New York: Pergammon.

10

THE USE OF SELF-MONITORING AS A TREATMENT INTERVENTION

CLAUDIA AVINA

Pepperdine University

CLINICAL APPLICATIONS OF SELF-MONITORING

The use of self-monitoring affords the opportunity to measure the presence of client symptoms, overall treatment progress, and clinician's effectiveness.

The clinical and empirical literature at times employs the concept of "self-monitoring" synonymously with other clinical behaviors such as self-management, homework, diary cards, and daily ratings. Research studies may evaluate the effectiveness of self-management (Barlow et al., 2005) or identify variables that enhance homework compliance (Burns & Auerbach, 1992) in which self-monitoring may comprise an essential component. Moreover, self-management may involve having the client continuously assess changes in the problem behavior *and* make appropriate behavioral changes in accordance with a larger treatment plan.

In this chapter, the concept of self-monitoring will be distinguished from other activities that describe behaviors in addition to the act of self-monitoring. The term "self-monitoring" will be used to describe the systematic recording by the client of his or her own behavior. Self-monitoring is appropriate for having a client report engagement in overt behaviors such as the number of alcoholic drinks consumed per day or acts of self-injurious behavior. It can also be used in having the client monitor internal emotional states such as levels of depression, anxiety, suicidal ideation, and urges to consume alcohol or engage in some other ineffective strategy. Additionally, clients can also self-monitor homework compliance and/or self-management behavior. For example, one of the essential treatment strategies of cognitive-behavioral therapy (CBT) for panic disorder is the use of exposure (Barlow et al., 1989). Clients are exposed to anxiety-provoking stimuli (imaginal and/or in vivo) during therapy sessions. They are also requested to engage in exposure outside of session (i.e., homework). Clients may be asked to report the amount (duration and frequency) of out-of-session exposures. Alternatively, in the treatment Dialectical Behavior Therapy (DBT; Linehan, 1993), clients are asked to keep track of the use of effective and ineffective clinical behaviors. They may be asked to report suicidal urges *and* their behavioral responses to those urges. In other words, the client will give an account of attempts to cope with distressing emotions through skillful behavior such as mindfulness meditation or attempts to self-soothe.

Effective clinical practice necessitates the incorporation of a systematic evaluative method for assessing progress (Costin, 1997). The integration of a scientific attitude that approaches clinical issues empirically provides for better informed treatment decisions. Self-monitoring is a therapeutic strategy that allows for the empirical evaluation of how a client's problems are progressing over the course of treatment. First, self-monitoring allows for the objective assessment of client symptoms and treatment targets. A client is able to objectively report information that is potentially more accurate than emotionally charged information (Craske & Barlow, 2001). For example, clients may provide more reliable reports regarding the assessment of depressive symptoms such as the number of hours slept, the incidence of social interactions, and a numerical rating of the level of depression experienced daily. Information obtained on a daily rating of depression may provide a better representation of changes and fluctuations in this feeling than the subjective experience of "I feel miserable all the time, it doesn't matter what is going in my life. Nothing I do helps," which is influenced by feelings of hopelessness that circumstances will remain the same. A client's continuous verbal report that he/she feels "depressed" provides different information than a daily rating which demonstrates that some days the client experiences a "6" on a 1–10 scale whereas a "10" on others.

Furthermore, ongoing objective assessment of the client's psychological issues informs the client and therapist about the client's progress. More specifically, it allows the therapist to assess "Am I having the desired impact on *this* client?" such that the prescribed treatment strategies are resulting in effective change. The therapist can then make appropriate adjustments to the treatment when the intervention is not working. It may be that the therapist's initial understanding of the source of the problems was incorrect. For example, the therapist may hypothesize that his/her client has withdrawn from his/her family, friends, and opportunities for social reinforcement because of feelings of depression and worthlessness. However, it may be that the client has withdrawn because of social anxiety and the consequent limited social interaction has resulted in the client feeling depressed. In this case, treating the depression first may not be the most effective strategy. The client would need to be taught how to manage his/her anxiety and distress produced by social situations so that he/she would be motivated to be less withdrawn.

Self-monitoring simultaneously informs the client about his/her treatment progress. He/she can evaluate from the objective data whether the therapy is working for him/her. In the case of a client receiving treatment for substance abuse, he or she can notice decreases in urges to use and actual use of alcohol or drugs. This can help motivate the client to continue participating in the treatment and follow the therapist's recommendations. In essence, this can increase treatment compliance and effectiveness. In contrast, when a client determines that the desired changes have not occurred, he/she may make appropriate adjustments to his/her behavior based on this information. This may be illustrated by the client who actively avoids triggers of thoughts and images associated with a traumatic event but continues to experience intrusive images. Self-monitoring the occurrence of intrusive images may help the client recognize that his/her avoidance behavior has not resulted in any reductions in the distressing experience and may be more willing to follow treatment recommendations to reprocess the event by purposely thinking and talking about it. The following section will review empirical data that supports the effectiveness of self-monitoring as an intervention.

REVIEW OF THE OUTCOME DATA

Current research providing validation of the sole use of self-monitoring is limited [see Korotitsch and Nelson-Gray (1999) for a full review]. It seems that the clinical application of this procedure is an extension of considerable research conducted in the 1970s demonstrating that the frequency of a behavior changes when it is observed and recorded (Hayes & Nelson, 1983; Kazdin, 1974; Willis & Nelson, 1982) including addictive behaviors such as smoking (Lipinski et al., 1975), overeating (Romanczyk, 1974), and alcohol use (Fremouw & Brown, 1980; Sobell & Sobell, 1973). More recent research has demonstrated that "consistent" self-monitoring of mood and pleasant activities, occurring throughout the day, resulted in positive changes on self-ratings of both these dimensions in depressed individuals (Harmon et al., 1980). The act of recording food intake has also been shown to have positive effects on successful weight loss in adults (Baker & Kirschenbaum, 1993; Boutelle & Kirschenbaum, 1998) and adolescents (Saelens & McGrath, 2003).

Many empirical studies have evaluated the effectiveness of treatments that explicitly incorporate self-monitoring techniques as an adjunctive part of the intervention such as CBT (Butler et al., 2006; Kubany et al., 2004; Linehan et al., 2006; Murphy et al., 1998). In this particular therapy, the client is taught skillful behavior (e.g., thoughts, coping skills, interpersonal skills) to use in the place of problem behaviors. A collaborative relationship is established in which the client is responsible for recognizing when problem behaviors are occurring or are about to occur outside of session and replace them with the skills learned throughout the therapy (Huppert et al., 2006). As previously noted, one of the important benefits of self-monitoring is the accurate assessment of a behavior that can then be targeted by the therapist and/or client. As the client self-monitors, he or she is provided with a cue to change his/her behavior. It can also provide information about whether the therapist's recommendations are being implemented. For example, Beck's *Cognitive Therapy of Depression* (Beck et al., 1979) requests that the client detect changes in depressed mood, describe influencing factors such as ineffective thoughts and environmental events, provide more effective thoughts used in the situation, and finally recognize corresponding changes in mood. The above information is systematically recorded in a written format. In other treatments, self-monitoring may directly provide some of the intervention as is the case in treatments that require exposure to anxiety-provoking stimuli (Huppert et al., 2006). The cognitive-behavioral treatment for anxiety requires systematic exposure to events, thoughts, and feelings that induce anxiety in the client. When a client is asked to provide a numerical rating for his/her internal feelings of anxiety (i.e., self-monitor), he/she may be inherently focusing on thoughts and physical symptoms that contribute to the anxiety, and the activity results in the client experiencing anxiety in that moment. In essence, self-monitoring provides an exposure opportunity.

There is extensive research to support the effectiveness of cognitive-behavioral-based treatments that use self-monitoring as a critical component across a spectrum of psychological disorders such as substance abuse (Leigh, 2000), eating disorders (Allen & Craighead, 1999; Cash & Hrabosky, 2003), depression (Hollon & Shelton, 2001; Jacobson et al., 2001), anxiety (Barlow et al., 2005; Craske & Barlow, 2001), posttraumatic stress disorder (Foa & Meadows, 1997; Kubany et al., 2004), and borderline personality disorder (Scheel, 2000). More generally, self-monitoring is suggested as part of many empirically supported treatments including those that are not cognitive-behavioral (Korotitsch & Nelson-Gray, 1999). It has also been shown to be effective in psychological problems that do not meet diagnostic criteria for a disorder such as anger (Beck & Fernandez, 1998). Demonstrated empirical support in addition to the universal and popular use of self-monitoring by clinicians provides further support for the validity of this technique (Korotitsch & Nelson-Gray, 1999).

There is also research to support the use of self-monitoring as a component of interventions for medical populations. For example, there is some evidence to suggest that self-monitoring (when used in conjunction with other intervention techniques) results in significant reductions in fluid intake for hemodialysis patients (Sagawa et al., 2003; Welch & Thomas-Hawkins, 2005). An empirical literature review demonstrated that treatments that included self-monitoring as one of various components had positive results in six separate studies (Welch & Thomas-Hawkins, 2005). However, the reviewed studies did not evaluate self-monitoring independently, and thus, it is unknown what amount of influence self-monitoring had on this outcome. In a separate study, self-monitoring was an explicit component of a cognitive-behavioral treatment that provided the patient reinforcement for attaining contracted fluid intake objectives

(Sagawa et al., 2003). Self-monitoring was necessary to determine when the reinforcement intervention should be administered. The positive results demonstrated in the study may have been due to the continuous recording of behaviors and emotions related to fluid intake (i.e., self-monitoring), the effect of reinforcement, or a combination of both. Self-monitoring may also be beneficial in increasing physical activity, which is considered vital in decreasing the development of chronic health problems (Aittasalo et al., 2006; Pate et al., 1995), when used in combination with mailed feedback from a physiotherapist (Aittasalo et al., 2006). This provides some preliminary support for the use of self-monitoring in medical interventions that target preventative treatments.

COST EFFICIENCY

Self-monitoring techniques are very inexpensive to administer as a stand-alone or adjunctive treatment. Providers may provide forms for the client to record ratings or ask that the client provide these forms by himself/herself in a personal log, journal, notebook, etc. Additionally, electronic technology such as personal computerized devices and the Internet may be used to eliminate these costs. There are no costs to scoring the information from these forms as there might be for self-report questionnaires or psychological assessments. The most costly aspect may be the therapist's or medical provider's time necessary for reviewing the information and providing appropriate feedback to the client. However, the client's self-monitoring data can supply rich information about the current state of the problem(s) being targeted in a very objective and simplified way. This can result in more accurate and efficient treatment planning. Although managed care companies determine third-party reimbursement according to clinical outcome research, self-monitoring can help provide a real-time assessment of treatment effectiveness of a specific therapy, by a particular mental health provider, and/or with a specific set of problems. It provides information about whether the current services being administered are functioning and thus whether they are cost-effective. Moreover, the potential increased effectiveness of mental health and/or physical health practices may maximize the benefits of the primary intervention being utilized.

KEY PROCESS VARIABLES

Self-monitoring can occur within a therapeutic session, as is the case when a client is asked to regularly report his/her level of anxiety experienced during an exposure exercise or when a client is asked to rate his/her level of emotional distress/dysregulation during a conversation about what prompted his/her last suicide attempt. It can also be utilized outside the therapy session as the client assesses frequency of daily panic attacks, overall level of depression experienced daily, and incidence of binging/purging episodes. In order for self-monitoring to provide an effective means of systematically and objectively assessing a targeted behavior, it is important that the client clearly understand the issue that is being measured. For example, for a client suffering from panic disorder that is monitoring the occurrence of panic attacks, a panic attack may need to be differentiated from anxiety resulting from the feeling that a panic attack may be imminent, or for a client that is receiving treatment for an eating disorder it will be important to know what constitutes a "binge" and/or a "purge." This can be accomplished by providing specific but comprehensive criteria for defining the behavior. The therapist could define a binge as the consumption of a specific number of calories during one eating episode. The goal is to decrease ambiguity about the variable being assessed so that the client's report can be reliable and accurate as well as ensuring that the client and the therapist are evaluating the same behavior(s). It would not be beneficial to the treatment for a client suffering from a restrictive type of eating disorder to report average-sized meals as binging episodes. It would likely be iatrogenic for the therapist to target these episodes as problematic eating behavior.

Another important element is that the client has a systematic method for evaluating and reporting the behavior. This issue is especially relevant when the client is evaluating internal states such as depression, anxiety, or suicidal ideation. Typically, numerical rating scales are used to provide the client with a quantifiable system for measuring the emotional experience. It is more critical that the client and the therapist use the rating system in the same manner than it is for the scale to include a specific range. Moreover, the therapist can implement a rating scale ranging from 1 to 10 *or* 0 to 100 as long as the specific numbers within the scale equate to the same clinical meaning for the client and the therapist. In other words, the therapist must instruct the client in the use of the rating system so that a "2" versus a "5" versus a "7" on a 1–10 scale reflect different experiences and the client and the therapist have a comparable understanding of what each of those numerical values reflect. The therapist should be sensitive to these issues at the outset of implementing self-monitoring as the clinician may not be readily available to the client during out-of-session monitoring for the purpose of clarifying or modifying the assessment instructions.

The most reliable self-monitoring information will result from having the client regularly monitor the behavior or experience. Research has shown that memory can be significantly inaccurate (Schacter, 1999) and affected by mood at the time that an individual is attempting to retrieve memories (Fiedler et al., 2001). This is particularly relevant when considering that a therapist is using information provided by the client in order to identify appropriate treatment targets and clinical strategies. Therefore, it is ineffective to ask the client to describe what has transpired over the course of the week without any objective data to prompt a more reliable account. You may be confronted by the client who feels particularly depressed at the time of the session and therefore remembers feeling this way throughout the previous week even though there may have been 1 or 2 days where he/she felt less depressed. The alternative may also be true; the client may feel less depressed at the time of the session and consequently reports an improvement in mood during the week and omits an elevation in suicidal ideation on one or more occasions. The client should be recording the behavior in temporal proximity to the occurrence of the behavior. If he/she is providing a daily rating of depression or anxiety, then he/she should reflect on his/her emotional experience and record his/her rating each day (not once every several days). If he/she is recording the frequency of a behavior such as panic attacks or instances of self-injurious behavior, then he/she should record the occurrence of each instance soon after it occurred before other circumstances negatively affect his/her ability to recall. The therapist and the client should work out a system that allows the client to quickly and efficiently record the information.

The client should be instructed on how to resume self-monitoring when he/she has failed to systematically observe and record the requested information. Each instance in which the client has missed an opportunity may facilitate continual noncompliance with the process. For instance, the client fails to record when having difficulties coping after an argument with a significant other on Day 1. He/she is sufficiently distressed that he/she is not motivated to complete the self-monitoring form. On Day 2, his/her mood has greatly improved such that he/she feels that it would not be worthwhile to record "a good day." One Day 3 he/she simply forgets. Consequently, by Day 4, he/she may rationalize that because he/she has missed approximately one-half of the week, it will be best to discontinue monitoring for that week and begin again after his/her next session. Clinically relevant information is lost. Additionally, for certain psychological problems and interventions, this process may be therapeutically harmful. In the case of exposure therapies for disorders such as phobias, panic disorder, and post-traumatic stress disorder (PTSD), avoidance of anxiety-provoking stimuli is negatively reinforced and maintains the disorder. In other words, when a client avoids evaluating his/her anxious experience (provided by a daily rating), he/she is avoiding thoughts believed to induce anxiety. The client feels short-term relief but the behavior contradicts the treatment recommendations to approach these opportunities in order to learn more skillful behavior (instead of escape and avoidance) for coping with the anxiety.

The therapist should encourage the client to regularly complete the monitoring form as best he/she can. The therapist can help educate the client about the importance of the information obtained for the treatment and enhance the client's belief in his/her ability to complete the task. The client can also be instructed to complete the evaluation regardless of how many opportunities have been missed. It would be therapeutically beneficial for the therapist to additionally request that the client document any noticeable factors that may have interfered with the completion of the record (e.g., argument with a family member, emotional difficulties, avoidance, and forgetting). These issues can then be addressed during the next session so that the client would have problem-solving strategies available to him/her the next time that the issues present themselves.

The proper use of the self-monitoring intervention allows for a reliable and accurate record of the client's progress in treatment. As previously discussed, the systematic recording of psychological issues and treatment targets allows the therapist to have a better assessment of what is occurring outside of session than relying on a general verbal recollection when the client comes to session. Inaccurate reporting may lead to an exacerbation of the problem because of the client's faulty perception (of severity and/or frequency) and consequent anxiety about future occurrences (Craske & Barlow, 2001; Rapee, Craske & Barlow, 1990). Self-monitoring can help circumvent this problem. Additionally, the client is providing information about his/her experience outside of session during real-world interactions, which are significantly greater in number and perhaps more meaningful than the limited opportunities for observing behavior that are available during 1 or 2 hours per week, during therapy sessions. It can inform the therapist that the treatment he/she is employing is effectively working with this particular client. If the treatment is ineffective then appropriate changes can be made to the treatment. Finally, self-monitoring may allow for the efficient and appropriate prioritization of session objectives. It provides the therapist with rich data to determine how to allocate time during the therapy session.

ROLE IN THE TREATMENT PLAN AND COORDINATION ISSUES

Significant attention has been given to the use of self-monitoring in cognitive-behavior therapies because of the explicit integration of this technique within these specific treatments. In fact, self-monitoring procedures are essential to the competent delivery of cognitive-behavior therapy. However, in light of the above discussion regarding the utility of self-monitoring for problem assessment and treatment planning, the procedure is very amenable to other treatment models. Self-monitoring can be tailored to meet the needs of the client and/or the therapist. It can be customized such that it remains consistent with the treatment being provided. While following some of the recommendations discussed about how to implement the technique, the therapist can determine the important therapeutic variables that need to be monitored. Self-monitoring may provide information about the state of the client's problems that the therapist uses to make desirable therapeutic changes according to his/her preferred model.

Self-monitoring also has vast flexibility in regard to the type and severity of the problem with which it can be used. It is appropriate for many psychological problems ranging from depression and anxiety to addictive disorders. It is also appropriate for lower-level problems such as relationship discord, inadequate physical activity, and unhealthy dietary intake; as well as more pervasive problems including parasuicidal behavior and disturbed perceptual experiences (e.g., delusions and hallucinations).

The empirical literature has shown that self-monitoring has a generally immediate and reliable effect on behavior (Korotitsch & Nelson-Gray, 1999). As a result of its potential influence of behavior and its amenability as an adjunct to various psychotherapy treatments, self-monitoring can be implemented during any phase of assessment or treatment. The client may be requested to engage in self-monitoring during the assessment phase in order to gather information necessary for developing an appropriate treatment plan. It can also be initially recommended before commencing treatment, as it may be solely sufficient for behavior to change. Positive outcomes may result from the client more readily noticing problematic behaviors in the moment that they are occurring and making appropriate changes. In these cases, treatment may not be warranted. If no such change occurs, self-monitoring continues to provide systematic information for evaluating changes in the identified issue(s). Self-monitoring can be incorporated as part of very short-term therapies in order to encourage the rapid positive effect on behavior change. It can be assumed that the continued use of self-monitoring during a longer-term treatment may maintain the therapeutic benefits of allowing the client and the therapist to monitor (1) the frequency of the problem behavior, (2) opportunities for the client to engage in recommended strategies, (3) attempts to replace problem behavior with more effective behavior, and (4) overall effect(s) of the treatment. Regardless of the length of treatment, self-monitoring can be continued throughout the therapy given its important function of accounting for progress and therapy effectiveness.

The treatment provider should continuously assess whether the ratings are reliable and accurate because the client either is not monitoring at the recommended intervals (e.g., he/she completes his/her form only once just before coming to session) or incorrectly monitors a specified factor (e.g., he/she ignores all urges to consume alcohol other than those leading to actual drinking behavior). There is also the possibility that the client inaccurately reports in a positive direction. Otherwise, information obtained through self-monitoring presents a misleading picture to the client and the therapist about what is occurring. In the most extreme case, a therapist continues with a treatment that is harmful to the client. This could occur if a client inaccurately reports low suicidal urges because he/she mistakenly confuses urges with suicidal acts. The therapist may not be aware that the client is experiencing an unchanged or higher level of urges. Some time may be necessarily allocated to addressing why the client is not completing the self-monitoring activity as requested. The therapist may need to assess whether noncompliance results from lack of motivation, confusion, and/or emotional barriers (e.g., shame or anxiety) as each may require a different strategy. Some of these may be circumvented by designating an appropriate amount of time to possible obstacles at the beginning stage of introducing the self-monitoring intervention as discussed in the section above.

RESEARCH AGENDA

There is an insufficient amount of research investigating which elements make self-monitoring the most effective. There are numerous factors that may influence whether clients comply with this recommended activity and whether the technique results in the positive effects noted in the literature. Research should attempt to identify the required level of client's motivation, belief in one's ability to carry out the procedure, education, and/or understanding necessary to participate in effective self-monitoring. Although the technique appears to be very popular among clinicians (Korotitsch & Nelson-Gray, 1999), it is important to evaluate whether it should be applied universally across clients. Additionally, more research should specify how the recording activity needs to be performed in order to achieve positive results. For example, one study demonstrated that self-monitoring in overweight adolescents did result in weight loss when the individuals recorded a sufficient amount of overall consumed meals per day, but this outcome was not significantly related to more detailed recording (Saelens & McGrath, 2003). In other words, more specific tracking did not provide a better predictor of successful weight loss. Similarly, self-monitoring has been shown to positively affect depressed mood and occurrence of engaging in pleasant activities when both were monitored regularly throughout the day as opposed to only once per day (Harmon et al., 1980). In addition to examining the necessary factors required for self-monitoring to reach a minimal level of effectiveness, it may also be useful to identify those factors that enhance its effects. More research of this type needs to be conducted in order to better understand how self-monitoring techniques should be utilized in treatment.

Research should further investigate therapist factors that influence self-monitoring effectiveness in order to delineate what constitutes competent delivery of this adjunctive treatment. There are few studies examining the relationship between these influencing variables and the broader category of "homework" (Kazantzis et al., 2004) of which self-monitoring may be one technique. Therapist's adherent ability to review homework as part of cognitive therapy for depression has been shown to be related to positive therapeutic outcomes (DeRubeis & Feeley, 1990). Although therapist's competent focus on homework more generally has not been shown to be significantly related to overall homework compliance, review of homework in previous session does appear to be related to future homework completion (Bryant et al., 1999). Although recommendations for the proper use of homework in psychotherapy may be generalized to self-monitoring, empirical validation of these variables is imperative for informing clinical guidelines. In this way, clinicians can be properly trained to conduct psychotherapy with the greatest possibility of improving the lives of clients.

DISSEMINATION AGENDA

The use of self-monitoring has a strong history in behavioral research and behaviorally oriented therapies. Yet, the intervention has immense portability to a diversity of theoretical orientations and treatments. The technique can be modified to fit conceptually with seemingly contrasting psychotherapies. Also, it is completely appropriate to use for behavioral health issues. In the current age of managed care that mandates provider accountability, it seems vital to integrate self-monitoring into mental and behavioral health treatments as a continual measure of treatment progress and effectiveness. Self-monitoring can provide immediate feedback to the client and the clinician about the current state of the problem, whereas more formal assessments can be implemented at the institutional level. It seems logical that if the therapist modifies their behavior accordingly in response to the instant feedback they are receiving from self-monitoring records of specific targets that clinical effectiveness will be demonstrated at the larger level (i.e., psychological outcomes, health outcomes, etc.).

Self-monitoring is a cost-effective adjunctive treatment in numerous ways. First, it is incredibly inexpensive. It simply requires a form for the client to record his/her behaviors. It does not require costly inventories, questionnaires, or administration programs. Self-monitoring occurs outside of appointments and thus, does not require institutional resources (e.g., staff, location, time) to administer. Additionally, these resources are not necessary for scoring or interpretation. The provider can examine the documented information and incorporate it seamlessly into practice. Secondly, as described above, self-monitoring encourages the use of effective practice. Because treatment will be modified to achieve the greatest immediate benefit, treatment will be efficient and successful. These factors encourage the viable and rapid dissemination of this technology.

REFERENCES

Aittasalo, M., Miilunpalo, S., Kikkonen-Harjula, K., & Pasanen, M. (2006) A randomized intervention of physical activity promotion and patient self-monitoring in primary health care. *Preventive Medicine*, *42*, 40–46.

Allen, H.N. & Craighead, L.W. (1999). Appetite Monitoring in the treatment of binge eating disorder. *Behavior Therapy, 30*(2), 253–272.

Baker, R.C. & Kirschenbaum, D.S. (1993). Self-monitoring may be necessary for successful weight control. *Behavior Therapy*, *24*, 377–394.

Barlow, D.H., Craske, M.G., Cerny, J.A., & Klosko, J.S. (1989). Behavioral treatment for panic disorder. *Behavior Therapy*, *20*, 261–282.

Barlow, J.H., Ellard, D.R., Hainsworth, J.M., et al. (2005). A review of self-management interventions for panic disorders, phobias, and obsessive-compulsive disorders. *Acta Psychiatrica Scandinavica*, *222*, 272–285.

Beck, A.T., Rush, A.J., Shaw, B.F., & Emery, G. (1979). *Cognitive Therapy of Depression.* New York: Guilford Press.

Beck, R. & Fernandez, E. (1998). Cognitive-behavioral self-regulation of the frequency, duration, and intensity of anger. *Journal of Psychopathology and Behavioral Assessment*, *20*, 217–229.

Boutelle, K.N. & Kirschenbaum, D.S. (1998). Further support for consistent self-monitoring as a vital component for successful weight control. *Obesity Research*, *6*, 219–224.

Burns, D.D. & Auerbach, A.H. (1992). Does homework compliance enhance recovery from depression? *Psychiatric Annals*, *22*, 464–469.

Butler, A.C., Chapman, J.E., Forman, E.M., & Beck, A.T. (2006). The empirical status of cognitive-behavioral therapy: A review of meta-analyses. *Clinical Psychology Review*, *26*, 17–31.

Bryant, M.J., Simons, A.D., & Thase, M.E. (1999). Therapist skills and patient variables in homework compliance: Controlling an uncontrolled variable in cognitive therapy outcome research. *Cognitive Therapy and Research*, *23*, 381–399.

Cash, T.F. & Hrabosky, J.I. (2003). The effects of psychoeducation and self-monitoring in a cognitive-behavioral program for body-image improvement. Eating Disorders: *The Journal of Treatment & Prevention, 11*(4), 225–270.

Costin, A. (1997). Research and counseling practice: Issues of application and integration. In P.K.S. Patrick (Ed.), *Contemporary Issues in Counseling* (pp. 99–121). Boston, MA: Pearson Education Inc/Ally & Bacon.

Craske, M.G. & Barlow, D.H. (2001). Panic Disorder and Agoraphobia. In D.H. Barlow (Ed.), *Clinical Handbook of Psychological Disorders: A Step-by-Step Treatment Manual* (3rd Ed.), pp. 1–59. New York: Guilford Press.

DeRubeis, R.J. & Feeley, M. (1990). Determinants of change in cognitive therapy for depression. *Cognitive Therapy and Research*, *14*, 469–482.

Fiedler, K., Nickel, S., Muehlfriedel, T., & Unkelback, C. (2001). Is mood congruency an effect of genuine memory or response bias? *Journal of Experimental Social Psychology*, *37*, 201–214.

Foa, E.B. & Meadows, E.A. (1997). Psychosocial treatments for post-traumatic stress disorder: A critical review. *Annual Review of Psychology*, *48*, 449–480.

Fremouw, W.J. & Brown, J.P. (1980). The reactivity of addictive behaviors to self-monitoring: A functional analysis. *Addictive Behaviors*, *5*, 209–217.

Jacobson, N.S., Martell, C.R., & Dimidjian, S. (2001). Behavioral activation treatment for depression: Returning to contextual roots. *Clinical Psychology: Science and Practice*, *8*, 255–270.

Harmon, T.M., Nelson, R.O., & Hayes, S.C. (1980). Self-monitoring of mood versus activity by depressed clients. *Journal of Consulting and Clinical Psychology*, *48*, 30–38.

Hayes, S.C. & Nelson, R.O. (1983). Similar reactivity produced by external cues and self-monitoring. *Behavior Modification*, *7*, 183–196.

Hollon, S. & Shelton, R. (2001). Treatment guidelines for major depressive disorder. *Behavior Therapy*, *32*, 235–258.

Huppert, J.D., Roth Ledley, D., & Foa, E.F. (2006). The use of homework in behavior therapy for anxiety disorders. *Journal of Psychotherapy Integration*, *16*, 128–139.

Kazantzis, N., Deane, F.P., & Ronan, K.R. (2004). Assessing compliance with homework assignments: Review and recommendations for clinical practice. *Journal of Clinical Psychology*, *60*, 627–641.

Kazdin, A.E. (1974). Reactive self-monitoring: The effects of response desirability, goal setting, and feedback. *Journal of Consulting and Clinical Psychology*, *42*, 704–716.

Korotitsch, W.J. & Nelson-Gray, R.O. (1999). An overview of self-monitoring research in assessment and treatment. *Psychological Assessment*, *11*, 415–425.

Kubany, E.S., Hill, E.E., Owens, J.A., et al. (2004). Cognitive trauma therapy for battered women with PTSD (CTT-BW). *Journal of Consulting and Clinical Psychology*, *72*, 3–18.

Leigh, B.C. (2000). Using daily reports to measure drinking and drinking patterns. *Journal of Substance Abuse, 12*, 51–65.

Linehan, M.M. (1993). *Cognitive-Behavioral Treatment of Borderline Personality Disorder*. New York: Guilford Press.

Linehan, M.M., Comtois, K.A., Murray, A.M., et al. (2006). Two-year randomized controlled trial and follow-up of dialectical behavior therapy vs therapy by experts for suicidal behaviors and borderline personality disorder. *Archives of General Psychiatry*, *63*, 757–766.

Lipinski, D.P., Black, J.L., Nelson, R.O., & Ciminero, A.R. (1975). Influence of motivational variables on the reactivity and reliability of self-recording. *Journal of Consulting and Clinical Psychology*, *43*, 637–646.

Murphy, M.T., Michelson, L.K., Marchione, K., et al. (1998). The role of self-directed in vivo exposure in combination with cognitive therapy, relaxation training, or therapist-assisted exposure in the treatment of panic disorder with agoraphobia. *Journal of Anxiety Disorders*, *12*, 117–138.

Pate, R.R., Pratt, M., Blair, S.N., et al. (1995). Physical activity and public health: A recommendation from the Centers for Disease Control and Prevention and the American College of Sports Medicine. *Journal of the American Medical Association*, *273*, 402–407.

Rapee, R.M., Craske, M.G., Barlow, D.H. (1990). Subject described features of panic attacks using self-monitoring. *Journal of Anxiety Disorders*, *4*(2), 171–181.

Romanczyk, R.G. (1974). Self-monitoring in the treatment of obesity: Parameters of reactivity. *Behavior Therapy*, *5*, 531–540.

Saelens, B.E. & McGrath, A.M. (2003). Self-monitoring adherence and adolescent weight control efficacy. *Children's Healthcare*, *32*, 137–152.

Sagawa, M., Oka, M., & Chaboyer, W. (2003). The utility of cognitive behavioral therapy on chronic haemodialysis patients' fluid intake: A preliminary examination. *International Journal of Nursing Studies*, *40*, 367–373.

Schacter, D.L. (1999). The seven sins of memory. *American Psychologist*, *54*, 182–203.

Scheel, K.R. (2000). The empirical basis of dialectical behavior therapy: Summary, critique, and implications. *Clinical Psychology: Science and Practice*, *7*, 68–86.

Sobell, L.C. & Sobell, M.F. (1973). A self-feedback technique to monitor drinking behavior in alcoholics. *Behaviour Research and Therapy*, *11*, 237–238.

Welch, J.L. & Thomas-Hawkins, C. (2005). Psycho-educational strategies to promote fluid adherence in adult hemodialysis patients: A review of intervention strategies. *International Journal of Nursing Studies*, *42*, 597–608.

Willis, S.E. & Nelson, R.O. (1982). The effects of valence and nature of target behavior on the accuracy and reactivity of self-monitoring. *Behavioral Assessment*, *4*, 401–412.

11

EXPRESSIVE WRITING

DEBORAH NAZARIAN AND JOSHUA SMYTH

Syracuse University

Journaling has long been a common strategy for expressing strong emotion through the written word (Riordan, 1996). Although journaling is often utilized both personally and in therapy (e.g., Progoff's intensive journaling; see Smyth & Greenberg, 2000), it is only recently that investigators have examined the effects of writing about emotional experiences on mental and physical health. One approach in particular that is a recent topic of growing research and clinical interest is to express one's thoughts and feelings through writing in a personal and often confidential fashion. We will use the term "expressive writing" to refer to the process of disclosure writing discussed in this chapter. This is in large part to clearly distinguish the type and process of writing that has typically been used in clinical studies (discussed herein), from a wider array of writing processes and exercises that are used in a variety of settings and range from self-initiated and self-structured (e.g., diary or journal writing) to highly prescriptive writing used in the context of other therapies (e.g., written "homework" in therapy).

Expressive writing is a psychosocial intervention that promotes written emotional disclosure of stressful or traumatic events in a structured and confidential manner. Written emotional disclosure has been used as an intervention to foster emotional expression without regard to social stigma, and encourages individuals to approach and express their emotions through writing in an experimental setting. Participants typically write about a stressful or traumatic experience for approximately 20 minutes across 3–5 days (e.g., Pennebaker & Beall, 1986; Smyth, 1998). The effects of this emotional disclosure are usually compared to writing about emotionally neutral writing topics (such as an objective description of time planning).

The use of writing as a form of therapy appears to have evolved from psychotherapeutic traditions that espoused emotional expression. Most traditional talk therapies, regardless of theoretical orientation, consist of some form of interpersonal disclosure that includes identifying, labeling, and disclosing emotional experiences (Smyth & Helm, 2003). There can, however, be barriers to interpersonal disclosure that limit the capacity or willingness for emotional expression. Although people may have a desire to express and/or discuss negative events, social constraints may force them not to (e.g., Lepore et al., 1996). Some negative life events may have a social stigma attached to them, reducing the likelihood that the event is shared with others. Additionally, many individuals may not have access to sympathetic or supportive listeners in their lives. Others might have access to a support network, but receive support that is perceived as inappropriate or insensitive (e.g., Wortman & Silver, 1989), and subsequently decide to refrain from discussing the trauma further. Expressive writing thus provides a means of expressing and processing emotions that can help avoid the barriers and/or negative consequences that might accompany interpersonal disclosure.

Structured expressive writing (as opposed to unstructured) focuses on a specific topic of writing, such as stressful or traumatic life experiences. The majority of experimental studies utilize this form of structured writing within the controlled setting of the laboratory. In the prototypical writing study, disclosure is induced in the laboratory by randomly assigning participants to either an expressive writing group or an emotionally neutral writing condition. Participants in both groups are usually assured of confidentiality and encouraged to write without regard to spelling, style, or grammar. The time and attention is matched between conditions in an attempt to equalize all factors except for the experimental manipulation. Therefore, the sole (intended) difference between the experimental and the control groups are the writing instructions.

Individuals in the experimental condition are most commonly encouraged to identify and explore their cognitions and emotions surrounding a stressful experience. Instructions typically take the following form:

> During each of the writing days, we would like you to write about the most stressful or upsetting experiences of your entire life. You can write on different topics each day or on the same topic for all three days. Don't worry about grammar, spelling, or sentence structure. The important thing is that you write about your deepest thoughts and feelings about the experience. You can write about anything you want, but whatever you choose, it should be something that has affected you very deeply. It is critical, however, that you let yourself go and touch those deepest emotions and thoughts that you have.

Control participants are instructed to write about emotionally neutral topics, such as to write about their plans (framed as time management). Session 1 typically focuses on the previous week, session 2 on the previous 24 hours, and session 3 on the upcoming week. Prior studies that have utilized these instructions demonstrated that participants view the exercise as valid and report it as valuable, although there is no evidence that it influences mental or physical health outcomes (e.g., Hockemeyer & Smyth, 2002). For example, instructions for the first day of writing are as follows:

> During each of the three writing days, we would like you to write about an assigned topic. You should write about the specific topic in detail without discussing any of your thoughts and feelings surrounding the topic, but rather focus on a factual description. Today we want you to write about your plans for the **previous week**. Again, describe them in detail without referring to your thoughts or feelings associated with them.

BENEFICIAL OUTCOMES OF WRITTEN EMOTIONAL DISCLOSURE

Relatively early in the development of this literature, a quantitative review of the research was conducted. A meta-analysis of 13 randomized experiments that utilized experimental manipulation of written emotional disclosure revealed that the writing intervention produced beneficial health outcomes across several domains (each of which was measured several months postwriting; Smyth, 1998). A meta-analysis consists of statistical methods for generating an estimate of effect size by cumulating information from all available studies. Expressive writing groups tended to do "better" than neutral writing groups across a wide range of outcomes (Smyth, 1998). The outcome types that have been influenced by the writing task were grouped into five general categories: (1) Physiological outcomes (e.g., natural killer cell activity, viral antibodies, liver enzyme function); (2) Psychological well-being (e.g., positive/negative mood, depression); (3) Reported health (e.g., health center visits, symptom reports, URI reports); (4) Academic/employment [e.g., absenteeism, reemployment, grade point average (GPA)]; and (5) Health behaviors (e.g., alcohol or drug use, exercise, sleep, diet).

The overall effect size for the writing intervention was $d = 0.47$, which is comparable to other psychological interventions, such as psychotherapy (Smyth, 1998). The mean weighted effect size for each outcome is presented in Figure 11.1. As is evident from the figure, the effect sizes differed across outcome types. Relative to other outcomes, reported health behaviors had the lowest effect size and were not statistically significant. In addition to the five outcome types, a mean effect size was also calculated for short-term distress because most studies reported an increase in pre- to postwriting distress among

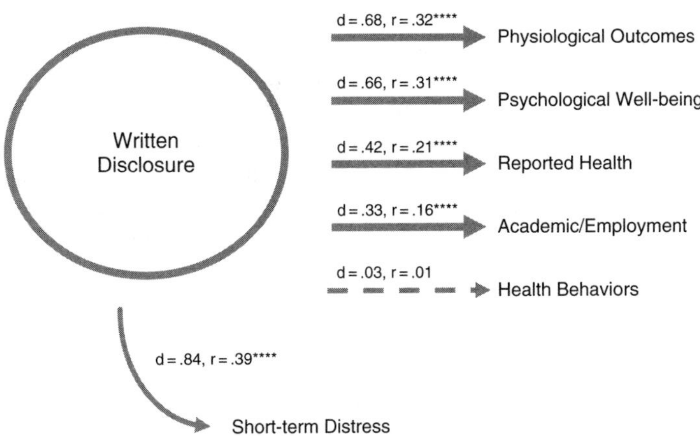

FIGURE 11.1 Effect sizes by outcome type from meta-analysis (Smyth, 1998).

experimental participants who engaged in the writing task, as compared with controls (Smyth, 1998).

Several moderator variables were examined in order to determine their relationship to outcomes, including student status, age, gender, number of sessions, length of sessions, length of time over which the writing sessions were spaced, publication status, and writing instructions (Smyth, 1998). Participants who were students (vs nonstudents) had significantly higher effects within the psychological well-being outcomes. Conversely, age was not related to well-being outcomes. The overall effect size was moderated by two variables: Gender and the length of time over which writing sessions were spaced. More specifically, higher mean effect sizes were related to studies that included a higher percentage of males and studies that had the writing sessions spaced over a longer period of time. These results suggest that writing may be more effective for males. Additionally, studies that used longer time spans over which the writing was spaced (e.g., once a week rather than on consecutive days) demonstrated somewhat larger effects.

The results of a more recent quantitative review provide continuing evidence for the beneficial effects of expressive writing (Frattaroli, 2006). The comprehensive meta-analysis included 146 randomized expressive writing interventions and found that the unweighted average effect size of the intervention was $r = .075$ (Cohens $d = .151$). Separate unweighted mean effect sizes were also computed for six outcome types as follows: psychological health ($r = .056$), physiological functioning ($r = .059$), reported health ($r = .072$), health behaviors ($r = .007$), subjective impact of the intervention ($r = .159$), and general functioning/life outcomes ($r = .046$). The effect size for health behaviors did not approach significance, which is consistent with Smyths (1998) meta-analysis. Furthermore, although these effect sizes were more moderate than those identified in the meta-analysis by Smyth (1998), they indicate that expressive writing is an effective intervention with beneficial effects across a wide range of outcomes.

The recent meta-analysis also examined several moderating variables that were grouped into the following categories: report information (e.g., publication status), setting, participant characteristics, methodology, and implementation of treatment (Frattaroli, 2006). A number of variables were found to moderate the effects of experimental disclosure. For example, effect sizes had a tendency to be larger for studies that had more male participants, did not include a college student sample, and included only participants with a history of trauma or stressors. Features of the disclosure setting also moderated the effect of expressive writing. In particular, the privacy of the disclosure setting (i.e., more privacy led to greater benefit) moderated both the overall and psychological effect sizes. Furthermore, some variables that were significantly related to effect size in the meta-analysis by Smyth (1998) did not moderate the effects of expressive writing in Frattarolis (2006) meta-analysis (e.g., spacing of disclosure sessions, age of participants). Taken together, the effect size computations and moderator analyses of the aforementioned quantitative reviews provide evidence for the beneficial effects of expressive writing. Nonetheless, they underscore the need to experimentally manipulate and examine variables of interest in future research in order to improve the efficacy of the intervention.

OUTCOME DATA

COST-EFFICIENCY

There is a growing movement to use supplements or alternatives in the direct delivery of mental and physical health care. Proponents of structured writing as complementary or supplemental treatment have argued that face-to-face delivery of verbal treatment is inherently inefficient (e.g., L'Abate, 1999). It limits the number of respondents (individuals, couples, and families) who can receive treatment from mental health professionals, and comes at (often significant) cost. A major appeal of the expressive writing intervention lies in its ease of administration, cost-effectiveness, and potential reach of administration. The minimal materials required for the intervention (paper and pen) makes it easily accessible to people who are willing and able to write for a moderate amount of time (e.g., 15–20 minutes). Although current research on expressive writing has yet to support its use as a stand-alone intervention in clinical populations (i.e., in lieu of in-person treatment), it has tremendous potential to serve as a supplement or adjuvant to existing treatment.

Through supplementing traditional psychotherapeutic treatments with expressive writing in its various structures, some of the therapeutic process can be achieved outside the limits prescribed by direct, verbal, face-to-face contact between a professional and a respondent. The inclusion of these supplements and alternatives, then, hopefully will lead to more cost-effective treatments, through treatment of a greater numbers of respondents with fewer sessions and on an out-patient basis (L'Abate, 1999). The inclusion of writing concurrent with standard psychotherapy contact may, even in the absence of reducing visits or costs, improve the effectiveness of care and client prognosis.

DEMONSTRATED RANGE OF APPLICABILITY

Investigators have examined the generalizability of expressive writing by examining the effects of the intervention on various clinical and medical samples. The large majority of evidence suggests that expressive writing produces beneficial results across various outcomes among different samples. It appears that asking people to write about stress and/or traumatic experiences, or other powerful emotions, is something most are willing and able to do. Writing is a powerful disclosure mechanism across samples without well-developed writing or literacy skills. Populations have included children to elderly participants with varying education levels (including medical patients, honor students, maximum security prisoners, and many others). The range of traumatic topics has been considerable as well, including death of a loved one, personal illness or injury, injury or illness of someone close, physical assault or abuse, rape, sexual abuse, and relationship problems. Several studies, however, indicate the intervention may not be particularly effective or even appropriate for some samples as a standalone treatment. For example, very preliminary evidence does suggest that the disclosure intervention may not be particularly beneficial for participants experiencing great distress (e.g., posttraumatic stress disorder; Gidron et al., 1996), at least in the absence of additional support of some sort (e.g., psychotherapy). Additionally, expressive writing may not be an effective grief intervention for bereaved individuals (e.g., O'Connor et al., 2004; Stroebe et al., 2002).

Expressive Writing among Chronically Ill Populations

The expressive writing intervention has produced robust effects in producing beneficial results among physically healthy individuals (e.g., Smyth, 1998). However, the extension of the paradigm to chronically ill populations is a growing area of research that has produced somewhat inconsistent results. In one of the first such published randomized trials, community residents with chronic asthma or rheumatoid arthritis were randomly assigned to write about either the most stressful events of their life or neutral topics (Smyth et al., 1999). Health assessments were conducted at baseline, and at 2 weeks, 2 months, and 4 months postwriting. Medically relevant and objectively verifiable disease outcomes were included to supplement self-reported health and symptoms. As such, asthma patients' pulmonary function was assessed using spirometry and rheumatoid arthritis patients had clinical examinations conducted by a rheumatologist. All assessments were performed "blind" to condition. In addition to the statistical significance of these results, clinically significant changes were also observed. Asthma patients showed a 15% change from baseline (FEV_1) and rheumatoid arthritis patients had a shift in their rating category of severity (asymptomatic/mild/moderate/severe/very severe).

The effects of expressive writing have also been examined in other medically ill populations. The breadth of samples have included women with breast cancer (Stanton et al., 2002; Walker et al., 1999), patients with rheumatoid arthritis (Kelley et al., 1997), patients with fibromyalgia (Gillis et al., 2006; Smyth & Nazarian, 2006), HIV (Mann, 2001; Petrie et al., 2004), men diagnosed with prostrate cancer (Rosenberg et al., 2002), women with chronic pelvic pain (Norman et al., 2004), patients undergoing bladder papilloma resection (Solano et al., 2003), and patients with renal cell carcinoma (de Moor et al., 2002). Although several of these studies found beneficial effects as a result of the writing intervention, many had more equivocal results.

In an attempt to clarify these inconsistent findings in clinical populations, a recent meta-analysis examined the effects of written emotional disclosure on the health outcomes of clinical samples in nine studies (Frisina et al., 2004). The mean weighted effect size in clinical populations was $d = 0.19$, suggesting modest improvement in these samples. Additionally, these analyses suggested that the expressive writing intervention produced more improvement on physical rather than psychological health outcomes (Frisina et al., 2004). The results from this meta-analysis and those by Smyth (1998) and Frattaroli (2006) meta-analysis provide an important source of information about the parameters of the expressive writing intervention that may then be used to examine its utility in the clinical context. Overall, evidence suggests that expressive writing can be used in clinical populations and that it has modest, but fairly reliable, beneficial effects. Perhaps as important, there is little evidence of potential harm in its use when conducted under highly controlled research settings.

Efficacy Versus Effectiveness Research

Although previous research suggests that people are willing to write about personal topics within the laboratory, the benefits of expressive writing have been more inconsistent when writing was conducted outside of the laboratory or medical clinic. This raises two separate issues with regard to completing expressive writing outside of the clinical setting—feasibility (Will people adhere to instructions and complete the exercise?) and effectiveness (Does expressive writing confer beneficial results when conducted outside of traditional settings?). Efficacy trials conducted in highly controlled and formalized conditions have demonstrated the robust effects of expressive writing. Researchers have yet to demonstrate the effectiveness of this intervention using the same scientific rigor. In addition, some results also suggest that compliance with the intervention may be a particular point of concern when writing is conducted in less-structured settings, such as participants' homes (e.g., Gallagher & Maclachlan, 2002; Sheffield et al., 2002).

The distinction between efficacy and effectiveness research is an important one in intervention and treatment outcome research (e.g., Neal & Smyth, 2004). Efficacy research evaluates treatment outcomes in the highly controlled conditions of the laboratory. Effectiveness research demonstrates that a treatment promotes change in clinical or "real-life" settings. Although efficacy research is necessary to demonstrate that an intervention is responsible for differential change between a treated group and an untreated group (internal validity), it often does so at the expense of external validity (e.g., Neal & Smyth, 2004). Thus, effectiveness research demonstrates the generalizability of the intervention in more diverse settings that are less structured than the highly controlled scientific settings of the laboratory. The effectiveness of the structured expressive writing task in naturalistic settings is unclear. Taking expressive writing out of the laboratory and into the field signifies an important step toward effectiveness, which would immensely benefit the potential reach of administration.

A controlled trial conducted by Hockemeyer and Smyth (2002) supported both the feasibility and effectiveness of a multicomponent self-administered stress management workbook. Individuals with asthma were randomly assigned to a treatment group or to a placebo control group. The workbook intervention consisted of three components: A tape-recorded deep-breathing relaxation exercise, a cognitive-behavioral treatment, and a 20-minute written emotional disclosure exercise. The matched placebo workbook was composed of three sets of parallel exercises, which differed in content but not by process. Participants completed the workbook exercises at home over the course of 4 weeks, and were not contacted or prompted by the experimenters. Results revealed that the treatment group significantly improved in measures of lung function following completion of the workbook (as compared with the placebo group; Hockemeyer & Smyth, 2002).

A handful of studies have more explicitly examined the feasibility and effectiveness of the expressive writing protocol in medical settings. Broderick and colleagues (2004) conducted an effectiveness trial that translated the expressive writing intervention into a community-based intervention in the form of a videotaped program that was distributed to patients with rheumatoid arthritis. Although the format of this intervention differed from traditional efficacy trials, the standard writing instructions did not produce an effect. There were no significant differences between the groups for change in Disease Activity Rating or psychological impact of the intervention. Schilte and colleagues (2001) randomly assigned patients who frequently attended general practice with somatizing symptoms, to either a disclosure intervention condition or a control group (that consisted of usual care). Participants in the disclosure condition were visited two to three times by a trained "disclosure doctor" in their home and encouraged to discuss an emotionally significant experience. There were no significantly different changes in outcome measures during 2 years of follow-up between the disclosure and the control group (Schilte et al., 2001). Despite the scientific rigor and sound strategy of this study, the findings suggest that it may not be particularly beneficial to have general practitioners (GPs) play two different roles. Additionally, the nonstandard disclosure intervention (which involved talking about a significant emotional experience to an "expert") differs from traditional disclosure studies that ask participants to write privately about a stressful experience. Solitary disclosure may remove the social pressure of speaking to an expert about a private experience and enables individual to determine their own dose (Pennebaker, 2002).

KEY PROCESS VARIABLES

The robust efficacy of expressive writing was established early in the development of expressive writing (e.g., Smyth, 1998), but there is considerably less clarity regarding the underlying mechanisms responsible for the observed effects of the intervention. Multiple mechanisms that contribute to the effectiveness of expressive writing have been proposed and examined (see Lepore et al., 2002; Sloan & Marx, 2004). Regardless of the specific model, several points should be kept in mind. The writing intervention does not appear to be constrained to the actual writing session. The thoughts, emotions, and experiences that are disclosed may linger long beyond the 20 minutes of writing. Thus, it is challenging to tease apart exactly which mechanisms are responsible and at what point in the process they take place. Additionally, it is important to distinguish between evidence that is consistent with the purported model (correlational support) rather than in support of the model (experimental support).

THE INHIBITION MODEL

Early work focused a great deal on the role of inhibition on health outcomes. Active inhibition is a form of physiological work, which results in autonomic and central nervous system arousal—a chronic low-level stressor. This model posits that inhibition increases the risk of illness and other stress-related problems (e.g., Pennebaker et al., 1987). To the extent that the constraint of thoughts, feelings, or behaviors is stressful, disclosing thoughts and feelings should, in theory, reduce the stress of inhibition. However, previous disclosure and pre- and postwriting changes in inhibition are not consistently related to improvement (e.g., Greenberg & Stone, 1992). Hence, the role of inhibition in written disclosure is not clearly understood. Since this early explanation, a number of alternative theoretical perspectives have been proposed and, to a degree, examined.

INTEGRATED MODEL FOR THE BENEFITS OF WRITTEN DISCLOSURE

Another early explanation focused on the structure of traumatic or stressful memories. The forced transduction of memories from a sensory or affective format to a linguistic format is presumed to promote a narrative formation and organization. Although this transduction process can initially increase distress, it may allow a modification of the fear structure associated with the trauma, in turn facilitating the integration of the traumatic memory. Integrated memories should no longer cause intrusive reexperiencing, a change that will allow the attenuation of conditioned fear responses. The chronic hyperarousal associated with intrusion and fear responses should be eliminated, ultimately leading to reductions in psychological and physiological symptomatology. In effect, this results in a reduction in intrusions, ruminations, and associated physiological arousal, as well as reduced symptomatology (Smyth, 1998; Smyth & Pennebaker, 1999). Alternatively, there is some evidence that stress-or trauma-related intrusions might still persist after the intervention, but that the emotional impact of such thoughts is attenuated (e.g., Lepore, 1997; Smyth et al., 2002). That is, people may continue to have unbidden and/or unwanted thoughts about a stressful or traumatic experience but, when they do, they find them less distressing.

EXPERIENTIAL MODEL

Consistent with the experiential model of disclosure, and the early work of Janet (e.g., 1909), there is evidence consistent with an experiential aspect of writing. In an experiential model of therapy, processing of stressful or traumatic events is guided by schemas. Such schemas include cognitive representations of these events, affective responses, and specific patterns of autonomic arousal related to these events (Greenberg & Safran, 1987). Strong unresolved emotions related to a stressful or traumatic event can be held, in part, as somatic states (e.g., tension, arousal; Gendlin, 1996; Greenberg & Safran, 1987). According to this model, processing a stressful or traumatic event enables an individual to reexperience stress-related thoughts, emotions, and sensations, and come to see the problem in a new—less threatening—manner (Lutgendorf & Ullrich, 2002). Findings suggest that the combination of cognitive and emotional processing, along with a moderate level of emotional arousal, is required to produce change (Lutgendorf & Ullrich, 2002). The depth of processing that occurs during disclosure is an important component of this model, as it is thought to directly relate to better psychological and immune functioning through cognitive restructuring and release of somatic tension.

SELF-REGULATION

Several models have been proposed involving the regulation of thought, behavior, and most notably, affect. Dysregulated emotion is problematic because it may be either excessively controlled or excessively undercontrolled. Writing may normalize an emotional experience and possibly subsequent experiences and emotional behaviors. Research supports the view that emotion dysregulation (either excessive or inadequate control over emotional experience, expression, physiology, or behavior) can negatively impact mental and physical health. Expressive writing influences attention, habituation to stressful stimuli and to negative emotions, and may influence restructuring of cognitions related to stressors and stress responses (Lepore et al., 2002). Recent empirical evidence suggests that repeated exposure to specific stimuli (i.e., repeatedly writing about the same traumatic experience) might be more effective than requiring individuals to write about different traumatic events during each writing session (Sloan et al., 2005). Evidence consistent with emotion regulation processes has been demonstrated in several writing studies. Regulation may also occur in broader contexts, such as effective goal pursuit (King, 2002).

LANGUAGE USE

The Linguistic Inquiry and Word Count (LIWC), a computerized text analysis, is a computational examination of language that yields quantitative information using written text (Pennebaker et al., 1997). The LIWC computes language statistics (e.g., word count, sentence length, use of "big" words) and linguistic dimensions (e.g., pronouns). Additionally, information about psychological processes is also provided by counting related words in written text. These include the use of positive and negative words in each essay, as well as words indicative of causal or insight thinking (e.g., cause, effect, reason, because). The relativity of each writing sample may also be measured by computing the use of past, present, or future tense words.

Pennebaker and colleagues have used the LIWC to analyze the content of essays from several writing studies (Pennebaker & Francis, 1996; Pennebaker et al., 1997). Linguistic predictors of improved physical health included more positive emotion word use, moderate negative emotion word use, and an increase in causal and insight words (e.g., cause, effect, reason, because) over the course of writing. Individuals who benefit most from the writing appear to progress from using relatively few causal and insight words to using them more often by the last day of writing (Pennebaker et al., 1997). The authors note that people who showed this pattern of language use appeared to be telling a story over the course of writing. Although this research support is correlational, it suggests that narrative formation is a critical part of the writing process (Pennebaker et al., 1997). Smyth et al. (2001) experimentally manipulated narrative levels and found that narrative structure (stories with a clear start, middle, and finish) was necessary to produce beneficial changes, as participants expressing thoughts and feelings in an unstructured (fragmented) format were indistinguishable from participants writing about emotionally neutral topics.

COGNITIVE PARAMETERS

Ongoing work suggests core cognitive capacities are involved in the writing task. Both historical trauma and current stress are related to impaired core cognitive function, including working memory and executive processing. Intrusive thoughts are related to impaired core cognitive function (e.g., working memory) and partially mediate the relationship between stress and cognition. Some evidence suggests that expressive writing interventions can improve working memory and changes in working memory mediate other improvements (such as GPA; Klein, 2002). As already mentioned, the role of intrusions is less clear. It has not been determined whether the writing intervention has any effect on intrusions, results in fewer intrusions, or may be related to equal rates of intrusion, but with less of an impact (e.g., Lepore, 1997; Smyth et al., 2002).

BIOLOGICAL PARAMETERS

There is abundant evidence that writing influences a variety of biological parameters, including autonomic activity, endocrine function, and immune function (e.g., Esterling et al., 1990; Lutgendorf et al., 1994; McGuire et al., 2005; Pennebaker et al., 1988; Sloan & Epstein, 2005). Whether this is an "upstream" or "downstream" effect with regard to health outcomes has yet to be determined. That is, does writing lead to physiological changes that promote health, or does writing (through some alternate pathway) lead to improved health that subsequently alters (improves) physiological function? Such temporal sequencing is difficult to determine, as the cognitive/emotional/physiological systems are clearly dynamic and recursive (e.g., Blalock, 1984), but such demonstrations are critical to improve our understanding of potential mechanisms. Central in the role of biology, however, is clearly emotional experience and expression. The degree to which writing can influence emotional states, emotional expression, and emotional reactions to ongoing or future stimuli will have implications for physiological processes.

FINAL COMMENT ON MECHANISMS

Although there is a desire for a clear answer and a tendency to reduce the results to a single mechanism, it is quite possible that the writing intervention involves many or all the mechanisms reviewed here. The beneficial effects of structured expressive writing may be due to the cumulative effects of many small changes, or there may be different mechanisms present in different people or different situations. Many studies examining mechanisms have primarily focused on only one potential mechanism, and found little or equivocal support. In contrast, a preferable method may rely on a more pluralistic approach to mediation, widely assessing the range of possible mechanisms that may occur in concert with one another within individuals, or differentially between individuals.

ROLE IN COMPREHENSIVE TREATMENT PLAN OR STEPPED CARE AND COORDINATION ISSUES

Expressive writing may be implemented as an adjunctive treatment in a number of different ways. The intervention could be used to help individuals who are reluctant to seek psychological services because of the stigma associated with psychotherapy. Expressive writing may help promote emotional expression and potentially facilitate entry into face-to-face services. It could also be used to extend client contact in traditional psychotherapy settings, with clients writing on their own time, as homework, or utilizing structured writing outside of the session for topic generation. It may extend contact between therapist and client because it facilitates expression of emotion and experiences that may not be discussed during a session (either due to time constraints or the client's difficulty in verbally disclosing a particular issue). Although the majority of writing studies have involved writing longhand about a stressful or traumatic experience, typing has garnered increasing attention as a viable alternative to writing. Recent research has examined the effects of utilizing different modalities of writing, particularly with respect to eliciting differential affective arousal (Brewin & Lennard, 1999; Sharp & Hargrove, 2004). Conflicting evidence in the literature suggests that additional research is required before specific recommendations can be confidently made regarding the advantage of utilizing one modality as opposed to the other.

Alfred Lange and colleagues have developed a novel program called "Interapy" or "Internet therapy," which utilizes structured writing through the Internet (e.g., Lange et al., 2002, 2003). This procedure combines structured expressive writing with therapist feedback and instructions in the delivery of mental health services (Lange et al., 2002). In one such study that utilized Interapy, participants suffering from posttraumatic stress symptoms were randomly assigned to either a treatment group (Interapy) or a waiting list control group (Lange et al., 2002). Results indicated that participants assigned to the treatment condition, as compared with the control group, reported significant improvements in trauma-related symptoms and general psychopathology. It is also interesting (and somewhat surprising) to note that many participants reported that they would prefer electronic (remote) counseling to face-to-face therapy. These findings are encouraging and suggest that written emotional disclosure delivered through the Internet has the potential to serve as an effective supplemental treatment.

In addition to the clinical setting, the expressive writing intervention might also be used as an adjunctive treatment within the primary care setting. Limited evidence supports the feasibility of utilizing expressive writing as an intervention in primary care (Hannay & Bolton, 1999; Klapow et al., 2001). Klapow and colleagues (2001) evaluated the feasibility of the expressive writing protocol among older primary care patients. Findings supported the feasibility of using the expressive writing protocol as a primary care intervention. Only descriptive outcomes were reported, however, which precludes drawing any conclusions from these data. A variation of the writing paradigm was utilized in a separate study by Hannay & Bolton (1999), in which GPs were trained to disseminate writing guidelines (of a more unstructured nature than that typically used in expressive writing studies) to patients who were identified as anxious and depressed. Although only descriptive data were provided, the investigators indicate that therapeutic writing was feasible and acceptable in general practice (Hannay & Bolton, 1999).

These encouraging results must be evaluated with caution in light of subsequent findings that demonstrated that even though expressive writing was generally well-received by doctors and patients in primary care settings, there were no significant differences in outcomes between the disclosure and the control groups (Schilte et al., 2001). Although the aforementioned studies were all conducted within a primary care setting, the variations in the protocol and implementation of the intervention prohibit direct comparisons among these three studies (Hannay & Bolton, 1999; Klapow et al., 2001; Schilte et al., 2001). There is clearly a need to conduct additional experimental research in order to better understand the efficacy and effectiveness of utilizing expressive writing in primary healthcare settings. It is also imperative that researchers investigate which patients would be most likely to benefit from the intervention in such settings, and which staff (e.g., physicians, nurses, others) are the most efficacious treatment providers.

RESEARCH AGENDA

Much of the more recent work on expressive writing, particularly in the last 5 years, has been conducted in different ways or with different goals, which has produced both strengths and weaknesses. For example, several studies have tried to establish boundary conditions of the intervention by testing it in new populations or in new settings. Others have explored theoretical questions and have altered the content of the intervention (e.g., different instructional content). These variations in procedure provide important information about the generalizability of expressive writing, which might increase the potential reach of the intervention, or even increase intervention efficacy. Despite these advances, recent research has also been characterized by inconsistent scientific and reporting rigor. Many studies have lacked theoretical justifications and/or frameworks and have included multiple and poorly specified dependent variables.

Researchers have altered multiple procedural components of the intervention (e.g., investigator, sample, instructions) without regard for potential consequences. The effects of these inconsistent procedures may produce artifacts that can threaten the validity of expressive writing studies. In fact, the frequency with which these variations in procedure are conducted (and the differences in the quality of reporting such alterations) conveys an implicit notion in the literature that altering procedural components of the intervention do not matter. Many investigators have interpreted the ease of administering the expressive writing intervention to mean that it can be carried out anywhere, by anyone, at any time. This "one-size-fits-all" attitude may be inaccurate and detrimental to the quality of the intervention and the literature as a whole (Smyth, 2006). This may further promulgate poor scientific reporting of such changes because such alterations are assumed to be inconsequential.

Researchers must improve several areas within the expressive writing literature before it can confidently be identified and evaluated as an evidence-based behavioral medicine intervention. The heterogeneity of the administration and implementation of the intervention suggests the need to standardize the intervention. One suggested approach is to develop and distribute a manual that provides guidelines for running an expressive writing study. Such a manual might include writing instructions, explicit directions on protocol, and suggestions on how to handle potential issues that might arise during and/or after administration of the intervention. A similar version, currently available on Pennebaker's website (Pennebaker, 1994), primarily draws on anecdotal evidence from his own experiences conducting expressive writing studies. This existing manual may provide a starting point for developing a more updated and professional version that cites scientific evidence to support the suggestions that are made.

Despite the rapid advances that have taken place in expressive writing research, numerous questions still remain and several issues must be considered before the writing paradigm is formally transferred to the clinical setting. An issue of considerable concern is how practitioners can ensure the safety of clients when writing is conducted outside of the laboratory. Although the majority of individuals may be able to safely self-regulate their emotional responses to writing, a subset of individuals may not have the internal or external resources to do so. It is thus imperative to continue investigations that explore for whom and under what circumstances expressive writing is most effective.

DISSEMINATION AGENDA

As expressive writing continues to garner attention and evidence as an effective adjunctive treatment, various issues necessitate deliberate research and clinical consideration. These issues have implications for designing future research within the area of expressive writing as well as for its use as a supplemental psychosocial intervention. Despite the apparently increasing popularity of the expressive writing intervention, it is imperative that researchers prioritize quality before quantity. Investigators should aspire to conduct a few well-controlled studies as opposed to publishing a large number of poorly controlled and poorly reported studies. It is essential that researchers clearly report any variations to the expressive writing intervention in order to more carefully document their effects and whether they might serve as potential moderators of overall efficacy of the intervention.

In addition to reporting variations in procedure, it is also suggested that researchers describe the experimental context of expressive writing studies, which includes both the status of study personnel (i.e., those with participant contact) and the location of writing. Recent empirical evidence suggests that the experimental context can affect the results of an expressive writing intervention, and different samples may respond differentially to contextual variables (e.g., location of writing and legitimate authority of investigator; Nazarian & Smyth, 2006). The issue is not whether alterations to these factors are necessarily appropriate (although evidence suggests that they have an impact). Rather, it is incumbent upon researchers to describe the context of their studies (e.g., setting and location of writing, the status and training of research staff) to allow the careful examination (and meta-analytic modeling) of these issues.

Contextual variables may also have significant clinical implications, particularly if clinicians suggest that clients complete the intervention in naturalistic settings that are less formalized and structured than that of the laboratory (e.g., at home). This raises concern about the safety and well-being of clients when the intervention is administered in a self-help format outside of the laboratory (Smyth & Helm, 2003). These and other issues must be considered and evaluated on an individual basis before suggesting that clients utilize expressive writing in an unsupervised and less-structured environment than that of the laboratory and/or clinical setting.

Although the most common mode of writing reported in expressive writing trials is longhand, a small percentage of studies utilize typing, which is another viable alternative to writing. Researchers and clinicians must be cognizant of the effects that this different mode of writing might have on both the process and the outcomes of expressive writing and must be careful not to assume that mode of writing is inconsequential. Rather, it is imperative to take into account any factors that accompany alterations made to the mode of writing and consequently might affect the intervention (e.g., typing skill and speed, computer literacy, topic of writing, interacting with mode of writing). These various factors should be considered and accounted for when suggesting that clients use different modes of writing.

It is again worth noting that researchers stand to learn a great deal from any modification made to the expressive writing intervention. Such alterations to the intervention offer valuable information about boundary conditions, moderators of clinical effectiveness, translational characteristics, and other important issues. Therefore, the procedure of altering parameters is not a problem, per se. Rather, it is the erroneous assumption that altering parameters of the intervention does not matter and, as a result, said alterations are often not clearly reported or evaluated as to their impact on outcomes. The preceding guidelines highlighted several suggestions that were directed at both researchers and clinicians within the area of expressive writing research. The ensuing discussion highlights general suggestions for implementing the intervention as an adjunctive treatment specifically within the clinical setting.

THE USE OF EXPRESSIVE WRITING IN THE CLINICAL SETTING

Within clinical settings, the nature of expressive writing should be clarified ahead of time in order for clients to decide whether their writing will be private or shared. Although writing interventions can "work" without therapist feedback, it is unclear whether having a therapist and/or feedback would be useless. Participants who write about their personal experiences in the context of scientific studies write, to some extent, with a presumed audience in mind. Participants are aware that their writing will be viewed by the researchers (although they are assured that their name will not be associated with their writing). Results suggest that the greater the presumed audience, however, the more filtered the disclosure (e.g., Wortman & Silver, 1989). Thus, care should be taken in the manner in which writing is integrated into other therapeutic modalities and the degree to which it involves sharing writing with others.

Therapist involvement and feedback may be deemed appropriate on an individual basis. Feedback might play a trivial role for clients who are ready to improve on their own or if there is a poor match between the therapist and the clients (such as different goals, mismatch between approach). Conversely, some individuals may require more formal assistance. Many people do not benefit from "self" administered writing, and there may possibly be some identifiable subgroups that would benefit from assistance (e.g., alexithymics; Lumley et al., 2002). Therapists might facilitate benefit for some of these individuals by clarifying the process and goals, providing appropriate feedback, and regulating the "dose" of writing. It may also be prudent for the clinician to touch base with clients after the first writing session to address any questions and concerns.

It is recommended that clients complete their writing in a safe, quiet location without disruptions. Approximately 30–45 minutes should be allotted for each session, with about the first half devoted to writing and a few minutes left afterwards to compose oneself. Clients should be encouraged to write continuously for the allotted time without regard to spelling, style, grammar, or the "polish" of their writing. When therapists and clients select the number of writing sessions, it is important to note that there is no magical number—some individuals benefit from a single session, whereas others are likely to require more. Nonetheless, a comfortable number of sessions should be selected, ranging from three to four. It is also unclear what the optimal spacing of sessions is, and most likely varies by individual characteristics. Sessions might be conducted daily, or spaced out over several weeks (or even months).

Therapists should encourage the exploration of thoughts and feelings regarding the experiences or thoughts that are important to the client. Topics to consider during writing sessions may include how the stressful experience relates to the client's current condition/situation and how it relates to other aspects of life (e.g., relationships, childhood, goals, who the client is). Almost writing focuses solely on topics that might increase negative affectivity (i.e., traumatic or stressful negative events), topics can also focus on positive events. These might include writing about the positive aspects of negative events, future positive goals, intensely positive experiences, or other topics deemed helpful (e.g., Burton & King, 2004; King & Miner, 2000). Although some efforts have been made to improve the intervention by imposing writing guidelines (such as narrative structure, processing, word use), these studies have produced mixed results and pose the danger of too much structure (whereupon the writer is consumed with following restrictive instructions and focus on emotional and cognitive content is impaired). It appears critical, however, to include both thoughts and feelings (cognition and affect), as including only one appears to undermine the benefit of writing (Smyth & Pennebaker, 1999). Additionally, it appears useful to generally emphasize the narrative structure, coherence, and story-like features of writing (e.g., Smyth et al., 2001).

Although expressive writing proffers many benefits, barriers exist in its implementation. Clients may not be willing to revisit a painful experience by writing about it and may stop writing when they experience distress or discomfort. Data suggest that individuals who write about a stressful or traumatic event experience greater distress during writing and after writing, as compared with participants who write about neutral topics (Smyth, 1998). Thus, it is important to understand how to help participants cope with this distress if writing is completed in an unmonitored setting. Some individuals may not initially recognize the utility of revisiting a past upsetting experience by writing about it. In such instances, practitioners might highlight the findings of expressive writing studies and refer patients to lay publications that may provide further information (e.g., Desalvo, 1999; Pennebaker, 1997).

Furthermore, many clients may present with disabilities that precludes utilizing the traditional expressive writing task. Practitioners and researchers alike must be sensitive to physical disabilities, learning disabilities, literacy issues, and the role of these factors in the willingness and ability to write. Individuals who are unable to write might be encouraged to privately disclose their experiences into a tape recorder (Kelley et al., 1997; Murray et al., 1989; Murray & Segal, 1994). Irrespective of the specific guidelines that are provided to clients, it is imperative that clinicians make sound clinical judgments and adopt an ideographic approach when incorporating expressive writing as an adjunct treatment. If used judiciously, however, expressive writing is a widely available, low-cost adjuvant treatment that has the potential to improve health and well-being.

REFERENCES

Blalock, H.M. (1984). Contextual-effects models: Theoretical and methodological issues. *Annual Review of Sociology, 10*, 353–372.

Brewin, C.R. & Lennard, H. (1999). Effects of mode of writing on emotional narratives. *Journal of Traumatic Stress, 12*, 355–361.

Broderick, J.E., Stone, A.A., Smyth, J.M., & Kaell, A.T. (2004). The feasibility and effectiveness of an expressive writing intervention for rheumatoid arthritis via home-based videotaped instructions. *Annals of Behavioral Medicine, 27*, 50–59.

Burton, C.M. & King, L.A. (2004). The health benefits of writing about intensely positive experiences. *Journal of Research in Personality, 38*, 150–163.

de Moor, C., Sterner, J., Hall, M., et al. (2002). A pilot study of the effects of expressive writing on psychological and behavioral adjustment in patients enrolled in a Phase II trial of vaccine therapy for metastatic renal cell carcinoma. *Health Psychology, 21*, 615–619.

Desalvo, L. (1999). *Writing As a Way of Healing: How Telling Our Stories Transforms Our Lives.* San Francisco, CA: Harper Press.

Esterling, B.A., Antoni, M.H., Kumar, M., & Schneiderman, N. (1990). Emotional repression, stress disclosure responses, and Epstein-Barr viral capsid antigen titers. *Psychosomatic Medicine, 52*, 397–410.

Frattaroli, J. (2006). Experimental disclosure and its moderators: A meta-analysis. *Psychological Bulletin, 132*, 823–865.

Frisina, P.G., Borod, J.C., & Lepore, S.J. (2004). A meta-analysis of the effects of written emotional disclosure on the health outcomes of clinical populations. *Journal of Nervous and Mental Disease, 192*, 629–634.

Gallagher, P. & Maclachlan, M. (2002). Evaluating a written emotional disclosure homework intervention for lower-limb amputees. *Archives of Physical Medicine and Rehabilitation, 83*, 1464–1466.

Gendlin, E.T. (1996). *Focusing-Oriented Psychotherapy: A Manual of the Experiential Method.* New York: Guildford Press.

Gidron, Y., Peri, T., Connolly, J.F., & Shalev, A.Y. (1996). Written disclosure in posttraumatic stress disorder: Is it beneficial for the patient? *Journal of Nervous and Mental Disease, 184*, 505–507.

Gillis, M.E., Lumley, M.A., Mosley-Williams, A., et al. (2006). The health effects of at-home written emotional disclosure in fibromyalgia: A randomized trial. *Annals of Behavioral Medicine, 32*, 135–146.

Greenberg, L. & Safran, J. (1987). *Emotion in Psychotherapy: Affect, Cognition and the Process of Change*. New York: Guilford Press.

Greenberg, M.A. & Stone, A.A. (1992). Emotional disclosure about traumas and its relation to health: Effects of previous disclosure and trauma severity. *Journal of Personality and Social Psychology, 63*, 75–84.

Hannay, D. & Bolton, G. (1999). Therapeutic writing in primary care: A feasibility study. *Primary Care Psychiatry, 5*, 157–160.

Hockemeyer, J. & Smyth, J. (2002). Evaluating the feasibility and efficacy of a self-administered manual-based stress management intervention for individuals with asthma: Results from a controlled study. *Behavioral Medicine, 27*, 161–172.

Janet, P. (1909). *Les Névroses*. Paris.

Kelley, J.E., Lumley, M.A., & Leisen, J.C.C. (1997). Health effects of emotional disclosure in rheumatoid arthritis patients. *Health Psychology, 16*, 331–340.

King, L.A. (2002). Gain without pain? Expressive writing and self-regulation. In S.J. Lepore & J.M. Smyth (Eds.), *The Writing Cure: How Expressive Writing Promotes Health and Emotional Well-Being* (pp. 119–134). Washington, DC: American Psychological Association Press.

King, L.A. & Miner, K.N. (2000). Writing about the perceived benefits of traumatic events: Implications for physical health. *Personality and Social Psychology Bulletin, 26*, 220–230.

Klapow, J.C., Schmidt, S.M., Taylor, L.A., et al. (2001). Symptom management in older primary care patients: Feasibility of an experimental, written self-disclosure protocol. *Annals of Internal Medicine, 134*, 905–911.

Klein, K. (2002). Stress, expressive writing, and working memory. In S.J. Lepore & J.M. Smyth (Eds.), *The Writing Cure: How Expressive Writing Promotes Health and Emotional Well-Being* (pp. 135–155). Washington, DC: American Psychological Association Press.

L'Abate, L. (1999). Taking the bully by the horns: Beyond talk in psychological interventions. *Family Journal: Counseling and Therapy for Couples and Families, 7*, 206–220.

Lange, A., Schoutrop, M., Schrieken, B., & van de Ven, J.P. (2002). Interapy: A model for therapeutic writing through the Internet. In S.J. Lepore & J.M. Smyth (Eds.), *The Writing Cure: How Expressive Writing Promotes Health and Emotional Well-Being* (pp. 215–238). Washington, DC: American Psychological Association Press.

Lange, A., Rietdijk, D., Hudcovicova, M., et al. (2003). Interapy: A controlled randomized trial of the standardized treatment of posttraumatic stress through the Internet. *Journal of Consulting and Clinical Psychology, 71*, 901–909.

Lepore, S.J. (1997). Expressive writing moderates the relation between intrusive thoughts and depressive symptoms. *Journal of Personality and Social Psychology, 73*, 1030–1037.

Lepore, S.J., Greenberg, M.A., Bruno, M., & Smyth, J.M. (2002). Expressive writing and health: Self-regulation of emotion-related experience, physiology, and behavior. In S.J. Lepore & J.M. Smyth (Eds.), *The Writing Cure: How Expressive Writing Promotes Health and Emotional Well-Being* (pp. 99–117). Washington, DC: American Psychological Association Press.

Lepore, S.J., Silver, R.C., Wortman, C.B., & Wayment, H.A. (1996). Social constraints, intrusive thoughts, and depressive symptoms among bereaved mothers. *Journal of Personality and Social Psychology, 70*, 271–282.

Lumley, M.A., Tojek, T.M., & Macklem, D. (2002). Effects of written emotional disclosure among repressive and alexithymic people. In S.J. Lepore & J.M. Smyth (Eds.), *The Writing Cure: How expressive Writing Promotes Health and Emotional Well-Being* (pp. 75–95). Washington, DC: American Psychological Association Press.

Lutgendorf, S.K., Antoni, M.H., Kumar, M., & Schneiderman, N. (1994). Changes in cognitive coping strategies predict EBV-antibody titre change following a stressor disclosure induction. *Journal of Psychosomatic Research, 38*, 63–78.

Lutgendorf, S.K. & Ullrich, P. (2002). Cognitive processing, disclosure, and health: Psychological and physiological mechanisms. In S.J. Lepore & J.M. Smyth (Eds.), *The Writing Cure: How Expressive Writing Promotes Health and Emotional Well-Being* (pp. 177–196). Washington, DC: American Psychological Association Press.

Mann, T. (2001). Effects of future writing and optimism on health behaviors in HIV-infected women. *Annals of Behavioral Medicine*, *23*, 26–33.

McGuire, K., Greenberg, M.A., & Gevirtz, R. (2005). Autonomic effects of expressive writing in individuals with elevated blood pressure. *Journal of Health Psychology*, *10*, 197–209.

Murray, E.J., Lamnin, A.D., & Carver, C.S. (1989). Emotional expression in written essays and psychotherapy. *Journal of Social and Clinical Psychology*, *8*, 414–429.

Murray, E. & Segal, D. (1994). Emotional processing in vocal and written expression of feelings about traumatic experiences. *Journal of Traumatic Stress*, *7*, 391–405.

Nazarian, D. & Smyth, J.M. (2006). The role of context in the effectiveness of an expressive writing intervention. In A. Stanton (Ed.), *Theory to Practice in Expressive Writing Interventions: Effects of Experimental Context and Participant Attributes*. Symposium conducted at the Annual Meeting of the American Psychosomatic Society, Denver, CO.

Neal, D.J. & Smyth, J. (2004). Treatment efficacy versus effectiveness. In A. Christensen, R. Martin, & J. Smyth (Eds.), *Encyclopedia of Health Psychology*. New York: Kluwer Academic Press.

Norman, S.A., Lumley, M.A., Dooley, J.A., & Diamond, M.P. (2004). For whom does it work? Moderators of the effects of written emotional disclosure in a randomized trial among women with chronic pelvic pain. *Psychosomatic Medicine*, *66*, 174–183.

O'Connor, M.-F., Allen, J.J.B., & Kaszniak, A.W. (2004). Emotional disclosure for whom? A study of vagal tone in bereavement. *Biological Psychiatry*, *68*, 135–146.

Pennebaker, J.W. (1994). Some suggestions for running a confession study. Available at: http://www.psy.utexas.edu/Pennebaker (accessed April 2006).

Pennebaker, J.W. (1997). *Opening Up: The Healing Power of Expressing Emotions*. New York: Guilford Press.

Pennebaker, J.W. (2002). Solitary disclosure allows people to determine their own dose. *British Medical Journal*, *324*, 544.

Pennebaker, J.W. & Beall, S.K. (1986). Confronting a traumatic event: Toward an understanding of inhibition and disease. *Journal of Abnormal Psychology*, *95*, 274–281.

Pennebaker, J.W. & Francis, M.E. (1996). Cognitive, emotional, and language processes in disclosure. *Cognition and Emotion*, *10*, 601–626.

Pennebaker, J.W., Hughes, C.F., & O'Heeron, R.C. (1987). The psychophysiology of confession: Linking inhibitory and psychosomatic processes. *Journal of Personality and Social Psychology*, *52*, 781–793.

Pennebaker, J.W., Kiecolt-Glaser, J.K., & Glaser, R. (1988). Confronting traumatic experience and immunocompetence: A reply to Neale, Cox, Valdimarsdottir, and Stone. *Journal of Consulting and Clinical Psychology*, *56*, 638–639.

Pennebaker, J.W., Mayne, T.J., & Francis, M.E. (1997). Linguistic predictors of adaptive bereavement. *Journal of Personality and Social Psychology*, *72*, 863–871.

Petrie, K.J., Fontanilla, I., Thomas, M.G., et al. (2004). Effect of written emotional expression on immune function in patients with HIV infection: A randomized trial. *Psychosomatic Medicine*, *66*, 272–275.

Riordan, R.J. (1996). Scriptotherapy: Therapeutic writing as a counseling adjunct. *Journal of Counseling and Development*, *74*(3), 263–269.

Rosenberg, H.J., Rosenberg, S.D., Ernstoff, M.S., et al. (2002). Expressive disclosure and health outcomes in a prostate cancer population. *International Journal of Psychiatry in Medicine*, *32*, 37–53.

Schilte, A.F., Portegijs, P.J., Blankenstein, A.H., et al. (2001). Randomised controlled trial of disclosure of emotionally important events in somatisation in primary care. *British Medical Journal*, *323*, 1–6.

Sharp, W.G. & Hargrove, D.S. (2004). Emotional expression and modality: An analysis of affective arousal and linguistic output in a computer vs. paper paradigm. *Computers in Human Behavior*, *20*, 461–475.

Sheffield, D., Duncan, E., Thomson, K., & Johal, S.S. (2002). Written emotional expression and well-being: Result from a home-based study. *Australasian Journal of Disaster & Trauma Studies*. Available at: http://www.massey.ac.nz/~trauma/issues/2002-1/sheffield.htm (accessed May 2006).

Sloan, D.M. & Epstein, E.M. (2005). Respiratory sinus arrhythmia predicts written disclosure outcome. *Psychophysiology*, *42*, 611–615.

Sloan, D.M. & Marx, B.P. (2004). Taking pen to hand: Evaluating theories underlying the written disclosure paradigm. *Clinical Psychology: Science and Practice*, *11*, 121–137.

Sloan, D.M., Marx, B.P., & Epstein, E.M. (2005). Further examination of the exposure model underlying the efficacy of written emotional disclosure. *Journal of Consulting and Clinical Psychology*, *73*, 549–554.

Smyth, J.M. (1998). Written emotional expression: Effect sizes, outcome types, and moderating variables. *Journal of Consulting and Clinical Psychology*, *66*, 174–184.

Smyth, J.M. (2006). Expressive writing: Bargain or boutique intervention? In A. Stanton (Ed.), *Theory to Practice in Expressive Writing Interventions: Effects of Experimental Context and Participant Attributes*. Symposium conducted at the Annual Meeting of the American Psychosomatic Society, Denver, CO.

Smyth, J.M. & Greenberg, M.A. (2000). Scriptotherapy: The effects of writing about traumatic events. In P.R. Duberstein & J.M. Masling (Eds.), *Psychodynamic Perspectives on Sickness and Health* (pp. 121–160). Washington, DC: American Psychological Association.

Smyth, J.M. & Helm, R. (2003). Focused expressive writing as self-help for stress and trauma. *Journal of Clinical Psychology/In Session: Psychotherapy in Practice*, *59*, 227–235.

Smyth, J., Hockemeyer, J., Anderson, C., et al. (2002). Structured writing about a natural disaster buffers the effects of intrusive thoughts on negative affect and physical symptoms. *Australasian Journal of Disaster and Trauma Studies*, *1*. Available at: http://www.massey.ac.nz/~trauma/issues/2002-1/smyth.htm (accessed April 2006).

Smyth, J.M. & Nazarian, D. (2006). Development and preliminary results of a self-administered intervention for individuals with fibromyalgia syndrome: A multiple case control report. *Explore: The Journal of Science and Healing*, *2*, 426–431.

Smyth, J.M. & Pennebaker, J.W. (1999). Sharing one's story: Translating emotional experiences into words as a coping tool. In C. Snyder (Ed.), *Coping: The Psychology of What Works* (pp. 70–89). New York: Oxford University Press.

Smyth, J.M., Stone, A.A., Hurewitz, A., & Kaell, A. (1999). Effects of writing about stressful experiences on symptom reduction in patients with asthma or rheumatoid arthritis: A randomized trial. *Journal of the American Medical Association*, *281*, 1304–1309.

Smyth, J.M., True, N., & Souto, J. (2001). Effects of writing about traumatic experiences: The necessity for narrative structuring. *Journal of Social and Clinical Psychology*, *20*, 161–172.

Solano, L., Donati, V., Pecci, F., et al. (2003). Postoperative course after papilloma resection: Effects of written disclosure of the experience in subjects with different alexithymia levels. *Psychosomatic Medicine*, *65*, 477–484.

Stanton, A.L., Danoff-Burg, S., Sworowski, L.A., et al. (2002). Randomized, controlled trial of written emotional expression and benefit finding in breast cancer patients. *Journal of Clinical Oncology*, *20*, 4160–4168.

Stroebe, M., Stroebe, W., Schut, H., et al. (2002). Does disclosure of emotions facilitate recovery from bereavement? Evidence from two prospective studies. *Journal of Consulting and Clinical Psychology*, *70*, 169–178.

Walker, B.L., Nail, L.M., & Croyle, R.T. (1999). Does emotional expression make a difference in reactions to breast cancer? *Oncology Nursing Forum*, *26*, 1025–1032.

Wortman, C.B. & Silver, R.C. (1989). The myths of coping with loss. *Journal of Consulting and Clinical Psychology*, *57*, 349–357.

12

Holistic and Alternative Medicine as Adjunctive to Psychotherapy

Janet L. Cummings and Nicholas A. Cummings

University of Nevada, Reno and The Nicholas and Dorothy Cummings Foundation

Since the mid-1960s, alternative medicine, which encompasses a large array of approaches, has been booming. Although most of these potions, nostrums, and interventions are unverified, it has grown into a multibillion dollar industry, with adherents who would resent paying out of pocket for ordinary medical care eager to fork over whatever the cost inasmuch as most health insurance plans do not cover alternative or holistic medicine. The very term itself ranges from the obvious (e.g., exercise, pure air and water, nutritional diet) and the efficacious or verified (e.g., acupuncture, biofeedback) on the one hand, to the outright outrageous on the other (e.g., feng shui, crystal therapy), and a wide range of verified and unverified interventions in between. Separating the wheat from the chaff is controversial, as it flies in the face of adherents who promote St John's Wort for depression and Echinacea for the common cold, long after controlled studies have called them into serious question. These are only two examples of widely heralded holistic substances that have been shown to be ineffective or, at best, minimally effective, yet continue to have proponents. Consumers cannot rely on the Food and Drug Administration (FDA) inasmuch as the courts have ruled that much that is swallowed in alternative medicine are so-called natural substances that cannot be regulated as drugs.

Often included in alternative medicine are such widely disparate procedures as relaxation techniques, yoga, New Age approaches, spiritual healing, and prayer. The latter often includes prayers offered by others on behalf of someone who does not know he or she is being prayed for. Because those who dispense alternative and holistic medicine often are not health professionals, but often mystics, cultists, self-appointed experts, and even health spa employees; the public is not accorded the protections found in the regulated healthcare system.

The authors have often stated that contemporary alternative medicine is the most varied collection of gold and feces ever assembled in healthcare. This chapter addresses the need for alternative and holistic medicine while striking a note of caution to both the unwary consumer and the well-meaning professional. Psychotherapists are often called upon to make recommendations, or to otherwise comment on various alternative treatments that the client may be considering or already partaking. As a licenced provider, you may be held accountable should there be untoward effects on your client from such use after you have given your positive or even implied recommendation. With appropriate knowledge, however, alternative medicine can be a valuable adjunct to psychotherapy.

HISTORICAL PERSPECTIVE

The wide range of interventions that might be termed "alternative medicine" have taken many twists and turns throughout the centuries; yet, the primary thrust of providing an alternative to contemporary medicine has remained constant. Exercise, fresh air, pure water, herbs, and healthy nutrition have survived the ages, being the very essence of medicine beginning with Hippocrates and Galen. Currently, these take a back seat to more aggressive methods such as medications and surgery, and are being championed as natural remedies. Nonetheless, the ancient physicians could never have envisaged health food store shelves lined with hundreds of packages containing herbal products, the overwhelming majority of which have never been subjected to scientific scrutiny. And in their zeal for pure water, they could not have anticipated that people would be paying $2 a pint for bottled water, even after time and time again it has been shown that it was no more pure than tap water, and in some instances even inferior to it.

During the Middle Ages, even the seemingly ubiquitous belief in fresh air and pure water waned. It was widely believed that night air was deleterious, so windows were tightly shut after dark and people went outdoors as little as possible after sundown. Bathing was considered so dangerous that it was a rare event and it had best be prescribed by a physician. Perfumes were concocted to mask body odors, a practice that continued in France until well after World War II. Even in the United States, the bath was considered a weekly Saturday-night event until well into the twentieth century.

Few today are aware that in the United States during the 1800s homeopathy was the predominant form of medicine, while allopathic medicine, which is the mainstream healthcare today, was still in its infancy. In-time consumers lost confidence in homeopathy, and it declined as allopathic medicine gained ascendancy. The last homeopathic medical school closed in 1923. Today, homeopathy is an alternative medicine, and there are once again a number of homeopathic and naturopathic schools as alternative medicine continues to gain adherents.

It is interesting to note that at one point a psychiatric treatment ran afoul of the laws governing quackery. Wilhelm Reich's orgone box, in which a patient sat to receive some kind of therapeutic emanations from the surroundings, was banned and confiscated by the government. This has gone down in history as the only "psychotherapy" technique to be prohibited by health regulations. Before it was banned, Reich even developed a portable orgone box that could be shared, or accompany the traveler. Recent attempts to revive the orgone box failed to generate much interest.

Chiropractors, many of whom during the 1930s were associated with low-voltage therapy treatments, unnecessary spinal adjustments, and even such outlandish practices as prescribing colored underwear that was personality compatible, as well as other highly questionable treatments, have worked diligently to upgrade their profession in the public's perception. Today, chiropractors are among the strongest proponents of alternative medicine, and many of their followers reflect their chiropractors' resentment of the medical establishment. In their zeal for alternative medicine, some of their practices may be problematic. For example, popular and widely syndicated radio shows such as that of "Doctor Bob" Martin promote so many herbal and other holistic products that if one were to swallow even half of those recommended there would be no room in the patient's life for food.

THE DEMOGRAPHIC SHIFT

Just as consumer loss of interest in homeopathy resulted in its near disappearance at the end of the nineteenth century, it is the consumers in the early twenty-first century that are driving the economic boom in alternative medicine. A $30–40 billion market may not seem impressive when compared with the $1.6 trillion spent in America on allopathic medical care, but it looms large when one realizes it equals or exceeds the entire mental health and substance abuse budget. There are a number of factors driving this boom, listed as follows, but principal among them is a dramatic shift in the demographics of the United States.

- The generation whose mantra was "never trust anyone over thirty" is aging, an event that was not supposed to happen. As the boomers enter their fifties and sixties, there is an almost desperate rush to stay young: Botox, liposuction, antiwrinkle creams, and all sorts of cosmetic surgery and dentistry. Many physicians and dentists devote their entire practices to cosmetics, and it is estimated that 25% of all medical practice is absorbed by cosmetic rather than by critical healthcare. Alternative medical interventions that promise to prevent aging are in vogue, and the previous generation that believed one should "grow old gracefully" (Snowden, 2001) has been replaced by the cry "defy aging" (Brickey, 2000).

- This same generation has witnessed the greatest medical advances in the history of the world, resulting in unprecedented longevity, along with an expectation of medical miracles. But even modern advances in medical care have limitations, and when confronted by the reality that longevity does not mean eternal youth, these consumers uncritically rush to espouse dubious alternatives that are willing to make unsubstantiated promises.
- Widely used FDA-approved medications that later were shown to be harmful and even deadly (e.g., Vioxx, Fen-Phen, the brand name for combination of fenfluramine and phentermine) have received broad media coverage, and have contributed to a growing distrust. This skepticism has been further fueled by reports that the pharmaceutical industry spends $13 billion annually on advertising (Freudenheim, 2007), resulting in the fear that the medical profession, the FDA, and Big Pharma are too cozy, jeopardizing consumer safety and welfare. One of the effects of this fear has been a renewed interest in natural remedies.
- Many boomers have confided the fear that considerable drug use during the Hippie hey day has damaged their bodies and in the need to purify them they often turn uncritically to holistic remedies.
- The generation that in the 1960s and 1970s uncritically trusted the street drug pusher now has transferred this questionable judgment into trust of unverified and dubious practices and practitioners. This would be paradoxical, were it not for a common thread: The propensity of the boomers to trust the unregulated peddler (street drug pusher, health food store operator, self-appointed guru) over the establishment (Obama, 2007).

The recent revival of holistic and alternative treatments and on such a large-scale, and all in the name of healthcare, raises alarms, especially because fads and cults have proliferated. Most of the techniques remain unverified and their proponents rely on junk science or testimonials from the "cured" to lure the public. Certain persons are particularly vulnerable to these fads and the allure of charismatic gurus. Among these are individuals with thought disorders who seek to control the disordered thinking with cultish solutions. Individuals with somatization disorders are susceptible to promises of "cure" after they have been disappointed by the medical profession's inability to do so (Cummings and Sayama, 1995). Griffin (1996), along with other dangers, lists a number of commonly used herbs that can cause serious problems such as kidney failure and stroke.

Perhaps the greatest danger lies in the promises of cure without medication side effects or the pain of radiation or surgery that might cause the patient to forego necessary treatment in favor of ineffective approaches. The authors are sadly aware of all too many instances in their practices in which patients had succumbed to extravagant promises of questionable practitioners, only to awaken too late to the futility of their choices.

Despite the dangers inherent in some alternative treatments and the precariousness of relying on nonvalidated techniques while rejecting validated ones, many alternative treatments have merit, especially when used as adjuncts to traditional medical treatments and even psychotherapy. This chapter addresses a number of these, describing the extent to which they have been verified, and their appropriate use. Purposely omitted are a number of New Age practices that have vociferous adherents, but lack verification, rely on junk science, testimonials, and even gullibility; and when subjected to controlled studies yield effectiveness scores below the very minimum expected by the placebo effect alone. Among them are aroma therapy, copper bracelets, feng shui, holding crystals, and magnets inserted in shoes.

THE PLACEBO EFFECT: THE IMPORTANCE OF BELIEF

The placebo effect, defined as the propensity for recovery and improvement resulting from a belief in the efficacy of the intervention, may be regarded as an ally or an adversary, depending on the setting. In drug research, the task is to demonstrate the effectiveness of the medication above and beyond the placebo effect, whereas in treatment, it may comprise nature's own healing process and comprise a substantial portion of the improvement. The early history of medicine may actually be reflective of the placebo effect, for unlikely treatments such as lizard's blood, crushed insects, leeches, blood letting, and blistering were reported to effectively treat disease (Kemeny, 1996). These substances and practices probably did no more than to create expectations of a cure.

The placebo effect has been known and subsequently well-documented since the classic work of Beecher (1955), *The Powerful Placebo*. This placebo response has been generally accepted to be about 35%, although it can vary from 10 up to 70% (Beecher, 1955; Kemeny, 1996). The influence of placebo has been known in some instances to reach 100% (Kemeny, 1996; Shapiro & Morris, 1978). As some examples, placebo has been shown to heal gastric ulcers in 40–70% of patients and to be 50–75% effective in stopping acute upper gastrointestinal bleeding. Belief can be upto 50% as effective as an injection of morphine by causing endorphin release. Angina is 30–40% responsive to placebo treatment and about 40% responsive to mock surgery. The placebo effect is particularly high in rheumatoid arthritis patients (89%) and about 85% of patients with high blood pressure will show a significant drop with placebo alone.

Not surprisingly, the best predictor of the magnitude of a placebo effect is the provider of the treatment rather than the treatment itself (Kemeny, 1996; Shapiro & Morris, 1978). The more the practitioner believes the treatment will work, the better this belief can be instilled in the patient. Along with the provider's confidence in the treatment, the attributes of enthusiasm, optimism, warmth, and caring further enhance the transfer of the provider's confidence in the treatment. In this also lies danger, in that charisma and enthusiasm, along with the abundance of personal attention they accord their followers, may account for the ability of certain gurus to "cure" some patients with techniques that of themselves have no ability to heal. The placebo effect can also be maximized in intensely emotional group ceremonies conducted by shamans and other faith healers.

Of importance also is the atmosphere and the paraphernalia that surround the healer. One should not underestimate the props that proffer the healer as an expert: The white coat, the stethoscope around the doctor's neck, the diplomas and licences hanging on the wall, the intensity of the hospital setting, and the professionalism of the provider and his/her staff. The pecking order of the medical system also assures the physician will get a greater response than the nurse when administering the same placebo for the same condition. Impressive new apparatus such as an MRI or CAT-scan will further enhance the placebo effect. In short, a number of studies with a number of conditions and treatments demonstrate that patients improve more when medical personnel appear more professional, convey an air of confidence, genuinely believe in the efficacy of their procedures, and care about their patients (O'Brien, 1996).

SPIRITUALITY

Recently, there has been a surge of interest in the benefits of prayer and spiritual beliefs on health. In his now classic review of a number of well-controlled studies, Cooper (1995) distinguishes between *extrinsic* and *intrinsic* belief. The former consists of membership in a religious organization, rote recitation of liturgy, or intellectual affirmation of beliefs, whereas the latter is a profound spiritual commitment, devotion to a transformed life, and heartfelt prayer. He further delineates intrinsic belief to embody two elements: A leap of faith initiating a life-changing belief and the belief that the body's ability to be healthy grows gradually with personal discipline. He lists six characteristics of persons who demonstrate positive health benefits from their spiritual beliefs:

(1) They believe their bodies are good and worthy of being treated as a creation of God.
(2) They believe they have a personal responsibility to help prevent the onset of disease.
(3) They believe they possess a natural inner power to promote the healing of a disease.
(4) They are open to receiving spiritual support from others.
(5) They have a relatively firm and stable philosophy of life.
(6) They are willing to stay committed to a personal fitness program despite the changes and new findings that regularly occur in the scientific research.

From these personal characteristics, it is apparent why individuals of faith repeatedly are revealed to be healthier and happier than those who are strictly secular or those who are extrinsically religious and are passively waiting for a higher power to heal them. Their health cannot be attributed to a placebo effect alone, as they take an active role in maintaining healthy life styles as well. The studies that Cooper (1995) cites demonstrate the positive health benefits of intrinsic belief: Optimism with decreased incidence of depression, less smoking, less alcohol and drug abuse, fewer medical complications in maternity patients as well as their newborns, decreased incidence of colon and rectal cancer, higher self-esteem and emotional maturity, reduced levels of stress, lower blood pressure, increased survival following a heart attack, and a greater ability to maintain healthy eating habits that overcome obesity.

POSITIVE PSYCHOLOGY

Another development in recent years has been the rise of positive psychology, with the accompaniment of a decline in victimology. Positive psychology breeds optimism, whereas the victimology that pervaded psychology for at least the 1980s and 1990s was counterproductive (Zur, 2005). Seligman (1975) pioneered positive psychology over 30 years ago and has been its leading proponent, but his optimistic emphasis did not take hold in psychology until c. 1990–2000 (see Seligman et al., 2004). Seligman now has a website from which subscribers receive regular psychoeducational messages in positive psychology.

Peterson and Bassio (1993) see optimism as contributory to good health and define it as an active participation in one's own health with the expectation that their behavior will impact on their health. In conjunction with such a belief, optimists take concrete steps to improve and maintain their own health. That this works is revealed in longitudinal and empirical research that demonstrates people with this type of optimism are healthier overall (Peterson & Bassio, 1993).

USES AND MISUSES OF THE PLACEBO EFFECT

It is apparent from the foregoing that natural healing has three components that are interrelated: (1) a belief system, (2) optimism, and (3) personal responsibility. All ultimately combine in varying degrees to result in what might be termed the placebo effect. In recent years, healthcare thinking has moved toward accepting the placebo effect as part of nature's healing mechanism and to enhance it whenever possible. However, not all holistic and alternative techniques are *ipso facto* equally helpful, and validation is as important in holistic healthcare as it is in the regulated medical system.

Practitioners who utilize only on unvalidated techniques that rely on placebo or belief alone often do a disservice to their patients by denying them the healing which modern medicine and surgery afford. On the other hand, practitioners who fail to understand and appreciate the power of patients' beliefs rob their patients of this healing force. Although it may be unethical for healthcare professionals to advocate particular unvalidated alternative techniques or to impose their religious–spiritual beliefs on their patients, they would do well to encourage patients to develop their own belief systems and to use whatever religious–spiritual beliefs they have in the service of good health while continuing to seek the most up-to-date medical care available.

The exception to the physician's or psychotherapist's insistence on verified alternative treatments may be seen in the approach to the dying patient. When surgery, radiation, chemotherapy and other drastic treatments have failed so that the patient is awaiting imminent death, such a patient may be comforted by the belief that an alternative technique, such as a certain combination of herbs, will accomplish what the intensive medical treatments failed to do. This may be part of nature's way of helping the patient remain optimistic and somewhat comforted while dying, and it would be unfortunate for the physician or psychotherapist to insist on scientific validity in the face of the patient's need for optimism.

Although many alternative treatments work solely because of their placebo effect, others have been scientifically validated for use with particular conditions. As such, they can be valuable adjuncts to traditional medical treatments, and the practitioner needs to be aware of them. It would be impossible to address every available holistic treatment, and the following have been selected as examples of techniques that have been verified for use with certain conditions. Glaringly absent will be such fanciful, though often quite popular, techniques that defy empirical verification, as aroma therapy, feng shui, copper bracelets, and the holding of crystals.

NUTRITION

That a high-fat diet is associated with susceptibility to certain cancers, especially of the colon, breast, and prostate, has been documented for years (Gershwin et al, 1985; Kemeny, 1996). Family history and other risk factors exist, but nutrition is one risk factor well within the individual's control. For example, Nicholson (1996) reports that the rate of breast cancer drops significantly in women who consume only 309% or fewer of their daily calories from fat, and that it is almost unheard of in women who consume less than 10% or fewer of their daily calories from fat.

There is considerable evidence that certain plant foods reduce breast cancer risk and lung cancer risk because they include fiber, indoles, flavonols, vitamins C and E, beta carotene, selenium, and other important nutrients (Gershwin et al, 1985; Kemeny, 1996; Nicholson, 1996). Similar lower rates associated with nutrition have been found for stomach, esophageal, rectal, pancreatic, cervical, and lung cancer, and iodine deficiency has been associated with cancer of the thyroid. Selenium may also protect against cardiomyopathy and other cardiovascular diseases (Badmaev et al., 1996). For menopausal women, hot flashes can be reduced by avoiding caffeine, alcohol, spicy foods, carbonated beverages, and excess sugar, indicating that holistic treatment may be able to control these symptoms without the risks of estrogen replacement therapy (Soffa, 1996). Granted that a low-fat, high-fiber, vitamin-rich diet is unlikely to cure existing cancer, it certainly can substantially lower the risk for new cancers. It may be that a healthy diet can provide better prevention for cancer than anything modern medicine has to offer.

There exists today a plethora of nutritional information, ranging from websites such as WebMD and RevolutionHealth.com to the Harvard or Mayo health letters for anyone who may not be computer literate, all available to those who wish to take responsibility for their own health. Two diametrically opposed attitudes may have the similar effect of impeding nutritional health. Many Americans have the attitude that they can do any damage to their bodies but modern medicine will fix it, whereas other Americans would prefer fanciful, unverified passive holistic solutions to the self-responsibility of a healthy diet. This is where a psychotherapist's intervention is essential to address issues that are psychological impediments to progress.

EXERCISE

One of the most beneficial natural remedies is also the one most widely neglected. The importance of exercise is widely disregarded in the sedentary lifestyle that has become the norm in our society. That regular moderate exercise mitigates both stress and depression, often exceeding the positive effects of antianxiety and antidepressive medications and with no drug side effects, should be of interest to psychotherapists. They would do well to make exercise a therapeutic issue, encouraging their patients to design, adopt, and maintain a regimen of their choosing. Yet, in attempting to include this as a therapeutic issue in training of psychotherapists meets with resistance from trainees who themselves have become sedentary (Cummings et al., 2007).

Obesity has been declared an epidemic by the US Surgeon General, and not surprisingly the sales of books purporting to help individuals lose weight are booming as fad diets promising weight loss are proliferating. The latest psychologist to jump on the bandwagon is none other than Judith Beck (2007), daughter of pioneer cognitive behaviorist Aaron T. Beck, with her new book, *The Beck Diet Solution: Train Your Brain to Think Like a Thin Person.* As of to prove that nothing under the sun is new, one is reminded of Robert Coe who in the 1920s had millions of Americans chanting five times before their mirrors each morning, "Every day in every way I am getting better and better." The financial success of these diet messages rests upon one premise: People will espouse any diet or regimen proffered, no matter how outlandish, as long as it does not include exercise. Hence, we have contradictory fads ranging from the grapefruit diet, the Atkins diet, the high calorie to the low calorie diets, all embraced with vigor until each is shown to be ineffective or not lasting.

In the face of this public resistance, studies continue to overwhelmingly reveal that exercise, coupled with healthy nutrition, is indispensable in changing the sedentary, over-eating life style that results in obesity and diabetes. The following are only a sampling of the definitive evidence that established exercise as paramount years ago even though psychotherapists continue to disregard it. In the meantime, their patients increasingly turn to psychotropic, pain, and sleep medications for anxiety and depression.

- Exercise can diminish certain types of pain by strengthening muscles, increasing endurance, releasing endorphins, and giving a sense of control over the pain (Kemeny, 1996).
- Regular exercise relieves general body pain as well as specific joint pain in arthritis patients. It also strengthens the muscles and other structures around individual joints, which provides stability to the joints and relieves pain. It helps keep bones and cartilage strong, which in turn lessens arthritic pain (O'Koon & Morrow, 1995).
- Regular aerobic exercise can help relieve symptoms of depression in patients with minor depression, major depression, and premenstrual depression (Byrne & Byrne, 1993; Sachs, 1993). This seems to be accomplished by the release of endorphins and norepinephrine, rendering a sense of accomplishment and mastery (Kemeny, 1996).
- Aerobic exercise also lessens symptoms of anxiety by reducing excess levels of blood glucose, epinephrine, and oxygen (Byrne & Byrne, 1993; Hardy, 1970).
- People who exercise regularly are less likely to adopt unhealthy ways of coping with stress, such as smoking, over-eating, and alcohol abuse (Sachs, 1993).
- Although excessive exercise can actually decrease the functioning of the immune system, regular moderate exercise has been shown to increase immune cells for a period of time after each episode of exercise. However, it is unknown whether this increase is large enough and long-lasting enough to significantly increase the body's ability to fight infectious diseases (Sachs, 1993).

Although exercise alone may not relieve the pain of arthritis completely, it certainly can lessen the pain and reduce the need for analgesic medication in many patients. Even though exercise alone may not cure severe depression or anxiety, it can relieve minor cases of depression and anxiety without the use of psychotropic medications. In more severe cases, it can serve as a very helpful adjunct to pharmacologic and psychotherapeutic treatments. A number of recent variations such as yoga and aerobic dance classes have made exercise more popular among a growing number of devotees, especially women, and running and biking, although less popular than the 1990s ago, continue to be so with both genders.

MASSAGE THERAPY

The kneading motion of muscle massage is beneficial to a variety of conditions and situations. It can relieve arthritic pain by bringing warmth to the affected areas through increased blood circulation (O'Koon & Morrow, 1995). It can also smooth out muscle knots and help joints attain their full range of motion. Massage has been scientifically demonstrated to lessen pain in children with rheumatoid arthritis or burns and in adults with fibromyalgia, perhaps because it raises the levels of natural pain killers, or endorphins and enkephalins (Griffin & Gallagher, 1995).

Massage is popular in strenuous activities such as sports and ballet because it shortens the time it takes for the body to recover. The pressure and warmth associated with massage cause the cells to release histamine, which causes the nearby capillaries to dilate, which in turn increases blood circulation to the muscles. Thus, the muscles receive more oxygen and nutrients, and metabolic wastes and toxins are removed more quickly (Griffin & Gallagher, 1995).

Because massage switches off the sympathetic nervous system, there is a calming effect on the body. Not surprisingly, therefore, massage mitigates against insomnia, enabling fussy babies, restless children, adults under stress, and adults with chronic fatigue syndrome to fall asleep sooner (Griffin & Gallagher, 1995).

It has been speculated that massage therapy can ward off colds and other viruses because some studies reveal it increases the number and activity of the natural killer cells. This increase in immune functioning is likely due to the reduced levels of stress hormones such as cortisol brought about by massage (Griffin & Gallagher, 1995; Keremy, 1996). However, it has yet to be demonstrated whether these changes in immune functioning are large and long-lasting enough to actually increase resistance to viruses (Keremy, 1996).

Massage therapy does not have to be expensive as it can be given by nonprofessionals, such as parents to children, and spouses to each other. Thus, the cost of a trained professional need not be an impediment.

ACUPUNCTURE

Acupuncture was developed in China approximately 5000 years ago, but it was not introduced into the United States until c. 1965. After a slow start, it gained in popularity after physicians began referring patients once empirical studies began to demonstrate its efficacy. Twenty-five years after its introduction, it was estimated that over 12 million treatments were performed in the United States (Harvard Medical School, 1995). By the twenty-first century, a number of states had statutory recognition and regulation of acupuncture, and most managed healthcare policies pay for treatments by a licenced or certified acupuncturist. The day may not be far off before acupuncture transitions from alternative to mainstream medicine.

Acupuncture is now being used in a large number of illnesses, including allergies, anxiety, arthritis, asthma, back pain, digestive problems, dizziness, fatigue, headaches, high blood pressure, neck pain, premenstrual syndrome, sciatica, sexual dysfunction, stress, tendonitis, urinary tract problems, viral infections, and vision problems. However, only a few of these uses have been validated in controlled studies (Harvard Medical School, 1995). In these randomized trials, although the experimental group received acupuncture, the control group received "sham acupuncture," or a procedure resembling acupuncture in every respect except that the needles were inserted in the wrong places. These studies demonstrated (Harvard Medical School, 1995):

- *Menstrual cramps*: Nine months after treatment, subjects in the treatment group showed 91% reduction in symptoms, whereas the control group showed only a 40% reduction.
- *Chronic low back pain*: In one study, 81% of treatment subjects and 31% of control subjects showed improvement 1 month after treatment. Nine months later, 53% of treatment subjects and no control subjects reported significant pain relief.
- *Neck pain*: 80% of treatment subjects and 23% of control subjects demonstrated significant improvement 12 weeks following treatment.
- *Alcohol abuse*: Several studies demonstrate that treatment subjects have fewer drinking episodes and hospital detoxifications than the control subjects.

The landmark Harvard studies show that acupuncture triggers the release of chemicals with pain-relieving properties (enkephalins and endorphins), and it is possible it may also trigger the release of the neurotransmitter serotonin, which is associated with decreased depression. Additionally, O'Koon and Morrow (1995) point out that acupuncture may stimulate nerves in a way that they sense the presence of the needle rather than the presence of pain.

BIOFEEDBACK

Like acupuncture, biofeedback began to capture the attention of alternative medicine c. 1960. By the 1980s, it became a standard procedure in military medical centers, was found in most hospitals, and may one day transition from alternative to mainstream medicine.

This is a technique that involves teaching the patient to relax by controlling his or her body's reactions to pain and stress. Special monitoring equipment attached to the body measures heart rate, blood pressure, galvanic skin response (GSR), temperature, and muscle tension. Using this feedback, a trained professional helps the patient gain control over these physical responses (O'Koon & Morrow, 1995).

Schwartz and Schwartz (1993) outlined five types of biofeedback and their uses:

- *Electromyographic* (EMG) biofeedback measures muscle tension and is used for tension headaches, physical rehabilitation, chronic muscle pain, incontinence, temporomandibular joint (TMG) pain, and general relaxation.
- *Thermal* biofeedback, which measures skin temperature, is used for Raynaud's disease, migraines, hypertension, anxiety, and general relaxation.
- *Electrodermal activity* (EDA) biofeedback measures very minute changes in sweat activity and is used for anxiety and hyperhidrosis (over-active sweat glands).
- *Finger pulse* biofeedback measures pulse rate and force. It is used for hypertension, anxiety, and cardiac arrhythmias.
- *Breathing* biofeedback measures breath rate, volume, location, and rhythm. It is used for asthma, anxiety, hypertension, and general relaxation.

A growing number of neuroscientists and neuropsychologists are experimenting with biofeedback for conditions believed to be due to irregular brain wave patterns, including attention deficit disorder (ADD) and attention deficit hyperactivity disorder (ADHD), as well as certain types of epilepsy. The results are promising, and some preliminary findings suggest improvement (Schwartz & Schwartz, 1993; neuropsychologists Ralph Reitan and J. Lawrence Thomas, personal communication, 2006).

All uses for biofeedback have been extensively studied, and most reveal significant diminution of symptoms. However, two uses are so well-documented that they have become treatments of choice for those conditions: Muscle tension headaches and Raynaud's disease (Schwartz & Schwartz, 1993). For these, biofeedback is perhaps no longer regarded as alternative medicine. Raynaud's disease involves a constriction of blood vessels in the fingers and toes, thus giving the patient the uncomfortable sensation of cold extremities.

There are now reasonably priced home biofeedback instruments that enable a person to do self-training. These are not as extensively used as was originally anticipated, and the results are often disappointing. Perhaps the low rate of success at home versus the doctor's office has more to do with the placebo effect (or lack of it) than the instrument itself.

RELAXATION, HYPNOSIS, GUIDED IMAGERY, AND MEDITATION

Although it may seem as if disparate techniques are being lumped together, all of these have three features in common that warrants their being addressed together:

- They shut down the activity of the sympathetic nervous system, decrease the stress response, and create a state of relaxation.
- They create a distraction from pain, focusing attention on pleasant images instead of on pain.
- They have been demonstrated to boost the immune system by increasing both the number and the activity of natural killer cells. However, it is not known whether these changes in the immune system are large enough or long-lasting enough to reduce susceptibility to infectious diseases (Kemeny, 1996).

These techniques do help patients manage pain by relaxing the painful areas and by creating a pleasant distraction from the pain (O'Koon & Morrow, 1995). However, they do not cure pain, but then neither does analgesic medication which also must be repeated. There are at least two advantages of these techniques over medication: There are no drug side effects and there is no addictive potential. With the introduction of new, safer over-the-counter pain relievers, the use of these alternative techniques has declined.

Meditation has existed in Eastern religions for centuries, but it became popular in the United States c. 1960 along with most other alternative medicine techniques. For a time a controversy raged as to whether meditation itself had efficacy, or whether it had to be transcendental meditation, with the latter having achieved almost a cult status.

Historically, hypnosis has been a subject of psychiatry for over 200 years, experiencing periodic resurgence with subsequent declines. Sigmund Freud rejected it early in his career, preferring free association. Milton Erickson, however, made it an integral part of his therapy, but his successors in Ericksonian therapy are now using it less as time goes on. Hypnosis received considerable bad publicity in the 1990s, when it was discovered that over-zealous therapists were actually implanting false memories of incest in their patients. A number of fathers went to prison following faulty psychological testimony, and subsequently, the courts released them as some practitioners lost their licences in the decade-long controversy. At the present time, hypnosis is still used by some practitioners in stop-smoking programs, with a reported success rate of about 30%.

Relaxation and guided imagery continue to be useful in the management of anxiety, including panic and generalized anxiety disorders. With continued practice of these techniques, patients become more adept at diminishing the stress response and creating a state of relaxation. Even though these techniques must be practiced regularly for a period of time in order for anxious patients to learn to use them proficiently, the learning that occurs eventually allows patients to relax themselves quickly without performing the complete exercise (Hardy, 1970).

SOCIAL SUPPORT

It is generally accepted that thoughts, either positive or negative, can have an impact on physical health, for better or for worse (Azur, 1996). The effectiveness of psychoeducational programs in preventing and treating disease is discussed by the authors (Cummings and Cummings) in a separate chapter in this book. Furthermore, the effectiveness of psychotherapy in treating somatization disorders and in offsetting medical and surgical costs is also well-documented (Cummings, 1991a, 1991b, 1993, 1994, 1996a, 1996b; Cummings and Follette, 1976; Cummings and VandenBos, 1981; Cummings et al., 1993; Strain, 1993). However, the impact of support groups and social support in general on disease has not been as widely addressed.

In his definitive review of a broad range of studies, Spiegel (1995) demonstrates the health benefits of social support. Replicated studies consistently reveal that married persons are substantially healthier and have a lower mortality than unmarried people. They are found to be happier in general, and this seems to translate into such specifics that married cancer patients have significantly lower mortality rates than unmarried cancer patients. Another study found that the number of social supports that subjects had could predict the probability of mortality over the next 9 years. Other studies confirm that socially isolated people are two to three times more likely to die over the course of the longitudinal study than those who are least socially isolated.

According to Spiegel, social isolation is as strong a risk factor as smoking, and he cites several reasons why social support may positively benefit health:

- Those who believe that others care about them may be more likely to take active steps toward staying healthy.
- People who interact well with friends and family may also interact well with their healthcare providers, encouraging their providers to do all possible for them.
- Social support may directly reduce the levels of stress hormones in the body, thus enhancing the functioning of the immune system.

In other words, support groups may be effective because (1) they counter isolation and (2) they allow people to feel as though they can help each other, making them feel competent rather than helpless in the face of extended illness. Effective social support is found in a close-knit extended family, a happy long-term marriage, active religious affiliation with a warm congregation, a circle of close friends, Alcoholics Anonymous (AA) and other 12-step groups, and it even extends to the remarkable comradeship that is found among military units in combat zones.

The effect of support groups on breast cancer has been the most widely researched of all medical conditions (see summaries by Spiegel, 1995, and Spiegel et al., 1989). It has been found consistently that women with breast cancer who attended breast cancer support groups lived twice as long as women with the same illness who did not attend such a support group. In another study, patients who attended the support groups showed improved psychological adjustment, better coping skills, better compliance with treatment regimens, and enhanced immunological functioning compared with controls who did not attend a breast cancer support group (Sleek, 1995).

REFERENCES

Azur, B. (1996, October). Intrusive thoughts proven to undermine our health. *Monitor on Psychology*, *27*, 34.

Badmaev, V., Majeed, M., & Passwater, R (1996). Selenium: A quest or better understanding. *Alternative therapies*, *2*, 59–67.

Beecher, H.K. (1955). The powerful placebo. *Journal of the American Medical Association*, *159*, 1602–1606.

Beck, J.S. (2007). *The Beck Diet Solution: Train Your Brain to Think Like a Thin Person*. Philadelphia: The Beck Institute.

Brickey, M. (2000). *Defy Aging*. Columbus, OH: New Resources Press.

Byrne, A. & Byrne, D.G. (1993). The effect of exercise on depression, anxiety and other mood states: A review. *Journal of Psychosomatic Research*, *17*, 565–574.

Cooper, R.H. (1995). *It's Better to Believe*. Nashville, TN: Thomas Nelson.

Cummings, N.A. (1991a). Brief, intermittent psychotherapy throughout the life cycle. In J.K. Zeig & S.G. Gillian (Eds.), *Brief Therapy: Myths, Methods and Metaphors*. New York: Brunner/Mazel.

Cummings, N.A. (1991b). Arguments for the psychological efficacy of psychological services in health care settings. In J.J. Sweet, R.G. Rozensky, & S.M. Tovian (Eds.), *Handbook of Clinical Psychology in Medical Settings* (pp. 113–126). New York: Plenum.

Cummings, N.A. (1993). Somatization: When physical symptoms have no medical cause. In D. Coleman & J. Gurin (Eds.), *Mind-Body Medicine* (pp. 221–232). Yonkers, NY: Consumer Reports.

Cummings, N.A. (1994). The successful application of medical cost offset in program planning and in clinical delivery. *Managed Care Quarterly*, *2*, 1–6.

Cummings, N.A. (1995). Impact of managed care on employment and training: A primer for survival. *Professional Psychology: Research and Practice*, *26*, 10–15.

Cummings, N.A. (1996a). Does managed mental health care offset costs related to medical treatment? In A. Lazarus (Ed.), *Controversies in Managed Mental Health Care* (pp. 213–227). Washington, DC: American Psychiatric Press.

Cummings, N.A. (1996b). The impact of managed care on employment and professional training: A primer for survival. In N.A. Cummings, M.S. Pallak, & J.L. Cummings (Eds.), *Surviving the Demise of Solo Practice: Mental Health Practitioners Prospering in the Era of Managed Care*. Madison, CT: Psychosocial Press.

Cummings, N.A., Dorken, H., Pallak, M.S., & Henke, C.J. (1993). The impact of psychological intervention on health care costs and medical utilization: The Hawaii Medicaid Project. In N.A. Cummings & M.S. Pallak (Eds.), *Medicaid, Managed Behavioral Health and Implications for*

Public Policy, Vol. 2: Healthcare and Utilization Cost Series (pp. 3–23). South San Francisco: Foundation For Behavioral Health.

Cummings, N.A. & Follette, W.T. (1976). Brief psychotherapy and medical utilization: An eight-year follow-up. In H. Dorken (Ed.), *The Professional Psychologist Today* (pp. 126–142). San Francisco: Jossey-Bass.

Cummings, N.A., O'Donohue, W.T., & Cummings, J.L. (2007). *Clinical Strategies for Becoming a Master Psychotherapist*. New York: Brunner-Routledge.

Cummings, N. & Sayama, M. (1995). *Focused Psychotherapy: A Casebook of Brief Intermittent Psychotherapy Throughout the Life Cycle*. New York: Brunner/Mazel.

Cummings, N.A. & VandenBos, G.R. (1981). The twenty year Kaiser-Permanente experience with psychotherapy and medical utilization: Implications for national health policy and national health insurance. *Health Policy Quarterly, 1*, 159–175.

Freudenheim, M. (2007). AOL founder hopes to build a new giant among a bevy of health care web sites. *New York Times,* 1 and 14.

Gershwin, M.E., Beach, R.S, & Hurley, L.S. (1985). *Nutrition and Immunity*. New York: Academic Press.

Griffin, K. (1996). The new doctors of natural medicine. *Health, 10*, 61–68.

Griffin, K. & Gallagher, D. (1995). Hands on healing. *Health, 9*, 59–63.

Hardy, A. (1970). *The Terrap Manual for the Treatment of Agoraphobia*. Menlo Park, CA: Terrap.

Harvard Medical School (1995). Acupuncture. *Harvard Women's Health Watch, 3*, 4–5.

Kemeny, M.E. (1996a). A new model of physician-patient communication: West Haven, CT: Miles Institute for Health Care Communication.

Kemeny, M.E. (1996b). *Psychology of Mental Control*. Presented at Mind Matters Seminar, Phoenix, Arizona.

Nicholson, A. (1996). Diet and the prevention and treatment of breast cancer. *Alternative Therapies in Health and Medicine, 2*, 32–38.

Obama, B. (2007). *The Audacity of Hope: Reclaiming the American Dream*. New York: Crown.

O'Brien, A. (1996). Mind matters. *Vim & Vigor*, July/August, 46–50.

O'Koon, M. & Morrow, S. (1995). When rheumatology meets psychology. *Arthritis Today,* November/December, 28–33.

Peterson, G. & Bassio, L.M. (1993). Healthy attitudes: Optimism, hope, and control. In D. Goleman & J. Gurin (Eds.), *Mind/body Medicine* (pp. 351–366). Yonkers, NY: Consumer Reports.

Sachs, M.H. (1993). Exercise for stress control. In D. Goleman & J. Gurin, *Mind/body medicine* (pp. 315–327). Yonkers, NY: Consumer Reports.

Schwartz, M.S. & Schwartz, N.M. (1993). Biofeedback: Using the body's signals. In D. Goleman & J. Gurin (Eds.), *Mind/body medicine*. Yonkers, NY: Consumer Reports.

Seligman, M.E.P. (1975). *Helplessness: On Depression, Development and Death*. San Francisco: W.H. Freeman.

Seligman, M.E.P., Linely, P.A., & Joseph, S. (2004). *Positive Psychology in Practice*. New York: Wiley.

Shapiro, D.E. & Morris, L.A. (1978). The placebo effect in medical and psychological therapies. In S.L. Garfield & A.E. Bergin (Eds.), *Handbook of Psychotherapy and Behavioral Change* (2nd Ed.). New York: Wiley.

Sleek, S. (1995). Rallying the troops inside our bodies. *APA Monitor, 26*(I), 24–25.

Snowden, D. (2001). *Aging With Grace*. New York: Bantam Books.

Soffa, V.M. (1996). Alternatives to hormone replacement for menopause. *Alternative Therapies, 2*, 34–39.

Spiegel, D. (1995). Social support and cancer. In N.R.S. Hall, F. Altman, & S.J. Blumenthal (Eds.), *Mind Body Interactions and Disease*. Tampa, FL: Health Dateline.

Spiegel, D., Bloom, J.R., & Kraemer, H.C. (1989). Effect of psychosocial treatment on survival of patients with metastatic breast cancer. *Lancet, 2*, 888–890.

Strain, J.J. (1993). Psychotherapy and medical conditions. In D. Goleman & J. Gurin, *Mind/body Medicine*. Yonkers, NY: Consumer Reports.

Zur, O. (2005). The psychology of victimhood. In W.H. Wright & N.A. Cummings, *Destructive Trends in Mental Health: The Well-Intentioned Path to Harm* (pp. 45–64). New York: Routledge (Taylor and Francis).

13

ADJUNCTIVE TREATMENTS FOR CHILDHOOD DISORDERS

BRIE A. MOORE*† AND LAUREN W. TOLLE*

*University of Nevada, Reno, Department of Psychology and
†UCLA Semel Institute for Neuroscience and Behavior

INTRODUCTION

Practitioners interested in the evidence-based treatment of childhood disorders are likely confronted by a myriad of presenting concerns, ranging from Separation Anxiety Disorder, to Attention Deficit Hyperactivity Disorder (ADHD), to Pervasive Developmental Disorders. Despite the nearly 15% of children with behavioral health concerns that cause significant impairment, there is limited existing research on evidence-based treatments for children and adolescents (Roberts et al., 1998). Therefore, it is not surprising that only one in five children gain access to services by appropriately trained mental health professionals (Centers for Disease Control, 2004).

To date, a number of cognitive-behavioral therapy (CBT) approaches have gained empirical support for treating individual-level symptoms. Most notably, manualized CBT-based treatments for anxiety disorders, Oppositional Defiant Disorder (ODD), and ADHD have been well-validated (Christophersen & Mortweet, 2001; Hibbs & Jensen, 2004). Treatment components such as psychoeducation, behavior modification, cognitive restructuring, habit reversal, and exposure with response prevention have a strong empirical base (APA, 2006). These interventions are recommended as the first line of defense in the treatment of child behavioral health concerns. However, additional treatment approaches may oftentimes be warranted to augment treatment outcomes and promote generalization.

This chapter reviews a number of empirically based approaches that, when used as an adjunct to primary treatment approaches, serve to enhance treatment outcomes and promote long-term behavior change. Evidence-based adjunctive treatments provide the practitioner with a means to intervene at multiple levels within the child's environment. In this chapter, we discuss three evidence-based treatments: (1) Classroom Interventions, (2) Social Skills Training (SST); and (3) Multisystemic Therapy (MST). Additional approaches including mentoring programs, summer camps, physical activity programs, and religious involvement are also reviewed. When used as adjuncts to primary treatment approaches, these interventions have been found to augment treatment outcomes and promote long-term maintenance of skill acquisition.

CLASSROOM INTERVENTIONS

NEED FOR CLASSROOM INTERVENTIONS

Managing children's behavior in the classroom has long been a concern of teachers and school personnel. Behaviors that are disruptive in the classroom include inattention, hyperactivity, and noncompliance among others (Goldstein, 1995). Children who exhibit problem behaviors in the classroom have vastly different experiences at school from their peers. They are reprimanded much more frequently, praised less frequently, are less likely to be called on academically and are therefore less likely to be able to give correct answers, all of which can contribute to increasing defiant behavior (Gunter et al., 1993; Morgan, 2006; Van Acker et al., 1996). Children with problem behaviors have less positive interactions with their teachers, and their teachers oftentimes have lower expectations of them (Farmer & Farmer, 1999; Morgan, 2006).

Approximately 20% of school-aged children meet criteria for ADHD (American Psychiatric Association, 1994), a disorder characterized by problems with sustained attention, impulsivity, and overactivity. ADHD can result in difficulty completing assigned work, following instructions, and following general classroom rules (Ervin et al., 1998). Children with ADHD often experience performance difficulties in school and have been found to be at a higher risk of grade retention and drop out as compared with non-ADHD children. As many as two-thirds of children meeting criteria for ADHD also meet criteria for a learning disability (Carlson et al., 1997; Frick & Silverthorn, 2004).

Approximately 16% of children meet criteria for ODD (American Psychiatric Association, 1994), a disorder characterized by a pattern of negativistic, hostile, disobedient, and defiant behavior. It is not uncommon for children to meet criteria for both ADHD and ODD concurrently, as comorbidity rates range from as high as 65 to 90%. Given these high prevalence rates, the need for effective interventions in the classroom is apparent (Abikoff & Klein, 1992; American Psychiatric Association, 1994; Coleman & Webber, 2002; Little, 2003).

There are several techniques that have been empirically supported in managing disruptive classroom behavior. Several factors should be taken into consideration when selecting which techniques should be implemented including (1) the type of disruptive behavior present; (2) the severity of the problems; (3) the level of involvement of a psychologist (or other behavioral health professional) in the classroom; and (4) the acceptability of interventions to teachers (Little, 2003; Mitchum et al., 2001). Teachers are most likely to decide to adopt and continue to use interventions, which they find acceptable, effective, efficient, and least intrusive (Kazdin, 1981; Mitchum & Young, 2001).

INTERVENTION COMPONENTS

There are a number of effective techniques for managing problem behaviors in classrooms. The literature has outlined several empirically supported behavioral interventions which include but are not exclusive to effectively giving commands, establishing clear rules, giving praise, giving positive reinforcement using tokens, response cost procedures, self-management, and group contingencies (Amato-Zech et al., 2006; Lambert et al., 2006; Little, 2003; Matheson & Shriver, 2005; Morgan, 2006).

Giving Commands and Setting Rules

Establishing rules is an essential component to a successful classroom intervention. Rules provide structure in the classroom-setting and establish expectations regarding how order in the classroom will be maintained. Although rules alone are not sufficient in achieving effective behavioral control in the classroom, they can serve as a fundamental base to any behavioral management plan. For example, compliance is maximized when students clearly understand and remember positively stated and specific rules regarding observable and quantifiable behavior. Furthermore, rules are maximally effective when linked to consistent and predictable consequences. Characteristics of effective rules for classroom behavior management are presented in Table 13.1.

TABLE 13.1 Characteristics of Effective Rules for Classroom Behavior Management

1) Keep rules to a maximum of five in number
2) Keep rules simple
3) Word rules positively, stating what students should *do* rather than *not do*
4) Keep rules specific
5) Keep rules limited to observable behaviors
6) Use rules that are measurable and can be monitored quantifiably
7) Keep rules publicly posted in a highly visible place
8) Keep rules connected to both positive and negative consequences
9) Include a compliance rule (e.g., do what the teacher asks you to do)
10) Expect all students to follow the rules without exceptions

Adapted from Little, 2003; McGinnis et al., 1995.

TABLE 13.2 Characteristics of Effective Commands—for Parents and Teachers

1. Mean it—always intend to follow through with a command
2. State the command as a declarative, not as a question or favor
3. Present the command in a neutral tone of voice
4. Give the child time to respond
5. Present the preplanned consequence if the child does not follow the command after stating it a second time
6. Maintain eye contact while giving the command
7. Be specific so that the command is clear and understandable
8. Reinforce compliance verbally, immediately following the desired behavior

Adapted from Barkley (2006)

Effectively giving commands in the classroom can be measured by the behavior of the child. If the command results in the desired behavior, then the command may be said to have been effective. Research on effective parent command-giving has identified effective commands as those that are stated directly, are specific and consist of one step, are developmentally appropriate, and are positively worded, much like the characteristics of effective rules (Forehand & McMahon, 1981; Matheson & Shriver, 2005). Although these guidelines for giving commands were initially developed to be utilized by parents, they can easily be adapted for teachers to use in their classroom to maintain behavior compliance (Little, 2003). These guidelines are described in Table 13.2.

Positive Reinforcement, Token Reinforcement, and Response Cost

Although a negative reprimand is often a teacher's response to disruptive behavior, it has not been found to lead to behavior change over time; in fact, it has been found to increase disruptive behavior (DuPaul & Weyandt, 2006). Instead, the use of positive reinforcement, as well as token reinforcement, has been found to decrease disruptive behavior (Reitman et al., 2004; Robinson et al., 1981). Contingency management procedures with positive reinforcement, though when used alone may not be effective in decreasing disruptive behavior, have been found to be effective if used in conjunction with other behavioral management plans (i.e., response cost). Many positive reinforcers are naturally occurring in the classrooms, such as positive attention from the teacher and earning good grades, although others are frequently used as well including tangible reinforcers such as badges, stickers, prizes, etc.; privilege reinforces such as being allowed to sit in a special desk, help the teacher, monitor other students; or generalized reinforcers such as points or tokens (Little, 2003). This last type of reinforcer has gained much attention in the literature for reducing disruptive behaviors in the classrooms and is referred to as token reinforcement.

Two forms of token reinforcement are frequently used to improve classroom behaviors: The use of home-based reinforcement for school behavior and response cost (DuPaul & Weyandt, 2006). Home-based reinforcement involves daily school report cards that teachers fill out on the child's behavior for that day as to whether they met certain behavioral goals (e.g., stayed in seat). These goals are rated on a scale (1 = did not meet goal; 5 = met goal perfectly), and the ratings are then converted to points that are redeemable for positive reinforcers provided at home (e.g., access to TV, favorite meal). Response cost strategies involve the removal of positive reinforcement contingent on inappropriate behavior (e.g., the removal of points, tokens, or an enjoyable activity in the presence of an inappropriate behavior). Response cost techniques can increase the effectiveness of token reinforcement strategies (Little, 2003).

Self-management

Self-management strategies are implemented by the student and are designed to increase self-control over behavior. Self-management strategies may include self-monitoring, self-monitoring combined with self-reinforcement, goal setting, self-evaluation, and self-reinforcement alone (DuPaul & Weyandt, 2006; Reid, Trout & Shwartz, 2005). Some self-management programs utilize a recording sheet for students to record their academic progress or behavior, whereas others have involved self-evaluation and the degree to which a student's self-evaluation matches with that of their teacher's evaluation of them. Self-monitoring studies have been conducted in preschool where students are instructed to use a thumbs-up or a thumbs-down to reflect the degree to which they believe they are meeting classroom expectations (Miller et al., 1993; Mitchem & Young, 2001).

Group Contingencies

Group contingencies operate similarly to the use of token reinforcement with response cost, with the main difference being that group membership parameters determine reinforcement and response cost (Stage & Quiroz, 1997). There are three different types of group contingencies—interdependent, independent, and dependent. When interdependent group contingencies are used, reinforcers are given to members of the group contingent upon the group meeting a specified criterion. With dependent group contingencies, only some of the group members are selected to perform to a specific standard, making other members of the group dependent on those who were selected to gain their reinforcers. Finally, independent group contingencies require each member of the group to perform to a set standard and reinforcement is not dependent on the behavior of other group members (Stage & Quiroz, 1997).

EMPIRICAL SUPPORT

The efficacy of the aforementioned behavioral interventions has been well-established in the literature. Specifically, much support has been found for the use of token reinforcement strategies in successfully decreasing disruptive behavior in classroom settings (Pelham et al., 1998). Support for the use of token reinforcement interventions has been found for preschoolers and young children, as well as elementary school-aged children and even adolescents (Moore et al., 2001; Musser et al., 2001; Stollar et al., 1994; Swiezy et al., 1992).

Numerous studies have also demonstrated the effectiveness of self-management or self-monitoring strategies in improving attention, academic productivity, and decreasing off-task behavior in the classroom (Amato-Zech et al., 2006; McDougall et al., 2004; Mitchem & Young, 2001). Much research focusing on self-management has been on self-monitoring of attention to task, which has been effective in both decreasing disruptive behavior and increasing on-task behavior (Dalton et al., 1999; Lam et al., 1994). Self-monitoring has also been found to be effective across a broad range of populations including students with emotional and behavioral problems, learning disabilities, autism, and mild to severe cognitive impairments (Alberto et al., 1999; Harrower & Dunlap, 2001; McDougall & Brady, 1995; Prater et al., 1992).

Much research is available that lends empirical support to the use of group contingencies in decreasing disruptive, problem behavior in classrooms. Specifically, research has found support for the use of interdependent group contingencies in both decreasing inappropriate classroom behaviors and increasing academic achievement (Popkin & Skinner, 2003). The Good Behavior Game (GBG) is a form of an interdependent group contingency that was developed originally by dividing a classroom into two teams and team members would earn marks for their team for inappropriate behavior (e.g., talking out of turn or getting out of one's seat) and the team with the fewest marks would win the game and receive privileges (Barrish et al., 1969). Since its inception, GBG has received much empirical support in reducing problem behaviors (Davis & Witte, 2000; Kellam & Anthony, 1998; Swiezy et al., 1992; Tingstrom, 1994). Studies have also found support for the use of dependent group contingencies in increasing on-task behavior in classrooms (Heering & Wilder, 2006; Kelshaw-Levering et al., 2000) Some studies have found when comparing the three types of group contingencies against each other, that interdependent and dependent groups were more effective than independent groups in managing disruptive classroom behavior (Gresham & Gresham, 1982), whereas others have found no difference among the three types of groups, in that all three were dramatically successful at improving on-task behavior compared with control groups (Theodore et al., 2004).

Extant literature also supports the use of effective command-giving and setting clear, effective rules in improving compliance and academic engagement (Little, 2003; Malone & Tietjens, 2000; Matheson & Shriver, 2005). Although the dearth of literature demonstrating children responding to effective commands comes from parenting research, some research has demonstrated correlations between a well-managed classroom and a student engagement in academic tasks, a more rapid progression through course materials and even higher levels of academic achievement (Brophy, 1983; Gettinger, 1986; Matheson & Shriver 2005).

Several reviews and meta-analyses have been conducted that examined the effectiveness of classroom interventions, yielding much empirical support for the behavioral interventions mentioned above. Specifically, Skiba and Casey (1985) conducted a meta-analysis to determine effective classroom interventions for improving behavioral and academic achievements, and of the 41 studies that were included in the meta-analysis, it was reported that the average effect size across interventions was 0.93. Of the eight interventions identified in this study, the highest effect size was found for reinforcement, with an effect size of 1.38 (Skiba & Casey, 1985). Subsequent meta-analyses on interventions designed to decrease disruptive classroom behavior have found similarly high effect sizes for behavioral interventions. In a meta-analysis of 99 studies, behavioral approaches were found to be more effective than interventions from other theoretical orientations, with group contingencies ($ES = 1.02$), self-management ($ES = 0.97$), and reinforcement strategies ($ES = 0.95$) the most effective interventions in the study (Stage & Quiroz, 1997).

In addition, Kratochwill and Stoiber (2000) reported that of over 300 studies that have been conducted with children aged 2 to 18, meta-analyses conducted of these studies have reported average effect sizes between 0.70 and 0.90 with all of the meta-analyses concluding that interventions based on applied behavior analysis, behavior therapy, or CBT have been superior to all other methods (Kazdin et al., 1990; Weiss et al., 1995).

AVAILABILITY, DISSEMINATION, AND FUTURE DIRECTIONS

With the assistance of school psychologist, applied behavior analyst, or school social work consultants, teachers can easily be trained in using these behavioral interventions and implementing them in their classrooms. One problem that has been seen in not implementing these behavioral strategies is the perceived unacceptability of some of these strategies to teachers. Specifically, teachers have seen consultants' recommendations as "socially invalid" for use in the classroom (Kazdin, 1981; Stoiber & Kratochwill, 2000). Understanding teacher's perceptions of acceptable classroom interventions with regard to effectiveness, timeliness of effect, a cost–benefit ratio, or even the social validity of the intervention should be important considerations when devising a classroom intervention plan (Curtis et al., 2006). In addition, studies have examined alternative mediums for implementing classroom interventions aside from the teacher, who may already be overburdened with managing an overfull classroom. Specifically, the use of peers, computer-based programs, and even other children with behavioral problems have gained some efficacy (DuPaul & Weyandt, 2006). In addition, the use of functional assessment to individualize behavior management plans may allow practitioners the opportunity to notice particular antecedents and consequences of an inappropriate behavior for a specific student, which has the potential to lead to a more time-efficient and effective treatment (DuPaul & Weyandt, 2006).

Carol Webster-Stratton and colleagues have also developed a series of tools to assist teachers in implementing these classroom interventions, and their tools have gained empirical support in improving on-task behavior and minimizing problematic behavior (Webster-Stratton et al., 2004). The program materials include DVDs with classroom vignettes, a leader manual, a book for teachers, *How to Promote Children's Social and Emotional Competence*, and other supplemental materials (Reid & Webster-Stratton, 2001). Helpful books for teachers in implementing classroom interventions include

- *effective school interventions: Strategies for enhancing academic achievement and social competence* (Rathvon, 2003);
- *school-based interventions: The tools you need to succeed* (Lane, 2003);
- *living with children: New methods for parents and teachers* (Patterson, 1977).

SOCIAL SKILLS TRAINING

NEED FOR SOCIAL SKILLS TRAINING

Establishing relationships with peers is a central developmental task of childhood. To establish friendships, children must learn to navigate a variety of complex social interactions and demands. Adapting flexibly to diverse social contexts requires the child to integrate behavioral, cognitive, and affective skills (Bierman & Welsh, 2000). However, many children lack this rich interpersonal repertoire. Some children struggle in social interactions, experience peer victimization, and are rejected by their same-aged peers. A growing body of evidence indicates that deficits in social skills and social competence play a significant role in the development and maintenance of a number of behavioral and emotional disorders of childhood and adolescence (Spence, 2003). Social skills deficits are evident in children diagnosed with pervasive developmental disorders, such as Autism and Asperger's Disorder (Frankel et al., 2007); in children diagnosed with Fetal Alcohol Spectrum Disorders (O'Connor et al., 2006); in children with behavioral disorders such as ADHD, Conduct Disorder (CD), and ODD (Frankel et al., 1997); in emotional disorders such as Social Anxiety Disorder (Spence & Marziller, 1981); in pediatric obesity (Wilfley et al., under review); and in children who experience social concerns such as peer rejection and victimization. SST is often an integral component of the prevention and treatment of these disorders.

INTERVENTION COMPONENTS

Adaptive social responding involves the complex interplay of social knowledge interpersonal problem-solving skills, processing of social information, perspective taking, attention to social contingencies, and affect regulation

(Spence, 2003). Not surprisingly, given the complexity of this required repertoire, SST methods have adopted a multimodal and integrated approach (Frankel & Myatt, 2003; Spence, 1995). These interventions aim to teach a range of fundamental social skills to deal with interpersonal situations that typically present a challenge for children and adolescents. Typically, both cognitive (e.g., self-talk) and behavioral strategies (e.g., modeling, behavioral rehearsal, feedback and reinforcement) are employed to enhance social perception skills, self-regulation and social problem solving (Spence, 2003). For example, Children's Friendship Training (CFT; Frankel & Myatt, 2003) is a standardized 12-week cognitive-behavioral social skills package in which children receive didactic training sessions, behavioral rehearsal, coaching to reduce maladaptive behaviors and promote pro-social interactions skills. Parents are also taught about core deficits in their child's diagnosed disorder and given companion information to their children's intervention in order to facilitate and support behavior change. Children's Friendship Training is distinct from other social skills approaches in its emphasis on (1) incorporating parents as an integral part of the intervention; (2) including homework assignments as part of the treatment sessions; (3) teaching socially valid skills; and (4) structuring play dates to be maximally effective in promoting best friendships. Skills taught in CFT discriminate socially skilled children from their socially unsuccessful peers.

For example, Frankel and colleagues described in detail an empirically-validated, 12-week SST group (O'Connor et al., 2006). Each 60-minute session involved the training and practice of unique skills for adaptive social interaction tailored to the unique needs of children and their parents. Parent and child sessions were held concurrently but separately. In session 1, group moderators discussed the rules of the group and elements of good communication. Children learned and practiced elements of good communication by introducing themselves to one another. Simultaneously, parents were provided with psychoeducation regarding the goals and methods of treatment and the importance of their role in the intervention was highlighted. In session 2, children learned and practiced skills for exchanging information in a two-way conversation. Parents were provided with strategies for helping their children develop reciprocal communication. Sessions 3 and 4 focused on "slipping in" or group entry skills and handling rejection from a group. Parents learned how to support their child's development of new friendships by allowing time for play dates. In the next two sessions, 5 and 6, children learned the fundamentals of "being a good sport," whereas parents learned more about appropriate activities for play dates. Children and parents gained additional information about play dates in session 7, including how to be a good "host" during indoor games. Session 8 focused on teaching children how to handle teasing and reduce the likelihood of its occurrence in the future. Next, in session 9, children learned how to handle situations when they are unjustly accused of bad behavior by an adult, whereas adults learn how to respond appropriately and effectively to other adults who complain about their child's behavior. In session 10, children and parents learned how to be a "good winner." Children learned how to handle "bullies," avoid conflict, and practice strategies for conflict resolution in session 11. Parents learned how to support their child's use of strategies for defusing confrontations with another child. Lastly, in session 12, children were praised for their participation and families engaged in a graduation ceremony. Throughout all sessions, behavioral strategies, including modeling, coaching, behavioral rehearsal with feedback, and reinforcement of adaptive social behavior, were used to facilitate the acquisition and generalization of social skills. A comprehensive description of the manualized treatment can be found in Frankel and Myatt (2003).

EMPIRICAL SUPPORT

Empirical studies have shown SST to be effective in increasing the performance of specific social skills with children and adolescents who present with a range of emotional, behavioral, and developmental concerns. Of the various intervention components of typical SST approaches, behavioral strategies, including modeling, coaching, rehearsal, feedback, and reinforcement of skill use, have received the most empirical support (McIntosh et al., 1991). Results of meta-analytic studies have been varied, with effect sizes ranging from small (0.19) to moderate (0.40; Schneider, 1992; Quinn et al., 1999). However, results of these analyses may have differed considerably because of the type of intervention, measures used, length of follow-up, and presenting concern of the child (Spence, 2003).

In contrast, in a number of recent studies, Frankel and colleagues have validated Children's Friendship Training in the treatment of deficits associated with a variety of disorders (Frankel, 2005). Outcomes of these studies indicate that the 12-week cognitive-behavioral intervention (described above) was effective in improving social skills in children with a wide variety of developmental, emotional, and behavioral disorders. This parent-assisted SST approach has been found to remediate social deficits in children diagnosed with pervasive developmental disorders, such as Autism and Asperger's Disorder (Frankel et al., 2007; Macintosh & Dissanayake, 2006), in children diagnosed with Fetal Alcohol Spectrum Disorders (Frankel et al., 2006; O'Connor et al., 2006), in children diagnosed with behavioral disorders such as ADHD (Frankel et al., 1997), CD (Spence & Marziller, 1981), and ODD (Frankel & Feinberg, 2002), in pediatric obesity (Wilfley et al., under review), and in children who experience social concerns such as peer rejection and peer victimization. Together, results indicated that children in families who received CFT demonstrated improvement in their knowledge of appropriate social behavior, improved social skills, and fewer problem behaviors than children who did not receive the intervention.

AVAILABILITY, DISSEMINATION, AND FUTURE DIRECTIONS

Both practitioners and parents interested in the application of SST can easily gain access to materials outlining an empirically validated treatment approach. Practitioners are directed to the manualized treatment, Frankel and Myatt's (2003)

Children's Friendship Training. Professionals interested in prescribing empirically based psychoeducational materials to families who may benefit from SST are encouraged to refer to Frankel's 1996 text, *Good Friends are Hard to Find: Help Your Child Find, Make, and Keep Friends*. In addition, Webster-Stratton and colleagues have developed empirically supported materials to improve social skills in children called *The Dinosaur child training curriculum* that includes instructional DVDs and engaging supplemental materials to assist children in acquiring new social skills (Webster-Stratton & Hammond, 1997). Although professionals, paraprofessionals, and family members may be able to easily acquire and implement this knowledge, future research investigating the effectiveness of these materials as a self-help approach to the treatment of social skills deficits and investigating treatment fidelity and therapist competence in the delivery of these materials is warranted.

MULTISYSTEMIC THERAPY

THE NEED FOR MULTISYSTEMIC THERAPY

Drug use and violence represent two prevalent problems in adolescence with widespread social ramifications (Randall & Cunningham, 2003). The Office of Juvenile Justice and Delinquency Prevention has reported that the nation's number one problem is substance abuse (Ericson, 2001). Reports on adolescent substance use have stated that among adolescents aged 12–17 years, an estimated 1.1 million meet criteria for dependence on illicit drugs, with an estimated 915 000 dependent on alcohol (National Household Survey on Drug Abuse, 1998). The recent violence in schools has demanded the attention of mental health professionals to turn toward evidence-based approaches that are effective at preventing violence and recidivism in adolescents.

MST began in the 1980s as an intensive, time-limited, home- and family-focused treatment approach for adolescents who had been referred to mental health professionals from the juvenile criminal justice system (Burns et al., 2000). MST has a clearly defined theory with volumes of empirical research to support it. MST has demonstrated effectiveness in both short- and long term and has been used across diverse populations including suicidal, adolescent sexual offenders, violent, antisocial, substance abusing, and conduct-disordered adolescents (Hinton et al., 2003; Randall & Cunningham, 2003; Sheidow & Woodford, 2003). Most recently, MST has been used to improve treatment adherence in adolescents with type 1 diabetes and HIV (Ellis et al., 2005, 2006).

INTERVENTION COMPONENTS

MST is a pragmatic and solution-focused treatment that targets factors in an adolescent's life that are triggering problematic, delinquent behavior (Randall & Cunningham, 2003). Oftentimes, these factors are within the adolescent's social network, and thus, MST strives to enhance interactions with aspects of that network (i.e., improve caregiver's discipline effectiveness, increase quality of caregiver and adolescent relationship, minimize contact with delinquent peers and increase contact with positive peers, improve youth vocational or academic experiences, involve adolescents in recreational activities, increase supports outside of the immediate family to provide support to the family) and to maintain those changes (Burns et al., 2000).

MST is delivered in the adolescent's natural environment (i.e., home, school, community) and the treatment plan is developed in collaboration with the family, making it a family-driven rather than therapist-driven approach, although therapists are available 24 hours a day, 7 days a week (Burns et al., 2000). The family is assigned to an MST team that usually consists of a supervisor and three clinicians who are responsible for assisting the needs of the family through treatment or navigating support services, and clinicians may be seeing as many as 4–6 families at a time. The typical duration of MST is 4 months with multiple weekly contacts between the therapist and the family that add up to an average of 40–60 hours of face-to-face clinical contact throughout the course of treatment (Burns et al., 2000).

One of the fundamental goals of MST is family preservation, and so, many of the treatment targets revolve around parent–adolescent interactions, and targeting barriers that might be interfering with better communication and conflict resolution (e.g., substance abuse, high stress, low social support, anger management) (Henggeler et al., 1998). Another important component of MST that adds to its effectiveness is the attention to cultural competence. MST therapists try to ensure that the MST team for a family includes therapists that reflect the ethnic and cultural background that the family identifies with. This has been found to be a large contributing factor to the efficacy of MST, with outcomes across racial/ethnic groups largely attributable to the cultural competence considerations that went into the treatment plans (Burns et al., 2000; Henggeler et al., 1992).

EMPIRICAL SUPPORT

Outcome studies testing the effectiveness of MST began in the mid-1980s with delinquent youths and showed promising results with decreased behavior problems and improved family relations (Henggeler et al., 1986). Subsequent randomized controlled trials with juvenile offenders using MST elicited similarly positive results, with adolescents at posttreatment who were involved in the MST condition showing reduced rearrest rates by 43%, which was maintained 2 years posttreatment (Borduin et al., 1995; Elliot, 1998; Henggeler et al., 1992). Following this, MST was extended across different populations, and was found to be effective with adolescent substance abusers and dependent juvenile offenders with severe emotional disturbances (Brown et al., 1999; Randall & Cunningham, 2003; Shoenwald et al., 1996), juvenile sexual offenders (Borduin et al., 1990), suicidal and homicidal adolescents (Shoenwald et al., 2000), and maltreating families where child neglect or abuse is present (Allin et al., 2005). MST is also gaining empirical support in chronic disease management research, specifically, with improving treatment adherence in adolescents with type 1 diabetes as well as HIV (Ellis et al., 2005, 2006).

MST has been consistently superior to control groups among numerous psychosocial variables including improved family relationships and family functioning, decreased adolescent substance abuse, increased school attendance, decreased rates of recidivism, and also decreased psychiatric symptoms (e.g., suicidality, depression, anxiety, antisocial behaviors), with recent studies reporting as high as 97–98% success rates of treatment completion (Sheidow & Woodford, 2003).

Not only has MST been established as an empirically supported treatment in reducing delinquent behaviors in adolescents, improving family relationships, and enhancing adolescent's social structure to help prevent recidivism, but also has shown to be cost-effective. Researchers at the Washington State Institute on Public Policy reviewed programs that were aimed at reducing violence in juveniles and found MST to be the most optimal program included, and with an estimated cost of $5000 per family, and an average effect size of −0.31, they saved system costs in the long run of over $100 000 per youth (Aos et al., 2001).

AVAILABILITY, DISSEMINATION, AND FUTURE DIRECTIONS

MST is a labor-intensive treatment to train and implement, which led to some problems with dissemination at the start of MST. Since then, MST developers have trained therapists across the country in MST, which has broadened the areas where MST services are available, and has also ensured treatment fidelity and consistency as the training was originally conducted by MST developers (Burns et al., 2000). MST has licensed network organizations in over 34 states across the United States, and in nine other countries, allowing MST services to reach more than 8000 families a year (Multisystemic Services, 2007).

An in-depth training manual for MST has been developed and is available that guides clinicians through assessing family functioning, modifying peer relationships, promoting academic and extra-curricular activities in and after school, assisting families in broadening their social networks, and using various behavioral modification strategies to maintain positive changes (Burns et al., 2000; Henggeler et al., 1998). The MST training process, however, is ongoing in that continual supervision and fidelity checks are conducted to ensure that the treatment is being delivered as initially intended (Burns et al., 2000). The potential benefits of continuing to expand accessibility to this treatment are clear, although what is unclear is how continued treatment fidelity of such a tightly controlled and monitored program will be conducted. Developing alternative fidelity measures will be an important next step to further the dissemination of MST. Although currently MST is not offered in a stepped care fashion, alternatives to MST that target problem behaviors in adolescence such as violence recidivism, substance use, and communication problems are available for adolescents who may not have access to MST including

- *Pathways to Self-Discovery and Change: Criminal Conduct and Substance Abuse Treatment for Adolescents: The Participant's Workbook* (Milkman & Wanberg, 2004).
- *Managing the Defiant Child: A Guide to Parent Training* (DVD) (Barkley, 2006).
- *Anger Management Workbook for Kids and Teens* (Bohensky, 2001).

ADDITIONAL APPROACHES

In addition to the interventions presented above, a variety of other adjunctive approaches for various childhood problems exist. Recent data support that children with chronic problems report less participation in community activities compared with other children (Blanchard et al., 2007). Several community-based programs including mentoring programs, spiritual involvement, organized sports, and camp-based treatments are reviewed briefly here. Due to their widespread availability and low cost, many of these community-based approaches represent viable adjuncts to psychotherapy.

Mentoring programs, such as Big Brothers Big Sisters (BBBS), are effective in improving a number of psychosocial factors in children from single-parent homes. When compared to peers from two-parent households, children from single-parent households are more likely to experience poverty, behavioral and emotional problems, physical health problems, problems with peer and family relationships, and poor academic achievement (De Wit et al., 2007). Outcome studies have found that children who were matched with an adult mentor demonstrated improved academic achievement, improved relationships with peers and family, and less early experimentation with drugs and alcohol than their peers (Rhodes et al., 1999, 2005; Tierney et al., 1995). In addition to the benefits mentioned above, mentoring programs are also cost-efficient. Enrollment for children in these programs is free, and volunteer mentors are largely unpaid (De Wit et al., 2007).

Children and families often also have access to a number of community-based religious and spiritual organizations and activities. Spirituality and religion have been found to promote resilience in children with a wide variety of psychological and medical concerns. Involvement in a religious or spiritual community has been found protective for children exposed to war (Kanji et al., 2007), violence (Ai & Park, 2005), and other potentially traumatic events. Religion and spirituality may also play a facilitative role in the treatment of substance abuse among adolescents (Knight et al., 2007). In addition to the treatment of psychological and behavioral health concerns, spiritual care is also an integral part of the comprehensive treatment of children with terminal illnesses, particularly pediatric cancer (Hutchinson et al., 2003). Religion and spirituality have direct, positive benefits for children in terms of mental health outcomes and can also improve the child's health and well-being indirectly through parent and family functioning (Mabe & Josephson, 2004). Practitioners are advised to carefully evaluate the goodness of fit between the child's presenting concern and the family's religious beliefs or practices when developing an integrated treatment plan that involves spiritual care as an adjunct.

Other community programs, such as summer camps, are also effective in improving a number of psychosocial factors. Summer camps have been found to be effective in addressing a wide variety of behavioral health concerns in children, including learning disabilities, social skills deficits, poor self-esteem, and aggression (Brookman et al., 2003; Hektner et al., 2000; Michalski et al., 2003). Children with chronic illnesses have also benefited from summer camps. Summer camps have been found to be a useful environment to assist psychologists in addressing comorbid psychosocial problems (i.e., social skills deficits, problems with peer and family relationships, behavioral problems), as well as psychosocial problems that are commonly associated with the illness (i.e., disease management, grief and bereavement, coping with medical procedures, and adherence to recommended treatments). As an additional benefit, children with chronic illnesses often benefit from being around other children coping with the same disease for social support and to reduce stigma of having an illness. Camps for children with diabetes, cancer, asthma, epilepsy, and kidney disorders have been found to improve knowledge about the illness, improve treatment adherence, increase the use of effective coping strategies, improve adjustment to the illness, and improve self-efficacy (Briery & Rabian, 1999; Hunter et al., 2006; Rubin & Geiger, 1991; Singh et al., 2000). Camps have also been found to be an important respite for parents of children with chronic illness, giving parents time to recuperate and take care of themselves so that they might be more refreshed caretakers able to better assist their children (Meltzer & Johnson, 2004).

Lastly, participation in organized sports may also be considered as an adjunct to psychotherapy for a number of common psychological and behavioral concerns in children. Participation in organized sports has been associated with improvement in self-esteem, social competence, reduction in symptoms of depression, and promotion of overall psychosocial adjustment (Crews et al., 2004; Dykens et al., 1998; McHale et al., 2001) in typically developing children and in children with developmental disabilities. Furthermore, implementing interventions within the context of organized athletics have been found to be effective in reducing disordered eating and substance abuse in adolescents (Elliot et al., 2006). More broadly speaking, the positive effects of regular physical activity on health and well-being have been well-documented (Crews et al., 2004; *Physical Activity* this book).

CONCLUSION

Taken together, the interventions presented in this chapter represent a fraction of available, empirically supported treatments that can be used as an adjunct for primary treatments of childhood disorders. The strong empirical research supporting these interventions, as well as the high prevalence of the disorders addressed, make these optimal adjunctive treatments. In addition, many of the intervention components can be useful for a broad range of childhood behavioral problems. One example is the use of effective rule-setting, command-giving, and reinforcement strategies that can be adapted and used for parents as an alternative adjunct to ameliorating problem behaviors in the home environment. The adaptability and transportability of behavioral strategies used in SST and MST are also important for evidence-based practitioners who are looking to improve skills in effective communication, problem-solving, and social functioning in children. Finally, given the high comorbidity between chronic illnesses and behavioral problems, it is clear how children could benefit from these treatments as adjuncts to medical care (Harris et al., 1995).

Families in rural or underserved areas that do not have equal access to psychological care can benefit from the community-based approaches and activities described above. In addition, typically underserved families may benefit from stepped care treatments such as bibliotherapy for anxiety (Rapee et al., 2006), telehealth for pediatric pain (Holden et al., 2003), videoconferencing for depression (Nelson et al., 2003), and online cognitive-behavioral intervention to improve child behavior and social skills (Wade et al., 2006). As technology and research advance, additional opportunities for dissemination of evidence-based treatments for childhood disorders will surely become available.

REFERENCES

Abikoff, H. & Klein, R.G. (1992). Attention-deficit hyperactivity disorder and conduct disorder: Comorbidity and implications for treatment. *Journal of Consulting and Clinical Psychology*, *60*, 881–892.

Ai, A.L. & Park, C.L. (2005). Possibilities of the positive following violence and trauma: Informing the coming decade of research. *Journal of Interpersonal Violence*, *20*(2), 242–250.

Alberto, P.A., Taber, T.A., & Frederick, L.D. (1999). Use of self-operated auditory prompts to decrease aberrant behaviors in students with moderate mental retardation. *Research in Developmental Disabilities*, *20*, 429–439.

Allin, H., Wathem, C.N., & MacMillan, H. (2005). Treatment of child neglect: A systematic review. *Canadian Journal of Psychiatry*, *50*(8), 497–504.

Amato-Zech, N.A., Hoff, K.E., & Doepke, K.J. (2006). Increasing on-task behavior in the classroom: Extension of self-monitoring strategies. *Psychology in the Schools*, *43*(2), 211–221.

American Psychiatric Association (1994). *Diagnostic and Statistical Manual of Mental Disorders* (4th Ed.). Washington, DC: American Psychiatric Association.

Aos, S., Phipps, P., Barnoski, R., & Lieb, R. (2001). *The Comparative Costs and Benefits of Programs to Reduce Crime*. Olympia, WA: Washington State Institute for Public Policy.

APA Working Group on Psychoactive Medications for Children and Adolescents. (2006). Report of the Working Group on Psychoactive Medications for Children and Adolescents. Psychopharmacological, psychosocial, and combined interventions for childhood disorders: Evidence base, contextual factors, and future directions. Washington, DC: American Psychological Association.

Barkley, R. (2006). *Managing the Defiant Child: A Guide to Parent Training*. New York: Guilford Press.

Barrish, H.H., Saunders, M., & Wolf, M.W. (1969). Good Behavior Game: Effects of individual contingencies for group consequences on disruptive behavior within a classroom. *Journal of Applied Behavioral Analysis*, *2*, 119–124.

Bierman, K. & Welsh, J.A. (2000). Assessing social dysfunction: The contributions of laboratory and performance-based measures. *Journal of Clinical Child Psychology*, *29*, 526–539.

Blanchard, L.T., Gurka, M.J., & Blackman, J.A. (2007). Emotional, developmental, and behavioral health of American children and their families: A report from the 2003 National Survey of Children's Health. *Pediatrics*, *117*(6), 1202–1212.

Bohensky, A. (2001). *Anger Management Workbook for Kids and Teens*. New York: Growth Publishing.

Borduin, C.M., Henggeler, S.W., Blaske, D.M., & Stein, R.J. (1990). Multisystemic treatment of adolescent sexual offenders. *International Journal of Offender Therapy & Comparative Criminology*, *34*(2), 105–113.

Borduin, C.M., Mann, B.J., Cone, L.T., et al. (1995). Multisystemic treatment of serious juvenile offenders: Long term prevention of criminality and violence. *Journal of Consulting and Clinical Psychology*, *63*(4), 569–578.

Briery, B.G. & Rabian, B. (1999). Psychosocial changes associated with participation in a pediatric summer camp. *Journal of Pediatric Psychology*, *24*, 183–190.

Brookman, L., Boettcher, M., Klein, E., et al. (2003). Facilitating social interactions in a community summer camp setting for children with autism. *Journal of Positive Behavior Interventions*, *5*(4), 249–252.

Brophy, J.E. (1983). Classroom organization and management. *The Elementary School Journal*, *83*, 265–285.

Brown, T.L., Henggeler, S.W., Shoenwald, S.K., et al. (1999). Multisystemic treatment of substance abusing and dependent juvenile delinquents. Effects on school attendance at posttreatment and 6 month follow-up. *Children's Services: Social Policy, Research and Practice*, *2*(2), 81–93.

Burns, B.J., Shoenwald, S.K., Burchard, J.D., et al. (2000). Comprehensive community based interventions for youth with severe emotional disorders: Multisystemic therapy and the wraparound process. *Journal of Child and Family Studies*, *9*(3), 283–314.

Carlson, C.L., Lahey, B.B., & Frick, P.J. (1997). Attention deficit disorders: A review of research relevant to diagnostic classification. In T.A. Widiger, A.J. Frances, H.A. Pincus, R. Ross, M.B. First, & W. Davis (Eds.), *DSM-IV sourcebook*. Vol. 3 (pp. 163–188). Washington, DC: American Psychiatric Association.

Centers for Disease Control. (2004). National Center for Health Statistics: National health interview survey. Washington, DC: Centers for Disease Control.

Christophersen, E.R. & Mortweet, S.L. (2001). Treatments that work with children: Empirically supported strategies for managing childhood problems. Washington, DC: American Psychological Association.

Coleman, M.C. & Webber, J. (2002). *Emotional and Behavioral Disorders: Theory and Practice* (4th Ed.). Boston: Allyn & Bacon.

Crews, D.J., Lochbaum, M.R., & Landers, D.M. (2004). Aerobic physical activity effects on psychological well-being in low-income Hispanic children. *Perceptual Motor Skills*, *98*(1), 319–324.

Curtis, D.F., Pisecco, S., Hamilton, R.J., & Moore, D.W. (2006). Teacher perceptions of classroom interventions for children with ADHD: A cross-cultural comparison of teachers in the United States and New Zealand. *School Psychology Quarterly*, *21*, 171–196.

Dalton, T., Martella, R.C., & Marchand-Martella, N.E. (1999). The effects of a self-management program in reducing off-task behavior. *Journal of Behavioral Education, 9*(3–4), 157–176.

Davis, S. & Witte, R. (2000). Self-management and peer monitoring within a group contingency to decrease uncontrolled verbalizations of children with attention deficit hyperactivity disorder. *Psychology in the Schools*, *37*, 147–153.

De Wit, D.J., Lipman, E., Manzano-Munguia, M., et al. (2007). Feasibility for a randomized controlled trial for evaluating the effectiveness of the Big Brothers Big Sisters community match program at the national level. *Children and Youth Services Review*, *29*, 383–404.

DuPaul, G.J. & Weyandt, L.L. (2006). School-based intervention for children with attention deficit hyperactivity disorder: Effects on academic, social and behavioral functioning. *International Journal of Disability, Development and Education*, *53*(2), 161–176.

Dykens, E.M., Rosner, B.A., & Butterbaugh, G. (1998). Exercise and sports in children and adolescents with developmental disabilities. Positive physical and psychosocial effects. *Child and Adolescent Psychiatric Clinics of North America*, *7*(4), 751–771.

Elliot, D.L., Moe, E.L., Goldberg, L., et al. (2006). Definition and outcome of a curriculum to prevent disordered eating and body-shaping drug use. *Journal of School Health*, *76*(2), 67–63.

Elliot, D.S. (1998). *Blueprints for Violence Prevention* (Series Ed.). Boulder: University of Colorado, Center for the Study and Prevention of Violence, Blueprints Publications.

Ellis, D.A., Frey, M.A., Naar-King, S., et al. (2005). The use of multisystemic therapy to improve regimen adherence among adolescents with chronic poor metabolic control: A randomized controlled trial. *Diabetes Care*, *28*, 1604–1610.

Ellis, D.A., Naar-King, S., Cunningham, P.B., & Secord, E. (2006). Use of multisystemic therapy to improve antiretroviral adherence and health outcomes in HIV-infected pediatric patients: Results of a pilot program. *AIDS Patient Care and STDs*, *20*(2), 112–121.

Ericson, N. (2001). *Substance abuse: The nation is number one health problem.* Washington, DC: U.S. Department of Justice, Office of Juvenile Justice and Delinquency Prevention.

Ervin, R.A., DuPaul, G.J., Kern, L., & Friman, P.C. (1998). Classroom based functional and adjunctive assessments: Proactive approaches to intervention selection for adolescents with attention deficit hyperactivity disorder. *Journal of Applied Behavioral Analysis*, *31*, 61–78.

Farmer, E.M.Z. & Farmer, T.W. (1999). The role of schools in outcomes for youth: Implications for children's mental health services research. *Journal of Child and Family Studies*, *4*, 377–396.

Forehand, R. & McMahon, R. (1981). Helping the noncompliant child: A clinician's guide to parent training. New York: Guilford.

Frankel, F. (2005). Parent-assisted children's friendship training. In E.D. Hibbs & P.S. Jensen (Eds.), *Psychosocial Treatments for Child and Adolescent Disorders: Empirically Based Approaches* (2nd Ed.) (pp. 693–715). Washington, DC: American Psychological Association.

Frankel, F. (1996). *Good Friends are Hard to Find: Help Your Child Find, Make, and Keep Friends.* Los Angeles: Perspective Publishing.

Frankel., F. & Feinberg, D. (2002). Social problems associated with ADHD vs. ODD in children referred for friendship problems. *Child Psychiatry & Human Development*, *33*(2), 125–146.

Frankel, F. & Myatt, R. (2003). *Children's Friendship Training*. New York: Brunner-Routledge Publishers.

Frankel, F., Myatt, R., & Cantwell, D.P. (1995). Training outpatient boys to conform with the social ecology of popular peers: Effects on parent and teacher ratings. *Journal of Clinical Child Psychology*, *24*, 300–310.

Frankel, F., Myatt, R., Cantwell, D.P., & Feinberg, D.T. (1997). Parent assisted children's social skills training: Effects on children with and without attention-deficit hyperactivity disorder. *Journal of the Academy of Child and Adolescent Psychiatry*, *36*, 1056–1064.

Frankel, F., Myatt, R., & Feinberg, D. (2007). Parent-assisted friendship training for children with autism spectrum disorders: Effects associated with psychotropic medication. *Child Psychiatry and Human Development*, *37*(4), 337–346.

Frankel, F., Paley, B., Marquart, R., & O'Connor, M.J. (2006). Stimulants, neuroleptics and children's friendship training in children with fetal alcohol spectrum disorders. *Journal of Child and Adolescent Psychopharmacology*, *16*(6), 777–789.

Frick, P.J. & Silverthorn, P. (2004). Psychopathology in children. In H.E. Adams & P.B. Sutker (Eds.), *Comprehensive Handbook of Psychopathology* (3rd Ed.). New York: Springer.

Gettinger, M. (1986). Issues and trends in academic engaged time of students. *Special Services in the Schools, 2*, 1–17.

Goldstein, S. (1995). *Understanding and Managing Children's Classroom Behavior.* New York: Wiley.

Gresham, F.M. & Gresham, G.N. (1982). Interdependent, dependent and independent group contingencies for controlling disruptive behavior. *Journal of Special Education, 16*, 101–110.

Gunter, P.L., Denny, R.K., Jack, S.L., et al. (1993). Aversive stimuli in academic interactions between students with serious emotional disturbance and their teacher. *Behavioral Disorders, 18*, 265–274.

Harris, E.S., Canning, R.D., & Kelleher, K.J. (1995). A comparison of measures of adjustment, symptoms and impairment among children with chronic medical conditions. *Journal for the American Academy of Child and Adolescent Psychiatry, 35*(8), 1025–1032.

Harrower, J.K. & Dunlap, G. (2001). Including children with autism in general education classrooms: A review of effective strategies. *Behavior Modification, 25*, 762–784.

Heering, P.W. & Wilder, D.A. (2006). The use of dependent group contingencies to increase on-task behavior in two general education classrooms. *Education and Treatment of Children, 29*(3), 459–468.

Hektner, J.M., August, G.J., & Realmuto, G.M. (2000). Patterns and temporal changes in peer affiliation among aggressive and nonaggressive children participating in a summer school program. *Journal of Clinical Child Psychology, 29*(4), 603–614.

Henggeler, S.W., Melton, G.B., & Smith, L.A. (1992). Family preservation using multisystemic therapy: Long-term follow up to a clinical trial with serious juvenile offenders. *Journal of Consulting and Clinical Psychology, 60*(6), 953–961.

Henggeler, S.W., Rodick, J.D., Borduin, C.M., et al. (1986). Multisystemic treatment of juvenile offenders: Effects on adolescent behavior and family interactions. *Developmental Psychology, 22*(1), 132–141.

Henggeler, S.W., Shoenwald, S.K., Borduin, C.M., et al. (1998). *Multisystemic treatment of antisocial behavior in children and adolescents*. New York, NY: Guilford Press.

Hibbs, E.D. & Jensen, P.S. (Eds.) (2004). Psychosocial treatments for child and adolescent disorders: Empirically based strategies for clinical practice (2nd Ed.). Washington, DC: American Psychological Association.

Hinton, W.J., Sheperis, C., & Sims, P. (2003). Family based approaches to juvenile delinquency: A review of the literature. *The Family Journal: Counseling and Therapy for Couples and Families, 11*(2), 167–173.

Holden, G., Bearison, D.J., Rode, D.C., et al. (2003). Pediatric pain and anxiety: A meta-analysis of outcomes for a behavioral telehealth intervention. *Research on Social Work Practice, 13*(6), 693–723.

Hunter, H.L., Rosnov, D.L., Koontz, D., & Roberts, M.C. (2006). Camping programs for children with chronic illness as a modality for recreation, treatment, and evaluation: An example of a mission based program evaluation of a diabetes camp. *Journal of Clinical Psychology in Medical Settings, 13*(1), 67–80.

Hutchinson, F. King, N., & Hain, R.D. (2003). Terminal care in pediatrics: Where we are now. *Postgraduate Medicine, 79*(936), 566–568.

Kanji, Z., Drummond, J., & Cameron, B. (2007). Resilience in Afghan children and their families: A review. *Pediatric Nursing, 19*(2), 30–33.

Kazdin, A. (1981). Acceptability of child treatment techniques: The influence of treatment efficacy and adverse side effects. *Behavior Therapy, 12*, 493–506.

Kazdin, A.E., Bass, D., Ayres, W.A., & Rodgers, A. (1990). Empirical and clinical focus of child and adolescent psychotherapy research. *Journal of Consulting and Clinical Psychology, 58*, 729–740.

Kellam, S.J. & Anthony, J.C. (1998). Targeting early antecedents to prevent tobacco smoking: Findings from an epidemiological based randomized field trial. *American Journal of Public Health, 88*, 1490–1495.

Kelshaw-Levering, K., Sterling-Turner, H.E., Henry, J.F., & Skinner, J.H. (2000). Randomized interdependent group contingencies: Group reinforcement with a twist. *Psychology in the Schools, 37*, 523–533.

Knight, J.R., Sherritt, L., Harris, S.K., et al. (2007). Alcohol use and religiousness/spirituality among adolescents. *Journal of Southern Medicine, 100*(4), 349–355.

Kratochwill, T.R. & Stoiber, K.C. (2000). Uncovering critical research agendas for school psychology: Conceptual dimensions and future directions. *School Psychology Review, 29*, 591–603.

Lam, A.L., Cole, C.L., Shapiro, E.S., & Bambara, L.M. (1994). Relative effects of self-monitoring on-task behavior, academic accuracy and disruptive behavior in students with behavior disorders. *School Psychology Review, 23*(1), 44–58.

Lambert, M.C., Cartledge, G., Hewart, H.L., Lo, Y. (2006). Effects of response cards on disruptive behavior and academic responding during math lessons by fourth grade urban students. *Journal of Positive Behavior Interventions, 2*, 88–99.

Lane, K.L. (2003). *School-Based Interventions: The Tools You Need to Succeed.* New York: Allyn & Bacon.

Little, S.G. (2003). Classroom management. In, W. O'Donohue, J. Fisher, & S. Hayes (Eds.) *Cognitive Behavior Therapy: Applying Empirically Supported Techniques in your Practice.* New Jersey: Wiley.

Macintosh, K. & Dissanayake, C. (2006). Social skills and problem behaviors in school aged children with high functioning autism and asperger's disorder. *Journal of Autism and Developmental Disorders, 36*(8), 1065–1076.

McIntosh, R., Vaughn, S., & Zaragoza, N. (1991). A review of social interventions for students with learning disabilities. *Journal of Learning Disabilities, 24*, 451–458.

Malone, B.G. & Tietjens, C.L. (2000). Re-examination of classroom rules: The need for clarity and specified behavior. *Special Services in the Schools, 16*, 159–170.

Matheson, A.S. & Shriver, M.D. (2005). Training teachers to give effective commands: Effects on student compliance and academic behaviors. *School Psychology Review, 34*(2), 202–219.

Mabe, P.A. & Josephson, A.M. (2004). Child and adolescent psychopathology: Spiritual and religious perspectives. *Child and Adolescent Psychiatric Clinics of North America, 13*(1), 111–125.

McDougall, D., Farrell, A., & Hoff, K.E. (2004). Research on self-management techniques used by students with disabilities in general education settings: A promise fulfilled? Manuscript submitted for publication.

McDougall, D. & Brady, M.P. (1995). Using audio-cued self-monitoring for students with severe behavior disorders. *Journal of Educational Research, 88*, 309–318.

McGinnis, J.C., Frederick, B.P., & Edwards, R. (1995). Enhancing classroom management through proactive rules and procedures. *Psychology in the Schools, 32*, 220–224.

McHale, S.M., Crouter, A.C., & Tucker, C.J. (2001). Free-time activities in middle childhood: Links with adjustment in early adolescence. *Child Development, 72*(6), 1764–1778.

Meltzer, L.J. & Johnson, S.B. (2004). Summer camps for chronically ill children: A source of respite care for mothers. *Children's Health Care, 33*(4), 317–331.

Michalski, J.H., Mishna, F., Worthington, C., & Cummings, R. (2003). A multi-method impact evaluation of a therapeutic summer camp program. *Child and Adolescent Social Work Journal, 20*(1), 53–76.

Milkman, H.B. & Wanberg, K.W. (2004). *Pathways to Self-Discovery and Change: Criminal Conduct and Substance Use for Adolescents: The Participant's Workbook.* Boston, MA: Sage Publications.

Miller, L.J., Strain, P.S., Boyd, K., et al. (1993). The effects of classwide assessment on preschool children's engagement in transition, free play, and small group instruction. *Early Education and Development, 4*, 162–181.

Mitchum, K.J., Young, K.R., West, R.P., & Benyo, J. (2001). CSPASM: A classwide peer assisted self-management program for general education classrooms. *Education and Treatment of Children, 24*, 111–140.

Moore, J.W., Tingstrom, D.H., Doggett, R.A., & Carlyon, W.D. (2001). Restructuring an existing token economy in a psychiatric facility for children. *Child and Family Behavior Therapy, 23*, 53–59.

Morgan, P.L. (2006). Increasing task engagement using preference or choice-making: Some behavioral and methodological factors affecting their efficacy as classroom interventions. *Remedial and Special Education, 27*(3), 176–187.

Multisystemic Services (2007). MST Programs. http://www.mstservices.com/mst_programs.php

Musser, E.H., Bray, M.A., Kelhle, T.J., & Jensen, W.R. (2001). Reducing disruptive behaviors in students with serious emotional disturbance. *School Psychology Review, 30*, 294–304.

National Household Survey on Drug Abuse (1998). DHHS Publication No. (SMA) 99-3328. Rockville, MD: Office of Applied Studies, Substance Abuse and Mental Health Services Administration.

Nelson, E., Barnard, M., & Cain, S. (2003). Treating childhood depression over videoconferencing. *Telemedicine Journal and E-health, 9*(1), 49–55.

O'Connor, M.J., Frankel, F., Paley, B., et al. (2006). A controlled social skills training for children with fetal alcohol spectrum disorders. *Journal of Consulting and Clinical Psychology, 74*, 639–648.

Patterson, G.R. (1977). *Living With Children: New Methods for Parents and Teachers*. Illinois: Research Press.

Pelham, W.E., Wheeler, T., & Chronis, A. (1998). Empirically supported psychosocial treatments for attention deficit hyperactivity disorder. *Journal of Clinical Child Psychology, 27*, 190–205.

Popkin, J. & Skinner, C.H. (2003). Enhancing academic performance in a classroom serving students with serious emotional disturbance: Interdependent group contingencies with randomly selected components. *School Psychology Review, 32*(2), 282–295.

Prater, M.A., Hogan, S., & Miller, S.R. (1992). Using self-monitoring to improve on-task behavior and academic skills of an adolescent with mild handicaps across special and regular educational settings. *Education and Treatment of Children, 15*, 43–55.

Quinn, M., Kavale, K., Mathur, S., et al. (1999). A meta-analysis of social skills interventions for students with emotional or behavioral disorders. *Journal of Emotional and Behavioral Disorders, 7*, 54–64.

Randall, J. & Cunningham, P.B. (2003). Multisystemic therapy: A treatment for violent substance abusing and substance-dependent violent offenders. *Addictive Behaviors, 28*, 1731–1739.

Rapee, R.M., Abbott, M.J., & Lyneham, H.J. (2006). Bibliotherapy for children with anxiety disorders using written materials for parents: A randomized controlled trial. *Journal of Consulting and Clinical Psychology, 74*(3), 436–444.

Rathvon, N. (2003). *Effective School Interventions: Strategies for Enhancing Academic Achievement and Social Competence*. New York: Guilford Press.

Reid, R., Trout, A.L., & Schartz, M. (2005). Self-regulation interventions for children with Attention Deficit/Hyperactivity Disorder. *Exceptional Children, 71*(4), 361–377.

Reid, J. & Webster-Stratton, C. (2001). The incredible years parent, teacher, and child intervention: Targeting multiple areas of risk for a young child with pervasive conduct problems using a flexible, manualized treatment program. *Cognitive and Behavioral Practice, 8*, 377–386.

Reitman, D., Murphy, M.A., Hupp, S.D.A., & O'Callahagn, P.M. (2004). Behavior change and perceptions of change: Evaluating the effectiveness of a token economy. *Child and Family Behavior Therapy, 26*(2), 17–36.

Rhodes, J.E., Haight, W.L., & Briggs, E.C. (1999). The influence of mentoring on the peer relationships of foster youth in relative and nonrelative care. *Journal of Research on Adolescence, 9*(2), 185–201.

Rhodes, J.E., Reddy, R., & Grossman, J.B. (2005). The protective influence of mentoring on adolescent substance use: Direct and indirect pathways. *Applied Developmental Science, 9*(1), 31–47.

Roberts, R.E., Atkinson, C.C., & Rosenblatt, A. (1998). Prevalence of psychopathology among children and adolescents. *American Journal of Psychiatry, 155*(6), 715–725.

Robinson, P.W., Newby, T.J., & Ganzell, S.L. (1981). A token system for a class of underachieving hyperactive children. *Journal of Applied Behavior Analysis, 14*, 307–315.

Rubin, B.K. & Geiger, D.W. (1991). Pulmonary function, nutrition, and self-concept in cystic fibrosis summer camps. *Chest, 100*, 649–654.

Schneider, B.H. (1992). Didactic methods for enhancing children's peer relations: A quantitative review. *Clinical Psychology Review, 12*, 363–382.

Sheidow, A.J. & Woodford, M.S. (2003). Multisystemic therapy: An empirically supported, home-based therapy approach. *The Family Journal: Counseling and Therapy for Couples and Families, 11*(3), 257–263.

Shoenwald, S.K., Ward, D.M., Henggeler, S.W., et al. (1996). Multisystemic therapy treatment of substance abusing or dependent adolescent offenders: Costs of reducing incarceration, inpatient, and residential placement. *Journal of Child and Family Studies, 5*(4), 431–445.

Shoenwald, S.K., Ward, D.M., Henggeler, S.W., & Rowland, M.D. (2000). Multisystemic therapy versus hospitalization for crisis stabilization for youth: Placement outcomes 4 months postreferral. *Mental Health Services Research, 2*(1), 3–12.

Singh, R.H., Kable, J.A., Guerrero, N.V., et al. (2000). Impact of a camp experience on phenylalanine levels, knowledge, attitudes and health beliefs relevant to nutrition management of phenylketonuria in adolescent girls. *Journal of the American Dietetic Association 100*, 797–803.

Skiba, R. & Casey, A. (1985). Interventions for behaviorally disordered students: A quantitative review and methodological critique. *Behavioral Disorders, 10*, 239–252.

Spence, S.H. (1995). *Social Skills Training: Enhancing Social Competence in Children and Adolescents*. Windsor, UK: The NFER-NELSON Publishing Company Ltd.

Spence, S.H. (2003). Social skills training with children and young people: Theory, evidence and practice. *Child and Adolescent Mental Health, 8*(2), 84–96.

Spence, S.H. & Marzillier, J.S. (1981). Social skills-training with adolescent male offenders: II. Short-term, long-term and generalized effects. *Behavior Research and Therapy, 19*, 349–368.

Stage, S.A. & Quiroz, D.R. (1997). A meta-analysis of interventions to decrease disruptive classroom behavior in public education settings. *School Psychology Review, 26*(3), 333–368.

Stoiber, K.C. & Kratochwill, T.R. (2000). Empirically supported interventions and school psychology: Rationale and methodological issues. *School Psychology Quarterly, 15*(1), 75–105.

Stollar, S.A., Collins, P.A.D., & Barnett, D.W. (1994). Structured free-play to reduce disruptive activity changes in Head Start classroom. *School Psychology Review, 23*, 310–322.

Swiezy, N.B., Matson, J.L., & Box, P. (1992). The good behavior game: A token reinforcement system for preschoolers. *Child and Family Behavior Therapy, 14*, 21–32.

Theodore, L., Bray, M., & Kehle, T. (2004). A comparative study of group contingencies and randomized reinforcers to reduce disruptive classroom behavior. *School Psychology Quarterly, 19*, 253–271.

Tierney, J.P., Grossman, J. & Resch, N.L. (1995). *Making a difference: An impact study of Big Brothers Big Sisters*. Philadelphia, PA: Public/Private Ventures.

Tingstrom, D.H. (1994). The good behavior game: An investigation of teachers' acceptance. *Psychology in the Schools, 31*, 57–65.

Van Acker, R., Grant, S.H., & Henry, D. (1996). Teacher and student behavior as a function of risk for aggression. *Education and Treatment of Children, 19*, 316–334.

Wade, S.L., Carey, J., & Wolfe, C.R. (2006). The efficacy of an online cognitive-behavioral family intervention in improving child behavior and social competence following pediatric brain injury. *Rehabilitation Psychology, 51*(3), 179–189.

Webster-Stratton, C. & Hammond, M. (1997). Treating children with early onset conduct problems: A comparison of child and parent training interventions. *Journal of Consulting and Clinical Psychology*, *65*(1), 93–109.

Webster-Stratton, C., Reid, M.J., & Hammond, M. (2004). Treating children with early onset conduct problems. Intervention outcomes for parent, child, and teacher training. *Journal of Clinical Child and Adolescent Psychology*, *33*(1), 105–124.

Weiss, J.R., Han, S.S., Granger, D.A., & Morton, T. (1995). Effects of psychotherapy with children and adolescents revisited: A meta-analysis of treatment outcome studies. *Psychological Bulletin 117*, 450–468.

Wilfley, D., Stein, R., Saelens B., Mockus, D., Matt G., et al. (2007). Efficacy of maintenance treatment approaches for childhood overweight. *Journal of the American Medical Association, 298*, 1661–1673.

14

Adjunctive Therapies with Ethnically Diverse Populations

Aditi Vijay, Melanie P. Duckworth, and Ireon Lebeauf

University of Nevada, Reno

As the United States population diversifies, many health care providers have adopted a philosophy of valuing client diversity and have implemented a variety of initiatives intended to effectively identify and manage the needs of the current and projected population of ethnically diverse health care recipients. However, whether health care providers subscribe to, or even understand, the principles and dynamics of what it means to be culturally competent remains a largely unanswered question (Tackey, 2001). Health care systems and health care providers are being required by federal mandates, and by realities related to disease morbidity and mortality rates experienced by persons of ethnically diverse backgrounds, to attend to diversity issues and the impact of such issues on health care provision.

Health care providers who hope to retain persons from ethnically diverse backgrounds in treatment must create a therapeutic environment where diversity is accepted, rather than tolerated, and should find a way to integrate principles of cultural competency into standard health care practice. The health care provider who is culturally competent is able to provide insight regarding the influence of race and ethnicity on mainstream health care practices and adjunctive treatments, and is able to translate theory into practice, this translation manifested by the design and execution of culturally appropriate interventions. There are standards of multicultural competency that every health care provider should continually strive to adhere to as a professional (Arredondo et al., 1996). Culturally skilled therapists are aware of how their own cultural background and experiences have influenced attitudes, values and biases (Arredondo et al., 1996), and maintain a heightened awareness of the challenges that socio-race, racial identity development, gender bias, and age present for clients undergoing treatment.

There are multiple components and domains to consider when working effectively with diverse populations, and diversity is not limited to ethnicity. The culturally competent provider needs to take mental health status and physical health issues into account when treating a client. This chapter will focus on the physical and mental health challenges faced by individuals of ethnically diverse groups as well as subsequent treatment-seeking behaviors. A number of different adjunctive treatments are utilized to manage a variety of physical and mental disorders. To effectively treat members of ethnically diverse populations, it is imperative that providers are knowledgeable about the possible adjunctive therapies that may be utilized.

As a mental health provider, the importance of multicultural competency cannot be emphasized enough, if one desires to be an effective practitioner. Therapists are professionally and ethically bound to "actively attempt to understand the diverse cultural backgrounds of the clients with whom they work. This includes, but is not limited to, learning how the therapist's own cultural/ethnic/racial identity impacts his/her values and beliefs about the counseling process" (American Counseling Association, 1995, Section A.2.b., p. 2).

Cornel West (as cited in Parham & Austin, 1994) reminds us that whenever there exists a social reality where underrepresented groups must fight for legitimacy and self-affirmation, there will be instances of unjustified suffering, unmerited pain, and undeserved harm; the question is not whether hardship will come, but rather how will people deal with it. All psychotherapy is cross-cultural, and if the therapist is to bridge the gap, then grappling with racial identity is indeed an integral part of the process. Both the therapist and the patient reactions to each other are potentially influenced by the psychological qualities (e.g., attitudes, values, perceptions) that were acquired in response to racial socialization (Helms & Cook, 1999). However, the effective, culturally competent therapist is able to exhibit skills that are embedded with cultural intentionality, and is able to initiate a dialogue on how issues of multiculturalism are impeding the psychotherapeutic process.

As previously explained, it is unwise for therapists to assume that the client's perceptions are identical to their own. Therefore, an examination of the therapist's attitudes toward the members of the client's racial group is an ongoing part of the assessment process (Helms & Cook, 1999). If the therapist is conscious of the impact of racial identity development, then there will be (a) an awareness of the sociopolitical forces that have impacted the minority client; (b) an understanding of the challenges that differences in class, culture, and language bring to the psychotherapeutic process; (c) recognition of how the clients' worldviews and receptivity to counseling are affected by their perceptions of the therapist's expertness, trustworthiness, and lack of similarity; (d) an emphasis on how the clients' worldview guides their phenomenology; and

(e) an understanding of culture- and subculture-bound communication styles between and within racial groups (Sue & Sue, 1990).

Rather than viewing culturally competent service delivery to ethnically diverse patients as an isolated treatment consideration, providing culturally appropriate interventions strategies should become a standard path of treatment and intervention. A critical part of providing culturally appropriate treatment includes accessing information and resources. The American Psychological Association provides information and guides to working with racial and ethnic groups on their website (www.apa.org/pi/oema), which provides a place to start. However, the most skilled therapist could not possibly be aware of every study or piece of information on a specific group of people. Therefore, the next question becomes how do we, as therapists, work effectively with all clients? The answer includes seeking consultation when necessary and becoming familiar with ethical guidelines in the service of recognizing one's own biases and potential barriers to effective treatment (Duckworth & Iezzi, 2006). Hays (1996) posits a model that allows for the therapist to systematically explore cultural influences while allowing for the client to identify the influences that are most salient for them. Following such a model allows for therapists of varying degrees of cultural competence to work with people of different backgrounds in a culturally sensitive manner.

As the United States population diversifies, utilization of adjunctive therapies in the treatment of ethnically diverse populations has increased substantially (Keith et al., 2005). Individuals have sought adjunctive forms of treatment for help with mental and physical health issues. In order for clinicians to be able to provide the most effective treatment, they must be cognizant of these trends. This chapter will provide an overview of mental and physical health issues in ethnically diverse populations followed by a review of adjunctive therapies that are most commonly utilized.

MENTAL HEALTH ISSUES

MENTAL HEALTH ISSUES IN AFRICAN AMERICANS

It is estimated that approximately 34 million people who self-identify as African Americans reside in the United States, which accounts for 12% of the national population (Baker & Bell, 1999; DHHS, 2001). However, this is assumed to be an underestimation of the actual population, because of the overrepresentation of African Americans in hard-to-reach populations (e.g., homeless and incarcerated persons). As is the case with many demographic categories, African American is a seemingly homogeneous term; yet, it encompasses individuals with different geographic and cultural ancestries and histories. African Americans comprise a significant portion of the US population, and therefore, it is imperative for researchers and clinicians to be aware of the diverse mental health needs within this community.

In the United States, there is a long and disturbing history of racist and discriminatory practices toward African Americans. The legacy of these practices is evident in present society and continues to have measurable, harmful consequences to the mental health of African Americans. Although a review of these practices is outside the scope of this chapter, it would be inaccurate to discuss issues pertaining to African American mental health without considering the current sociopolitical context. Although US society has attempted to address the inequitable treatment of African Americans in numerous and varied ways, significant disparities persist. These disparities are evident throughout a number of domains (income, education, health care, etc.) and have a significant impact on the psychological well-being of African Americans.

Currently, 53% of African Americans live in the South, 37% live in primarily urban areas in the Northeast or Midwest, and approximately 15% live in rural areas. Many African Americans live in segregated neighborhoods, and consequently, poor African Americans are likely to reside along side other poor African Americans. There is evidence to indicate that poor neighborhoods tend to be underresourced as reflected by high unemployment rates, higher rates of homelessness, crime and substance abuse, which, in turn, impact the overall well-being of the residents (DHHS, 2001).

Recent research suggests that there is no longer a significant gap in rates of high school graduation between African Americans and Whites (DHHS, 2001). Additionally, the rate of college enrollment among African Americans has increased by 50% over the last 20 years (DHHS, 2001). However, differences between African Americans and Whites in general levels of academic achievement and the quality of academic curricula completed persist.

African Americans have experienced great strides in income levels over the past 30 years. From 1967 to 1997, the US Census Bureau reported a 31% increase in the median income of African Americans (DHHS, 2001). By 1997, approximately 32% of African Americans lived in the suburbs and were part of the middle class (DHHS, 2001). Despite these gains, aggregate measures indicate that African Americans are relatively poor, with approximately 22% currently living below the poverty line. African Americans are three times as likely as Whites to live in severe poverty. This dramatic range in economic status from severe poverty to significant prosperity has resulted in a polarized African American community (Snowden, 2001). Evidence suggests that poor mental health is more common among impoverished populations than those who are more affluent (DHHS, 2001). Given the higher rates of poverty within the African American community, it is plausible that there are mental health issues yet to be addressed.

Significant disparities exist in access to health care resources and subsequent utilization of those resources (Duckworth, 2005). Utilization of mental health care in the African American community is characterized by low rates of outpatient care and high rates of emergency services (Bell & Barker, 1999; DHHS, 2001; Snowden, 2001). There are several variables that are potentially related to reluctance to seek treatment. First, lack of access to services is a significant barrier to utilization. A lack of health insurance can make obtaining services unaffordable and therefore remains as a critical obstacle to receiving treatment. Nearly one-fourth of African Americans are uninsured. However, addressing financial barriers is not sufficient to ensuring provision of services or even that treatment will be sought (DHHS, 2001). Attitudes toward mental health services impact a person's willingness to seek treatment. The stigma surrounding mental health services in general within the African American community can serve to dissuade interested individuals from seeking appropriate services. The availability of service providers also effects treatment-seeking behaviors. Research indicates that African Americans would prefer to receive services from someone in their community and are more likely to seek treatment from a primary care physician than a mental health specialist (Bell & Barker, 1999). Additionally, African Americans are less likely to receive appropriate care when diagnosed with depression or anxiety. Furthermore, African Americans are less likely to receive accurate diagnoses when presenting to primary care physicians for psychological help (DHHS, 2001).

A long history of misdiagnosis followed by ineffective treatment contributes to a reluctance to utilize services (Snowden, 2001). For decades, it was assumed that the prevalence of schizophrenia in African American populations was significantly higher than the general population and the rates of affective disorders were significantly lower. On the basis of this assumption, many African Americans were incorrectly diagnosed with disorders such as schizophrenia, and then, based on inaccurate diagnosis, they were subjected to inappropriate treatments. This is due in large part to diagnostic and clinician bias (Baker & Bell, 1999). Diagnostic biases are partially due to lack of research of the prevalence of mental disorders in the African American communities as well as the limited exposure many clinicians have in working with this population. This history of misdiagnosis and ineffective or inappropriate treatment is related to the fact that African Americans are likely to terminate treatment prematurely (Sue et al., 1994).

The demographic data indicate that there are distal variables present within this population that may contribute to psychological distress. One example of a distal variable that impacts psychological health is violence exposure. Children who live in neighborhoods with higher crime rates are more likely to witness violence. There is an established link between exposure to violence and the subsequent development of psychological distress (Kessler et al., 1994). In fact, nearly one-fourth of African American children who were exposed to violence met criteria for a diagnosis of Posttraumatic Stress Disorder. Determining the separate and combined impact of the proximal and distal factors that are considered to contribute to psychological distress among African Americans is made difficult by the lack of research addressing these factors. Also, limiting our understanding of these relations is the persistently low rates of treatment-seeking evidenced by African Americans. Together, these circumstances combine to a dearth of epidemiological information to estimate the prevalence of mental disorders within the African American community.

MENTAL HEALTH ISSUES IN LATINOS/HISPANICS

Although Latino immigrants are often identified as a high-risk group for depression, anxiety, and substance abuse, the rates for psychiatric disorders such as bipolar disorder, schizophrenia, and other axis II diagnoses are fairly similar to the rates of mental illness in European American populations. With regard to gender, the prevalence of depression among Latino women is significantly higher (46%) than Latino men (19%). Suicide rates for Latino adults hover around 6% compared with 13% for non-Hispanic whites. In teenage populations, the rate of attempted suicide for Latino girls (14.9%) was one and half times that of African American or European American girls (National Alliance on Mental Illness, 2007).

Acculturation stress and place of birth has the most significant correlation for psychiatric disorders in the Latino community. Long-term residence in the United States significantly increased rates of mental disorders, with a dramatic increase in the rate of substance abuse. Foreign-born Latinos are at a significantly lower risk of suicide and depression than those born in the United States (National Alliance on Mental Illness, 2007).

MENTAL HEALTH ISSUES IN ASIAN AMERICANS

Asian Americans and Pacific Islanders (APIs) constitute one of the fastest growing ethnic groups in the United States; they currently comprise 3.6% of the American population (Chen et al., 2003; Iwasama & Hilliard, 1999; Kim & Chan, 2004; Kramer et al., 2002; Suen & Morris, 2006). The demographic category of API implies homogeneity within this group; thus, it is important to note that the term API encompasses over 25 distinct ethnic groups and more than 125 languages (Lin & Cheung, 1999). As this population continues to grow, it is even more important for mental health practitioners to become aware of different needs and traditions within this population in order to serve them effectively. In the past, APIs were widely perceived as the model minority. The high levels of educational, occupational, and financial success they achieved combined with low levels of mental health service utilization seemed to indicate that they did not require mental health services. With increased knowledge and exposure to API culture, it has become clear that there is an existing need for mental health services among API (Chung, 2002).

The lack of research and underutilization of mental health services by API contributes to the difficulty in estimating the prevalence of psychological disorders in this population. At this time, there are no aggregate estimates for the prevalence of mental disorder within API populations. However, it is estimated that 30% of elder Japanese Americans in retirement homes experienced some form of depression (Chen & Chen, 2002). Only 5% of their counterparts who reside in the family home experienced depression. Rates of anxiety in Japanese Americans were estimated to be even lower, with only 9% of Japanese Americans having experienced any form of anxiety or panic disorder (Iwasama & Hilliard, 1999). Currently, there are no prevalence data available to indicate rates of schizophrenia or bipolar disorder in Asian American populations (Bae & Kung, 2000).

In reality, the overall prevalence of mental illness among APIs seems to be similar to other communities in the United States. Despite average rates of mental disorder, APIs have historically presented to treatment at much lower rates than all other ethnic groups in the United States (Barreto & Segal, 2005). However, when API present to treatment, it is typically with severe symptoms (Chen et al., 2003). There are several hypotheses that may account for the reluctance on the part of many APIs to seek mental health services. Many Eastern traditions assert that the mind and body cannot be separated. This belief is in opposition to most Western philosophies and practices. This conceptualization, which is endorsed by many Asians currently living in the United States, makes seeking the services of any sort of mental health specialist seem unnecessary. Many Asian traditions contend that mental illness is caused by disharmony of emotions or evil spirits; thus, traditional psychotherapy is not the logical step when attempting to resolve these conflicts (Kramer et al., 2002). Alternatively, many APIs have had negative experiences with the health care system and are reluctant to seek treatment when they feel that their beliefs will not be respected (Kim et al., 2002).

When APIs do present for mental health services, there are still potential challenges to overcome in providing effective treatment. Key factors include language, level of acculturation, age, gender, occupational issues, and family structure. Clearly, language is a key component of effective treatment. In people of Asian descent living in the United States, there are over 125 languages and dialects represented (Lin & Cheung, 1999); therefore, it is important to ensure that language is not a barrier to treatment (Duckworth & Iezzi, 2006).

MENTAL HEALTH ISSUES IN AMERICAN INDIANS AND ALASKA NATIVES

The US Census Bureau estimates that 4.1 million American Indians/Alaska Natives (AI/AN) currently reside in the United States. AI/AN account for 1.5% of the US population and the majority live in urban, suburban, or rural nonreservation areas (DHHS, 2001). The relatively small size of this group is not indicative of the vast diversity within this group. The category of AI/AN includes 561 federally recognized tribes with over 200 indigenous languages spoken. This is simply one indicator of the heterogeneity that exists within this group and another factor that contributes to the challenge of providing mental health services effectively.

There are many significant barriers to effectively treating AI/AN for mental disorders. A critical component of this challenge is the dearth of empirical evidence regarding the prevalence of mental disorders in this population. The vast diversity of languages that are spoken within this population contributes to the challenges in appropriate assessment and treatment. In addition to the variety of languages spoken, the vocabulary is different. For example, there are no words in the majority of languages that have similar meanings to "depression" or "anxiety" which are in the English language. This difference in expression has results in critical challenges in a therapeutic setting. To address this, mental health practitioners need to be as well informed as possible, which points to the need for further research in this area.

As a result of limitations in collecting adequate sample sizes, epidemiological information is suggestive rather than conclusive. It is estimated that 20–30% of Native Americans have experienced depression during the course of their lifetime. Native American populations are more likely to endorse somatic symptoms associated with depression rather than affective components (Iwata & Buka, 2002). However, it has been noted that the rate of suicide is 1.5 times greater in the AI/AN population than in the general population (DHHS, 2001). This suggests that there are higher rates of psychological distress than have been previously documented. There is no empirical evidence regarding the phenomenology or prevalence of anxiety disorder. However, it is reasonable to assume given the prevalence of environmental stressors that a significant portion of this population suffers from anxiety-related disorders (DeCoteau et al., 2006). There is no data regarding the prevalence of bipolar disorder or schizophrenia within this population.

Whereas there is not specific information regarding the prevalence of mental disorder, there are distal factors present within this population that are associated with poor psychological health, thus emphasizing the need for further research in this area. It is possible that the most salient barrier to treatment is the long history of prejudicial practices and discriminatory treatment at the hands of the US government. This has established deep (and understandable) feelings of mistrust that make it difficult to enter into treatment. This must be carefully considered when working with this population.

PHYSICAL HEALTH ISSUES

The physical health of the larger US population would suggest that current rates of disease morbidity and mortality are largely a function of a cluster of predictors that include individual factors (age, gender, genetic inheritance) as well as lifestyle health behaviors that confer either increase risk or protection against chronic health conditions. On the basis of Whitfield et al. (2002), we have provided a brief overview of morbidity and mortality rates and health risk behaviors evidenced by persons representing diverse ethnic backgrounds.

The age- and gender-adjusted death rate from all causes of mortality is 60% higher among African Americans as a group when compared with Caucasians as a group. One of the major factors in this life expectancy gap is mortality from circulatory diseases. African Americans experience higher age-adjusted morbidity and mortality rates than Caucasians for coronary heart disease (CHD) and stroke. African Americans experience the most significant health burden from smoking. The prevalence of obesity among African American women is considered epidemic, with 53% of African American women being overweight and 34% of Caucasian women being overweight. African American alcohol use is characterized by both high rates of abstention and high rates of abuse.

Asian and Pacific Islanders (APIs) have one of the best health profiles in the United States. Heart disease and cancer are leading causes of death for adult API Americans. The little that is known suggests that Chinese Americans use less tobacco than people from other cultures. There may be lost health benefits for Asian Americans who opt to change to mainstream American diets rather than adhere to more traditional Asian diets. There is evidence that physical activity serves as a protective factor against chronic illness among Asian Americans from research on Japanese American men who participated in the Honolulu Heart Program. Physical activity is inversely related to diabetes, CHD morbidity, and mortality. Findings from the literature point to consistently low levels of alcohol consumption and drinking problems among the Chinese in America.

Latinos from households in which English was a second language (less acculturated) were less likely to be daily smokers and less likely to smoke more than 15 cigarettes a day than were those who were acculturated (those from households in which English was the primary language). Latinos have been found to be more likely than Caucasians to report inadequate intake of vegetables, problems with teeth or dentures that limited the kinds and amounts of food eaten, difficulty preparing meals, and lack of money needed to buy food. Data on the level of physical activity among Latinos are mixed. Some evidence suggests that Latinos are more physically active than other ethnic groups. The larger body of evidence suggests that Latinos do not differ from the low levels of physical activity reported in other ethnic groups. Prevalence rates of past heavy drinking among Mexican American and Puerto Rican males are approximately 3 times higher than rates reported for non-Latino male populations.

Mortality data reveal excess overall mortality among AI/AN, as well as excesses for specific causes of death, including accidents, diabetes, liver disease, pneumonia/influenza, suicide, homicide, and tuberculosis. There is almost a "deficit" of deaths noted for heart disease, cancer, and HIV infections in this population. Poor socioeconomic conditions, lack of education, and cultural barriers contribute to the enduring poor health status of AI/AN. Unusually high rates of smokeless tobacco use have been found in some AI/AN populations. As in other ethnic groups, diet has been implicated as a primary risk factor in the development of chronic diseases among American Indian tribes. There is concern that the dietary transition from traditional foods to more market (store-bought) foods among indigenous populations will bring about a rise in diet-related chronic disease. Current research suggests that American Indians do not participate in physical activity at levels sufficient to protect against the development of cardiovascular disease (CVD) risk factors, obesity, and noninsulin-dependent diabetes mellitus. Further research is necessary to address the issues of American Indians' drinking.

Together these data point to the importance of applying all available health care options, both traditional health care options and health care options that might be considered alternative or adjunctive, to the treatment of persons from diverse ethnic backgrounds who suffer from physical diseases. The trend toward increased utilization of adjunctive therapies for mental disorders and physical diseases supports the need to examine the effectiveness of these treatments as applied to ethnically diverse populations.

UTILIZATION OF ADJUNCTIVE THERAPIES

The prevalence of adjunctive therapies has increased substantially in the American population over the past 10 years (Clayton, 2005; Collinge et al., 2005; Druss & Rosenheck, 2000; Keith et al., 2005; Mamtani & Cimino, 2002). This chapter focuses on many of the widely used and researched adjunctive therapies, but it is not an exhaustive list. It is estimated that by 2010, at least two-thirds of the US population will utilize some form of complementary or adjunctive therapies for physical health issues and mental disorders (Patwardhan et al., 2005). The existence of adjunctive therapies in the United States has a long history, but it is more accepted by patients and practitioners at this point in time than ever before (Honda & Jacobson, 2005). The increased utilization of adjunctive therapies requires that therapist be familiar with these treatments and the potential benefits that may be derived from application of these treatments to client physical and psychological problems.

It is widely acknowledged that there are significant disparities between racial and ethnic groups in access to health care and mental health care and quality of services rendered (Coffey et al., 2000; Duckworth, 2005; Keith et al., 2005; Snowden & Yamada, 2005; Taylor, 2003; Whitfield et al., 2002). Individuals who are in poor health or who have had unsatisfactory experiences with the health care system are more likely to seek adjunctive treatments (Collinge et al., 2005). Typically, younger, well-educated, women living in the South or Western part of the United States and often without health insurance seek alternative treatments for physical and mental disorders (Keith et al., 2005; Mackenzie et al., 2003; Whitfield et al., 2002). Racial and ethnic groups utilize adjunctive treatments differentially. The rate of utilization for the general population is estimated to be 6.5%, depending on which treatments are included in this category. White Americans used complementary and alternative medicine (CAM) most often, whereas African Americans' use ranged from 4 to 33.1% and use by Latinos ranged from 6.5 to 24%. The pattern of use for Asian Americans was most similar to White Americans.

Although there is not much available information on factors associated with the use of alternative treatments, there is a positive correlation between self-reported mental illness and individuals seeking alternative treatments (Druss &

Rosenheck, 2000). Clinical populations utilize adjunctive therapies at a higher rate than the general population. One of these treatments that is used with the highest frequency is herbal treatment. There is no federally approved or otherwise mandated standard for herbal treatments; thus, consumers are not always aware of what they are purchasing or ingesting. The possibility of adverse drug interactions is present, making it more important for mental health service providers to become more knowledgeable of adjunctive treatments. Becoming more aware of the options for treatment and factors influencing the decision to seek services is imperative for practitioners who are working with these populations.

USE OF ADJUNCTIVE THERAPIES BY AFRICAN AMERICANS

Bibliotherapy, Psychoeducation, and Self-Help Groups

In the context of both mental and physical health, provision of care is sometimes defined by financial considerations rather than by empirical determinations regarding best care practice for a given complaint. In an effort to optimize affordable health care options, clinical researchers have attempted to establish the clinical effectiveness of low-cost care options such as self-help. Self-help strategies include but are not limited to bibliotherapy, e-health, and self-help groups. All these intervention strategies emphasize patient-driven acquisition and use of important health care information. The effectiveness of self-help strategies has been examined and supported in a variety of contexts, including depression experienced by older adults (Floyd et al., 2006), self-management abilities displayed by frail older adults (Frieswijk et al., 2006), panic disorder (Lidren et al., 1994), obsessive-compulsive disorder (Mataix-Cols & Marks, 2006), agoraphobia (Lovell et al., 2003), healthy sexual practices (van Kesteren et al., 2006) and general quality of life issues among persons who are HIV positive (Lechner et al., 2003), stress and anxiety (Reeves & Stace, 2005), and sleep problems (Yamatsu et al., 2004).

There are relatively few studies evaluating the effectiveness of self-help for imparting disease knowledge and managing the physical health of African Americans. Two of the physical health contexts in which the effectiveness of self-help strategies for African Americans has been examined include general quality of life issues among persons who are HIV positive and CVD risk (Laken et al., 2004; Lechner et al., 2003). The little empirical information that exists suggests that self-help in the form of psychoeducation and e-health can be effective in imparting health information to African Americans and other underserved populations.

Journaling/Expressive Writing, Self-Monitoring, and Self-Management

Journaling/Expressive Writing

There are relatively few studies that specifically evaluate the use of journaling or expressive writing as strategies for improving physical or psychological health outcomes of African Americans. Research examining journaling among African

Americans have centered on documenting racial and cultural issues as they impact both the instructional practices and principal teaching expectations of African American teachers (Derry, 2005) and documenting the relation of social support to medication adherence in a population of young HIV positive African American women (Edwards, 2006). Although a considerable number of research investigations of the health effects of expressive writing have been undertaken, few of these studies have evaluated the influence of expressive writing on the health outcomes of African Americans.

Self-monitoring and Self-management

Studies examining the use of self-monitoring by African Americans have generally been conducted in the context of physical health conditions such as diabetes and other chronic health conditions. Banister et al. (2004) determined that positive medical outcomes among African Americans and Hispanics with type II diabetes were associated with diabetes self-management training (DSMT) that emphasized self-monitoring of blood glucose as part of a broader array of strategies aimed at improving diabetic health indicators. Sixty-one percent of the 70 participants were described as experiencing positive medication outcomes. The authors concluded that DSMT can improve glycemic control achieved by individuals attending community clinics for management of type II diabetes. Sarkar et al. (2006) examined self-efficacy as a determinant of self-management behavior across various racial/ethnic groups. These researchers determined that improvements in self-esteem were related to improved diabetic self-management across all racial/ethnic groups.

Targeting enrollees of a managed care organization who were enrolled in a high-risk level diabetes disease management program, Welch and colleagues (2006) obtained baseline and follow-up survey data on eight preventative services from 1961 participating enrollees representing diverse racial/ethnic backgrounds. Participants were assigned to diabetic risk categories ranging from high to low and, based on the level of diabetic risk, participants were assigned to one of four intervention protocols that ranged in intensity from high intensity (review of educational materials and online materials related to diabetes disease management, at least monthly staff-initiated telephone calls, and more than once monthly reporting of vital statistics through participant-initiated telephone communication and online interactions) to low intensity (review of educational materials and online materials in the absence of staff-initiated telephone calls and in the absence of any reporting of vital statistics). Results of the study suggested that, at follow-up, the gap in utilization of preventative services widened between Blacks and Whites and narrowed between Whites and Hispanics. Data pertaining to engagement in self-management behavior were much more encouraging, with ethnically diverse groups engaging in more self-management behaviors than Whites at follow-up. The positive impact of self monitoring and self management behaviors on diabetes is supported by other ethnically diverse populations (Adams, et al., 2007).

Self-monitoring was identified by older adult African Americans as one of nine strategies they use to cope with chronic health conditions (Loeb, 2006). Loeb reported that a number of the 28 older adult African Americans participating in focus groups used self-monitoring to manage multiple chronic medical conditions and considered self-monitoring essential to maintaining health and evaluating changes in health status.

Together, these studies point to the benefit of self-monitoring and self-management training in managing chronic health conditions among African Americans and others with diverse cultural backgrounds. The findings also suggest that African Americans are as willing as Whites to engage in self-management strategies when training and monitoring equipment are available.

Physical Activity and Lifestyle Change

Lifestyle change that involves adequate nutrition and physical activity is critical to the long-term management of the chronic health conditions that constitute the largest threat to health among African Americans. Among the health conditions and diseases that constitute the top ten causes of mortality among Americans are cardiovascular disease (CVD), cancer, respiratory diseases, and conditions, such as Type II diabetes that are linked to lifestyle health behaviors and considered preventable. Any number of disease prevention and management initiatives have been undertaken to evaluate and facilitate African Americans' engagement in healthy nutrition and physical activity programs, including Project Power and Choose to Live, initiatives created by the American Diabetes Association, and the Power to End Stroke program and other State-specific initiatives sponsored by the American Heart Association.

African Americans are found to eat meals that are higher in fats and lower in fruits and vegetables than recommended (National Center for Health Statistics, 2007), these eating choices thought to be influenced by knowledge related to the relation of healthier food choices to disease risk, taste and food preparation preferences, and financial constraints. Regular physical activity has been associated with a number of beneficial health effects, including reduced risk of CVD, diabetes, and some forms of cancer (American Diabetes Association, 2006; American Heart Association/American Stroke Association, 2007; International Agency for Research on Cancer, 2002). Regular physical activity also impacts health status through its association with changes in other health risk behaviors such as obesity. On the basis of data from the 2005 Behavioral Risk Factor Surveillance System (BRFSS) survey (as cited in the Heart Disease and Stroke Statistics 2007 At-a-Glance), nearly 50% of adults do not engage in physical activity that is of the intensity, frequency, and duration recommended by public health authorities (American Heart Association/American Stroke Association, 2007). Among those factors predicting lower levels of physical activity are older age, lower educational attainment, being of a diverse ethnic or racial background, and lower socioeconomic status. Studies examining barriers to physical activity within the multiethnic populations have identified various sociodemographic variables to be associated with physical inactivity, including older age, female gender, being overweight and obese, lower acculturation, and being unemployed (Bennett et al., 2006; Wolin et al., 2006).

African Americans are among those persons who are at highest risk for physical inactivity (Marshal et al., 2007). Research studies and clinical initiatives have been undertaken to more fully explicate the relation of ethnicity and race to physical activity and to increase physical activity within at-risk African American populations. Fleury and Lee (2006) posit that interventions aimed at increasing physical activity engagement among African American women need to address the personal, social, environmental, and organizational factors that serve as "leverage points for influencing physical activity" among this population (p. 135). In additional to sociodemographic variables, the factors identified by Fleury and Lee as potential leverage points include perceptions of the benefit of physical activity and motivation to initiate and maintain physical activity; social support and social norms that reinforce physical activity; convenient and safe facilities for physical activity; and formal promotion of physical activity by community organizations and partnerships. Research studies support the role of these variables in increasing physical activity among African American women and other at-risk ethnically diverse populations (Albright et al., 2005; Sharma et al., 2005; Young & Stewart, 2006).

Relaxation, Meditation, and Stress Management

Relaxation

The term "relaxation" is used to capture a variety of procedures, including progressive muscular relaxation, meditation, and yoga. The effectiveness of relaxation is usually evaluated in the context of anxiety or stress management. A considerable number of comparative effectiveness studies have been conducted to document the utility of relaxation procedures in managing emotional distress and in managing the deleterious physiological effects of stress on healthy individuals and individuals with compromised health. Generally, these studies have demonstrated the effectiveness of relaxation strategies relative to wait-list control conditions (for a review, see Ernst et al., 2007). Several published studies of the effectiveness of relaxation have incorporated ethnically diverse samples; however, to our knowledge, very few studies have incorporated ethnicity as a primary variable of interest in establishing the effectiveness of such procedures.

Meditation

Meditation is a stress-reduction strategy that has been employed to manage distress related to a variety of psychosocial stressors. The attention devoted to the study of psychosocial stressors and their impact on the health of African Americans is a function of the differentially high rates of psychosocial stressors experienced by African Americans who live within the larger Eurocentric US culture; the increased incidence, morbidity, and mortality associated with

African Americans' experience of many of the most prevalent physical diseases; and the limited success of traditional medical treatments in managing these diseases. Researchers are attempting to modify CVD morbidity and mortality among African Americans by eliminating those psychosocial stressors that influence disease risk. Schneider and colleagues have dedicated years of clinical investigation to establishing the effectiveness of different stress-reduction strategies in reducing CVD risk among African Americans and other underserved populations. In a recent review, Schneider et al. (2005) summarized findings related to the effects of transcendental medication on CVD risk factors, events, and mechanisms. The review captured data from randomized clinical trials and meta-analyses and focused on African Americans and other underserved populations found to be at substantially higher risk for CVD morbidity and mortality. Across CVD risk factors including blood pressure, cholesterol, and smoking, transcendental medication was found to be an effective risk-reduction strategy. Across cardiovascular events and endpoints including myocardial ischemia, left-ventricular mass, and atherosclerosis, transcendental medication was found to be effective, increasing exercise tolerance and maximum work load and delaying the onset ST-segment depression, all of which may reduce stress-induced myocardial ischemia. Across physiological neuroendocrine mechanisms that contribute to cardiovascular compromise, including baseline levels of respiration and heart rate, spontaneous skin resistance, heart rate reactivity, sympathetic adrenergic receptor sensitivity, and basal and average cortisol levels, transcendental medication was found to be effective in reducing stress and in creating a state of relaxation that may impact the physiological and neurohormonal mechanisms that underlie cardiovascular health. On the basis of all the data reviewed, Schneider and colleagues concluded that transcendental meditation is an efficacious and cost-effective behavioral strategy for reducing CVD risk and improving outcomes.

Stress Management

Studies of African American use of and benefit from stress management procedures are few in number and, as with self monitoring and self management strategies, have been investigated in the context of chronic health conditions. Stress is a well-researched concept; however, research on the effects and clinical management of stress have targeted White males, with a very limited number of clinical trials performed to evaluate stress in African Americans. The importance of stress and stress management for African Americans is immediately apparent when rates of cardiovascular compromise and disease among African Americans are considered. Burt and colleagues (as cited in Schneider et al., 2005) determined that rates of hypertension among African American men and women are higher than the rates of hypertension evidenced by non-Hispanic White men and women and hypertension has been found to develop earlier and to be more severe among African Americans than Whites, with increased duration and severity of disease contributing to more negative clinical outcomes including mortality.

Researchers have posited that stressors associated with the life circumstances experienced by a proportion of African Americans in the United States contribute to elevated blood pressure and clinical hypertension among the life circumstances of African Americans (Schneider et al., 2001; Neighbors et al., 1995). Recently, research has been undertaken to determine the impact of stress management procedures on hypertensive outcomes among African Americans. Webb et al. (2006) evaluated the impact of stress management on blood pressure indices and stress-related variables among 33 African American women who were assigned to stress management or delayed treatment conditions. Although analyses of the impact of stress management on blood pressure and stress-related variables revealed trends in support of the possible effectiveness of stress management, differences between stress management and delayed treatment groups were not significant.

Support Groups

African American use of support groups has been evaluated in the context of chronic health conditions such as breast cancer, caregiving, and mental health concerns including substance abuse and partner violence. There is a plethora of studies examining the effects of support group participation on the psychological and physical well-being of breast cancer survivors. Study findings generally suggest that participation in support groups provides psychological benefits (Michalec, 2005). Findings regarding the effect of support group participation on physical health outcomes of breast cancer survivors are more equivocal. African Americans are underrepresented among breast cancer support groups. This underrepresentation of African Americans in breast cancer support groups and research studies evaluating the effects of such support groups has been attributed to (1) differential rates of provider recruitment across Whites and persons representing diverse ethnic backgrounds and (2) a more general tendency among African Americans away from participation in support groups. Until recently, this purported tendency had not undergone methodologically sound evaluation. Michalec et al. (2004) posited that the race gap in support group participation across African Americans and Whites is a function of methodological limitations that characterize most research into this question. Michalec and colleagues evaluated support group participation across African Americans and Whites using a population of breast cancer survivors rather than a population of support group participants to evaluate support group participation across the two racial groups. Phone interview data revealed that African Americans and Whites participated in breast cancer support groups at equal rates.

Research suggests that social support impacts mental health outcomes among African Americans. Social support has been found to mediate the effects of partner violence on the levels of anxiety and parenting distress experienced by battered African American women (Mitchell et al., 2006). Social networks have been established as conveying some protective benefit for African American drug users (Tobin et al., 2007). Participation by African Americans in formal support groups aimed at improving mental health may be influenced by group process variables as well as the informational content addressed by the group.

In an innovative approach to documenting those aspects of the support group process that are related to attendance and group engagement, Steward (2001) compared the group dynamics evidenced within an all-Black woman's support group to those evidenced within an all-White woman's support group. With respect to attendance, Black women were found to attend fewer group meetings, with academic and occupational demands, family problems, and illness or fatigue cited as explanations for nonattendance. With respect to expressions of affect, Black women were observed to be more responsive to expressions of positive affect and anger whereas White women were found to be more responsive to expressions of sadness, helplessness, and fear. Differences in the critical issues addressed during group meetings were also observed, with Black women concentrating their discussions on day-to-day issues that interfere with their ability to function and White women focusing on family-of-origin issues. These findings have implications for the development and structuring of support groups designed to serve persons from diverse ethnic backgrounds.

There is a fast-growing body of research addressing the well-being of caregivers. Establishing the support needs of African American care givers is essential for a number of reasons. African Americans are at higher risk of morbidity and mortality for a range of diseases, including but not limited to CVD, diabetes, some forms of cancer, and Alzheimer's disease. Higher rates of disease morbidity confer a greater care burden on the relatives and friends of impacted persons. African Americans are overrepresented among the uninsured and underinsured. As a consequence, much of the burden of nonacute and long-term care for these uninsured or underinsured African Americans is borne by relatives and friends. Even when adequately insured, many African Americans ascribe to cultural norms regarding the in-family care of persons who are afflicted with illness and disease.

Support groups are one avenue for ensuring that caregivers do not succumb to the multiple and significant stressors associated with serving as a primary source of care for an afflicted other. Caregivers of persons with Alzheimer's disease are among the most frequently studied caregivers. The sometimes enduring nature of the disease requires that services need to assist caregivers in managing the care demands of the patient with Alzheimer's disease be evaluated routinely and provided. Cox (1999) examined the pattern of support services use by 300 African American and White caregivers of persons with Alzheimer's disease. Although African American and White caregivers differed on a number of sociodemographic and caregiving variables (educational attainment, economic status, relationship of caregiver to person with Alzheimer's disease, duration of caregiving, and support satisfaction), these groups of caregivers evidenced similar levels of depression, burden, stress, and relationship strain. Both groups acknowledged support service needs and the intention to seek services; however, across African American and White caregivers use of services was poor. Given the higher rate at which African Americans are diagnosed with Alzheimer's disease, and given the clinically significant burden placed on the caregivers of persons with Alzheimer's disease, it is imperative that every effort be made to identify those factors that would predict adequate use of the support services that are available to African American caregivers.

Williams and Barton (2004) have forwarded a model of successful support groups for African American caregivers based on successes achieved within the Delaware chapter of the Alzheimer's Association, this chapter is headquartered in Philadelphia and serves a large number of African Americans. Williams and Barton (2004) summarized the key components of successful support groups for the African American community as including

- development of a working advisory committee including representatives of trusted and familiar providers of community *services, small* business, community leaders, elected officials, and churches;
- development and implementation of marketing strategies specifically for reaching African American family caregivers and personally inviting then to participate in the support group;
- activities to inform local small businesses such as barber shops, beauty and nail salons, corner pharmacies, markets, and the like that serve the African American community so they can pass on or post information about available caregiver support;
- recruitment and training of African American support-group facilitators.
- identification of a host location that is accessible, safe, and welcoming to caregivers and family members (p. 82).

FAITH-BASED HEALTH PROGRAMS: A SPECIAL INSTANCE OF HEALTH EDUCATION AND SUPPORT

A growing alternative to traditional medically managed health promotion and disease prevention programs are faith-based health programs. Faith-based health programs can be conceptualized as serving in a manner similar to support groups, but as having the added advantages of having health information imparted by a trusted authority and support for behavior change provided in the context of already established and trusted relationships. Faith-based health programs have been increasing in number and in complexity of health-related services since the mid-1980s. The growth of faith-based health programs is considered to be a function a heightened emphasis on health maintenance and disease prevention; increasing health care costs; and the growing number of community-dwelling persons who are considered to be particularly advantaged by community-based health services (e.g., older adults, persons with disabilities, and homeless individuals) (Cantanzaro et al., 2006).

The hypothesized relation of religion to health outcomes has shifted dramatically over time; however, more recent examinations of the relation of religiosity to health behaviors suggest modest to moderate beneficial effects of active membership in faith-based organizations on health behaviors (for a review, see (Peterson et al., 2002)). Methodologically sound examinations of the effectiveness of faith-based health programs are woefully few in number. In a review of studies examining the effectiveness of church-based health promotion (CBHP) interventions, Campbell and colleagues (2007) identified 13 studies that they considered to "demonstrate the characteristics and evaluative findings of most CBHP studies." On the basis of these studies, Campbell and colleagues concluded that there is evidence for the potential effectiveness of CBHP interventions in attaining behavior change among participants, with small to moderate effect sizes obtained for fruit and vegetable consumption and physical activity.

Establishing the effectiveness of faith-based health programs is particularly relevant for persons from diverse ethnic backgrounds. Briscoe and Prichert (as cited in Drayton-Brooks & White, 2004) highlighted the importance of culturally relevant approaches to providing health care access and ensuring improved health status among African Americans. Drayton-Brooks and White conducted an exploratory examination of the factors influencing health-promoting behaviors displayed by African American women with faith support. Study participants identified exercise, nutrition, and weight and stress reduction as behavioral health concerns and identified trusting, familiar, inclusive, and comfortable environments as critical to the success of behavior change efforts. The researchers identified spiritual fatalism among this group of respondents as of potential significance in explaining low rates of engagement in health-promoting behavior among this population. Campbell and colleagues (2007) suggested that effective CBHP interventions are characterized by the use of church members as lay advisors, facilitators, and peer educators, the provisions of culturally targeted and/or individually relevant self-help materials, and the inclusion of telephone counseling.

USE OF ADJUNCTIVE THERAPIES BY LATINOS/HISPANICS

Although Latinos are the largest ethnic minority population in the United States, there are few data available documenting the utilization rates of adjunctive therapies within this ethnic group. Latino patients are less likely than White and/or Asian Americans to utilize CAM or adjunctive therapies including but not limited to acupuncture, nutritional advice, massage therapy, herbal remedies, biofeedback, meditation training, homeopathic therapy, spiritual healing, hypnosis, and traditional cultural medicine (Keith et al., 2005). That is not to say that Latino/as are not pursuing adjunctive therapies outside of traditional health care systems. One study has found that Latino/as use the following adjunctive treatments most commonly: Herbs, prayer, dietary supplements, chiropractic care, massage, and acupuncture. However, self-reported use of these treatments was usually for somatic conditions such as headaches, insomnia, obesity, and diabetes rather than for relief of psychological distress.

In addition to herbal remedies, Latino clients frequently seek spiritual advisement from clergy and curandero/as (general practitioners of Mexican folk healing), espiritistas (Puerto Rican faith healers), santeros (Cuban faith healers), yerbistas (herbalists), and sobadores (massage therapists). Curanderismo is a nontraditional healing practice of Latino culture. Culturally bound disorders frequently seen in the Latino community include *susto* (fright), *nervios* (nerves), *mal de ojo* (evil eye), *ataque de nervios* (nervous attack), *bilis* (bile resulting from strong emotion), and embrujado (bewitchment) (Stanford.edu). Symptoms of these previously listed illnesses may include screaming uncontrollably, crying, trembling, verbal or physical aggression, dissociative experiences, seizure-like or fainting episodes, and suicidal gestures (SAMHSA). The curandero/a has advanced supernatural knowledge of the illnesses that the gods use to punish humans, and by mystical power and rituals are able to break the spells of disease that agitate their clients (Padilla et al., 2001). Additionally, traditional clergy members are often consulted for psychological and psycho-somatic symptoms by members of the Latino community.

Latino patients are less likely to receive specialized mental health care for conditions such as depression (Miranda & Matheny, 2000). When compared to evaluations of White patients, providers are less likely to recognize the psychological symptomatology in Latino patients, resulting in fewer clinical diagnoses and less data related to the assessment and treatment of psychological disorders occurring in this population. The rates of depression in Latino populations are estimated to be similar to those of Euro Americans (NAMI). However, Latino patients are less likely to receive prescriptions for depressive symptoms and are usually reluctant to ingest psychotropic medications if they are recommended. Acculturation stress and economic issues seem to contribute to clinical depression in Latino communities. Acculturation stress seems to be associated with country of origin. Mexican immigrants who lived in the United States for fewer than 13 years and Puerto Ricans who resided on the island of Puerto Rico rather than in the United States had lower prevalence rates of depression and other psychiatric disorders than did Mexican Americans who were born in the United States, Mexican immigrants who lived in the United States 13 years or more, or Puerto Ricans who lived on the mainland. These findings imply that the acculturation stress of living in the United States has a tremendous impact on the mental health and well-being of members of Latino populations.

Although the use of adjunctive therapies within the Latino population is believed to be relatively high, there is evidence to suggest that Latino patients believe that conventional medicine is superior to alternative remedies and/or spiritual advisement (Mikhail et al., 2004). However, the cultural norm of *fatalismo,* the belief that one can do nothing to alter fate, may steer Latino patients away from adjunctive therapies (Welch, 2000).

Bibliotherapy, Psychoeducation, and Self-help Groups

There are very few studies that investigate the use of bibliotherapy, psychoeducation, and self-help groups [e.g., Alcoholics Anonymous (AA)] within the Latino community. However, one study (Atkinson et al., 1994) has found that

Mexican American college students perceived AA to be an effective method of self-help in contrast to their Euro American counterparts. In the same study, the perceived effectiveness of AA was inversely related to acculturation.

Web and E-Health Support Groups

There are virtually no studies of web and e-health or support groups that address the use and effectiveness of such therapies in treating Latino populations. Perhaps the impact of socioeconomic status, access to technology, and language issues account for the lack of information regarding Latinos in the realm of web and e-Health. It is also worth noting that less than 1% of all mental health practitioners are Latino in descent and/or bilingual (NAMI), so it is easy to speculate that Latino patients are less likely to participate in support groups.

Physical Activity and Lifestyle Change

The research agenda on the effect of exercise as a complementary treatment has not been adequately examined in Latino patients, but there are several studies that have focused on health care disparities, barriers to exercise, obesity and diabetes control, self-esteem and body image (Guinn et al., 1997; Trevino et al., 2005). One study that investigated self-esteem, body weight, and body distortion in female Latino populations found significant positive relationships between self-esteem and body image and exercise involvement and a significant negative relationship between self-esteem and body fatness (Rutt & Coleman, 2001).

USE OF ADJUNCTIVE THERAPIES BY ASIAN AMERICANS

In reviewing the literature on the use of adjunctive therapies in Asian Americans, it is important to remember that this is a demographic category comprising a variety of cultural traditions and practices. The wide variety of languages is one indication of the magnitude of diversity that is evident within this group. In this community, psychological distress is often expressed as physical symptoms. The dichotomy between Eastern and Western traditions of conceptualizing mental illness could account for the initial differences in treatment-seeking (Chen et al., 2003; Manio & Hall, 1987; Miller, 1990). Korean Americans tend to select alternative forms of medical treatment initially because it is congruent with their personal beliefs (Kim & Chan, 2004). Over 40% of Chinese Americans seeking care in emergency rooms had tried a form of traditional medicine before seeking services at the hospital (Pearl et al., 1995). These trends are indicative of a larger pattern of Asian Americans who first try traditional medicine and utilize Western medical practices as a last resort (Gerber, 1994). The traditional medical practices can range from traditional Chinese medicine, which typically includes acupuncture and qi-gong to faith-based alternatives or Ayurveda, which are the traditional Indian healing practices. Although treatment-seeking practices are related to levels of acculturation, it seems that often Asian Americans are looking toward traditional methods first and Western practices are utilized second, when nothing else seems to have worked.

The prevalence of utilization of alternative treatments is high in this ethnic group. The factors influencing Asian Americans to seek adjunctive therapies are as varied as the cultural traditions that comprise this group. The most widely endorsed reason for Asian Americans seeking alternative therapies was the fact that they were the most congruent with their personal and philosophical beliefs (Pearl et al., 1995). Many Asian Americans embrace a philosophical view that embraces the connection between the mind and the body. In keeping with this philosophy, they prefer treating physical and mental problems in a holistic manner and feel that they are not able to receive this care in traditional Western medical settings (Rao, 2006). Another significant factor for influencing alternative treatment choices was ethnicity and level of acculturation. In keeping with the vast diversity of this group, there is variability in the types of treatment that are sought.

Bibliotherapy, Psychoeducation, and Self-help/Support Groups

Bibliotherapy and Psychoeducation

Bibliotherapy has not been studied extensively in Asian Americans. Preliminary findings indicate that bibliotherapy has been moderately successful in working through identity issues (Schulte, 2005). Identity development and levels of acculturation are associated with development and maintenance of mental distress; so, this is an area that warrants further investigation.

In the wake of the violence at the Virginia Technical Institute in 2007, the dearth in psychoeducation of mental illness in Asian American populations has become apparent. For decades, it has been a widely held belief that mental disorder is not prevalent within the Asian community and they have often been perceived as a "model" minority. Additionally, expressing psychological distress and subsequent treatment is stigmatized (Chen et al., 2003). Taken together, it is clear that there is a need for increased psychoeducation within this community as well as to providers who are likely to work with this group.

Self-help Groups/Support Groups

Currently, there is no empirical evidence to illuminate utilization rates of self-help or support groups in Asian Americans. As mentioned previously, there is a dearth of research in this population that makes it difficult to make conclusive statements. There are some fundamental obstacles that could make it difficult for Asian Americans to fully utilize these sorts of groups. Many Asian cultures revere the involvement and harmony of family and extended family. In this tradition, it sometimes manifests as individuals feeling uncomfortable to disclose personal information to other groups, which could potentially interfere with experiencing the benefits of this type of treatment (Manio & Hall, 1987). Clearly, further research in this area is necessary.

Journaling and Self-Monitoring

There is no literature at the present time documenting the use of self-monitoring in Asian Americans. Journaling has been studied to a greater extent. There are many potential benefits to utilizing of journaling in a therapeutic setting with Asian Americans. The most salient characteristic is that journaling is a private enterprise that could allow an individual to genuinely express themselves without worrying about the judgments of family or therapist. Although there is a gap in the literature that examines the efficacy of journaling or other forms of expressive writing within this population, there is research to suggest that this is an avenue worth pursuing. Keeling & Nielson (2005) examined the use of writing in an Asian Indian population as part of a larger study of the use of narrative within this population. In this sample of women who had recently emigrated from India, it was found that journaling was a positive adjunct to treatment. Journaling allowed for further work on relevant issues in relative privacy. This served to preserve and enhance the therapeutic relationship by allowing clients to "save face" that was ultimately an important part of the therapeutic process.

Physical Activity and Lifestyle Change

Physical health outcomes in Asian Americans are thought to be associated with cultural beliefs and levels of acculturation. The literature indicates that as a result of some traditional beliefs, Asian Americans are less likely to access health care resources. Additionally, differing ideas regarding self-care, the stress of immigration and family obligations and expectation, in the case of many women, can increase risk of health problems (Choudhry et al., 2002). Furthermore, higher levels of acculturation are related to an increase in health-promoting and prevention behaviors. The exact relationship between acculturation and health promotion behaviors needs further research to be fully explicated.

Although this does not fall strictly under the domain of physical health and lifestyle change, many Asian Americans are likely to seek alternative systems of care, either as an alternative or a complement to allopathic care. For practitioners who work with this population, these systems of medicine are important to be aware of. Among the most popular are traditional Chinese medicine and Ayurveda (traditional Indian medicine). Traditional Chinese medicine has existed as the primary form of treatment for the past 3000 years in China and has never been replaced by Western medicine. Consequently, many Chinese immigrants continue to seek those services. This system of medicine is based on the idea that opposite forces in the body (*yin* and *yang*) need to be in balance. When the *yin* and *yang* are unbalanced disease results. There are different ways to rebalance the body, some of which include the use of herbal treatments, acupuncture, or meditation. Ayurveda, which is the traditional form of medicine in India, is based on the belief that three life forces, *kapha*, *pitta*, and *vata*, are present in every living thing. When the life forces are imbalanced, it results in disease. Ayurvedic medicine believes that by making changes in diet and physical activity, and using herbal remedies can reintroduce harmony to the individual thus eradicating disease (Patwardhan et al., 2005).

The prevalence and efficacy of these systems of medicine are unclear. Clinical trials are underway to investigate these areas. In some cases, the severity of the illness can influence what type of services Asian Americans seek, and sometimes, they will seek help from a variety of practitioners. Chinese-, Japanese-, and Korean Americans are more likely to seek traditional healers for severe illnesses, whereas Indian Americans are more likely to seek help from allopathic doctors when an illness is more severe. However, the unity of the mind and body is the underlying principle of Traditional Chinese medicine and Ayurveda, which influences the expectations of caregivers in this population.

Relaxation, Meditation, and Stress Management

Mind/Body interventions focus on helping the individual achieve generalized relaxation. This is done through a repetitive focus on a word or sound and the adoption of a passive attitude toward intrusive thoughts, which is the foundation of yoga. There are different methods through which this can be achieved, and relaxation exercises have been found to be effective with reducing chronic pain or anxiety associated with stressful experiences. It has been found to be effective in reducing anxiety, insomnia, and panic disorders (Mamtani & Cimino, 2002). There are no data that indicate the utilization rates within the Asian American community.

USE OF ADJUNCTIVE THERAPIES BY AMERICAN INDIAN/ALASKAN NATIVES

Although there is a gap in the literature regarding the utilization of adjunctive therapies in Native Americans and Alaska Natives, preliminary indications are that they utilize adjunctive treatments in conjunction with Western medicine. Native Americans and Alaska Natives do not seem to conceptualize health and healing from a disease perspective and prefer to engage in treatments that work with the whole person rather than treating the symptoms. Adjunctive treatments that address many parts of the person seem to be more congruent with personal beliefs.

Bibliotherapy, Psychoeducation, and Self-help Groups/Support Groups

Bibliotherapy

Bibliotherapy is a technique through which the use of books is helpful in gaining insight into personal challenges (Heath et al., 2005). Research has found that bibliotherapy is effective in some cases (for a review of the literature, see Chapter 2). There are no data regarding the effectiveness of bibliotherapy in Native Americans, however, there is reason to believe that it could be especially effective within this group. Traditionally, Native Americans have imparted information through stories, dances, and songs (Hill, 1997), which indicates that it is possible for bibliotherapy could be utilized in a manner that is consistent with cultural practices and traditions.

Psychoeducation

Given the estimated prevalence of psychological distress, it is reasonable to assume that psychoeducational materials would be a useful way to reach a larger number of people. Preliminary research suggests that psychoeducational materials that address historical and cultural forces that impact the mental health of Native Americans were well-received in the community. This is one study and additional research is clearly necessary here to further evaluate the effectiveness.

Self-help Groups/Support Groups

At the present time, there is no empirical evidence to support the effectiveness of self-help groups or support groups within this population. The majority of studies in this area have been conducted to compare the rate at which Native Americans seek support groups in relation to primary care services in relation to substance use issues. Studies have found that Native Americans are likely to seek help in the form of traditional healing or 12-step programs at relatively equal rates. Native Americans are likely to find 12-step programs helpful when they are perceived as being in line with traditional beliefs (Beals et al., 2006).

There is anecdotal evidence that suggests that slight modifications to self-help and support groups can also be effective. In a report published by the Surgeon General (1999), one Vietnam veteran who is of Native American descent discussed how helpful it was to participate in a group that was made up exclusively of Native Americans. He reported feeling more comfortable with the norms surrounding sharing and disclosure than when he participated in a group at the local Veterans' Administration Hospital. This is positive preliminary evidence to suggest that modifications to existing support groups could serve to enhance treatment.

Journaling and Self-Monitoring

There are no data to demonstrate the effectiveness of self-monitoring and journaling within the AI/NA community. It would seem that there are multiple ways in which this can be utilized effectively within this population, but empirical evidence is needed for practitioners to be able to effectively implement these techniques.

Physical Activity and Lifestyle Change

There is increasing evidence to suggest that physical health problems are increasing in Native American populations and will soon reach epidemic proportions. The development and maintenance of these problems can be mediated through lifestyle changes that include modifications to diet and exercise. However, in order to bring about sustained lifestyle change, culturally relevant lifestyle changes must be implemented (Macvicar, 2002). There is preliminary evidence to suggest that culturally relevant prevention and intervention programs are effective in Native American populations. Clearly, further work is required to determine what is the most effective and how to effectively disseminate it within this population.

Relaxation, Meditation, and Stress Management

There are few studies documenting the effectiveness of meditation and relaxation techniques in Native Americans. Anecdotal evidence suggests that meditation and relaxation treatment in conjunction with psychotherapy can enhance the effectiveness of treatment (Khouzam, 2001). Further research in this area is necessary before it is possible to make conclusive statements.

IMPLICATIONS FOR THE FUTURE

The general trend toward increasing utilization of adjunctive therapies is evident within the general population and ethnically diverse populations. Furthermore, demographic information indicates that the US population is diversifying at increasing rates with Latinos and Asian Americans being the fastest growing ethnic groups. Taken together, these trends indicate that being knowledgeable about adjunctive therapies in ethnically diverse populations is important for the culturally aware therapist. The increasing utilization rates of adjunctive treatments provide an exciting opportunity for practitioners to reach a greater number of clients in multiple ways.

Despite these increased opportunities, there are also inherent challenges for the practitioner. A recurring theme throughout this chapter is the lack of empirical evidence within the relevant population. This dearth of information coupled with the well-documented fact that individuals from ethnically diverse backgrounds experience barriers to treatment for physical and mental problems in the United States make it difficult for practitioners to work effectively. Despite these challenges, the impetus is on practitioners to ensure that a lack of cultural knowledge and awareness of adjunctive treatments does not become an additional barrier to quality services.

REFERENCES

Adams, A.S., Trinacty, C.M., Fang, Z., et al. (2007). Medication adherence and racial differences in HbA1c control. *Diabetes*, *56* (Suppl. 1), A318–A318.

American Counseling Association (1995). Code of ethics and standards of practice. Alexandria, VA.

American Diabetes Association (2006). Standards of medical care in diabetes. *Diabetes Care*, *29* (Suppl. 1), S4–S42.

American Heart Association/American Stroke Association (2007). Heart Disease and Stroke Statistics: 2007 Update At-a-Glance.

Arredondo, P., Toporek, R., Jones, J., et al. (1996). Operationalization of the multicultural competencies. *Journal of Multicultural Counseling and Development*, *24*, 42–78.

Atkinson, D.R., Abreu, J., Ortiz-Bush, Y., & Brewer, S. (1994). Mexican American and European American rating of four alcoholism treatment programs. *Hispanic Journal of Behavioral Sciences*, *16*(3), 265–279.

Bae, S.-W. & Kung, W.M. (2000). Family intervention for Asian Americans with a schizophrenic patient in the family. *American Journal of Orthopsychiatry*, *70*(4), 532–541.

Baker, F.M. & Bell, C.C. (1999). Issues in the psychiatric treatment of African Americans. *Psychiatric Services,* 50(3), 362–368.

Banister, N.A., Jastrow, S.T., Hodges, V., et al. (2004). Diabetes self-management training program in a community clinic improves patient outcomes at modest cost. *Journal of the American Diabetic Association,* 104, 807–810.

Barreto, R.M. & Segal, S.P. (2005). Use of mental health services by Asian Americans. *Psychiatric Services,* 56(6), 746–748.

Beals, J., Novins, D.K., & Spicer, P. (2006). Help seeking for substance use problems in two American Indian reservation populations. *Psychiatric Services,* 57(4), 512–520.

Bennett, G.G., Wolin, K.Y., Puleo, E., & Emmons, K.M. (2006). Pedometer-determined physical activity among multiethnic low-income housing residents. *Medicine & Science in Sports & Exercise*, *38*, 768–773.

Berry, T.R. (2005). Black on black education: Personally engaged pedagogy for/by African American pre-service teachers. *The Urban Review*, *37*, 31–48.

Campbell, M.K., Hudson, M.A., Resnicow, K., et al. (2007). Church-based health promotion interventions: Evidence and lessons learned. *Annual Review of Public Health*, *28*, 213–234.

Cantanzaro, A.M., Meador, K.G., Koenig, H.G., et al. (2006). Congregational health ministries: A national study of pastors' views. *Public Health Nursing*, *24*, 6–17.

Chen, J.-P. & Chen, H. (2002). Depressive disorders in Asian American adults. *Western Journal of Medicine*, *176*, 239–244.

Chen, S., Sullivan, N.Y., Lu, Y.E., & Shibusawa, T. (2003). Asian Americans and mental health services: A study of utilization patterns in the 1990s. *Journal of Ethnic and Cultural Diversity in Social Work*, *12*(2), 19–42.

Choudhry, U.K., Jandu, S., Mahal, J., et al. (2002). Health promotion and participatory action research with South Asian women. *Journal of Nursing Scholarship*, *34*(1), 75–81.

Chung, H. (2002). The challenges of providing behavioral treatment to Asian Americans. *Western Journal of Medicine*, *176*, 222–223.

Clayton, A.H. (2005). Prevalence of complementary and alternative medicine use. *Primary Psychiatry*, *12(8)*, 25–35.

Collinge, W., Wentworth, R., & Sabo, S. (2005). Integrating complementary therapies into community mental health practice: An exploration. *The Journal of Alternative and Complementary Medicine*, *11*(3), 569–574.

Cox, C. (1999). Race and caregiving: Patterns of service use by African American and white caregivers of persons with Alzheimer's disease. *Journal of Gerontological Social Work*, *32*, 5–19.

DeCoteau, T., Anderson, J., & Hope, D. (2006). Adapting manualized treatments: Treating anxiety disorders among Native Americans. *Cognitive and Behavioral Practice*, *13*, 304–309.

Drayton-Brooks, S. & White, N. (2004). Health promoting behaviors among African American women with faith-based support. *The ABNF Journal*, *15*, 84–90.

Druss, B.G. & Rosenheck, R.A. (2000). Use of practitioner-based complementary therapies by persons reporting mental conditions in the United States. *Archives of General Psychiatry*, *57*, 708–714.

Duckworth, M.P. (2005). Behavioral health policy and eliminating disparities through cultural competency. In N.A. Cummings, W.T. O'Donohue, & M.A. Cucciare (Eds.), *Universal Healthcare: Readings for Mental Health Professionals*. Reno, NV: Context Press.

Duckworth, M.P. & Iezzi, T. (2006). Recognizing and dealing with cultural influences in psychotherapy. In W.T. O'Donohue (Ed.), *Clinical Strategies for Becoming a Master Psychotherapist.* Boston, MA: Elsevier.

Edwards, L.V. (2006). Perceived social support and HIV/AIDS medication adherence among American women. *Qualitative Health Research, 16*, 679–691.

Ernst, E., Pittler, M.H., Wider, B., & Boddy, K. (2007). Mind-body therapies: Are the trial data getting stronger? *Alternative Therapies, 13*, 62–64.

Fleury, J. & Lee, S.M. (2006). The social ecological model and physical activity in African American women. *American Journal of Community Psychiatry, 37*, 129–140.

Floyd, M., Rohen, N., Shackelford, J.A.M., et al. (2006). Two-year follow-up of bibliotherapy for depressed older adults. *Behavior Modification, 30*, 281–294.

Frieswijk, N., Steverink, N., Buunk, B.P., & Slaets, J.P.J. (2006). The effectiveness of bibliotherapy in increasing self-management ability of slight to moderately frail older people. *Patient Education and Counseling, 61*, 219–227.

Gerber, L. (1994). Psychotherapy with Southeast Asian refugees: Implications for treatment of Western patients. *American Journal of Psychotherapy, 48*(2), 280–293.

Guinn, B., Semper, T., & Jorgensen, L. (1997). Mexican American femaleadolescent self-esteem: The effect of body image, exercise behavior, and body fatness. *Hispanic Journal of Behavioral Sciences, 19*(4), 517–526.

Hays, P.A. (1996). Addressing the complexities of culture and gender in counseling. *Journal of Counseling and Development, 74*, 332–338.

Heath, M.A., Sheen, D., Leavy, D., et al. (2005). Bibliotherapy: A resource to facilitate emotional healing and growth. *School Psychology International, 26*(5), 563–580.

Helms, J.E. & Cook, D.A. (1999). *Using Race and Culture in Counseling and Psychotherapy.* Needham Heights, MA: Allyn & Bacon.

Hill, R.T.G. (1997). Methodological approaches to Native American narrative and the role of performance [Special issue: To hear the eagles cry: Contemporary themes in Native American spirituality. Part III-Historical Reflections]. *American Indian Quarterly, 21*, 111–147.

Honda, K. & Jacobson, J.S. (2005). Use of complementary and alternative medicine among United States adults: The influences of personality, coping strategies and social support. *Preventive Medicine, 40*, 46–53.

International Agency for Research on Cancer (2002). *Weight Control and Physical Activity.* Oxford University Press.

Iwasama, G.Y. & Hilliard, K.M. (1999). Depression and anxiety among Asian American elders: A review of the literature. *Clinical Psychology Review, 19*(3), 343–357.

Iwata, N. & Buka, S. (2002). Race/ethnicity and depressive symptoms: A cross cultural/ethnic comparison in university students in East Asia, North and South America. *Social Science and Medicine, 55*(12), 2242–2252.

Keeling, M.L. & Nielson, L.R. (2005). Indian women's experience of a narrative intervention using art and writing. *Contemporary Family Therapy, 27*(3), 435–452.

Keith, V.M., Kronenfeld, J.J., Rivers, P.A., & Liang, S. (2005). Assessing the effects of race and ethnicity on use of complementary and alternative therapies in the USA. *Ethnicity and Health, 10*(1), 19–32.

Kessler, R.C., McGonagle, K.A., Zhao, S., et al. (1994). Lifetime and 12-month prevalence of DSM-III-R disorders in the United States. *Archives of General Psychiatry, 51*, 8–19.

Khouzam, H.R. (2001). Religious meditation and its effect on posttraumatic stress disorder in a Korean war veteran. *Clinical Gerontologist, 22*(3–4), 125–131.

Kim, M., Han, H.-R., & Kim, K.B. (2002). The use of traditional and western medicine among the Korean-American elderly. *Journal of Community Health: The Publication for Health Promotion and Disease Prevention, 27*(2), 109–120.

Kim, J. & Chan, M.M. (2004). Factors influencing preferences for alternative medicine by Korean Americans. *The American Journal of Chinese Medicine, 32*(2), 321–329.

Kramer, E.J., Kwong, K., Lee, E., & Chung, H. (2002). Culture and Medicine: Cultural factors influencing the mental health of Asian Americans. *Western Journal of Medicine, 176*, 227–231.

Laken, M.A., Orourke, K., Duffy, N.G., et al. (2004). Use of the internet for health information by African-Americans with modifiable risk factors for cardiovascular disease. *Telemedicine Journal & E-Health, 10*, 304–310.

Lechner, S.C., Antoni, M.H., Lydston, D., et al. (2003). Cognitive-behavioral interventions improve quality of life in women with AIDS. *Journal of Psychosomatic Research, 54*, 253–261.

Lin, K.-M. & Cheung, F. (1999). Mental health issues for Asian Americans. *Psychiatric Services, 50*(6), 774–780.

Lidren, D.M, Watkins, P.L, Gould, R.A, et al. (1994). A comparison of bibliotherapy and group therapy in the treatment of panic disorder. *Journal of Consulting and Clinical Psychology, 62*, 865–869.

Loeb, S.J. (2006). African American older adults coping with chronic health conditions. *Journal of Transcultural Nursing, 17*, 139–147.

Lovell, K., Cox, D., Garvey, R., et al. (2003). Agoraphobia: nurse therapist-facilitated self-help manual. *Issues and Innovations in Nursing Practice, 43*, 623–630.

Mackenzie, E.R., Taylor, L., Bloom, B.S., et al. (2003). Ethnic minority use of complementary and alternative medicine (CAM): A probability survey of CAM utilizers. *Alternative Therapies, 9*(4), 50–56.

Macvicar, D.W. (2002). Self-reported physical activity and intention to exercise as predictors of health outcomes in Native American populations across Montana. *Dissertation Abstracts International: Section B, Sciences and Engineering, 63*(5-B), 2592.

Mamtani, R. & Cimino, A. (2002). A primer of complementary and alternative medicine and its relevance in the treatment of mental health problems. *Psychiatric Quarterly, 73*(4), 367–381.

Manio, E.B. & Hall, R.R. (1987). Asian family traditions and their influence in transcultural health delivery. *Children's Health Care, 15*(3), 172–177.

Marshall, S.J., Jones, D.A., Ainsworth, B.E., Reis, J.P., Levy, S.S., Macera, C.A. (2007). Race/ethnicity, social class, and leisure-time physical inactivity. *Medical and Science in Sports & Exercise, 39*, 44–51.

Mataix-Cols, D. & Marks, I.M. (2006). Self-help with minimal therapist contact for obsessive-compulsive disorder: A review. *European Psychiatry, 21*, 75–80.

Michalec, B. (2005). Exploring the multidimensional benefits of breast cancer support groups. *Journal of Psychosocial Oncology, 23*, 159–179.

Michalec, B., van Willigen, M., Wilson, K., et al. (2004). The race gap in support group participation by breast cancer survivors. *Evaluation Review, 28*, 123–143.

Miller, J.K. (1990). Use of traditional Korean health care by Korean immigrants to the United States. *Social Science Research, 75*, 38–43.

Mikhail, N., Wali, S., & Ziment, I. (2004). Use of alternative medicine among Hispanics. [Electronic version]. *The Journal of Alternative and Complementary Medicine, 10*(5), 851–859.

Miranda, A. & Matheny, K. (2000). Socio-psychological predictors of acculturative stress among latino adults. [Electronic version]. *Journal of Mental Health Counseling, 22*(4), 306–318.

Mitchell, M.D., Hargrave, G.L., Collins, M.H., et al. (2006). Coping variables that mediate the relation between intimate partner violence and mental health outcomes among low-income African American women. *Journal of Clinical Psychology, 62*, 1503–1520.

National Alliance on Mental Illness. Retrieved July 31, 2007 from "http://www.nami.org" www.nami.org.

National Center for Health Statistics (2007). Healthy People 2010 Nutrition and Overweight Progress Review. http://www.cdc.gov/nchs/about/otheract/hpdata2010/focusareas/fa19-nutrition.htm

Neighbors, H.W., Braithewaite, R.L., & Thompson, E. (1995). Health promotion and African-Americans: From personal empowerment to community action. *American Journal of Health Promotion, 9*, 281–287.

Padilla, R., Gomez, V., Biggerstaff, S., & Mehler, P. (2001). Use of curanderismo ina public healthcare system. [Electronic version]. *Archives of Internal Medicine, 161*(10), 1336–1340.

Parham, T. & Austin, N.L. (1994). Career development and African Americans: A contextual reappraisal using the Nigrescence construct. *Journal of Vocational Behavior*, *44*, 139–154.

Patwardhan, B., Warude, D., Pushpangadan, P., & Bhatt, N. (2005). Ayurveda and traditional Chinese medicine: A comparative overview. *Evidence Based Complementary and Alternative Medicine*, *2*(4), 465–473.

Pearl, W.S., Leo, P., & Tsang, W.O. (1995). Use of Chinese therapies among Chinese patients seeking emergency department care. *Annals of Emergency Medicine*, *26*(6), 735–738.

Peterson, J., Atwood, J.R., & Yates, B. (2002). Key elements for church-based health promotion programs: Outcome-based literature review. *Public Health Nursing*, *19*, 401–411.

Rao, D. (2006). Choice of medicine and hierarchy of resort to different health alternatives among Asian Indian migrants in a metropolitan city in the USA. *Ethnicity and Health*, *11*(2), 153–167.

Reeves, T. & Stace, J.M. (2005). Improving patient access and choice: Assisted bibliotherapy for mild to moderate stress/anxiety in primary care. *Journal of Psychiatric and Mental Health Nursing*, *12*, 341–346.

Rutt, C. & Coleman, K. (2001). The evaluation of a measurement model for the bodyimage questionnaire and the eating attitudes test in a hispanic population. *Hispanic Journal of Behavioral Sciences*, *23*(2), 153–170.

Sarkar, U., Fisher, L., & Schillinger, D. (2006). Is self-efficacy associated with diabetes self-management across race/ethnicity and health literacy. *Diabetes Care*, *29*, 823–829.

Schneider, R.H., Alexander, C.N., Salerno, J. et al. (2005). Stress reduction in the prevention and treatment of cardiovascular disease in African Americans: A Review of Controlled Research on the Transcendental Meditation Program. *Journal of Social Behavior & Personality*, *17*, 159–180.

Schneider, R.H., Castillo-Richmond, A., Alexander, C.N., et al. (2001). Behavioral treatment of hypertensive heart disease in African Americans: Rationale and design of a randomized controlled trial. *Behavioral Medicine*, *27*, 83–95.

Schulte, R. (2005). The effects of a biracial identity development program on feelings of alienation in biracial children. *Dissertation Abstracts International: Section B, Sciences and Engineering*, *65*(12-B), 6539.

Sharma, M., Sargent, L., & Stacy, R. (2005). Predictors of leisure-time physical activity among African American women. *American Journal of Health Behavior*, *29*, 352–359.

Sciarra, D. (1999) *Multiculturalism in counseling*. Itasca, IL: F.E. Peacock. Stanford University (n.d.) Retrieved from http://www.stanford.edu

Snowden, L.R. (2001). Barriers to effective mental health services for African Americans. *Mental Health Services Research*, *3*(4), 181–187.

Snowden, L.R. & Yamada, A. (2005). Cultural differences in access to care. *Annual Review of Clinical Psychology*, *1*, 143–166.

Steward, R.J. (2001). Black women and white women in groups: Suggestions for minority-sensitive group services on university campuses. *Journal of Counseling & Development*, *72*, 39–41.

Sue, D.W. & Sue, D. (1990). *Counseling the culturally different: Theory and Practice*. New York: John Wiley & Sons, Inc.

Sue, S., Zane, N., & Young, K. (1994). Research on psychotherapy on culturally diverse populations. In A. Bergin & S. Garfield (Eds.), *Handbook of Psychotherapy ad Behavior Change* (4th Ed.) (pp. 783–817). New York: Wiley.

Suen, L.-J. & Morris, D.L. (2006). Depression: Focus on Taiwanese American older adults. *Journal of Gerontological Nursing*, *32*(4), 28–36.

Tackey, N.D. (2001). Eliminating bias in performance management [Electronic version]. *British Journal of Administrative Management*, *27*, 12–18.

Taylor, J.S. (2003). Confronting "culture" in medicine's "culture of no culture". *Academic Medicine* *78*(6), 555–559.

Tobin, K.E., Hua, W., Costenbader, E.C., & Latkin, C.A. (2007). The association between change in social network characteristics and non-fatal overdose: Results from the SHIELD study in Baltimore, MD, USA. *Drug and Alcohol Dependence*, *87*, 63–68.

Trevino, R.P., Hernandez, A.E., Yin, Z., et al. (2005). Impact of bienestar health program on physical fitness in low-income mexican-american children. *Hispanic Journal of Behavioral Science*, *27*(1), 120–132.

U.S. Department of Health and Human Services. (2001). Mental health: Culture, race and ethnicity – A supplement to mental health: A report to the Surgeon General. Rockville, MD: U.S. Department of Health and Human Services, Substance Abuse and Mental Health Services Administration, Center for Mental Health Services.

van Kesteren, N.M.C., Kok, G., Hospers, H.J., et al. (2006). Systematic development of a self-help motivational enhancement intervention to promote sexual health in HIV positive men who have sex with men. *Aid Patient Care and STDs*, *20*, 858–875.

Webb, M., Beckstead, J., Meininger, J., & Robinson, S. (2006). Stress management for African American women with elevated blood pressure: A pilot study. *Biological Research for Nursing*, *7*, 187–196.

Welch, V.L., Oster, N.V., Gazmararian, J.A., et al. (2006). Impact of diabetes disease management program by race and ethnicity. *Disease Management and Health Outcomes*, *14*, 245–252.

Welch, T. (2000). Culture and the patient-physician relationship: Achieving cultural competency in health care. [Electronic version]. *Journal of Pediatrics*, *136*, 14–26.

Whitfield, K.E., Weidner, G., Clark, R., & Anderson, N.B. (2002). Sociodemographic diversity and behavioral medicine. *Journal of Consulting and Clinical Psychology*, *70*(3), 463–481.

Williams, P. & Barton, E. (2004). Successful support groups for African American caregivers. *Generations*, *27*, 81–83.

Wolin, K., Colditz, G., Stoddard, A.M., et al. (2006). Acculturation and physical activity in a working class multiethnic population. *Preventive Medicine*, *42*, 266–272.

Yamatsu, K., Adachi, Y., Kunitsuka, K., & Yamagami, T. (2004). Self-monitoring and bibliotherapy in brief behavior therapy for poor sleepers by correspondence. *Sleep and Biological Rhythms*, *2*, 73–75.

Young, D.R. & Stewart, K.J. (2006). A church-based physical activity intervention for African American women. *Family & Community Health*, *29*, 103–117.

15

ADJUNCTIVE TREATMENTS FOR RURAL POPULATIONS

DENNIS F. MOHATT, CANDICE M. TATE, AND MIMI MCFAUL

Western Interstate Commission for Higher Education (WICHE), Mental Health Program

MENTAL HEALTH IN RURAL AMERICA

Mental health treatment in rural America has received little attention over the past 40 years. Not only was rural America perceived to be an idyllic place with little strife, it was also assumed that urban-developed treatments would naturally transplant to rural settings. These myths serve to mask the realities that rural families face on a daily basis. It is a challenge for systems of mental health care to serve their spread-out populations with limited resources using whatever materials, treatments, and professionals are available.

Designing, implementing, and measuring a mental health treatment according to rigorous definitions is beyond the means of most rural mental health providers, even if they are lucky enough to have the minimum number of patients required for some treatments (i.e., groups). As a result, most practitioners take what they know and adapt it to their populations in the best way feasible. Most appear effective; however, without empirical data it is difficult to ascertain treatment impacts. In many cases, these clinical and adjunctive treatments do not have the necessary evidence-based components. Some, however, show great promise and with appropriate attention and support, are on the way to becoming full-fledged evidence-based practices (EBPs) and adjunctive treatments.

There are three sections to this chapter. The first section will review the various definitions of rural versus urban areas, epidemiologic facts and trends, and the prevalence of mental health disorders in rural areas of the United States as well as briefly address some of the resulting clinical, social, and policy implications. The second section will present a discussion of the three major barriers to rural mental health services. The third and final section of the chapter will discuss evidence-based adjunctive treatments (EBATs) and the issues surrounding the development of an EBAT in rural communities. In addition, we will present a hypothetical implementation of a telehealth system and address cultural issues.

WHAT IS "RURAL"?

> Rural America comprises 2,305 counties, contains 83 percent of the nation's land, and is home to just over 60 million Americans, 25 percent of this country's total population (McCabe & Macnee, 2002).

There are a myriad of ways to define "Rural," using different subjective and objective measures, different criterion, and different analyses. There is a general stereotype of Rural America as being simple farmland, separated physically from the bustle and purposeful activity of urban areas. According to the Economic Research Service Website, less than 10% of rural populations live on farms and people in rural areas are engaged in a wide range of activities. Many organizations have attempted to define rural with varying success. Each definition utilized has a profound impact on the economic, political, educational, and funding realities of rural and frontier populations and each paints a potentially different picture. Researchers and policy makers need to be aware of which definition is used and how it affects their work.

Three major Federal definitions are used for most research and practical purposes:

- *Department of Commerce's Bureau of the Census* roughly defines rural as being a population cluster of less than 2500 people with the density of the surrounding areas taken into account. For example, the Census will designate a small town of 2000 people with an adjacent suburb of 800 people as an urban cluster with a population of 2800. Considering a town of 5000 people with 500 outlying residents spread out over a vast area, the Census will classify the 500 as rural and the urban population would be just 4500.
- *White House's Office of Management and Budget (OMB)* uses a complex system for defining "core-based statistical areas" and divides the population into three types: Metropolitan areas (50 000 or more), micropolitan areas (at least 10 000 and less than 50 000), and noncore counties (everything not classified as micro or metro). OMB will classify a micro area as metro if more than 25% of its workers commute to a nearby metro area or if metro commuters perform more than 25% of work in the microcounty.
- *Department of Agriculture Economic Research Service* uses rural–urban continuum codes, ranging from 1 to 9. Rural (nonmetro) is anything between 4 and 9, where a designation score of 4 equals an urban population of 20 000 or more, adjacent to a metro area, and a score of 9 equals completely rural or urban population of fewer than 2500, not adjacent to a metro area.

These three definitions can create vastly different pictures of rural America. For example, in 2000 according to the *OMB* definition, rural America comprised 17% (49 million) of the population, compared with 21% (59 million) by the *US Census* definition and 48.8 million by the *USDA/ERS* definition. In some cases, it is necessary to break down the definition of rural a step further to emphasize "frontier" areas. Frontier appears to have a consistent definition of areas with a population density of less than seven people per square mile. Figure 15.1 illustrates the population density of the United States per square mile and the vast sections of the United States that can be considered frontier and rural.[1]

The President's New Freedom Commission on Mental Health, Subcommittee on Rural Issues (NFC-SRI, 2004) recommended the adoption of a single definition that was precise enough to capture the diversity of rural America. This would enable different state and federal agencies to target monies and resources to address specific rural needs. A number of publications present extensive discussions of the implications of this array of definitions on health and human services programs (Ciarlo et al., 1996; Hewitt, 1989; Wagenfeld et al., 1994).

PREVALENCE OF MENTAL DISORDERS AND SUBSTANCE ABUSE

Current prevalence rates show that mental health issues affect approximately 20% of the US population each year (Kessler et al., 1994). The National Institute of Mental Health (NIMH) reports 26.2% of Americans have a mental illness, which equates to approximately 57.7 million people. In a review of studies investigating the prevalence of psychiatric disorders in *rural* primary care settings, Sears and colleagues (2003) found that 34–41% of patients had a mental health disorder. Hauenstein and Boyd (1994) found that 41% of their sample of rural women reported depressive symptoms, which contrasts with the typical urban prevalence rates of 13–20%.

According to the National Survey on Drug Use and Health (Office of Applied Studies, 2005), the rate of substance abuse was lower in rural areas than in urban areas. The rates were 6.9% in rural areas and 8.4% in urban areas. The survey breaks down nonmetropolitan areas even further and reveals that urbanized counties had a rate of 7.8%, less urbanized counties had a rate of 6.5%, and completely rural counties had a rate of 5.1%.

These data appear to match a historical trend in substance use being more common in urban areas; however, recent statistical analyses reported in a 2007 report by the National Advisory Committee on Rural Health and Human Services found surprising differences. When the data were broken down into drug categories, several had significantly heavier rural use, in particular methamphetamine, OxyContin, tobacco, and alcohol.

[1] In-depth discussion of these three definitions can be found at: http://www.raconline.org/info_ guides/ruraldef/

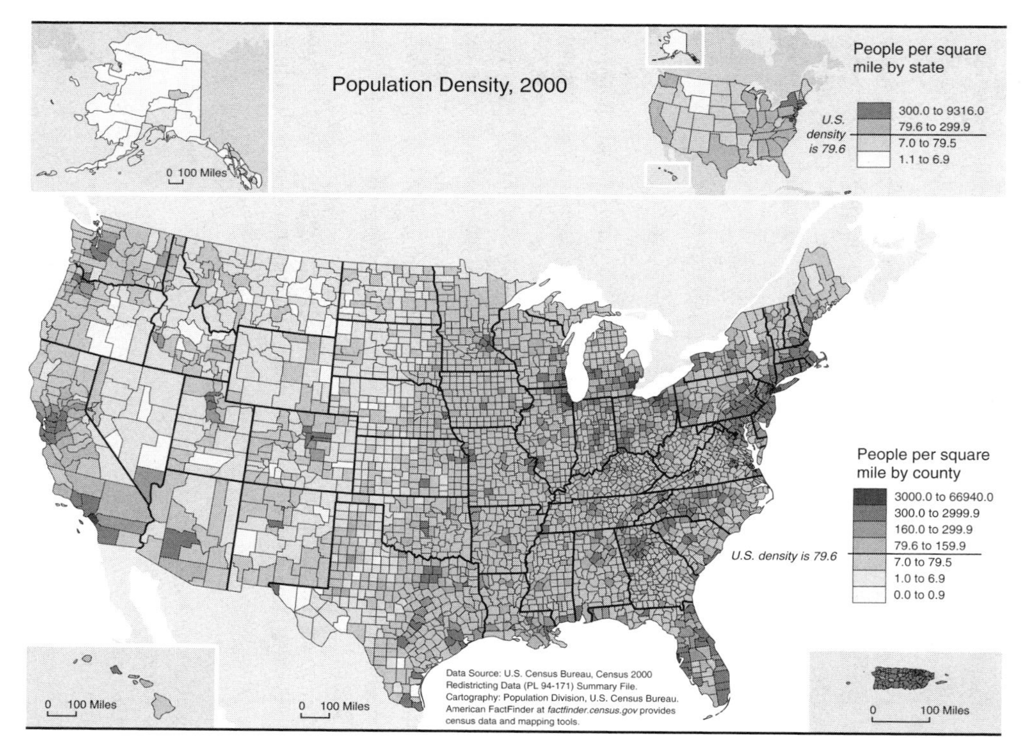

FIGURE 15.1 One can easily see by looking at the map that the majority of the Western states have vast areas with less than seven people per square mile

Results of studies of seriously mentally ill individuals indicate that rural residents have poorer outcomes (e.g., reliance on inpatient services, increased symptom severity) when compared with urban residents, especially if there are cooccurring substance abuse issues (Fischer et al., 1996; Rost et al., 1998). Rural families often experience stress because of the high poverty rates, high unemployment rates, and low educational opportunities (Champion et al., 2002; Human & Wasem, 1991). Women living in rural areas are particularly affected by these barriers of rural culture and are at a higher risk for domestic abuse (Boyd, 2000; Champion, 1999; Champion et al., 2002; Dimmitt & Davila, 1995). Because of the small size of rural communities and a lack of anonymity, it may be very difficult for women to leave abusive or dangerous relationships. Compounding this difficulty is a lack of mental health and other community services.

Despite all these facts, prevalence is still the science of estimation. However, we can safely say that regardless of this varying information on prevalence, the major barriers to effective mental health treatment remain the same. It is not a question of which population develops more symptoms, but rather, which one is healthier due to receiving adequate, appropriate, quality treatment. The overall numbers of individuals with serious mental illnesses may be small (Gale & Deprez, 2003), but these individuals often live across vast areas, making coordinated service delivery challenging. As a result, rural communities must address an equivalent prevalence of serious mental illnesses and clinical complexities with fewer resources to do so.

There is a general perception in our culture that rural areas are homogeneous. However, there is actually a rich diversity among rural communities in terms of geography and culture. In this sense, we use adjunctive treatments to help traditional therapy match the unique history, culture, and qualities of different communities (Mulder et al., 2003). Culturally, rural communities may rely much more on institutions outside of the traditional mental health system for mental health issues (Sears et al., 2003). Paraprofessionals, peer supports, natural healers, community leaders can be community assets in the pursuit of a mentally healthy community (Mulder et al., 2003). However, there has been little work done on how effective they are (i.e., evidence-based). Rural barriers are presented in the next section as information for professionals exploring adjunctive treatment in rural areas for mental health.

BARRIERS TO MENTAL HEALTH TREATMENT IN RURAL COMMUNITIES

Historically, rural America has lacked the necessary political influence and resources to promote effective rural mental health policy agendas (Ahr & Halcomb, 1985; Danbom, 1995; Dyer, 1997; Kimmel, 1992). Several Federal projects including Rural Healthy People 2010, the President's New Freedom Commission, Subcommittee on Rural Issues, and the 1990 Surgeon General's report on Mental Health have called attention to the existence of underserved mental health issues in rural communities and the need for stronger policies and increased resources.

Demographics, economics, and cultural values have a dynamic impact upon mental health and mental health care. The prevalence and incidence of adults with severe mental illnesses and children with serious emotional disturbances are not significantly different in rural and urban areas. What differs in rural America is the experience of individuals with mental illnesses and their families (Wagenfeld et al., 1994). Numerous barriers contribute to disparities in access to care, and utilization of services and treatment of mental health disorders for rural residents.

Fox et al. (1995) and the NFC-SRI (2004) indicate that obstacles to service use generally fall into three categories: Availability, accessibility, and acceptability. These variables led rural residents with mental health needs to enter care later in the course of their disease than do their urban peers, enter care with more serious, persistent, and disabling symptoms, and require more expensive and intensive treatment response (Wagenfeld et al., 1994).

Availability refers to the presence or absence of services and service providers. Accessibility refers to whether people can reach the services they need and their ability to pay for services. Acceptability indicates a person's attitude to mental health issues, willingness to seek services, and enter treatment.

AVAILABILITY

There is clear evidence that the availability of mental health services and the number of mental health providers in rural areas is severely inadequate. According to the National Advisory Committee on Rural Health (2007), of the 3075 rural counties in the United States, 55% had no practicing psychologists, psychiatrists, or social workers (NFC-SRI, 2004). It is often difficult to recruit and keep professionals in rural areas. In many areas, the number of mental health professionals is actually decreasing (Kane & Ennis, 1996), further exacerbating the issue of limited core services, such as case management, inpatient service, crisis response, and continuity of care (Kane & Ennis, 1996; Rohland & Rohrer, 1998; Shelton & Frank, 1995). Although there have been government subsidized programs (e.g., student loan repayment), they have only had a minimal effect in solving the mental health workforce shortage in rural areas. Lower salaries and a more limited range of social and other outlets may be disincentives to move to such areas or motivators to return to urban centers.

The availability of specialty mental health services (e.g., neuropsychology, geriatric) is even lower than that of general mental health services. Most specialty mental health services are available through larger centers or locally by periodic visits made by providers (Wagenfeld et al., 1994). Rural areas also contain fewer hospital-based inpatient and outpatient services for both psychiatric and substance abuse (Hartley et al., 1999). Often when inpatient care facilities release individuals to the community, there are few social services and rehabilitation agencies to provide follow-up care.

Primary care physicians and other general medical practitioners are often the first-line mental health providers for rural residents. Of those clients who do receive treatment in rural areas, approximately 40% receive care from a mental health specialist and 45% from a general medical practitioner (Regier et al., 1993). However, primary care physicians may not be adequately trained to identify and treat mental illness and behavioral disorders (Ivey et al., 1998; Little et al., 1998; Susman et al., 1995). In addition to training concerns, primary care physicians may also lack the time, training, and resources to diagnose mental health disorders adequately.

Although there has been increased national attention and support for EBPs, there have been only minor efforts to increase workforce development activities to enable rural mental health providers and systems to initiate such practices. There has been a steady decline in training programs that target rural mental health professionals (NFC-SRI, 2004; Wagenfeld et al., 1994).

ACCESSIBILITY

Despite comparable prevalence rates for mental disorders among rural and urban residents, rural residents are much less likely to have access to services or providers (Lambert & Agger, 1995). There are three significant components of access to mental health services for rural residents: Knowledge, transportation, and financing. The following paragraphs will briefly expand upon these issues.

KNOWLEDGE

An essential element of access is knowing when one needs care and where and what care options are available to address needs. In both respects, the rural experience differs from the urban one. Mohatt and Kirwan (1995) found that rural residents lacked an awareness of the need for mental health care, which leads to seeking care later in the course of their disorders. Consumers noting "they couldn't go because they didn't know," believe public education/marketing efforts should be among the top priorities for enhancing the rural mental health care system (Ralph & Lambert, 1999). Many outreach interventions in rural areas have failed to convince mentally ill individuals that they need to seek care (Fox et al., 1999).

TRANSPORTATION

The ability to travel to mental health services and to pay for those services if accessed is a significant barrier for rural Americans (NFC-SRI, 2004). Transportation barriers for people living in rural communities include the lack of personal transportation to travel to service providers, geographic barriers, and limited, inefficient, or inconvenient public transportation (Schauer & Weaver, 1993; the United States). In addition, the use of catchment areas can complicate access to services for rural residents. The catchment area system may require individuals to seek services in an area that they do not usually frequent because of the allocation of funding streams (Mulder et al., 2003). Rural consumers and families must often travel hundreds of miles weekly to access care available only in larger communities that serve as "regional centers of trade."

FINANCING

Inability to pay further hinders accessibility to mental health services, because of either insufficient insurance coverage or high copayments for appointments (Zevenbergen & Buckwalter, 1991). Of the people living in rural areas who do have health insurance, many do not have comprehensive benefits and do not have coverage for psychotherapy (NIMH, 2000). Many rural residents are self-employed or work for small businesses and, thus, may not have employer-based health insurance. As a result, more residents in rural areas pay out-of-pocket for basic primary care services (Hartley & Gale, 2003). Approximately one-fourth of the rural poor qualify for Medicaid, compared with 43% of low-income urban residents. When Medicare and Medicaid only partially reimburse health care costs, the remaining fees may be too expensive for some rural residents. In addition, rural programs often operate in areas with limited financial resources to leverage as matching funds for other grant support (NFC-SRI, 2004).

ACCEPTABILITY

Stigma, cultural beliefs, and values hinder the acceptability of mental health services in rural areas (Intermill & Rathbone-McCuan, 1991). Rural residents tend to value self-reliance and view help-seeking behavior in a more negative light than do urban residents (Rost et al., 2002). According to Rost et al. (1993), the more negative the labeling of rural individuals struggling with depression, the less likely they are to seek treatment. In addition, belief in self-reliance and limited anonymity combine to limit more significantly a rural person's likelihood of seeking services.

On the provider side, Roberts et al. (1999) described how rural caregivers face serious clinical ethical dilemmas every day. Rural clinicians commonly provide care without optimal supports, services, and safeguards for their patients. It is necessary at times to ration care; to provide care outside of their usual areas of expertise and competence; to deal with patients' "noncompliance" related to access problems; to respond to complaints about colleagues' impairments; and to make complex clinical decisions about reproductive, end-of-life and quality-of-life issues without the benefit of specialists.

Care requires addressing patients' potential for self-harm and violence; dealing with the heightened social stigma associated with mental disorders; protecting vulnerable patients from potential abuse or exploitation; and grappling with care planning for individuals with impaired decision-making capacity. These ethical issues are often more acute in rural or isolated health care settings primarily because usual practices to ensure ethical conduct are narrowed by limited health care resources, such as a scarcity of providers leading to potential for dual relationships and practicing outside the scope of training.

Mental health providers in rural areas need an understanding of and appreciation for cultural similarities and differences within, among, and between groups [National Rural Health Association (NRHA), Issue Paper, 1999]. A survey of rural mental health outreach programs by the National Association for Rural Mental Health (NARMH) found that even the best programs felt unprepared to meet the cultural and clinical needs of recent immigrants to rural areas (Lambert et al., 2001; NFC-SRI, 2004). Many ethnic minority individuals are unable to access providers who are of similar ethnic or cultural background, speak their native language, or are knowledgeable about their particular culture (Martin, 1997; NFC-SRI, 2004; U.S. Department of Health and Human Services, 2001). Because of this barrier, ethnic minority individuals may be more hesitant to enter treatment based on fear that the provider may not understand their culture and traditions.

Increasing educational campaigns and enhancing social and professional network referrals may reduce the stigma against mental disorders and encouraging individuals to seek treatment when needed (Kenkel, 2003). Understanding and utilizing the work of indigenous healers or other natural supports could be particularly helpful in this regard (Buckwalter, 1992; Neese et al., 1999). A more in-depth review of cultural populations and issues is presented in the last section.

SUMMARY

The mental health needs of rural Americans are vast, and it is beginning to be recognized at the Federal level that implementation of adequate mental health services in rural areas is a critical area of focus. Rural mental health has emerged as a priority area for policy makers, mental health professionals, and rural community-based service providers. The literature on mental health in rural communities clearly defines areas of unmet need for individuals with mental health issues including a lack of availability of services, a lack of access to these services, and a lack of acceptability by rural residents because of the ever-present stigma around mental illness.

EVIDENCE-BASED ADJUNCTIVE TREATMENTS IN RURAL POPULATIONS

Most public mental health programs and services in rural areas stem from urban models, experiences and research, and are applied with unsupported modifications to rural communities (Beeson et al., 1998; Bergland, 1988; Gamm, 2002; Larson et al., 1993; Mohatt, 2000; NFC-SRI, 2004). Over time, it becomes evident that policies and programs designed for urban mental health services often are not appropriate or feasible for rural mental health services. Mental health professionals are generally trained with urban-centered standards that may not directly apply to rural communities (Wagenfeld & Buffum, 1983), using EBPs[2] that have little relation to the conditions in which they were initially validated. This violates the fidelity of the original measure. Fidelity refers to the degree of implementation of the critical ingredients of an EBP, based on the underlying principles and methods of that EBP (Bond, webpage).[3] Adhering to and measuring fidelity gives the implementers of an EBP a better chance of achieving desired client outcomes (validity) in the new application. If they make changes to the critical ingredients of the implementation or structure of the program, then the original reliability and validity data are less applicable and may not produce the desired results.

Because general public awareness of the difference between rural and urban settings is relatively new, there has not been adequate time, money, or system resources for the development and testing of EBPs specifically for rural populations. Compounding limited resources is the fact that adhering to the established critical ingredients of an urban EBP in rural areas is often not feasible because of differing population sizes, cultures, and geography. These barriers closely parallel the mental health barriers discussed in the previous section.

It is critical to be aware that mental health services in rural areas cannot achieve certain economies of scale, and some EBPs are inefficient to deliver unless there is a critical mass of patients (e.g., assertive community treatment). In addition, fidelity can be difficult to achieve with severe workforce shortages and other availability barriers as discussed previously. The President's Commission recommends the judicious adaptation of EBPs through dissemination and demonstration projects. This recommendation is buttressed by the recent Institute of Medicine (IOM; 2005) report, which endorses using demonstration projects in rural communities, as such locations are smaller and have unique characteristics. Methods for introducing EBPs into service delivery systems include educating clinicians and consumers about the short- and long-term benefits of EBPs, support and promotion by leadership, and establishment of reimbursement policies requiring the use of EBPs.

[2] "Evidence-based practices are interventions for which there is consistent scientific evidence showing that they improve client outcomes." (Drake et al., 2001).

[3] Introduction to the Evidence-Based Practice Fidelity Scales (http://ebp.networkofcare.org/definitions/index.cfm?pageName=DefsFidelity).

Another critical point to remember in adoption of urban treatments is that it is essential to incorporate and better capture the unique properties of rural communities into research. Rural context and experience needs to ground rural mental health research. Although traditional randomized clinical research allows for causal relationships of factors that influence change, qualitative methods (e.g., ethnographic, process analyses) can more fully demonstrate participant and community perceptions and experiences (Anthony et al., 2003). Qualitative methodology (e.g., correlational and quasi-experimental) can be used to guide the development of studies using more traditional research methods (Anthony et al., 2003). It is important that the quantitative and qualitative research methods employed are complementary and not duplicative (Anthony et al., 2003; Office of Behavioral and Social Sciences Research, 2001).

Despite these barriers, rural communities have not been discouraged. Innovative programs offer new designs for services (Mohatt & Kirwan, 1995). Newer technology, such as telemental health, may improve rural access to expertise from urban professionals (Britain, 1996; LaMendola, 2000; Smith & Allison, 1998). Internet access, videoconferencing, and various computer applications offer an opportunity to enhance the quality of care in rural mental health services. Numerous rural practices are showing strong ability to produce specific clinical outcomes, but have not yet gathered the evidence needed to be an established EBP. Adjunctive therapies appear to be following the same pattern. There are certainly promising adjunctive treatments for rural communities, but part of the problem is that we do not know or have a way to chronicle those specific treatments for rural communities. It is important to note that there are no evidence-based rural EBP adjunctive treatments but that rural service providers do often use adjunctive treatments to enhance their service capacity.

TELEMENTAL HEALTH: MENTAL HEALTH CARE FROM A DISTANCE

According to the Office of Rural Health Policy (1997), telemental health is one of the five most common applications for telemedicine in rural hospitals. In a healthcare environment that is technology-oriented, providers and patients are recognizing the benefits of telemental health services. Technology has the potential to decrease the gap in services by increasing education, support, and connectedness between the client and the provider. Health care providers are leveraging the power of video networks to link patients, specialists, and clinicians, thus extending the reach of healthcare to rural regions (Graham, 1996). Due to the use of telemental health, patients experience lower out-of-pocket costs, less travel, and shorter wait times as they receive medical care.

Telemedicine is also useful for purposes other than therapy including case management, medication management, psychiatric consultations, and psychiatric referrals (Rost et al., 2002). Evaluations of provider–patient encounters through interactive two-way video have generally demonstrated that the reliability of psychiatric assessment is comparable with that of face-to-face interviews (Baer et al., 1995, 1997; Baigent et al., 1997; Doniger et al., 1986; Rost et al., 2002; Zarate et al., 1997).

Despite this glowing vision of the future, a recent review and survey of current grantees under the Federal Office for the Advancement of Telehealth (LaMendola et al., 2002) noted that the majority listed mental health as an area of service delivery. However, closer examination found that telehealth mental health care was a major component of less than a dozen projects, and few noted any formal link to the systems of mental health care. Frequently, hospital and primary care networks organize these projects around existing medical services that may lack strong collaborative traditions with the mental health systems of care.

More importantly, the study also found little data on telehealth mental health care performance beyond consumer satisfaction surveys and process measures. Proponents have held forth telehealth mental health care as a significant tool in improving the chronic lack of access to mental health services among rural populations. However, there are not enough data available to measure the ability of such telehealth strategies to enhance access and affect behavioral outcomes.

TELEHEALTH ISSUES

Despite the potential value of telemedicine technology, there are barriers to the successful integration of these advances from an administrative perspective. Graham (1996) detailed some of these obstacles, which include (1) initial and continuing operating costs of technology, (2) professional issues that require the field to reframe the doctor–patient relationship, and (3) legal and confidentiality issues. Furthermore, census data indicate that Americans' access to usage of the Internet varies greatly depending on socioeconomic level. Urban residents are more than two times as likely to have Internet access as those in rural areas at the same lower income levels (Ferrell & McKinnon, 2003).

Licensure, mobility, and reciprocity for healthcare disciplines are more complex in the age of telemedicine or telehealth, which the Federal government has acknowledged. For example, Jonason and colleagues (2003) reported that the Telehealth Improvement Act of 1999 and the Comprehensive Telehealth Act of 1999 created a Joint Working Group charged with compiling data on the number of health care providers performing telehealth services across state lines and tracking efforts to develop uniform national sets of standards for telehealth licensure. A provision of these Acts is that if states are not making progress in facilitating telehealth services across state lines by eliminating unnecessary requirements and adopting reciprocal licensing arrangements for such services, then the secretary of Health and Human Services should make recommendations concerning the scope and nature of Federal actions required to assist telehealth services.

Education and training can be difficult for all the reasons noted throughout this chapter (e.g., geographical distance, lack of funding). However, the use of technology and distance-learning programs is beginning to show promise in breaking down these barriers. As Deleon et al. (2003) observe, professional schools will likely develop innovative distance-learning (i.e., web-based) oriented degrees or continuing education modules. Clinical treatment through telemedicine has been growing rapidly since the introduction of telemedicine in the late 1980's. Frontier States, such as Alaska, use distance-learning approaches to train Alaska Natives in remote areas. Thus, Deleon et al. argue, "Telehealth compels us to conceive of boundaries in other than geographical terms."

The Western Interstate Commission for Higher Education (WICHE) Mental Health Program, through funding from SAMHSA, has been offering a series of live grand rounds webcasts on clinical topics through the Internet with a focus on rural mental health. In effect, the Internet serves as an "E-Classroom" in which speakers and participants can interact in real time to discuss issues. Presentations can also be stored for later-viewing, which helps busy rural providers get needed information as it fits their schedules.

A HYPOTHETICAL SYSTEM OF SERVICES PROVIDED THROUGH VIDEOCONFERENCING

The following section is an example of what evidence-based services may look like in a rural setting that expands its medical telehealth program to include behavioral health. The expansion of videoconferencing from medical to behavioral health may allow local health providers to provide two major types of services to those in outlying areas: Direct clinical services and training/supervision. Telemental health could provide two types of direct clinical services: intervention/therapy and consultation. The interventions would involve routine therapy directly with clients. Possible therapies suitable for adaptation include Cognitive Behavioral Therapy, Motivational Interviewing and Motivation Enhancement, Parent/Child Interactive Therapy Interpersonal Therapy for depression, and Dialectical Behavior Therapy. These are all considered EBPs in the mental health field. In addition, it would be possible to establish support groups targeted toward those recovering from substance abuse or trauma. This can be extremely helpful for those that finish treatment in an urban residential facility and subsequently need follow-up care in their communities. It allows the client to participate anonymously in groups that do not consist of fellow residents.

The other aspect of direct clinical services may involve consultation with psychiatrists and emergency room providers. Consultations typically involve psychiatric connections with clients in remote locations to do medication evaluations/prescriptions/management as well as oversight of client's clinical progress and outcomes. The psychiatrists can also provide consultation for local providers. In addition to psychiatric services during regular hours, professionals can use the videoconferencing system to consult on crisis intervention, mental health assessment/evaluation and triage by clinicians and staff psychiatrists as well as after-hours emergency consultations and admission arrangements.

The other main suggested component of the videoconferencing unit is workforce management or training/supervision. Videoconferencing is able to provide extensive regional training for staff in remote locations, licensing and certifications, staff supervision activities, and staff meetings. In multisite conferences, the display screens are able to handle multiple camera inputs by displaying the various participants in a Hollywood Squares or Brady Bunch style. In addition, behavioral health systems can provide preadmission support and stabilization services for clients who are on a waiting list for residential services, live in remote communities, and have a need for these services. The videoconferencing system is not limited to these main areas of use. There is a wide variety of potential applications limited only by provider flexibility.

ADVANTAGES AND DISADVANTAGES

The obvious advantages taken from the above section are the increased access to professional, anonymous care with a significant decrease in the disruption of major travel. Another major advantage is the cost savings to service providers, given the reduction in travel expenses for clients. Clients also have increased access to immediate care when needed without disruption to their jobs or home life.

There are a number of challenges to working with the system. Potentially not having a workforce dedicated to working on the videoconferencing system could be one of the larger issues. It can be frustrating to have the professionals and the clients ready, but not have the technical staff time available to operate the system. This lack of dedicated technical assistance can lead to scheduling challenges, if both the behavioral and the medical systems share the telehealth system. Although a system may have a myriad of connection sites, it is also a finite system with bandwidth limitations. Overuse of the system at peak hours can lower the reception and quality of the screen. The technology is constantly changing for the better; however, this leads to outdated technology needing upgrades, which can involve significant amounts of money. Finally, providers could encounter a number of possible client issues. Not everyone will be willing to use this new technology because of unfamiliarity with the system, although we presume that children are more likely to be open to the technology than older adults are. Confidentiality can be another issue that professionals will need to address at each end of the system and in transit. The live video data transported through the Internet are subject to Health Insurance Portability and Accountability Act (HIPPA) regulations. This prevents the use of inexpensive store-bought webcam systems, which are unencrypted and therefore susceptible to hackers.

EMPIRICAL SUPPORT

Telehealth is not an established evidence-based adjunctive practice. The NIMH and the National Institute on Drug Abuse (NIDA) are currently conducting research to establish the preliminary data needed to formally label telehealth as an EBP. This is an area where rural service providers could prove invaluable. Developing a systematic way to gather information from rural providers who have already successfully implemented telehealth into their services and assisting them in gathering the rigorous data needed to develop into an EBP will be an invaluable resource.

CULTURAL ADJUNCTIVE THERAPY

To illustrate the impact of culture on mental illness and treatment, this section focuses on American Indians and Alaska Natives (AI/ANs). Despite focusing on only one culture group, the following discussion is applicable to any minority culture in the United States. We have chosen to highlight culturally based adjunctive treatments in this chapter because Rural America contains a high degree of cultural diversity. Only 23% of the white population resides in rural areas, compared with nearly half of the Native American population (U.S. Census, 2002). Thus, it is important for beginning rural practitioners to know and understand the culture of the areas they will be working with.

Because AI/ANs comprise such a small percentage of the overall population, most studies do not generate sufficiently large samples to draw accurate conclusions regarding their need for mental health care. Even when researchers acquire large samples, the wide heterogeneity that characterizes the social and cultural ecologies of Native people limits the findings. There are 561 federally recognized tribes, with over 200 indigenous languages spoken (Fleming, 1992). Differences between some of these languages are as distinct as the differences between English and Chinese (Chafe, 1962). Similar differences abound among Native customs, family structures, religions, and social relationships. The magnitude of this diversity among Indian people has important implications for the development of mental health treatments.

American Indians and Alaska Natives have well-established cultural differences in the expression and reporting of mental health issues. These often compromise the ability of assessment tools to capture the key signs and symptoms of mental illness (Kinzie & Manson, 1987; Manson, 1994; Manson et al., 1985). Words such as "depressed" and "anxious" are absent from some American Indian and Alaska Native languages (Manson et al., 1985). This cultural difference also affects the selection and course of treatment. Thus, evaluating the need for mental health care and the appropriate course of action for AI/ANs require careful clinical inquiry that attends closely to culture.

There have been historical issues that have hindered the development of evidence-based treatments and adjunctive therapies for this population. Researchers need to be aware that the sensitive issues of alcoholism, substance abuse, and other related social issues affect not only the individual but the family and the community as well. This de-emphasis on individualism in treatment requires great respect and sensitivity.

Scientific research is hard to conduct on traditional healing programs because of (1) lack of reliable records, (2) logistical challenges of rural life,[4] (3) problem of finding the posttreatment participants, and (4) legitimate fear of authorities. In addition, Western therapies tend to be linear and reductionistic, boiling everything down to simple concrete terms. In Native culture, themes are more holistic, thus, there are difficulties operationalizing data and terms (i.e., what constitutes a positive outcome when dealing with the more abstract Native cultural concepts). In general, research writings pertaining to Native therapies included outcomes that were not specific, measurable, or objective because of the more spiritual approach. It can be tricky to know how to operationalize a sweat lodge or other traditional healing experience and measure the long-term impact. Some local communities have developed potentially successful treatments. However, the specific tribal cultures guide treatment design and thus treatment is not easily generalizable to other communities. Developed treatments need a very clear understanding of Native culture and the impact of racism issues on their clients. For example, in Alaska, being a native has historically carried very negative implications. Providers should seek to restore the cultural identity and pride and help reestablish the view that culture is a gift. An emerging application of an established EBP is beginning to show promise for use with cultural groups. Venner et al. adapted Motivational Interviewing (MI) in 2006 for use with AI/AN populations. MI is a client-centered, directive method for enhancing intrinsic motivation to change by exploring and resolving ambivalence. The developed manual allows for flexibility in adapting the treatment to match the local culture. For providers, this may involve adding weekly rites of passage that equip each participant with tools and support designed to last past the end of the program. These adjunctive treatments may include such things as making medicine bags for symbolic items, talking circles, specific ceremonies that match the level of change, sweat lodges, and solo journeys into the wilderness. In addition, a hypothetical program can draw strongly on the power of metaphor and Native American storytelling to embrace and transmit MI concepts.

SUMMARY

There are currently no evidence-based adjunctive therapies for rural populations. EBPs are continuing to be a focus of service delivery across mental health systems in the United States, but the applicability of these treatments to rural populations still needs to be determined. Designing, implementing, and measuring mental health treatments modified for rural populations is beyond the means

[4] A total of 34% of the Native population resides in rural areas, where many reservations are located (Census Bureau, American Indian/Alaska Native Heritage Month, 2003).

of most rural mental health providers, and without empirical data, it is difficult to ascertain treatment effects. Despite the difficulties, rural providers are beginning to show preliminary data that are on the way to establishing full-fledged rural-based EBPs. Complexities surround the best way to define rural populations and collect data. As a result, we have limited knowledge about the prevalence of mental illness and substance abuse in Rural America.

We do know that rural Americans face significant barriers in availability, accessibility, and acceptability of mental health services. These barriers have a significant impact on quality of life and productivity.

Telemental health is one of the most promising adjunct therapies for use in rural populations. Despite significant challenges, it remains a promising and cost-effective way of providing high-quality services, regardless of geographic barriers. Telemental health has a wide variety of potential applications in the mental health field that include both clinical and supportive applications. Few health providers are currently utilizing telehealth, which limits the availability of empirical data to support the efficacy of delivering services remotely. Several national agencies are currently conducting research to fill these data gaps, and we can look forward to a new resource for rural practitioners to implement with confidence.

RESOURCES

The following websites provide further discussion of the issues provided in this report:

RURAL MENTAL HEALTH

Annapolis Coalition: http://www.annapoliscoalition.org/rural_workforce_issues.php

Frontier Mental Health Services Network: http://wiche.edu/mentalhealth/frontier/index.htm

National Association of Rural Mental Health: http://www.narmh.org/

National Rural Health Association: http://www.nrharural.org/

New Freedom Commission on Mental Health: http://www.mentalhealthcommission.gov/papers/Rural.pdf

Office of Rural Health Policy: http://ruralhealth.hrsa.gov/

Office of Rural Mental Health Research: http://www.nimh.nih.gov/ormhr/index.cfm

Resource Center for Rural Behavioral Health, APA: http://www.apa.org/rural/homepage.html

TriWest Healthcare Alliance: https://www.triwest.com

University of Montana Rural Institute: http://ruralinstitute.umt.edu/index.asp

Western Interstate Commission for Higher Education: http://www.wiche.edu/mentalhealth/

TELEHEALTH

American Telemedicine Association: http://www.americantelemed.org/ICOT/sigtelemental.htm

Association of Telehealth Service Providers: http://www.atsp.org/publications/telemental_health_cdrom.asp

U.S. Department of Health and Human Resources: http://www.hrsa.gov/ telehealth/pubs/mental.htm

WICHE Telemental Health: http://www.wiche.edu/MentalHealth/northland/overview.asp

REFERENCES

Ahr, P.R. & Halcomb, W.R. (1985). State mental health directors' priorities for mental health care. *Hospital and Community Psychology*, *36*, 39–45.

Anthony, W., Rogers, E.S., & Farkas, M. (2003). Research on evidence-based practices: Future Directions in an Era of Recovery. *Community Mental Health Journal*, *39*(2), 101–114.

Baer, L., Elford, D.R., & Cukor, P. (1997). Telepsychiatry at forty: What have we learned? *Harvard Review of Psychiatry*, *5*(1), 7–17.

Baer, L., Cukor, P., Jenike, M.A., et al. (1995). Pilot studies of telemedicine for patients with obsessive-compulsive disorder. *American Journal of Psychiatry*, *152*(9), 1383–1385.

Baigent, M.F., Lloyd, C.J., Kavanagh, S.J., et al. (1997). Telepsychiatry: 'tele' yes, but what about the 'psychiatry'? *Journal of Telemedicine and Telecare*, *3*(1), 3–5.

Beeson, P.G., Britain, C., Howell, M.L., et al. (1998). Rural mental health at the millennium. In R.W. Manderscheid & M.J. Henderson (Eds.), *Mental Health United States 1998* (pp. 82–97). Rockville, MD: Center for Mental Health Services, SAMHSA, U.S. Department of Health and Human Services.

Bergland, B. (1988). Rural mental health: Report of the National Action Commission on the Mental Health of Rural America. *Journal of Rural Community Psychology*, *9*(2), 29.

Boyd, M.R. (2000). Predicting substance abuse and comorbidity in rural women. *Archives of Psychiatric Nursing*, *14*, 64–72.

Britain, C.S. (1996). Making the connection in rural mental health. *Behavioral Healthcare Tomorrow*, *5*, 67–69.

Buckwalter, K. (1992). *Mental and Social Health of the Rural Elderly*. Paper presented at the Health and Aging in Rural America: A National Symposium, San Diego, CA.

Chafe, W. (1962). Estimates regarding the present speakers of North American Indian languages. *International Journal of American Linguistics*, *28*, 162–171.

Champion, J.D. (1999). Life histories of rural Mexican American adolescents experiencing abuse. *Western Journal of Nursing Research*, *21*(5), 699–717.

Champion, J., Artnak, K., Shain, R., & Piper, J. (2002). Rural woman abuse and sexually transmitted disease: An ethical analysis of clinical dilemmas. *Issues in Mental Health Nursing*, *23*, 305–326.

Ciarlo, J.A., Wackwitz, J.H., Wagenfeld, M.O., & Mohatt, D.F. (1996). Focusing on "frontier": Isolated rural America. [On-line Letter to the Field No. 2.] *Frontier Mental Health Services Resource Network, WICHE Mental Health Program*. Retrieved June 14, 2007, from http://www.wiche.edu/MentalHealth/Frontier/index.htm

Danbom, D. (1995). *Born in the Country: A History of Rural America*. Baltimore: Johns Hopkins University Press.

Deleon, P.H., Crimmins, D.B., & Wolf, A.W. (2003). Afterword—The 21st Century has Arrived. *Psychotherapy: Theory, Research, Practice, Training*, *40*, 164–169.

Dimmitt, J. & Davila, Y. (1995). Group psychotherapy for abused women: A survivor group prototype. *Applied Nursing Research, 8*, 3–8.

Doniger, M., Tempier, R., Lalinec-Michaud, M., & Meunier, D. (1986). Telepsychiatry: Psychiatric consultation through two-way television. A controlled study. *Canadian Journal of Psychiatry, 31*(1), 32–34.

Dyer, J. (1997). *Harvest of Rage: Why Oklahoma City is on the Beginning*. Boulder, CO: Westview Press.

Drake, R.E., Goldman, H.H., Leff, H.S., et al. (2001). Implementing evidence-based practices in routine mental health service settings. *Psychiatric Services, 52*(2), 179–182.

Ferrell, S.P. & McKinnon, C. (2003). Technology and rural mental health. *Archives of Psychiatric Nursing, 17*(1), 20–26.

Fischer, E.P., Owen, R.R. Jr., & Cuffel, B.J. (1996). Substance abuse, community services use, and symptoms severity of urban and rural residents with schizophrenia. *Psychiatric Services, 47*(9), 980–984.

Fleming, C.M. (1992). American Indians and Alaska Natives: Changing societies past and present. In M.A. Orlandi, R. Weston, & L.G. Epstein (Eds.), *Cultural Competence for Evaluators: A Guide for Alcohol and Other Drug Abuse Prevention Practitioners Working with Ethnic/Racial Communities* (OSAP cultural competence series 1, pp. 147–171). Rockville, MD: U.S. Department of Health & Human Services.

Fox, J., Blank, M., Berman, J., & Rovnyak, V.G. (1999). Mental disorders and help seeking in a rural impoverished population. *International Journal of Psychiatry in Medicine, 29*(2), 181–195.

Fox, J., Merwin, E., & Blank, M. (1995). Defacto mental health services in the rural south. *Journal of Health Care for the Poor and Underserved, 6*(4), 434–468.

Gale, J.A. & Deprez, R.D. (2003). A public health approach to the challenges of rural mental health service integration. In B.H. Stamm (Ed.), *Behavioral Healthcare in Rural and Frontier Areas: An Interdisciplinary Handbook*. Washington, DC: APA Books.

Gamm, L. (2002). White Paper: Models for Meeting the Mental Health Needs of People Living in Rural Areas, a report to the Substance Abuse and Mental Health Services Administration, Rockville, MD. Southwest Rural Health Research Center, Texas A&M Health Science Center, College Station, TX.

Graham, A.M. (1996). Telepsychiatry in Appalachia. *American Behavioral Scientist, 39*(5), 602–615.

Hartley, D. & Gale, J. (2003). Rural Health Care Safety Nets. In R.M. Weinick. & J. Billings (Eds.), *Monitoring the Health Care Safety Net. Book III: Tools for Monitoring the Health Care Safety Net.* (AHRQ Pub. No. 03-0027). Rockville, MD: Agency for Healthcare Research and Quality.

Hartley, D., Bird, D., & Dempsey, P. (1999). Mental health and substance abuse. In T. Ricketts (Ed.), *Rural Health in the United States*. New York: Oxford University Press.

Hauenstein, E.J. & Boyd, M.R. (1994). Depressive symptoms in young women of the Piedmont: Prevalence in rural women. *Women and Health, 21*(2–3), 105–123.

Hewitt, M. (1989). *Defining "Rural" Areas: Impact on Health Care Policy and Research*. Washington, DC: Health Program, Office of Technology Assessment, Congress of the United States.

Human, J. & Wasem, C. (1991). Rural mental health in America. *American Psychologist, 46*(3), 232–239.

Institute of Medicine (2005). *Quality Through Collaboration: The Future of Rural Health*. The Committee on the Future of Rural Health Care; Board on Health Care Services. Washington, DC: The National Academies Press.

Intermill, N.L. & Rathbone-McCuan, E. (1991). *Mental Health Services for Elders in Rural America*. Kansas City, MO: National Resource Center for Rural Elderly.

Ivey, S.L., Scheffler, R., & Zazzali, J.L. (1998). Supply dynamics of the mental health workforce: Implications for health policy. *Milbank Quarterly, 76*, 25–58.

Jonason, K.R., DeMers, S.T., Vaughn, T.J., & Reaves, R.P. (2003). Professional Mobility for Psychologists Is Rapidly Becoming a Reality. *Professional Psychology: Research and Practice, 34*, 468–473.

Kane, C.F. & Ennis, J.M. (1996). Health care reform and rural mental health: Severe mental illness. *Community Mental Health Journal*, *32*(5), 445–462.

Kenkel, M.B. (2003). Rural women: Strategies and resources for meting their behavioral health needs. In B.H. Stamm (Ed.), *Rural Behavioral Health Care: An Interdisciplinary Guide* (pp. 181–192). Washington, DC: American Psychological Association Press.

Kessler, R.C., McGonagle, K.A., Zhao, S., et al. (1994). Lifetime and 12-month prevalence of DSM-III-R psychiatric disorders in the United States: Results from the national comorbidity study. *Archives of General Psychiatry*, *51*, 81–89.

Kimmel, W.A. (1992). *Rural Mental Health Policy Issues for Research: A Pilot Exploration.* Rockville, MD: National Institute of Mental Health, Office of Rural Mental Health Research.

Kinzie, J.D. & Manson, S.M. (1987). Self-rating scales in cross-cultural psychiatry. *Hospital and Community Psychiatry*, *38*, 190–196.

Lambert, D. & Agger, M. (1995). Access of rural Medicaid beneficiaries to mental health services. *Health Care Financing Review*, *17*(1), 133–145.

Lambert, D., Donahue, A., Mitchell, M., & Strauss, R. (2001). *Mental Health Outreach in Rural Area: Promising Practices in Rural Areas.* Rockville, MD: Center for Mental Health Services, Substance Abuse and Mental Health Services Administration.

LaMendola, W.F. (2000). Telemental Health Services In U.S. Frontier Areas. [On-line Letter to the Field No. 3.] *Frontier Mental Health Services Resource Network, WICHE Mental Health Program.* Retrieved June 14, 2007, from http://www.wiche.edu/MentalHealth/Frontier/index.htm

LaMendola, W.F., Mohatt, D.F., & McGee, C. (2002). *Telemental Health: Delivery Models and Performance Measurement.* WICHE Mental Health Program. Retrieved June 14, 2007, from http://www.wiche.edu/MentalHealth/northland/index.asp

Larson, M.L., Beeson, P.G., & Mohatt, D.F. (1993). *Taking Rural Into Account: A Report of the National Public Hearing on Rural Mental Health.* St. Cloud, MN: National Association for Rural Mental Health and the Federal Center for Mental Health Services.

Little, D.N., Hammond, C., Kollisch, D., et al. (1998). Referrals for depression by primary care physicians: A pilot study. *Journal of Family Practice*, *47*(5), 375–377.

McCabe, S. & Macnee, C. L. (2002). Weaving a new safety net of mental health care in rural America: a model of integrated practice. *Issues in Mental Health Nursing*, *23*(3), 263–78.

Manson, S.M. (1994). Culture and depression: Discovering variations in the experience of illness. In W.J. Lonner & R.S. Malpass (Eds.), *Psychology and Culture* (pp. 285–290). Needham, MA: Allyn and Bacon.

Manson, S.M., Shore, J.H., & Bloom, J.D. (1985). The depressive experience in American Indian communities: A challenge for psychiatric theory and diagnosis. In A. Kleinman & B. Good (Eds.), *Culture and Depression* (pp. 331–368). Berkeley, CA: University of California Press.

Martin, P. (1997). Immigration and the changing face of rural America. *Increasing Understanding of Public Problems and Policies* (pp. 201–212). Oak Brook, IL: Farm Foundation.

Mohatt, D.F. (2000). Access to mental health services in frontier areas. *Journal of the Washington Academy of Sciences*, *86*(3), 35–48.

Mohatt, D.F. & Kirwan, D. (1995). *Meeting the Challenge: Model Programs in Rural Mental Health.* Rockville, MD: Office of Rural Health Policy.

Mulder, P.L., Linkey, H., & Hager, A. (2003). Needs assessment, identification, and mobilization of community resources, and conflict management. In B. Hudnall Stamm (Ed.), *Rural Behavioral Health Care: An Interdisciplinary Guide* (pp. 67–79). Washington, DC: American Psychological Association.

National Advisory Committee on Rural Health and Human Services (2007, January). *The 2007 Report to the Secretary: Rural Health and Human Service Issues.* U.S. Department of Health and Human Services.

National Institute of Mental Health (2000, September). *Rural Mental Health Research at the National Institute of Mental Health.* U.S. Department of Health and Human Services. Retrieved June 14, 2007 from the National Institute of Mental Health website: http://www.nimh.nih.gov/publicat/NIMHruralresfact.pdf

National Rural Health Association (1999). *Mental Health in Rural America: An Issue Paper Prepared by the National Rural Health Association.* Retrieved on June 14, 2007, http://www.nrharural.org/advocacy/sub/issuepapers/ipaper14.html

Neese, J.B., Abraham, I.L., & Buckwalter, K.C. (1999). Utilization of mental health services among rural elderly. *Archives of Psychiatric Nursing*, *13*(1), 30–40.

New Freedom Commission on Mental Health (2004). *Subcommittee on Rural Issues: Background Paper*. DHHS Pub. No. SMA-04-3890. Rockville, MD.

Office of Applied Studies, (2005). *Results from the 2005 National Survey on Drug Use and Health: National Findings*. Rockville, MD: Dept. of Health and Human Services, Substance Abuse and Mental Health Services Administration.

Office of Behavioral and Social Sciences Research (2001). *Qualitative Methods in Health Research: Opportunities and Considerations in Application and Review* (NIH Publication No. 02-5046). Bethesda, MD: National Institutes of Health.

Office of Rural Health Policy (1997). Exploratory evaluation of rural applications of telemedicine: Final report (WA 390 [Q] UNI 1997 [98832]). Rockville, MD: Office of Rural Health Policy.

Ralph, R.O. & Lambert, D. (1999). Best practices in rural Medicaid managed behavioral health: Consumer issues. In *Working Papers Series*. Portland, ME: Muskie Institute, University of Southern Maine.

Regier, D.A., Narrow, W.E, Rae, D.S., et al. (1993). The de facto United States mental and addictive disorders services system. *Archives of General Psychiatry*, *50*(2), 85–94.

Roberts, L.W., Battaglia, J., & Epstein, R.S. (1999). Frontier ethics: Mental health care needs and ethical dilemmas in rural communities. *Psychiatric Services*, *50*, 497–503.

Rohland B.M. & Rohrer, J.E. (1998). Capacity of rural community mental health centers to treat serious mental illness. *Community Mental Health Journal*, *34*(3), 261–273.

Rost, K.M., Owen, R.R., Smith, J., & Smith, G.R., Jr. (1998). Rural–urban differences in service use and course of illness in bipolar disorder. *Journal of Rural Health*, *14*(1), 36–43.

Rost, K.M., Fortney, J., Fischer, E., & Smith, J. (2002). Use, quality, and outcomes of care for mental health: The rural perspective. *Medical Care Research and Review*, *59*(3), 231–265.

Rost, K.M., Smith, R., & Taylor, J. (1993). Rural–urban differences in stigma and the use of care for depressive disorders. *Journal of Rural Health*, *9*, 57–62.

Schauer, P.M. & Weaver, P. (1993). Rural elder transportation. In J.A. Krout (Ed.), *Providing Community-Based Services to the Rural Elderly* (pp. 42–64). Thousand Oaks, CA: Sage.

Sears, S.F., Jr., Evans, G.D., & Kuper, B.D. (2003). Rural social service systems as behavioral health delivery systems. In B.H. Stamm (Ed.), *Rural Behavioral Health Care: An Interdisciplinary Guide* (pp. 109–120). Washington, DC: American Psychological Association.

Shelton, D.A. & Frank, R. (1995). Rural mental health coverage under health care reform. *Community Mental Health Journal*, *31*(6), 539–552.

Smith, H. & Allison, R. (1998). *The National Telemental Health Report*. Washington, DC: Department of Health and Human Services, Center for Mental Health Services and the Office of Rural Health Policy.

Susman, J.L., Crabtree, B.F., & Essink, G. (1995). Depression in rural family practice. Easy to recognize, difficult to diagnose. *Archives of Family Medicine*, *4*, 427–431.

U.S. Department of Health and Human Services. (2001). *Mental Health: Culture, Race, and Ethnicity—A Supplement to Mental Health: A Report of the Surgeon General*. Rockville, MD: U.S. Department of Health and Human Services, Substance Abuse and Mental Health Services Administration, Center for Mental Health Services.

Venner, K.L., Feldstein, S.W., & Tafoya, N. (2006). *Native American Motivational Interviewing: Weaving Native American and Western Practices. A Manual for Counselors in Native American Communities*. On-Line Treatment Manual Retrieved June 14, 2007 from University of New Mexico, Center on Alcoholism, Substance Abuse, and Addictions website: http://casaa.unm.edu/mimanuals.html

Wagenfeld, M.O., Murray, J.D., Mohatt, D.F., & DeBruyn, J.C. (1994). *Mental Health and Rural America: 1980–1993* (NIH Publication No. 94-3500). Washington, DC: U.S. Government Printing Office.

Wagenfeld, M.O. & Buffum, W.E. (1983). Problems in, and prospects for, rural mental health services in the United States. *International Journal of Mental Health, 12*(1–2), 89–107.

Zarate, C.A., Weinstock, L., Cukor, P., et al. (1997). Applicability of telemedicine for assessing patients with schizophrenia: Acceptance and reliability. *Journal of Clinical Psychiatry, 58*(1), 22–25.

Zevenbergen, P. & Buckwalter, K.C. (1991). The mental health of rural elderly outreach project: Then and now. Paper presented at the Gerontological Society of American Annual Conference, San Francisco, CA.

16

ADJUNCTIVE TREATMENTS FOR SEVERE MENTAL ILLNESS (SCHIZOPHRENIA)

JENNIFER D. GOTTLIEB* AND KIM T. MUESER†

** Massachusetts General Hospital Schizophrenia Program and Harvard Medical School, Department of Psychiatry, and New Hampshire-Dartmouth Psychiatric Research Center, Department of Psychiatry*

† New Hampshire-Dartmouth Psychiatric Research Center, Departments of Psychiatry and Community and Family Medicine

Historically, people with severe mental illnesses such as schizophrenia, bipolar disorder, and severe depression were considered "un-treatable," with little potential for rehabilitation. Patients with schizophrenia were thought to be unable to contribute to their own care and recovery, thus rendering psychosocial treatment approaches ineffective. However, with the advent of psychotropic medications, such as antipsychotics, mood stabilizers, and antidepressants in the 1950s and 1960s, coupled with the subsequent deinstitutionalization movement from the 1960s to the present day, beliefs about the "treatability" and prognosis of severe mental illnesses have undergone a sea change.

A growing body of evidence has demonstrated that through psychosocial interventions, people with severe mental illness can actively participate in their own treatment, important coping and social functioning skills, obtain and benefit from employment, and improve their overall quality of life. However, despite these advances in psychiatric rehabilitation, and the changing perspectives of clients, families, clinicians, and the public, treatment remains dominated by the medical model. Medication is the mainstay in the treatment of schizophrenia and other severe mental illnesses, and many patients receive little or no rehabilitation in addition to their pharmacotherapy.

From this perspective, all psychosocial treatments for severe mental illnesses *besides* medication can be considered "adjunctive." It is from this vantage point that we have organized this chapter. Thus, the format of this section is likely different from the other chapters in this book, given the distinct historical and philosophical perspective that has surrounded the treatment of severe mental illnesses over the years. We discuss six evidence-based treatments here: Assertive Community Treatment (ACT), Supported Employment, Family Psychoeducation, Integrated Treatment for Dual Disorders, cognitive-behavioral therapy (CBT) for persistent symptoms, and illness management and recovery (IMR), which is a treatment package that contains several strategies shown to improve illness self-management. We use the term *severe mental illness* here to describe a range of psychiatric disorders associated with significant functional disability, primarily including schizophrenia-spectrum disorders, bipolar disorder, and treatment-refractory major depression. For most of the research cited below, the majority of study participants had a schizophrenia-spectrum disorder.

ASSERTIVE COMMUNITY TREATMENT

NEED FOR ASSERTIVE COMMUNITY TREATMENT AND TARGET POPULATION

ACT is an intensive community-based, integrated treatment approach for individuals with schizophrenia who have difficulty staying connected to standard outpatient treatment modalities (e.g., attending psychopharmacology appointments, participating in therapy groups) and who are at high risk for relapse and psychiatric hospitalization. ACT clients typically have a recent history of multiple and/or lengthy inpatient stays and tend to have extremely impaired psychosocial functioning that may require daily professional assistance. Studies have suggested that ACT services most benefit this particular subset of clients and therefore may not be as useful for all individuals with serious mental illness (Rosenheck et al., 1995). Although this treatment was developed for individuals with various types of serious mental illness (e.g., severe depression, bipolar disorder), given the often debilitating course and associated functional impairments seen with schizophrenia, the majority of clients treated with ACT usually have schizophrenia-spectrum diagnoses.

INTERVENTION COMPONENTS

The ACT program, developed in the 1970s as a response to the host of problems related to the deinstitutionalization process that began in the 1960s, takes a multidisciplinary, holistic approach to treatment (Stein & Santos, 1998). Clients are provided medication management, housing assistance, help in getting basic daily living needs met, financial entitlements and money management support, counseling, and crisis management by a team of multidisciplinary treatment providers. What is most unique about the ACT program compared with traditional case management is the intensity of treatment (with clinician: client ratios of 1:10 in ACT compared with that of 1:25 or more in traditional case management), the provision of most services in the community rather than at the clinic, and the sharing of caseloads across a multi-disciplinary team of clinicians who assume round-the-clock coverage for clients.

Compared to the structure of most mental health services, where a case manager working with a client may "broker services" to other providers (e.g., to a psychiatrist at one clinic, a vocational specialist at another, day treatment at still another facility), ACT providers work together as a team, such that all team members are in frequent contact with every client and are in direct communication with each other regarding clients' needs on a very regular basis. Most ACT teams comprise a psychiatrist, nurse, social worker, at least one case manager and rehabilitation counselor, and ideally a substance abuse counselor as well. As opposed to the large caseload that most individual mental health providers carry, ACT team caseloads tend to be a fraction of the size, allowing smaller patient–staff ratios. As a result of the team approach and reduced caseload, clinicians can provide a degree of continuity of care and individualized attention that most other services cannot.

ACT services take place in the community, with staff members conducting frequent home visits, rather than insisting that clients come to the mental health clinic for appointments. A rule of thumb for client contact is that 80% or more of appointments take place in the home or other community setting (Bond et al., 2001a). This allows for *in vivo* progress: clinicians can more effectively help clients solve everyday problems, such as organizing their home or increasing medication adherence, in the natural environment than they can simply talking about the problems in an office. Compared to many mental health providers who deliver services exclusively during the 8-hour work day and then refer out to standard emergency services after business hours, ACT offers "rapid access" to client emergencies. Team members respond quickly to crises, even when they occur in the evenings or on weekends. As the goal of ACT is to reduce mental health crises and the necessity of hospitalizations, it has been suggested that ACT teams tend to be able to anticipate emergency situations proactively and therefore prevent the need for 24-hour coverage (Witheridge, 1991).

EMPIRICAL SUPPORT

The ACT model has been widely tested, with over 30 randomized controlled trials evaluating its effectiveness (Bond et al., 2001). Research findings demonstrate that clients who participate in ACT programs have fewer psychiatric hospitalizations, reduced symptom severity, more stabilized community housing, and improved quality of life. ACT tends to have minimal effects on social functioning and time spent in jail. Criticisms of ACT suggest that its assertive outreach style may be too demanding and/or paternalistic for clients (Fischer & Ahern, 2000; Spindel & Nugent, n.d.). However, in addition to successful levels of client engagement (1-year retention rates in mental health services was 84% for ACT clients compared to 54% for treatment-as-usual clients) (Bond et al., 1995), evaluation of consumer satisfaction (although less thoroughly investigated) suggests that clients and their families were significantly more satisfied with ACT than with other types of services (Bond et al., 2001a).

One potential drawback of ACT is its cost, given the intensity of the services provided to each client. However, whereas studies have found that ACT services do not tend to reduce clients' use of outpatient services, the high overall ACT program costs are usually offset by the substantial reduction in hospitalization costs (Latimer, 1999).

AVAILABILITY AND DISSEMINATION

ACT programs have been implemented in at least 35 states and several countries including Sweden, Australia, England, and Canada. The actual configuration of each program differs to some degree in regard to target population (e.g., Veterans, dual-diagnosis clients), specific resources (e.g., urban versus rural environments), and treatment components (e.g., offering family interventions, vocational rehabilitation); however, the development and use of the Dartmouth Assertive Community Treatment Fidelity Scale (DACTS) (Teague et al., 1998) has allowed planners of various programs to evaluate their inclusion of core ACT components that are critical for achieving effective outcomes. Not surprisingly, research has found that programs that more closely adhere to DACTS components are more effective than those that do not (Teague et al., 1998). Of the multiple components of ACT, the most "active ingredients" have been found to be the inclusion of small client caseload size with explicit program admission criteria and assertive engagement, and the provision of *in vivo* services (Group, 2000).

FUTURE DIRECTIONS

Despite the strong empirical support, wide dissemination, and popularity among clients and advocacy organizations alike, the future of ACT is not without its uncertainties. Funding is an obvious roadblock for any mental health-based program in this day and age. This may be an even greater obstacle to the continued goal of disseminating ACT, as traditional funding tends to be devoted to the support of hospital and clinic-based services as opposed to the "in the field" care that ACT provides. Another issue is the need to ensure adherence to the empirically supported components of the ACT model. It can be tempting for independent mental health programs to adapt ACT to suit the individual needs of clients and their group's specific resources. However, as research has indicated, departure from the model compromises its effectiveness. Over time, ACT will certainly require modifications to address important issues such as clients' physical health problems, trauma histories, and involvement in the criminal justice system. In addition, methods for graduating clients from ACT to less intensive services have been developed and evaluated (Salyers et al., 1998) but have not been formally integrated into the ACT model (Table 16.1).

TABLE 16.1 Features of Assertive Community Treatment (ACT) versus Clinical Case Management

	Assertive community treatment (ACT)	Clinical case management
Staff to patient ratio	1:10	1 : 30+
Outreach to patients	High	Low
Shared caseload	Yes	No
24-Hour coverage	Often	No
Consumer input	Low	Low
Emphasis on skills training	Moderate (?)	Low
Frequency of patient contacts	High	Moderate
Locus of contacts	Community	Clinic
Integration of treatment	High	Moderate
Direct service provision	High	Moderate
Target population	SMI high service users	SMI

Note: (?) = area of model that is unspecified; SMI = severely mentally ill.
Source: Mueser, K.T., Bond, G.R., Drake, R.E., & Resnick, S.G. (1998). Models of community care for severe mental illness: A review of research on case management. *Schizophrenia Bulletin, 24*, 37–74.

SUPPORTED EMPLOYMENT

NEED FOR SUPPORTED EMPLOYMENT AND TARGET POPULATION

Given the often debilitating nature of severe mental illness, unemployment is particularly common in people with schizophrenia (Mueser et al., 2001). Symptoms of schizophrenia such as auditory hallucinations, delusions, negative symptoms, and cognitive deficits make obtaining and holding a job challenging. Clients' fear of losing much-needed public assistance benefits (e.g., SSI) can also be a deterrent to active job-seeking and employment. Despite some beliefs that individuals with severe mental illness do not want jobs or are "better off" not working because of potential job stress, most people very much want to work (Mueser et al., 2001). Furthermore, limited evidence suggests that clients who return to work experience a modest degree of symptom reduction and increased life satisfaction (Bell et al., 1993; Bond et al., 2001b).

Vocational rehabilitation programs have been developed to help clients with severe mental illness achieve the common goal of work. These programs have been spurred by the hypothesis that "work is good therapy" (Strauss et al., 1988). Although a wide range of different vocational rehabilitation programs have been developed, supported employment enjoys the most empirical support. Supported employment is designed to help clients obtain and maintain competitive jobs paying competitive wages in the community, working alongside non-disabled individuals.

Supportive employment programs for persons with severe mental illness operate on a "zero-exclusion" criteria basis, with the only criteria for enrollment in a program is the stated desire to work. Clients are not excluded because of symptom severity, clinician-perceived "un-readiness to work," or substance abuse problems. This is one of the many ways that supported employment differs from traditional vocational services for individuals with severe mental illness.

INTERVENTION COMPONENTS

The Individual Placement and Support model (IPS) (Becker & Drake, 1993, 2003) is the most widely studied model of supported employment program. The IPS model is based on several core principles, including (1) integration of vocational and clinical services, (2) rapid job search and no prevocational training, (3) attention to client preferences, and (4) provision of ongoing, time-unlimited supports to facilitate job retention or transition to other jobs.

In supported employment, vocational services are provided in an integrated fashion with the mental health treatment, with employment specialists participating in all treatment team meetings, and seen as integral members of the team. This allows for increased communication and support of clients' employment goals, and prevents clients from dropping out of vocational services because of temporary increases in symptoms or fluctuations in motivation.

Compared to other vocational programs, which often require extensive prevocational training, work readiness assessments, time-limited transitional jobs, or sheltered work, supported employment focuses on helping clients obtain permanent *competitive* employment as soon as possible, with the job search usually beginning within a few weeks of the client enrolling in the program. Another distinguishing feature of supported employment is the role of client choice and preferences. In addition to client choice determining whether the client can participate in supported employment, client preferences are important regarding the types of jobs they would like to have, and the nature of job supports provided. For example, some clients choose not to divulge their psychiatric illness to their employer, in which case the role of the employment specialists is strictly "behind the scenes."

Supported employment specialists provide a full range of vocational services to their clients, including job finding and support. To increase client participation and skill generalization, this model emphasizes assertive outreach (influenced by the ACT model) to deliver these services in the client's natural community environment rather than in the mental health clinic. Given the potential for client's work motivation to fluctuate over time, this assertive outreach is likely a crucial feature of supported employment. Also similar to ACT is the time-unlimited support that IPS offers. In many other vocational rehabilitation approaches, consumers are offered services for a limited period of time and then graduate from the program. As individuals with severe mental illness often have difficulty maintaining employment, support is offered indefinitely.

EMPIRICAL SUPPORT

Significant research has accumulated on the effects of supported employment for severe mental illness over the past 15 years, including both quasi-experimental and randomized controlled trial studies. Four studies have tested the effectiveness of converting traditional day treatment programs into supported employment programs (Bailey et al., 1998; Becker et al, 2001; Drake et al., 1994, 1996; Gold & Marrone, 1998). These studies involved closing down day treatment programs while developing supported employment and drop-in peer support centers. Compared to the sites that did not make the transition, the newly-converted sites saw significant increases in the percentage of clients who were working competitive jobs. The RCTs, conducted across the United States, have demonstrated similarly impressive effects (Bond et al., 1997), as summarized in Figure 16.1.

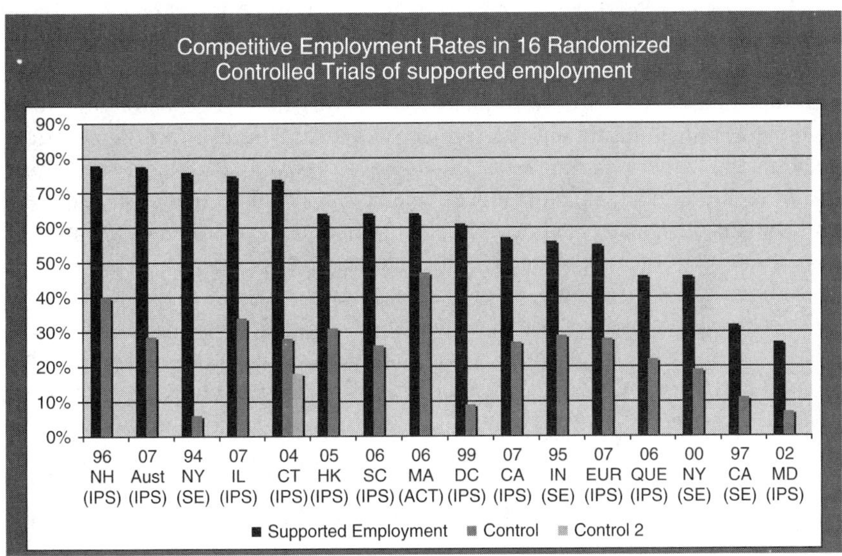

FIGURE 16.1 Rates of competitive employment in randomized controlled trials of supported employment for persons with severe mental illness (courtesy of Gary R. Bond).

AVAILABILITY, DISSEMINATION, AND FUTURE DIRECTIONS

As with the implementation of any new mental health service, cost is always an issue. However, this model is no more expensive than traditional vocational services (and clearly has been shown to be more effective). The average cost per client per year is $2449 (Latimer et al., 2004), which, when coupled with the suggestion that clients in supported employment services end up using fewer mental health services, is quite a reasonable expense (Clark et al., 1998).

In general, it has been the case that clients who want to work do not have access to supported employment services; unfortunately, most clients with schizophrenia (~75%) do not have access to any type of vocational service at all (Lehman & Steinwachs, 1998). Clearly, there have been several financial, organizational, and attitudinal barriers to implementing standardized supported employment programs across the country. Among these nationwide barriers are: disproportionate vocational rehabilitation department spending on assessment and other pre-employment training that has been found to be non-ideal with this population; minimal mental health funding for vocational services; fiscal and bureaucratic separation between mental health and vocational rehabilitation systems; and lack of Medicaid reimbursement for aspects of vocational services (Drake et al., 2006).

Fortunately, however, it appears as though the dissemination and therefore availability of supported employment programs are improving. Through the corporate–academic collaboration of Johnson & Johnson Company and Dartmouth Medical School, an intensive dissemination project was developed and positive results have recently been reported (Drake et al., 2006). Currently, seven states (Connecticut, the District of Columbia, Kansas, Maryland, Oregon, South Carolina, and Vermont) have implemented high-fidelity versions of supported employment programs through this project, and its successful effects demonstrate a substantial increase in number of clients served as well as a stable percentage (40%) of clients maintaining competitive employment. This unique and impressive merger of industry and academia certainly stands as a model to improve dissemination of other evidence-based treatments for serious mental illness.

As is the case for any other empirically supported for schizophrenia that is not quite yet in the mainstream of mental health services, advocates at all levels need to build these programs from the ground up. For clients and their families, this means knowing what good vocational services look like and banding together to demand these types of interventions.

FAMILY PSYCHOEDUCATION

NEED FOR FAMILY PSYCHOEDUCATION AND TARGET POPULATION

In large part because of improvements in antipsychotic medications over the years, most individuals with schizophrenia can be treated through outpatient services as opposed to the longer-term inpatient stays of the past. As a result, clients tend to have increased contact with family members, and many live with their relatives. Given that the impact of medications for schizophrenia is primarily on the psychotic symptoms, with little or no impact on negative symptoms (e.g., apathy, anhedonia) or cognitive functioning, impaired functioning continues to be a major problem.

Caring for a relative with schizophrenia often creates a sense of burden (Lefley, 1996), as well as confusion about the best way to cope with a relative's symptoms (Webb et al., 1998). In addition, caregiving is associated with significant stress in the family (Dyck et al., 1992), which has been linked to increased rates of relapse and rehospitalization in people with schizophrenia and major mood disorders (Butzlaff & Holey, 1998).

To address stress and burden in the family, and to reduce relapse rates, several types of family intervention have been developed and evaluated over the years for individuals with schizophrenia. The primary focus of these interventions is on teaching families about the nature of schizophrenia and its management in a respectful, collaborative manner that avoids blaming relatives (Glynn, 1993), and eschewing outdated theories that the family causes schizophrenia (Fromm-Reichman, 1948). The Schizophrenia Patient Outcomes Research Team (PORT) (Lehman & Steinwachs, 1998) has strongly recommended family psychoeducation programs for clients who have ongoing contact with their families, and has also highlighted that these interventions should not be limited to families where high levels of stress or interpersonal conflict are present. These guidelines were borne out of empirical findings that are discussed below.

INTERVENTION COMPONENTS

The nature, content, duration, and modality of psychosocial family interventions for schizophrenia vary from brief educational lectures (Smith & Birchwood, 1987) and psychoeducational groups (Leff et al., 1990) for relatives to more intensive single-family (Hogarty et al., 1991) and multi-family group therapy (McFarlane et al., 1995a) interventions, lasting anywhere from 2 months to 2 years.

Despite the differences between family intervention approaches, the most effective programs provide education about the symptoms of schizophrenia, strategies for more effective communication and solving problems, crisis management approaches, and the provision of emotional support. Clients with schizophrenia are routinely included in most or all family sessions. Most purely educational models utilize easy to understand handouts and present information in a non-judgmental manner, tailored to the particular issues of the individual family. In more intensive (and often longer-duration) types of family interventions, such as behavioral family therapy or management (Falloon et al., 1988; Mueser & Glynn, 1999), communication and problem-solving skills are taught using the principles of social learning, combined with the presentation of information about schizophrenia.

EMPIRICAL SUPPORT

Overall, evidence for the efficacy of family interventions for schizophrenia suggests that inclusion of relatives in psychosocial treatment reduces relapse and rehospitalization rates by at least 20% (Pitschel-Walz et al., 2001). Other findings across different trials of family intervention demonstrate improvement in knowledge about schizophrenia (e.g., Pitschel-Walz, 1997), better treatment compliance (e.g., McFarlane, et al., 1995), reduced tension and improved family quality of life (Zastowny, et al., 1992), and increased patient social and vocational adjustment (Bäuml, Kissling, & Pitschel-Walz, 1996).

The duration of family psychoeducation appears to be important. Shorter-term psychoeducational programs demonstrate limited impact on the course and severity of the disorder (Pitschel-Walz et al., 2001), whereas interventions lasting greater than 6 months tend to reduce relapse and readmission over 2 years or longer (Dixon et al., 2001; Pitschel-Walz et al., 2001). Both single- and multi-family group approaches are effective at reducing relapses and rehospitalizations (Baucom et al., 1998), with each modality having advantages and disadvantages. For example, it may be easier to engage families for clients with a first episode of psychosis in single-family treatment approaches (Montero et al., 2001), whereas multi-family interventions may provide more opportunities for social support and vicarious learning (Glynn et al., 2006).

Although the majority of family interventions have been created and implemented by professionals, the National Alliance for the Mentally Ill (NAMI) has developed trained peer family member-led groups that combine elements of education, skills training, and emotional support, and are focused on increasing family well-being. Limited research with these programs suggests participation benefits in knowledge increase, empowerment, self-care, and burden decrease (Dixon et al., 2004).

AVAILABILITY, DISSEMINATION, AND FUTURE DIRECTIONS

Given the strong empirical support and robust findings of the benefits of family involvement (and the risks of non-involvement), this treatment, perhaps more than any other, should obviously be first-line and not adjunctive. However, the PORT study found that only 31% of their sample of clients treated for schizophrenia reported that their family even received information about the illness (Lehman & Steinwachs, 1998), let alone formal family psychosocial treatment of any kind. A number of different explanations have been offered for the low access of family psychoeducation for clients with schizophrenia. Although economic considerations are important, limited research suggests that the costs of family psychoeducation are offset by reduced inpatient hospitalizations (Cardin et al., 1986; McFarlane et al., 1995b; Tarrier et al., 1991).

It has been suggested that explanations for the poor dissemination of adequate family interventions stem from family members' lack of ability or desire to participate, from consumers not wanting their family involved, and from providers feeling overburdened or untrained to provide appropriate family services. Unfortunately, however, little is known empirically about the actual barriers to the provision of sound family services for clients with severe mental illness. Besides the usual funding barriers that seem to befall the majority of evidence-based treatments for schizophrenia, other systems factors are at play.

Perhaps most importantly, there is lack of access to empirically supported family programs: a recently conducted national Veterans Administration survey found that *zero* VA institutions offer family services that conform to evidence-based practice guidelines (McCutcheon, 2003). A paucity of opinion leaders and detailed implementation plans has thwarted the adoption of family interventions for schizophrenia as well.

In addition to limited access to services, many have noted that families decline participation in family interventions at a surprisingly high rate (Barrowclough et al., 1999; Leavey et al., 2004). New evidence suggests that active recruitment and strong initial engagement of the client and his/her family members plays a crucial role in the acceptance and provision of family services.

Of great importance for the future of family-based psychoeducation for schizophrenia is improved dissemination to families of what the interventions actually involve, targeted at debunking long-held pejorative myths about family treatments for severe mental illness. This may improve interest in, acceptance of, and funding for empirically supported family programs. Although efforts to implement broad-based family programs are continuously being pursued, it is simultaneously important to initiate greater scientific study of the NAMI-based peer-led programs. Conceivably, these peer-led programs may contain active ingredients similar to the more formal, professionally run interventions, and could develop into highly feasible and cost-effective novel methods of family therapy.

INTEGRATED TREATMENT FOR DUAL DISORDERS

NEED FOR INTEGRATED TREATMENT AND TARGET POPULATION

Substance use disorders are widely recognized as the most common comorbid conditions in individuals with severe mental illness, with rates of lifetime abuse about 50%, and between 20 and 40% with current abuse problems (Mueser et al., 1992). Substance abuse in individuals with schizophrenia contributes to a wide range of negative outcomes, including elevated suicide risk, exacerbation of psychotic symptoms and more frequent hospitalizations, homelessness, violence, and increased risk for contracting infections like HIV (Drake et al., 1998). Traditionally, treatment for schizophrenia and substance use disorders has been organized as "sequential" (e.g., one cannot treat schizophrenia until the substance use problem is under control, or vice versa), or "parallel" (each problem is treated simultaneously, but with different providers often from different agencies, and frequently with different philosophies) (Mueser et al., 2003). The common result of these approaches has been lack of access to treatment either because clients are excluded from treatment or refuse to follow up on treatment referrals or because both types of services are delivered in a poorly integrated, sometimes contradictory fashion (Polcin, 1992).

Due to their unfortunately unique set of intermingling "dual-diagnosis" symptoms, clients with schizophrenia tend to do poorly in both traditional mental health programs and substance use treatment services—exclusion, early discharge, and drop-out from such programs is common, as are poor outcomes (Ridgley et al., 1990). As a result, there have been substantial efforts to develop effective interventions for this population. These types of integrated treatments accept clients with varying levels of motivation to change their substance use behaviors and/or manage their mental illness, and, in keeping with the well-supported stages of change model (Prochaska & DiClemente, 1984), meet each client "where they are" on that continuum. Thus, even for clients who have been dubbed "resistant" or "untreatable" within other intervention models, integrated treatment programs endeavor to effect change through a variety of stage-specific techniques.

INTERVENTION COMPONENTS

The hallmark feature of these interventions is that the same clinician provides both mental health and substance abuse treatment, and takes responsibility for working to seamlessly integrate interventions so that they are meaningful for the clients. This blending necessitates a consistent philosophy about and approach toward the two problems (Drake et al., 2004), and high-quality clinical skills to help clients effectively manage these entangled illnesses.

Of paramount importance in integrated treatment is to tailor the specific interventions to the client's stage of recovery. The stages of change concept has been proposed as a way of understanding the different motivational states all (or most) people progress through when changing health-related behaviors (Prochaska & DiClemente, 1984): *precontemplation* (the person is not thinking about change), *contemplation* (the person is thinking about change), *preparation* (the person is making plans to change), *action* (the person is making changes), and *maintenance* (the person is maintaining change). The stages of change have been adapted to stages of treatment to describe the discrete steps people with a dual disorder progress through when addressing their disorders in the context of treatment (Osher & Kofoed, 1989), including *engagement* (developing a therapeutic relationship with the client), *persuasion* (helping the client become motivated to address problems related to substance abuse or poorly managed mental illness), *active treatment* (helping the client change substance use or illness management behaviors), and *relapse prevention* (helping the client maintain a change). Understanding the client's stage of treatment is critical to selecting appropriate interventions that will facilitate movement onto the next stage (Mueser et al., 2003). For example, if the clinician does not yet have a therapeutic relationship with the client, attention first focuses on developing that relationship in a non-judgmental, empathic manner. Once a relationship is established, work focuses on developing motivation to change substance use behaviors (or to better manage psychiatric symptoms), before attempting to teach specific strategies designed to achieve those goals.

The importance of the stages-of-treatment concept is that it focuses the clinician on evaluating the client's motivation to change, and working with the client at that level. For example, a client may acknowledge the deleterious effects of untreated psychiatric symptoms and will be interested in actively working on that problem, yet simultaneously will be reluctant to talk about his or her use of marijuana or alcohol. In these cases, the clinician needs to address the specific problems the client wants to work on, while respectfully and nonjudgmentally exploring the client's substance use while providing basic information about the effects of substances on psychotic symptoms.

The specific strategies used to help clients progress through the stages of treatment depend on each stage. For example, at the engagement stage, possible strategies include assertive outreach, empathic listening, provision of practical assistance (e.g., access to housing, benefits, medical care, as necessary), and support to social networks. In the persuasion stage, the clinician's objective is to help the client develop an understanding of the negative consequences of substance use and to instill hope that positive behavior changes are possible. This may be accomplished by helping clients articulate personal goals, developing discrepancy between the client's current behavior and achieving those goals, and instilling hope that change is possible (i.e., *motivational interviewing*; Miller & Rollnick, 2002).

During the active treatment phase, clients are motivated to make changes in their behavior regarding their substance use (and/or improve management of their psychiatric symptoms) and are actively doing so. The clinician uses a variety of approaches to help clients achieve sobriety, such as developing plans for dealing with "high risk" situations for using substances, social skills training for dealing with substance use situations, cognitive-behavioral interventions to develop effective strategies for coping with symptoms instead of using substances, and teaching stress management and problem-solving skills. During relapse prevention, attention turns to maintaining awareness that a relapse could occur, whereas extending the recovery to other areas of functioning, such as family relationships, friendships and intimacy, and work. The strategies used at the different stages can be implemented using any combination of individual, group, and family modalities.

EMPIRICAL SUPPORT

Given the complex nature of integrated treatment (and the complexity of dual disorders themselves), there have been multiple attempts to develop effective treatments over the years. Not surprisingly, these treatments have encompassed many different types and combinations of intervention techniques and have evaluated several distinct domains of outcomes, making stringent evaluation of efficacy a challenge. Nevertheless, there are to date 51 general controlled dual disorder integrated treatment trials (experimental and quasi-experimental), with 16 randomized controlled trials that focus on clients with psychosis (Mueser et al., in press).

These studies evaluate the effects of individual psychotherapy, intensive outpatient rehabilitation, contingency management, group counseling, family intervention, care management, legal interventions, or residential treatment (Drake et al., 2004, in press).

Overall, research indicates that integrated treatments for dual disorders are effective and are superior to non-integrated treatments, with the most prominent achievement on the reduction of problematic substance use. In particular, contingency management-based programs and group counseling interventions enjoyed the most empirical support (Drake et al., in press). As it has been established that substance abuse is related to a host of very negative outcomes in individuals with serious mental illness, remission has been found to be associated with improvement in other important areas, such as fewer symptom relapses and increased stable housing in the community. Interestingly, even the specific treatments that did not demonstrate effectiveness in significantly diminishing substance abuse tended to promote positive change in other targeted functioning domains. For instance, motivational interviewing interventions improved treatment engagement, legal interventions curbed associated negative criminal justice outcomes, and care management led to increased time in the community.

Not surprisingly, brief interventions are not terribly effective, particularly for long-term outcomes, whereas longer duration (approximately 6–9 months in length) cognitive-behaviorally based treatments tend to be superior. However, maintenance of these positive gains has been less successful (Mueser et al., in press). Of note is that despite the plethora of integrated treatments for dual disorders that have been developed, there has not been a single standardized intervention that has been empirically evaluated more than once. This highlights the obvious need for more rigorous examination of already-existing interventions.

AVAILABILITY, DISSEMINATION AND FUTURE DIRECTIONS

As integrated treatment for dual disorders requires a comprehensive array of services, problems related to implementation and funding remain obstacles to their widespread adoption. However, studies have begun to assess strategies to finance integrated treatment programs, and some research suggests that the costs of integrated treatment may be offset by reductions in high-cost service utilization such as hospitalizations and emergency room visits (Dickey & Azeni, 1996). Key issues related to successful dissemination include developing evidence of longer-term cost effectiveness and ensuring clinician and program fidelity to the crucial effective components of this model (McHugo et al., 1999). Necessary and promising future directions for integrated treatments of dual disorders involve the continued honing of family interventions (Barrowclough et al., 2001; Mueser & Fox, 2002), increased attention toward effectiveness within minority groups (Mercer-McFadden et al., 1997), and exploration of unique treatment needs of special populations such as women with dual disorders and trauma histories (Goodman et al., 1997).

COGNITIVE BEHAVIORAL THERAPY

NEED FOR COGNITIVE BEHAVIORAL THERAPY AND TARGET POPULATION

Despite substantial advances in the effectiveness of antipsychotic medications over the past few decades, many individuals with schizophrenia continue to suffer from persistent psychotic symptoms. Even in medication-adherent individuals, studies have found that distressful delusions and hallucinations persist in about 25–50% of clients (e.g., Carpenter & Buchanan, 1994).

Although CBT was initially utilized by Beck in the 1950s to treat highly systematized paranoid ideation (Beck, 1952), in the intervening years it has most frequently been used for anxiety and depressive disorders. It was not until the 1980s that interest in CBT for psychotic symptoms resurfaced as successful outcomes began to be reported in the United Kingdom (Turkington et al., 2006). It has been suggested that inaction related to the advancement of CBT for schizophrenia was borne out of long-held skepticism as a result of past failed attempts at individual (mostly psychodynamic) psychotherapy with psychotic patients (Mueser & Berenbaum, 1990; Mueser & Noordsy, 2005). Furthermore, the notion that CBT was contraindicated for psychotic clients prevailed for several years and was underscored by assumptions that they lacked the reasoning skills or that their cognitive deficits were too severe to participate meaningfully in CBT. Nevertheless, CBT has gained both rapid popularity and empirical support in the past 15 years, and is becoming a more commonly used adjunct to medication management.

CBT is a shorter-term, structured treatment primarily geared toward alleviating distress related to psychotic symptoms such as hallucinations and delusions. People with schizophrenia with these medication-refractory symptoms tend to receive the most benefit from CBT.

INTERVENTION COMPONENTS

Similar to other empirically supported interventions for schizophrenia, CBT is structured and goal-oriented. It is relatively short-term (ranging from approximately 4–24 sessions, often with additional booster sessions as needed) compared with other types of open-ended, supportive psychotherapies, and emphasizes several core components. Although clearly important in any therapy, client–therapist alliance and collaboration are crucial in CBT for psychosis. Given the pervasiveness of paranoia and suspiciousness in individuals with schizophrenia, developing a trusting relationship can be a challenge. However, taking an interested stance in the client's perceived personal experiences and related emotional reactions, and working to fully understand the nature of the delusional or hallucinatory experience (without colluding) not only demonstrates respect and empathy, but provides information for case formulation, which in turn sets the stage for specific CBT interventions for the symptoms.

After establishing the rationale for the Cognitive Model (the interrelationship between thoughts, emotions, and behaviors), and developing a "problem list" with the client [e.g., (1) I am afraid that terrorists are out to get me and I am not safe, (2) I may get kicked out of my apartment because I yell at the voices to get them to stop, (3) I do not have any friends], therapy goals can be created and systematically addressed.

For individuals who experience significant functional impairments because of delusional beliefs and/or hallucinations, a major goal of CBT is the reduction of the impact of positive symptoms. This is done through a variety of strategies including the development of alternative explanations for symptoms coupled with a "normalizing rationale" (Kingdon & Turkington, 1991). Inference-chaining regarding the deeper meaning of delusional beliefs (e.g., "What would it say about you if it turned out you weren't the King of Spain after all?") is a commonly used technique. Also taught in CBT is the skill of evaluating evidence to support (and refute) unusual thoughts or beliefs about hallucinations in conjunction with subsequent cognitive restructuring and activities involving the gathering additional evidence through "behavioral experiments." Depending on the client's problems and goals, later sessions can also focus on other areas, such as addressing negative symptoms, social skills training, relapse prevention, or medication adherence (Fowler et al., 1995).

CBT for psychosis is distinct from other types of individual psychotherapy for severe mental illness. Some traditional psychoeducation approaches, which are often based on the biomedical model of schizophrenia, emphasize the pathological nature of delusions and hallucinations as etiologically related to neurological abnormalities, and place importance upon the client's acknowledgement of schizophrenia as their diagnosis. CBT, however, while still providing education about the illness as applicable, is more focused on the client's individual experience with and their personal meaning of specific symptoms (rather than a diagnostic label). Supportive psychotherapy gives prominence to validating the distress and loss that comes with having schizophrenia, while providing practical support for dealing with problems (Penn et al., 2004). CBT involves a more active role on the part of the client (and the therapist), with the focus on specific interventions to reduce that distress and loss. This focus often involves challenging clients' beliefs that they are powerless over psychotic symptoms such as hallucinations or paranoid delusions, or are unable to overcome their inertia and make concrete changes to their lives (Kingdon & Turkington, 2004; Rector et al., 2005). And compared to psychoanalytic therapy, which tends to emphasize the causal role of early childhood experiences and family dysfunction in the development of schizophrenia through a more amorphous therapeutic environment, CBT is more structured, and focuses on the here-and-now, rather than past issues that may be overwhelming to clients (Turkington et al., 2006).

EMPIRICAL SUPPORT

Because of the mental health community's initial uncertainty about revitalizing individual psychotherapy for schizophrenia, proponents of CBT have been motivated to test its efficacy. As a result, there are more randomized controlled trials for CBT than for any other individual psychotherapeutic intervention for psychosis (Martindale et al., 2003). Results from these studies suggest moderate to large effect sizes for psychotic symptom change at the end of treatment as well as overall maintenance of therapeutic gains at follow-up (Gould et al., 2001; Zimmerman et al., 2005). Reduction of the severity of and distress caused by hallucinations and delusions has certainly been the most robust finding for CBT, whereas its effect on other problems, such as negative symptoms or social functioning deficits have been less consistent (Cather et al., 2005).

AVAILABILITY AND DISSEMINATION

Most randomized controlled trials of CBT for psychosis have been conducted in the United Kingdom, and the intervention is more widely available and widely practiced there than in the United States. It has been speculated that this discrepancy stems from the historical battle in the United States between the biological psychiatry movement and the psychoanalysts regarding the treatment of schizophrenia—the biological psychiatry model prevailed and as a result, there was substantial backlash against psychotherapy as a viable treatment for psychosis (Turkington et al., 2006). Relatedly, the universal healthcare system in the UK encourages psychotherapy research more than the current systems in the United States. In fact, in the UK, CBT has become an accepted component of treatment guidelines for schizophrenia (National Collaborating Center for Mental Health, 2003).

Nevertheless, modifications of traditional CBT for psychosis models have been implemented to account for limited financial resources and the particular structure of the US mental health system. For example, group CBT has begun to be evaluated as a feasible treatment modality with some promising results (Granholm et al., 2005).

FUTURE DIRECTIONS

As a result of early, largely unsuccessful attempts to implement psychodynamic treatment models for schizophrenia in the United States, progress in the development of alternative approaches has been slow. Nevertheless, CBT offers a distinct perspective and unique approach to the treatment of psychosis, and enjoys strong empirical support. As most of these trials have taken place in the UK, however, more controlled investigation is needed in the United States. In addition, the relative newness of applying CBT techniques to schizophrenia in a systematized manner is such that little is known about the active ingredients in CBT responsible for change, or which clients are most likely to benefit.

Given the profound functional impairment associated with schizophrenia, another important next step in CBT is to expand its primary focus on psychotic symptoms to address negative symptoms, social functioning, and role functioning (e.g., work, parenting). Finally, if CBT for psychosis is going to become more widely available in the U.S., it will be crucial to develop standardized training programs for clinicians to ensure competent treatment. In the long run, it may be desirable to develop processes for certifying or credentialing clinicians in the provision of CBT to ensure high standards of care.

ILLNESS MANAGEMENT AND RECOVERY

NEED FOR IMR AND TARGET POPULATION

Past conceptualizations of schizophrenia were dominated by the belief that clients were unable to care for themselves, develop and pursue personal goals, or be active participants in their own treatment. These assumptions naturally thwarted the rehabilitation movement. However, in recent years, these hopeless attitudes have been challenged, driven by a combination of consumer advocacy groups comprising individuals with severe mental illness and their families (Frese & Davis, 1997), and the movement toward shared decision-making in medicine (Fenton, 2003; Wennberg, 1988). The predominant viewpoint now is that clients with schizophrenia have the desire and capability of learning how to manage their illness in collaboration with others, and to make progress toward meaningful personal goals. As a result of this new and more positive perspective, the concept of "recovery" has been redefined from a medical term meaning complete symptom remission to developing a personally meaningful life, and having hope and confidence in one's own abilities (Anthony, 1993; Bellack, 2006).

The notion that clients with schizophrenia are capable of learning how to better manager their illness has led to the development of a range of interventions designed to teach basic self-management skills. One program, IMR (Gingerich & Mueser, 2005) has recently been developed that was designed to explicitly incorporate specific empirically supported practices for illness self-management into a single cohesive program. Unlike some of the other interventions discussed in this chapter that are geared toward specific subpopulations of clients with psychotic disorders (e.g., those who are at very high-risk for relapse or who have persistent distressing psychotic symptoms, or who struggle with substance abuse), IMR was designed to be appropriate for practically all individuals with severe mental illness and diagnoses of schizophrenia, schizoaffective disorder, major depression, or bipolar disorder. The basic rationale underlying the IMR program is that any person with a severe mental illness can learn how to better manage one's own mental illness in the service of setting and pursuing personally meaningful, functional goals (Mueser et al., 2003).

INTERVENTION COMPONENTS

The IMR program was developed based on a systematic review of research on different strategies for helping people with severe mental illness understand their illness, detect and prevent relapses, manage persistent symptoms, and more fully collaborate with mental health professionals about treatment decisions (Mueser et al., 2002). The recovery component of the program was introduced as a way of instilling hope in clients and mental health professionals that change is possible in individuals with severe mental illness, that each person can develop his or her own definition of what recovery would mean to him/her, and that based on this definition practical goals can be established aimed at improving quality of life in areas such as relationships, work or school, independence, health, or leisure activities. Motivation to learn better illness self-management skills can then be harnessed as clients perceive such skills as relevant to achieving their personal goals.

The core components of the IMR program include five treatment strategies based on a review of the research that have direct relevance to improve management of severe mental illness. *Psychoeducation* is aimed at improving knowledge about mental illness, such as information about the stress-vulnerability model of schizophrenia, common symptoms, and facts about medication and other treatment strategies. *Medication-adherence strategies* include motivational interviewing (examining the role that antipsychotics may play in personal goal attainment), cognitive (evaluating the accuracy of beliefs about the use of medication), and/or behavioral (utilizing behavioral tailoring to incorporate medication into the daily routine) approaches designed to increase adherence to antipsychotics and reduce nonadherence-related relapses (Buchanan, 1992). *Relapse prevention* training involves helping clients identify specific triggers and early warning signs of relapses, and developing a plan to respond to those triggers (e.g., call case manager, arrange meeting with doctor to consider increase in medication dosage) in order to prevent relapses or minimize their severity. *Coping skills training* involves teaching clients skills for managing stress and for dealing with persistent symptoms such as hallucinations, anxiety, or depression. Finally, the IMR program incorporates *social skills training* as a strategy for increasing social support, which has been shown to buffer the negative effects of stress and to contribute to a better course of illness (Bebbington & Kuipers, 2002; Norman et al., 2005).

Other illness self-management programs have been developed that teach similar information and skills, but without the emphasis on helping clients identify personal "recovery" goals as a strategy for increasing motivation to learn the skills. For example, the Skills for Independent Living (SILS) program includes a variety of different group-based social skills training "modules" covering different topic areas relevant to illness self-management (Liberman et al., 1993), including medication management, symptom management, and basic conversational skills. Hogarty (2002) developed "Personal Therapy," an individual psychotherapy approach that incorporates a range of illness self-management strategies, such as psychoeducation and stress management.

EMPIRICAL SUPPORT

In a comprehensive review of illness self-management studies, Mueser et al. (2002) identified 25 randomized controlled trials evaluating either specific components of illness self-management or comprehensive programs. This review indicated that studies of purely psychoeducational methods significantly improve clients' knowledge about mental illness, but do not affect their medication adherence, reduce relapse, or improve functioning (Macpherson et al., 1996). Medication adherence programs focused more on cognitive-behavioral techniques such as behavioral tailoring tend to greatly affect the degree to which clients take medication as prescribed (e.g., Cramer & Rosenheck, 1999). All the programs addressing relapse prevention planning have demonstrated decreases in relapse or rehospitalization (e.g., Herz et al., 2000). Symptom severity reduced considerably in the studies where cognitive-behavioral-based techniques were utilized to increase clients' coping skills (e.g., Lecomte et al., 1999). Although these core components of illness self-management are incorporated into the IMR program described above, controlled trials of IMR have not yet been completed. However, preliminary research supports the feasibility and clinical promise of the intervention (Mueser et al., 2006).

Research does provide some support for other comprehensive illness self-management programs. For example, multiple studies have demonstrated that the skills training modules of the SILS program result in improved social functioning, although its effects on symptoms and relapses are less certain (Liberman, 2007). One controlled study of Personal Therapy also demonstrated improvements in functioning, mainly for clients living with relatives (Hogarty et al., 1997a, 1997b). Thus, comprehensive illness self-management programs appear to confer some benefits to clients in terms of social adjustment and quality of life.

Overall, research reviews of illness self-manage interventions conclude that although improving knowledge about schizophrenia does not in and of itself appear to affect behavior (Mueser et al., 2002), the wisdom gained from psychoeducational interventions may open the door for clients to take a more active role in future treatment decisions. Given the memory impairments that are associated with schizophrenia (Saykin et al., 1991), it is not surprising that more active techniques such as behavioral tailoring have a direct affect on medication adherence. The findings from studies of illness self-management programs also demonstrate that individuals with schizophrenia can in fact play an active role in their own care, as they are able to learn and execute important coping skills and relapse prevention strategies in their daily lives that make a big difference in their functional outcomes.

AVAILABILITY, DISSEMINATION, AND FUTURE DIRECTIONS

Although some components of training in illness self-management are in place in some treatment settings (e.g., psychoeducation-based programs, CBT-based therapies, behavioral treatments for medication management), these interventions suffer the same fate as the others described in this chapter. Few mental health programs provide comprehensive training in the rudiments of illness self-management. There is a clear need to implement and evaluate user friendly training "packages" such as the IMR program that incorporate the broad range of strategies found to be effective at improving illness self-management.

In addition, although the components of illness self-management have a strong empirical basis, less attention has been given to the concept of "recovery," and how to foster it in persons with schizophrenia and other severe mental illnesses (Anthony et al., 2003; Frese et al., 2001). Evaluating both subjective (e.g., hope, self-efficacy) and objective (e.g., role functioning, quality of life) aspects of recovery may provide valuable information about the positive effects of training in illness self-management, and identify areas in need of more effective treatment. Finally, considering the stated importance by many clients of self-help and peer support to recovery (Frese & Davis, 1997), more systematic evaluation of the impact of self-help and peer-operated mental health services on progress toward recovery is needed (Corrigan, 2006).

CONCLUSIONS AND A LOOK TO THE FUTURE

Although these six evidence-based interventions differ in the specific problems they tackle, they all highlight the same important focus: that individuals with schizophrenia have the ability to be active participants in their own treatment, and by doing so they can gain better control of their illness, improve their relationships, work, and lead more rewarding and fulfilling lives. Of note is that the interventions described in this chapter are not an exhaustive list. In recent years, other adjunctive treatments have been in development or are currently building evidence bases. For example, cognitive rehabilitation (or remediation), aimed at improving the cognitive deficits common in schizophrenia, has shown some success (Krabbendam & Aleman, 2003; Roder et al., 2006; Twamley et al., 2003), as have models of supported housing designed to help clients maintain stable and independent living in the community (Rog, 2004).

Another new area of focus is health in people with schizophrenia. With evidence accumulating showing high mortality from diseases in this population (Brown, 1997; Miller et al., 2006) because of problems such as a sedentary lifestyle, poor diet, and high rates of smoking, attention has turned to helping clients with severe mental illness make lifestyle changes, such as smoking cessation (Evins et al., 2001, 2005) and weight control (Faulkner et al., 2003). These types of treatments are especially important in light of the metabolic side effects of antipsychotic medications, which are the mainstay in the treatment of schizophrenia.

As reviewed in the main body of this chapter, the majority of adjunctive interventions that have been shown to improve the course of schizophrenia are not implemented on a routine basis. The net result is that schizophrenia is not treated nearly as effectively as it could be (Drake et al., 2001)—a striking conclusion considering that the disorder is among the top ten leading causes of global disease burden in the world (Murray & Lopez, 1996). Continued problems in funding of psychosocial treatments has been a significant roadblock to the availability of effective treatment packages.

In response to this problem, the nationwide Implementing Evidence-Based Practices (EBPs) Project was developed by a panel of mental health service researchers, family advocates, clients with mental illness, administrators, and clinicians in order to improve the promotion of empirically-supported treatments (Mueser et al., 2003). This project was based on the premise that the successful implementation of EBPs requires standardized resource materials for each specific EBP, including: an introductory video, training video, practitioner manual, fidelity scale, outcome measures, and information brochures for clients, family members, clinicians, supervisors, and program managers. These standardized materials were packaged in the form of "toolkits," which were subsequently evaluated in a multi-site study using both quantitative and qualitative methods. Following the implementation study, the toolkit materials were modified. The analysis of the findings from the implementation study is currently under way. As of this writing, the original versions of the toolkit materials are available at the following website and are in the public domain: http://mentalhealth.samhsa.gov/cmhs/communitysupport/toolkits/illness/

With the continued improvement and evaluation of interventions for schizophrenia, coupled with increased success in implementation and dissemination, it is hoped that these empirically supported treatments will become more firmly integrated in the mental health system. In the near future, a major aspiration is that these interventions will shift in status from "adjunctive" to that of "standard practice" for individuals with schizophrenia.

REFERENCES

Anthony, W.A. (1993). Recovery from mental illness: The guiding vision of the mental health service system in the 1990s. *Psychosocial Rehabilitation Journal*, *16*, 11–23.

Anthony, W.A., Rogers, E.S., & Farkas, M.D. (2003). Research on evidence-based practices: Future directions in an era of recovery. *Community Mental Health Journal*, *39*, 101–114.

Bailey, E.L., Ricketts, S.K., Becker, D.R., et al. (1998). Do long-term day treatment clients benefit from supported employment? *Psychiatric Rehabilitation Journal*, *22*, 24–29.

Barrowclough, C., Haddock, G., Tarrier, N., et al. (2001). Randomized controlled trial of motivational interviewing, cognitive behavior therapy, and family intervention for patients with comorbid schizophrenia and substance use disorders. *American Journal of Psychiatry*, *158*, 1706–1713.

Barrowclough, C., Tarrier, N., Lewis, S., et al. (1999). Randomised controlled effectiveness trial of a needs-based psychosocial intervention service for carers of people with schizophrenia. *British Journal of Psychiatry*, *174*, 505–511.

Bäuml, J., Kissling, W., & Pitschel-Walz, G. (1996). Psychoedukative gruppen für schizophrene patienten: Einfluss auf wissensstand und compliance. *Nervenheilkunde*, *15*, 145–150.

Beck, A.T. (1952). Successful outpatient psychotherapy with a schizophrenic with a delusion based on borrowed guilt. *Psychiatry, 15*, 305–312.

Becker, D.R. & Drake, R.E. (1993). *A Working Life: The Individual Placement and Support (IPS) Program*. Concord, NH: New Hampshire-Dartmouth Psychiatric Research Center.

Becker, D.R. & Drake, R.E. (2003). *A Working Life for People with Severe Mental Illness*. New York: Oxford University Press.

Becker, D.R., Bond, G.R., McCarthy, D., et al., (2001). Converting day treatment centers to supported employment programs in Rhode Island. *Psychiatric Services, 52*, 351–357.

Bell, M.D., Milstein, R.M., & Lysaker, P.H. (1993). Pay and participation in work activity: Clinical benefits for clients with schizophrenia. *Psychosocial Rehabilitation Journal, 17*, 173–177.

Bellack, A.S. (2006). Scientific and consumer models of recovery in schizophrenia: Concordance, contrasts, and implications. *Schizophrenia Bulletin, 32*, 432–442.

Bond, G., McGrew, J., & Fekete, D. (1995). Assertive outreach for frequent users of psychiatric hospitals. *Journal of Mental Health Administration.*

Bond, G.R., Drake, R.E., Mueser, K.T., & Latimer, E. (2001a). Assertive community treatment for people with severe mental illness: Critical ingredients and impact on clients. *Disease Management and Health Outcomes, 9*, 141–159.

Bond, G.R., Resnick, S.G., Drake, R.E., et al. (2001b). Does competitive employment improve nonvocational outcomes for people with severe mental illness? *Journal of Consulting and Clinical Psychology, 69*, 489–501.

Carpenter, W.T., Jr., & Buchanan, R.W. (1994). Schizophrenia. *New England Journal of Medicine, 330*, 681–690.

Cather, C., Penn, D.L., Otto, M.W., et al. (2005). A pilot study of functional cognitive behavioral therapy (fCBT) for schizophrenia. *Schizophrenia Research, 74*, 201–209.

Clark, R.E., Xie, H., Becker, D.R., & Drake, R.E. (1998). Benefits and costs of supported employment from three perspectives. *Journal of Behavioral health Services and Research, 25*, 22–34.

Cramer, J.A. & Rosenheck, R. (1999). Enhancing medication compliance for people with serious mental illness. *Journal of Nervous and Mental Disease, 187*, 53–55.

Dixon, L., Lucksted, A., Stewart, B., et al. (2004). Outcomes of the peer-taught 12-week family-to-family education program for severe mental illness. *Acta Psychiatrica Scandinavica, 109*, 207–215.

Dixon, L., McFarlane, W., Lefley, H., et al. (2001). Evidence-based practices for services to family members of people with psychiatric disabilities. *Psychiatric Services, 52*, 903–910.

Drake, R., Becker, D., Goldman, H., & Martinez, R. (2006). The Johnson & Johnson – Dartmouth Community Mental Health Program: Disseminating evidence-based practice. *Psychiatric Services, 57*(3), 302–304.

Drake, R., O'Neal, E., & Wallach, M. (2007). A systematic review of research on interventions for people with co-occurring severe mental and substance use disorders. *Journal of Substance Abuse Treatment.*

Drake, R.E., Becker, D.R., Biesanz, B.A., et al. (1996). Day treatment versus supported employment for persons with severe mental illness: A replication study. *Psychiatric Services, 47*, 1125–1127.

Drake, R.E., Becker, D.R., Biesanz, J.C., et al. (1994). Rehabilitative day treatment vs. supported employment: I. Vocational outcomes. *Community Mental Health Journal, 30*, 519–532.

Drake, R.E., Mercer-McFadden, C., Mueser, K.T., et al. (1998). Review of integrated mental health and substance abuse treatment for patients with dual disorders. *Schizophrenia Bulletin, 24*, 589–608.

Drake, R.E., Mueser, K.T., Brunette, M.F., & McHugo, G.J. (2004). A review of treatments for clients with severe mental illness and co-occurring substance use disorder. *Psychiatric Rehabilitation Journal, 27*, 360–374.

Drake, R.E., O'neal E.L., Wallach M.A. (2007). A systematic review of psychosocial research on psychosocial interventions for people with co-occurring severe mental and substance use disorders. *Journal of Substance Abuse Treatment* [Epub ahed of print].

Evins, A.E., Cather, C., Deckersbach, T., et al. (2005). A double-blind placebo-controlled trial of bupropion sustained-release for smoking cessation in schizophrenia. *Journal of Clinical Psychopharmacology*, *25*(3).

Evins, A.E., Mays, V.K., Rigotti, N.A., et al. (2001). A pilot trial of bupropion added to cognitive behavioral therapy for smoking cessation in schizophrenia. *Nicotine and Tobacco Research*, *3*(4), 397–403.

Falloon, I., Mueser, K., Gingerich, S., et al. (1988). *Behavioural Family Therapy: A Workbook*. Buckingham, England: Buckingham Mental Health Service.

Fowler, D., Garety, P., & Kuipers, E. (1995). *Cognitive Behaviour Therapy for Psychosis: Theory and Practice*. Chichester, West Sussex, England: John Wiley & Sons.

Fromm-Reichman, F. (1948). Notes on the development of treatment of schizophrenics by psychoanalytic psychotherapy. *Psychiatry*, *1*, 263–273.

Glynn, S.M. (1993). Family-based treatment for major mental illness: A new role for psychologists. *The California Psychologist*, *25*, 22–23.

Glynn, S.M., Cohen, A.N., Dixon, L.B., & Niv, N. (2006). The potential impact of the recovery movement on family interventions for schizophrenia: Opportunities and obstacles. *Schizophrenia Bulletin*, *32*(3), 451–463.

Gold, M., & Marrone, J. (1998). Mass Bay Employment Services (a service of Bay Cove Human Services, Inc.): A story of leadership, vision and action resulting in employment for people with mental Illness. *Roses and Thorns from the Grassroots, Spring*.

Goodman, L.A., Rosenberg, S.D., Mueser, K.T., & Drake, R.E. (1997). Physical and sexual assault history in women with serious mental illness: Prevalence, correlates, treatment, and future research directions. *Schizophrenia Bulletin*, *23*, 685–696.

Gould, R.A., Mueser, K.T., Bolton, E., et al. (2001). Cognitive therapy for psychosis in schizophrenia: An effect size analysis. *Schizophrenia Research*, *48*, 335–342.

Granholm, E., McQuaid, J.R., McClure, F.S., et al. (2005). A randomized, controlled trial of cognitive behavioral social skills training for middle-aged and older outpatients with chronic schizophrenia. *American Journal of Psychiatry*, *162*, 520–529.

Group, T.L. (2000). Systems analysis of evidence-based assertive community treatment: state profiles and site-visit protocols. *Prepared for Health Care Financing Administration, and Substance Abuse and Mental Health Services Administration, Falls Church, VA*.

Hogarty, G.E., Anderson, C.M., Reiss, D.J., et al. (1991). Family psychoeducation, social skills training, and maintenance chemotherapy in the aftercare treatment of schizophrenia, II: Two-year effects of a controlled study on relapse and adjustment. *Archives of General Psychiatry*, *48*, 340–347.

Hogarty, G.E., Kornblith, S.J., Greenwald, D., et al. (1997a). Three year trials of personal therapy among schizophrenic patients living with or independent of family I: Description of study and effects on relapse rates. *American Journal of Psychiatry*, *154*, 1504–1513.

Hogarty, G.E., Greenwald, D., Ulrich, R.F., et al. (1997b). Three year trials of personal therapy among schizophrenic patients living with or independent of family II: Effects of adjustment on patients. *American Journal of Psychiatry*, *154*, 1514–1524.

Kingdon, D., & Turkington, D. (1991). The use of cognitive behavior therapy with a normalizing rationale in schizophrenia. *The Journal of Nervous and Mental Disease*, *719*(4), 207–211.

Krabbendam, L., & Aleman, A. (2003). Cognitive rehabilitation in schizophrenia: A quantitative analysis of controlled studies. *Psychopharmacology*, *169*, 376–382.

Latimer, E. (1999). Economic impacts of assertive community treatment: A review of the literature. *Canadian Journal of Psychiatry*, *44*, 443–454.

Latimer, E.A., Bush, P., Becker, D., et al. (2004). The cost of high-fidelity supported employment programs for people with severe mental illness. *Psychiatric Services*, *55*(4), 401–406.

Leavey, G., Gulamhussein, S., Papadopoulos, C., et al. (2004). A randomized controlled trial of a brief intervention for families of patients with a first episode of psychosis. *Psychological Medicine*, *34*, 423–431.

Lecomte, T., Cyr, M., Lesage, A.D., et al. (1999). Efficacy of a self-esteem module in the empowerment of individuals with schizophrenia. *Journal of Nervous and Mental Disease, 187*, 406–413.

Leff, J.P., Berkowitz, R., Shavit, N., et al. (1990). A trial of family therapy versus a relatives' group for schizophrenia: Two-year follow-up. *British Journal of Psychiatry, 157*, 571–577.

Lehman, A.F., & Steinwachs, D.M. (1998). Translating research into practice: The Schizophrenia Patient Outcomes Research Team (PORT) treatment recommendations. *Schizophrenia Bulletin, 24*, 1–10.

Liberman, R.P. (2007). Dissemination and adoption of social skills training: Social validation of an evidance-based treatement for the mentally disabled. *Journal of Mental Health, 16*, 595–623.

Macpherson, R., Jerrom, B., & Hughes, A. (1996). A controlled study of education about drug treatment in schizophrenia. *British Journal of Psychiatry, 168*, 709–717.

McCutcheon, S. (2003). Mental Health QUERI and family psychoeducation: The beginning of a translation journey. *VA Midwest Healthcare Network 23 Mental Health Service Line.*

McFarlane, W.R., Link, B., Dushay, R., et al. (1995a). Psychoeducational multiple family groups: Four-year relapse outcome in schizophrenia. *Family Process, 34*, 127–144.

McFarlane, W.R., Lukens, E., Link, B., et al. (1995b). Multiple-family groups and psychoeducation in the treatment of schizophrenia. *Archives of General Psychiatry, 52*, 679–687.

Mercer-McFadden, C., Drake, R.E., Brown, N.B., & Fox, R.S. (1997). The community support program demonstrations of services for young adults with severe mental illness and substance use disorders 1987-1991. *Psychiatric Rehabilitation Journal, 20*, 13–24.

Mueser, K., Bellack, A., & Blanchard, J. (1992). Comorbidity of schizophrenia and substance abuse. *Journal of Consulting and Clinical Psychology, 60*, 845–856.

Mueser, K.T., & Fox, L. (2002). A family intervention program for dual disorders. *Community Mental Health Journal, 38*, 253–270.

Mueser, K.T., & Glynn, S.M. (1999). *Behavioral Family Therapy for Psychiatric Disorders* (2nd Ed.). Oakland, CA: New Harbinger.

Mueser, K.T., Kavanagh, D.J., & Brunette, M.F. (in press). Implications of research on comorbidity and the nature and management of substance misuse. In P. Miller & D.J. Kavanagh (Eds.). *Translation of Addictions Science into practice: Update and Future directions*. Elsevier.

Mueser, K.T., Noordsy, D.L., Drake, R.E., & Fox, L. (2003). *Integrated Treatment for Dual Disorders: A Guide to Effective Practice*. New York: Guilford Press.

Mueser, K.T., Salyers, M.P., & Mueser, P.R. (2001). A prospective analysis of work in schizophrenia. *Schizophrenia Bulletin, 27*, 281–296.

Mueser, K.T., Torrey, W.C., Lynde, D., et al. (2003). Implementing evidence-based practices for people with severe mental illness. *Behavior Modification, 27*, 387–411.

Mueser, K.T., Kavanagh, D.J., & Brunette, M.F. (2007). Implications of research on comorbidity for the nature and management of substance misuse. In P. Miller & D.J. Kavanagh (Eds.) Translation of Addictions Science into Practice (pp. 277–320). Amsterdam: Elsevier.

National Collaborating Centre for Mental Health (2003). Schizophernia: Full National Clinical Guideline on Core Interventions in Primary and Secondary Care. London: Gaskell and the British Psychological Society.

Pitschel-Walz, G. (1997). Die Einbeziehung der Angelhorigen in die Behandlung schizophrener Patienten und ihr Einflub auf den Krankheitsverlauf. *Frankfurt am Main, Germany, Peter Lang.*

Pitschel-Walz, G., Leucht, S., Bäuml, J., et al. (2001). The effect of family interventions on relapse and rehospitalization in schizophrenia: A meta-analysis. *Schizophrenia Bulletin, 27*, 73–92.

Prochaska, J.O. & DiClemente, C.C. (1984). *The Transtheoretical Approach: Crossing the Traditional Boundaries of Therapy*. Homewood, IL: Dow-Jones/Irwin.

Rosenheck, R.A., Neale, M.S., Leaf, P., et al. (1995). Multisite experimental cost study of intensive psychiatric community care. *Schizophrenia Bulletin, 21*, 129–140.

Smith, J. & Birchwood, M. (1987). Specific and non-specific effect of educational interventions with families of schizophrenic patients. *British Journal of Psychiatry, 150*, 645–652.

Spindel, P. & Nugent, J. The trouble with PACT: Questioning the increasing use of assertive community treatment teams in community mental health. *Consumer organization and networking technical assistance center, Charleston, WV, Available at http://www.contac.org/nec.htm*; accessed 12/19/06.

Strauss, J.S., Harding, C.M., Silverman, M., et al. (1988). Work as treatment for psychiatric disorder: A puzzle in pieces. In J.A. Ciardiello & M.D. Bell (Eds.), *Vocational Rehabilitation of Persons with Prolonged Psychiatric Disorders* (pp. 47–55). Baltimore: Johns Hopkins Press.

Teague, G.B., Bond, G.R., & Drake, R.E. (1998). Program fidelity in assertive community treatment: Development and use of a measure. *American Journal of Orthopsychiatry*, *68*(2), 216–232.

Turkington, D., Kingdon, D., & Weiden, P.J. (2006). Cognitive behavior therapy for schizophrenia. *American Journal of Psychiatry*, *163*(3), 365–373.

Twamley, E.W., Jeste, D.V., & Bellack, A.S. (2003). A review of cognitive training in schizophrenia. *Schizophrenia Bulletin*, *29*, 359–382.

Webb, C., Pfeiffer, M., Mueser, K.T., et al. (1998). Burden and well-being of caregivers for the severely mentally ill: The role of coping style and social support. *Schizophrenia Research*, *34*, 169–180.

Witheridge, T.F. (1991). The 'active ingredients' of assertive outreach. *New Directions in Mental Health Services*, *52*, 47–64.

Zastowny, T.R., Lehman, A.F., Cole, R.E., & Kane, C. (1992). Family management of schizophrenia: A comparison of behavioral and supportive family treatment. *Psychiatric Quarterly*, *63*, 159–186.

Zimmerman, G., Favrod, J., Trieu, V.H., & Pomini, V. (2005). The effect of cognitive behavioral treatment on the positive symptoms of schizophrenia spectrum disorders: A meta-analysis. *Schizophrenia Research*, *77*, 1–9.

INDEX